ENCOUNTERING
THEOLOGY OF
MISSION

A. Scott Moreau, *series editor*

Also in the series:

ENCOUNTERING THEOLOGY OF MISSION

Biblical Foundations, Historical Developments, and Contemporary Issues

CRAIG OTT
STEPHEN J. STRAUSS
WITH TIMOTHY C. TENNENT

Baker Academic
a division of Baker Publishing Group
Grand Rapids, Michigan

Published by Baker Academic
a division of Baker Publishing Group
P.O. Box 6287, Grand Rapids, MI 49516-6287
www.bakeracademic.com

Printed in the United States of America

Library of Congress Cataloging-in-Publication Data

Ott, Craig, 1952–
    Encountering theology of mission : biblical foundations, historical developments, and contemporary issues / Craig Ott and Stephen J. Strauss, with Timothy C. Tennent.
        p.   cm. — (Encountering mission)
    Includes bibliographical references and index.
    ISBN 978-0-8010-2662-1 (pbk.)
    1. Missions—Theory. I. Strauss, Stephen J., 1955– II. Tennent, Timothy C. III. Title.
BV2063.O88 2010
266.001—dc22   2009052484

11   12   13   14   15   16   17   8   7   6   5   4   3   2

Contents

Preface

The theology of Christian mission has undergone, in David J. Bosch's analysis, paradigmatic shifts throughout the history of the church. However, none of them has been as far reaching as those of the twentieth century. Understandings of truth, biblical authority, the nature of non-Christian religions, the role of the local church, the place of social justice, spiritual dynamics, the growth of the majority world church, and many other concerns have evolved and evoked dramatic rethinking of mission in many different directions. There has seldom been a greater need for biblical clarity and global awareness regarding the mission of the church as it moves into the twenty-first century.

Our goal is to provide the reader with an overview of these developments and deliver a fresh, biblical reframing of our understanding of mission. We thematically take up the central questions of mission and examine them from a biblical, historical, and contemporary perspective, taking into account current developments at both the local and the global levels. This book deals with these themes in three parts: (1) Biblical Foundations, (2) Motives and Means for Mission, and (3) Mission in Global and Local Context.

Though not always explicit, we have sought to link theology of mission more directly with ecclesiology and eschatology. Our conviction is that the church as community of the kingdom is both the primary agent as well as the chief fruit of the *missio Dei* in this age. Furthermore, only a theology of mission that is rightly framed eschatologically will give proper place to the kingdom of God. The church as God's people lives as instrument, witness, sign, and anticipation of the kingdom that is already present but only to come in fullness upon Christ's return. The cross remains the fulcrum of history, the gospel the message of hope, and the Spirit the power of mission.

We make no apology that biblical authority is the North Star by which we have sought to navigate these turbulent waters. We are evangelical in our orientation but hope that these pages will be of value to all, and we have sought to treat divergent viewpoints with fairness. Our approach to this task is not that of strictly armchair theologians; rather, each author brings many years of practical experience in cross-cultural mission, which has tempered our scholarship. Craig Ott has authored the introduction and chapters 1–9, Steve Strauss chapters 10, 11, and 13, and Timothy Tennent chapter 12. (Material for chapter 12 was adapted from *Invitation to World Missions: A Trinitarian Missiology for the Twenty-first Century* by Timothy C. Tennent. © 2010. Published by Kregel Publications, Grand Rapids, MI.) Translations of quotations from non-English original sources are our own. Bible quotations, unless otherwise stated, are from the New International Version. Apart from references to the Divinity, proper names, and use in direct quotations, we have chosen to use lower case for terms such as the *church* (whether referring to the church local or the church universal), *scripture*, and the *kingdom of God*. The term *gospel* is capitalized only when referring to the four Gospels in the New Testament. Italics within quotations are as set in the original unless noted otherwise.

Most chapters provide teachers and readers with sidebars and case studies intended to stimulate further reflection, the formation of the learner's own viewpoint, or practical application of the subject at hand. These may be used for group discussion, class interaction, or independent study.

We are grateful to those who have read all or portions of the manuscript and given us valuable feedback. These include among others Stephen Bevans, John Cheong, George Hunsberger, David Ngaruiya, Jim Reapsome, Eckhard Schnabel, Ed Stetzer, and Tite Tiénou. Scott Moreau, series editor, and Jim Kinney of Baker Academic have demonstrated indefatigable patience as well as professional expertise in guiding this work to completion. We're also grateful for the research and editing assistance of Axel Fachner, Ben Stevens, and Amy Hay. Not least, we thank our spouses, who have patiently and faithfully supported us in this undertaking.

Our hope and prayer is that this volume will stimulate students, missionaries, academics, and ordinary Christians to a deeper understanding of and more faithful participation in the *missio Dei*.

Abbreviations

AG	Vatican Council II, *Ad Gentes*
CRESR	Consultation on the Relationship between Evangelism and Social Responsibility (sponsored by LCWE)
CWME	Commission on World Mission and Evangelism
ESA	Evangelicals for Social Action
GOCN	Gospel and Our Culture Network
IMC	International Missionary Conference
LCWE	Lausanne Committee for World Evangelization
LG	Vatican Council II, *Lumen Gentium*
LMS	London Missionary Society
LOP	Lausanne Occasional Paper
MM	Manila Manifesto (from Lausanne II)
RM	Pope John Paul II, *Redemptoris Missio* (encyclical letter)
SLSW	strategic-level spiritual warfare
SPCK	Society for Promoting Christian Knowledge
SPG	Society for the Propagation of the Gospel
WCC	World Council of Churches
WEA	World Evangelical Alliance
WEF	World Evangelical Fellowship (later renamed WEA)

Introduction

THE IMPORTANCE OF THEOLOGY OF MISSION TODAY

The living God, maker of heaven and earth, lover of our soul, the eternal Father, sends his people on a mission in this world. Having redeemed us by the blood of his Son, having given us his message in the Bible, and having equipped us with the Holy Spirit, he sends us to become his instruments for fulfilling his purposes in history. The more one contemplates this thought, the more awe inspiring and overwhelming it becomes; the deeper our sense of privilege, unworthiness, and inadequacy, the greater the urgency to make sure that we get it right. Theology of mission can be reduced to the wonderful yet challenging task of unpacking just what that means—to be sent by God on his assignment into the world.

And yet few topics evoke such a wide range of emotions, commitments, and convictions as Christian mission. Some Christians are enthusiastically and sacrificially committed to mission. They see it as the central calling of the church. Others become fearful or even hostile at the thought of mission, seeing it as arrogant or a threat to world peace. "Christian mission" is for some synonymous with a colonialist mentality, destruction of traditional cultures, and religious intolerance.

Even among mission advocates, opinions differ widely when they attempt to define the central task of mission. Is mission primarily a matter of preaching the gospel to those who have never heard? Or does mission include feeding the hungry? Perhaps mission should focus more on social justice and fighting "structural sin"? Or is mission simply a matter of quietly living out a life of integrity and love wherever one is—being a "silent witness"? Numerous other questions and issues swirl about the term *mission*: Is there still even a need or justification for sending missionaries? Who is a "missionary"? What right do

Christians have to suggest that Christianity is in any way superior to other religions? What about those who have never heard the gospel? Do we need better strategies or more spiritual power? The list goes on.

These questions only illustrate the confusion that surrounds the topic of Christian mission. Since the 1950s the necessity, definition, and justification of mission in its traditional sense have been seriously questioned. Walter Freytag's (1958, 138) statement of over fifty years ago still rings true today: mission doesn't have a problem, mission has *become* a problem!

There is little clear consensus on many of these issues—neither at the popular level in the local church, nor at the theological level in the seminary, nor at the strategic level in the mission agency. Yet local churches, mission organizations, Christian leaders, and individual Christians regularly make decisions based on their understanding of how these questions should be answered. These decisions have far-reaching consequences; they influence which projects get supported, which tasks are undertaken, how one prays, how people are counseled in Christian service, how one relates to people of other faiths, how Christian leaders are trained, what is emphasized in sermons, how missions is promoted, and so on.

In our rapidly globalizing world these questions have only become more complex. The world has become very small through increased travel, the ease of global communication, a growing variety of media options, the spread of international economic networks, and the international flow of immigrants, students, refugees, tourists, and businesspeople. Christians everywhere increasingly encounter people of other ethnic backgrounds, with other religions and other values. They are often our next-door neighbors or colleagues at work. The short-term mission phenomenon, whereby annually over one and a half million North Americans travel internationally on ministry trips, has not only increased enthusiasm for mission but has also raised concerns about mission. Majority world churches have also become significant missionary-sending bodies, often sending workers to lands traditionally considered Christian. Mission has literally become "from everywhere, to everywhere" (Nazir-Ali 1990). What are the implications of such developments for our understanding of mission?

THE TASK OF THEOLOGY OF MISSION

The task of theology of mission is to address such matters and provide biblical direction for the church's fulfillment of its missionary mandate. As trends in mission practice come and go; as new mission theories and strategies are aggressively marketed; as contemporary developments confound established understandings; as local congregations bypass traditional mission agencies; as conferences, workshops, and consultations on mission abound; the practical need has perhaps never been greater for biblical and theological reflection on the nature of mission. If our mission practice and passion are based solely on catchy slogans, trendy strategies, or contemporary social scientific discoveries, and not on sound biblical foundations, mission practice will be reduced to pragmatism, enthusiasm, or even political correctness. Evangelical warnings of the "de-theologizing of missiology" must be taken seriously (e.g., Rommen 1993).

The need is for nothing less than a biblically grounded theological perspective on God's work in the world and the participation of the church in that work today. If we believe that mission involves the very nature of God, his will for the church, and his plan for the nations—and this we most certainly do believe—then theology of mission must be the starting point for defining the nature of mission and discerning the practice of mission. A theology of mission must accomplish the following tasks.

Provide Clear Biblical Direction for the Task of Mission

Mission passion fueled by the power of the Holy Spirit is the locomotive pulling the train of Christian mission. Theology of mission, however, provides the rails upon which the train should ride. The rails give direction and stability, leading the train to its proper destination. Without rails the most powerful train will not travel far or in the right direction. So, too, without clear biblical theological direction, the greatest mission commitment and vision will not bring the work of mission to its God-given destination. Conversely, without the empowerment of the Holy Spirit, the most carefully and biblically articulated theology of mission will be as immobile as a train without a locomotive.

Accompany and Scrutinize the Foundations and Practice of Mission

Theology of mission not only gives direction but also must accompany the church as it embarks on its engagement with the world. In the words of David J. Bosch, "Missiology's task, furthermore, is critically to accompany the missionary enterprise, to scrutinize its foundations, its aims, attitude, message, and methods not from the safe distance of an onlooker, but in a spirit of co-responsibility and of service to the church of Christ. Missiological reflection is therefore a vital element in Christian mission—it may help to strengthen and purify it" (1991, 496–97).

Hold Forth the Missionary Dimension of the Gospel to Church and Academy

Because mission is rooted in the very nature of God—God is a missionary God—theology of mission has an important role to play in the broader disciplines of theology. Theology of mission not only continually reminds the church of its missionary calling, giving missionary practice biblical direction, but it is also the "gadfly in the house of theology" (D. J. Bosch 1991, 496). Theology of mission calls the church out of its comfort zone and the academy out of its ivory tower, holding the world ever before their eyes.

It lies in the nature of both church and academy for energy to gravitate toward narrowly defined "in-house" concerns and self-serving pursuits. But theology of mission has the task of stubbornly and biblically keeping the vision of God's purposes for the world before the eyes of theologians and pastors, academic institutions and congregations, Christian leaders and Christian novices. Thus the forging of a sound theology of mission must be considered central to a biblical understanding of God and his purposes for the church today.

MISSION, MISSIONS, AND MISSIONARIES

Surprisingly the words *mission* and *missionary* do not occur in most English Bible translations. One searches concordances in vain to find these terms and consider their biblical usages. This simple fact explains some of the confusion surrounding the terms. The word *mission* derives from the Latin word *mitto*, "to send," and *missio*, "sending." The word *mission* was first used in 1544 by the Jesuits Ignatius Loyola and Jacob Loyner to describe the spread of the Christian faith. In 1588 Loyola wrote, "By mission I mean journeys and undertakings carried on from town to town for the sake of the word of God" (cited in K. Müller 1987, 30). The term *mission* entered common usage in the seventeenth century. Previously one spoke more of the *apostolate*, or apostolic office (Ohm 1962, 38–39).

Though the terms may not occur in the English Bible, the concept of mission—sending—certainly does. The Greek New Testament uses two terms to describe sending: *pempo* and *apostello*. These terms are used more or less synonymously to describe God sending angels and prophets, the Father sending the Son, the sending of the Holy Spirit, and the sending of the disciples (Köstenberger 1998a, 97–111).

> If one wants to maintain a specifically theological meaning of the term *mission* as "foreign mission(s)," its significance is, in my opinion, that it keeps calling the Church to think over its essential nature as a community sent forth into the world. Seen in that light missionary work is not just one of its activities, but the criterion for all its activities. Missionary work reflects in a unique way, particularly in its passing boundaries in space and spirit, the very essence of the Church as a Church. It returns, as it were, to its origin, and is confronted with its missionary calling. It is exactly by going outside itself that the Church is itself and comes to itself.
>
> Johannes Blauw (1962, 122)

Until the 1950s the terms *mission* and *missions* were generally used synonymously to describe the spread of the Christian faith, usually by missionaries—persons sent by the church—with the explicit calling and mandate to preach the gospel to those who had never heard and gather converts into churches (sidebar I.1 offers additional definitions for consideration). This normally included crossing geographical or cultural barriers. Often attendant to this task, but usually considered secondary or supportive of it, was the establishment of schools, hospitals, and orphanages and various other works of compassion or economic development. This understanding has since undergone radical transformation in many circles.

Since the 1960s the term *mission* (singular) has come to be used more broadly to describe all of God's sending activity: God's mission in the world. Mission has come to describe not merely the tasks of missionaries, but the very sending mandate of the church as a whole. Stephen Neill claimed in 1966, "The age of missions is at an end; the age of mission has begun" (cited in D. J. Bosch 1991, 391).

The term *missions* (plural) has come to be more narrowly used to describe the various specific efforts of the church to carry out the task of mission in the world, usually related to the spread of the gospel and the expansion of the kingdom of God. This distinction, though not unproblematic, will generally be maintained throughout this book. We will use the term *mission* to describe *the sending activity of God with the purpose of reconciling to himself and*

SIDEBAR I.1
DEFINING MISSION

Consider the following definitions of Christian mission:

The word "mission" . . . is properly a comprehensive word, embracing everything which God sends his people into the world to do. (Stott 1975, 35)

Mission is the people of God giving witness to the reality of God through the church as the sign, foretaste, and presence of the kingdom. (Roxburgh 2000, 179)

Mission is the self-sending creative and redemptive action of the triune God for the [sic] mankind and the world. Its ultimate goal is the completion of the Kingdom of God and salvation of the people of God. (Yoshimoto 2005)

"Mission" is the divine activity of sending intermediaries whether supernatural or human to speak or do God's will so that God's purposes for judgment or redemption are furthered. (Larkin 1996, 534)

REFLECTION AND DISCUSSION

1. Which definition do you think most accurately reflects a biblical understanding of mission and why? What passages of scripture support your choice?
2. What are the strengths and weaknesses of each definition?
3. What difficulties might arise from adopting an inadequate or inaccurate definition of Christian mission?

SIDEBAR I.2
GLOSSARY OF TERMS

Many terms, such as *missional,
contextualization*, and *religious pluralism*, will be
defined in detail later in this volume. We
offer here a brief glossary of terms used
in this text that may be unfamiliar to the
reader.

CONCILIAR. A reference to churches,
denominations, and mission
organizations associated with the
World Council of Churches (WCC,
est. 1948) and other ecumenical
councils preceding it dating back to
Edinburgh 1910. Various conferences
and commissions of the WCC, such
as the Commission on World Mission
and Evangelism, have shaped conciliar
theology of mission (see www
.oikoumene.org).

DOXOLOGY. A term derived from Greek
meaning "glorification" in the sense of
glorifying God. Used in this text with
broad reference to the worship, praise,
and honor of God, not narrowly as an
element of the Christian liturgy.

ENLIGHTENMENT. An intellectual and social
movement generally associated with
the eighteenth century, but influencing
Western culture subsequently. It
advocates individual rights, natural law,
and the sufficiency of human reason
alone (apart from religious authority)
to understand reality and solve human
problems. Scientific inquiry should dispel
superstition, and religion is relegated to
the private, personal sphere of life.

ESCHATOLOGY. Theology pertaining to the
course of history with emphasis on the
coming of the kingdom of God, the
return of Christ, and the end of history.

EVANGELICAL. Protestant Christians,
churches, and organizations that hold to
the full authority and reliability of the

Bible, teach the necessity of personal
conversion through faith in Christ, and
emphasize personal piety and activism.
Used in this text broadly to include
Pentecostals and charismatics, and
those in various other churches with
evangelical convictions (see www
.worldevangelicals.org).

GLOBALIZATION. The phenomenon
whereby the world is becoming
economically, culturally, intellectually,
and technologically interconnected
through travel, communication,
immigration, commerce, and education.
Local life is increasingly influenced by
and interdependent with events, people,
and powers around the globe.

INDIGENOUS CHURCH. A church comprised
primarily of people native to a region
and historically defined as being
self-propagating, self-governing,
and self-supporting. More recently,
characteristics such as self-theologizing
and contextualized have been added to
the definition, with the church giving
local expression to the gospel.

LAUSANNE MOVEMENT. An organization
to promote broad evangelical
cooperation in mission growing out of
the International Congress on World
Evangelization held in Lausanne,
Switzerland, in 1974. The Lausanne
Covenant (1974) is the theological and
missiological basis of the movement.
Ongoing working groups, consultations,
conferences, and reports have
significantly shaped evangelical mission
thinking and practice (see www
.lausanne.org).

MAJORITY WORLD. Africa, Asia, and
Latin America. Replaces outdated
terms such as *third world* or *developing*

world, emphasizing that these regions now comprise not only the majority population of the world but also the majority of Christians in the world.

MILLENNIUM. The thousand-year period of the binding of Satan and the reign of Christ described in Revelation 20:1–8.

PENTECOSTAL/CHARISMATIC. Christians, churches, and organizations that emphasize the ecstatic personal experience of the Holy Spirit, often evidenced by speaking in tongues, and who believe in the ongoing presence and importance of supernatural spiritual gifts such as miracles and healing.

PREMILLENNIALISM. Belief that Christ will return bodily to earth, initiating a literal thousand-year reign of peace. Prior to Christ's return, Satan and the forces of evil on earth will not be ultimately defeated and the kingdom of God cannot be fully realized.

POSTMILLENNIALISM. Belief that Christ will bodily return to earth at the end of the millennium, which is understood as a period of gradual expansion and realization of the kingdom of God on earth, defeating Satan, leading up to Christ's return.

SYNCRETISM. The phenomenon whereby one religion becomes mixed with another so that its essential character is fundamentally changed or compromised.

UNREACHED PEOPLE. An ethnic or linguistic group that has little or no access to the gospel. Also sometimes defined as a people group without an indigenous church able to communicate the gospel in a culturally relevant and understandable way.

VATICAN II. The Second Ecumenical Council of the Vatican, 1962–65, which passed major reforms in Roman Catholic teaching and practice. Two important documents were drafted relating to the mission of the church: *Lumen Gentium* and *Ad Gentes*.

WESTERN. *Western* is used in this text primarily to describe cultural, intellectual, and social influences of European origin. Today Western culture is often (though not exclusively) associated with individualism, modernization, industrialization, free-market capitalism, and Enlightenment philosophy. The Western church is generally understood as the churches of Europe and people of European descent, particularly in North America.

bringing into his kingdom fallen men and women from every people, nation, and tongue. The church is God's primary agent for mission in this age. One of the most important tasks of this text will be to more carefully define the purpose and task of mission.

The term *missionary* was first associated with the office of an apostle. The Greek term *apostolos* means simply "sent one" or "emissary." Early missionaries were considered to be continuing in the tradition of the original twelve apostles, who were called and sent by Jesus to preach the gospel in all the world and make disciples of all nations. Though there is also confusion regarding the meaning of the term *missionary*, we will generally use the term to describe people who have been commissioned by the church or a Christian mission agency dedicated explicitly and intentionally to the work of missions (see chapter 10; we provide very basic definitions for additional terms used in the book in sidebar I.2).

In recent years the term *missional* has become popular in missiological and ecclesiological writing. As Christopher J. H. Wright defines it, "*Missional* is simply an adjective denoting something that is related to or characterized by mission, or has the qualities, attributes or dynamics of mission" (2006, 24). Simply put, *missional* focuses on the *doing* of mission. The term has become associated with the concept of the "missional church," which emphasizes that the church does not merely send missionaries, but the church *itself* is sent by God with a missionary mandate. The church is on mission wherever it finds itself.

MISSIONAL THEOLOGY, THEOLOGY OF MISSION, MISSIOLOGY

A useful distinction can be made between the terms *missional theology, theology of mission, missiology,* and *biblical theology of mission.*

Missional Theology

Missional theology, sometimes called mission theology, refers to the missional dimension of various theological disciplines. In a sense all theology is mission theology in that nearly all biblically oriented theology will, or should, in one way or another relate to God's missional purposes in the world and the missionary character of God.

In the words of Martin Kähler, "The earliest mission became the mother of theology because it attacked the contemporary culture" ([1908] 1971, 190). Historically viewed, much theology (particularly in the New Testament) developed in the context of the spread of the Christian faith. The encounter with other religions, idolatry, false teaching, syncretism, and ethical challenges faced by new believers served as the anvil on which theology was forged. Thus Martin Hengel can claim that the history and theology of the early church are all "mission history" and "mission theology" (1983, 53). At a deeper level all Christian theology proceeds from God's self-revelation and saving acts climaxing in Jesus Christ; therefore, all biblical theology has a missional dimension. Wright has argued persuasively for a missional hermeneutic of the Bible, whereby mission becomes the focus of hermeneutical coherence: "Mission is what the Bible is all about; we could as meaningfully talk of the missional basis of the Bible as of the biblical basis of mission" (C. J. H. Wright 2006, 29).

Missional theology seeks to delineate more clearly the missional aspects of theology as a whole, placing God's mission as a central integrating factor. In the words of Bosch, "We are in need of a missiological agenda for theology rather than just a theological agenda for mission" (D. J. Bosch 1991, 494). Missional theology is thus concerned with providing an interpretive frame of reference by which we understand the message of scripture and the mission of the church in its entirety.

At the same time, missional theology is dependent on the other theological disciplines, learning from them and building upon them, and then bringing them into relation with God's mission in the world. Missiology apart from a sound theology is a dangerous and speculative undertaking. Not only does theology help us to correctly interpret the scriptures, but it also provides the larger framework of biblical understanding with which a theology of mission must be in harmony.[1]

Theology of Mission

Theology of mission, as a subset of missional theology, examines the theological foundations, guidelines, and dimensions of mission in particular. It is a theological reflection on the *nature* and *task* of mission. In this regard theology of mission begins with the explicit biblical teaching on mission but moves on to apply that teaching to the various issues that confront the church in fulfilling its missionary calling. Theology of mission thus becomes a dialogue between biblical text and missionary context: "The theology of mission is a disciplined study which deals with questions that arise when people of faith seek to understand and fulfill God's purposes in the world, as these are demonstrated in the ministry of Jesus Christ. It is a critical reflection on attitudes and actions adopted by Christians in pursuit of the missionary mandate. Its task is to validate, correct and establish on better foundations the entire practice of mission" (Kirk 2000, 21). This means that theology of mission, as we define it, addresses a broad range of topics relating to God's mission in the world and the challenges of mission practice, reflecting on these topics biblically. It includes the freedom to theologically explore contemporary issues and challenges in mission that may not be explicitly addressed in the Bible or in traditional theological inquiry.

Kevin Vanhoozer defines theology in general as "biblical interpretation that aims at knowledge of God" (2000, 81). He expands on the practical implications of theology: "Theology yields instructions for deliberating well about the gospel—for deliberating well about what God has done in Christ, for deliberating well about what the church is to say about God and do in the name of God in particular situations, for deliberating well about how we can live well, as individuals and as communities, in light of the gospel" (2000, 82–83). He argues that theology must move beyond *theoria* (good conceptual logic) to wisdom, what he calls *phronesis* (practical reason resulting in right action). If we follow Vanhoozer's definition of theology, then a theology of mission will yield instructions for deliberating well about the nature of God as a missionary God in Christ, about the nature of the church as a missionary community, and about how we as individuals and communities wisely fulfill our mission mandate in light of the gospel.

---

1. For a discussion of how mission should profit from theology, see Kähler ([1908] 1971, 184–221).

Missiology

Related to these terms is the comprehensive term *missiology*, which includes theology of mission as well as history of mission, anthropology and intercultural studies, mission strategy, world religions, church growth, religious demographics, and related fields of study. "Missiology's task in every age is to investigate scientifically and critically the presuppositions, motives, structures, methods, patterns of cooperation and leadership which the churches bring to their mandate" (Verkuyl 1978, 5). If this is the task of missiology, then the task of theology of mission is to provide the theological foundations and guidelines for missiology. Theology of mission is the intersection of missiology and mission theology (see fig. I.1).

FIGURE I.1: THEOLOGY OF MISSION VISUALIZED

Theology of Mission
Theology pertaining to the task of mission, where missiology and mission theology intersect.

Missiology
Theology, history, social sciences, strategy, etc. pertaining to the task of mission.

Missional Theology
The missional dimension of all theology.

Biblical Theology of Mission

Biblical theology of mission can be considered a subcategory of biblical theology and a subcategory of theology of mission. Biblical theology (in general) is not merely theology based on the immediate teaching of the Bible, but theology that gives particular attention to the historical development of theological themes within the biblical canon and examines the setting and contributions of the individual biblical books or authors in the context of the whole Bible. Biblical theology of mission is thus an examination of the historical development of the theme of mission within the biblical canon, noting the particular contributions of various biblical books or authors.

Biblical theologies of mission have been written by both missiologists (e.g., Peters 1972, Glasser et al. 2003) and by biblical scholars (e.g., Senior and Stuhlmueller 1983, Larkin and Williams 1998, C. J. H. Wright 2006). Andreas J. Köstenberger and Peter T. O'Brien's *Salvation to the Ends of the Earth: A Biblical Theology of Mission* (2001) is a good example of a work by biblical scholars. As New Testament theologians, they discuss the scriptural teaching on mission by examining the history, literature, and theology of the various biblical books and authors. Their method is primarily inductive and exegetical. Their discussion is, in keeping with the biblical theological approach, limited almost exclusively to the immediate teaching of the biblical texts in their original contexts, though they recognize a unifying, salvation-historical theme. Eckhard Schnabel's monumental two-volume *Early Christian Mission* (2004) examines encyclopedically the historical, social, geographical, and theological aspects of mission in the New Testament.

Missiologists writing biblical theology of mission usually give less attention to technical concerns of Old and New Testament scholarship and devote more attention to themes relating to mission practice. Because these authors and others have already provided detailed biblical theologies of mission, this volume will only briefly summarize the fruit of such studies in chapters 1 and 2, and then in later chapters discuss more systematically specific issues of a theology of mission.

SOURCES FOR DOING THEOLOGY OF MISSION

There are many avenues that one might take to forge a theology of mission. We have chosen four avenues of inquiry in our attempt to bring clarity to these questions.

The Bible

First and foremost, the Bible, God's inspired Word, serves as our primary source in discovering the purposes and revealed will of God. We need not speculate nor are we left to our own imagination on questions of such magnitude. God has spoken. Admittedly our interpretation of scripture is imperfect, and we are not entirely free from our own blind spots and preconceptions. We also recognize much room for difference of opinion among Christ-honoring students of the Bible. Yet we are of the conviction that the Bible does offer *adequate* clarity and direction on the subject. Scripture will serve as our ultimate authority, and our desire is to allow the Bible to speak to these issues (see C. J. H. Wright 2006, 51–58). All other sources are secondary and subordinate to biblical teaching.

Biblical theology of mission provides the North Star by which the ship of mission must navigate. Though storms may rage and currents may pull, the ship of mission can stay its intended course as long as it reorients itself on the fixed point. Trends and fads, political correctness, popular opinion (inside and outside the church), ethnocentrism and myopia, and a host of other forces would blow this ship off course. The scriptures as the revealed Word of God must remain the fixed point by which we navigate the ship of mission.

History

A second line of inquiry and source of insight is history. We seek to learn from both the history of the expansion of Christianity throughout the world and, more particularly, from the history of Christian thought on the subject of mission. Many of the issues and questions that seem unique to our day are in fact surprisingly similar to issues faced by Christians in previous eras. Others have gone before us in both the practice of mission and the theological reflection on the issues of mission. Many of the debates have been hammered out on the anvil of earlier crises; many of the theories have been tested and refined in the fires of previous missionary practice. While God has spoken in scripture, he is at work in history, and we are foolish if we fail to learn from it. Knowing from whence we have come also helps us understand where we are presently headed and why and may also help us realize if our course needs correction. We desire to stand on the shoulders of those who have gone before, not to uncritically accept their conclusions, but in humility to gain a broader and longer perspective as we develop a fresh vision for our generation.

Social Sciences

Third, we look to the social sciences to aid us in understanding the complexity of culture and the human experience. While strictly speaking we do not view social science as a source for mission theology, it does provide an important backdrop and conversation partner for it. Mission concerns God's work in human lives, families, communities, and societies; thus, we must understand the nature of those lives and communities. The social sciences can provide us with disciplined methods of inquiry to grow in such understanding. But social theories cannot be allowed to undermine biblical teaching; they cannot become a social-scientific tail wagging the theological dog, as unfortunately often happens. Instead, within the framework of a biblical worldview, such inquiry can help us better discern the complexities of communication, life change, social transformation, and an array of other human factors that influence the understanding and fulfillment of biblical mission.

Voices of the Global Church

A fourth route of inquiry is to listen carefully to the voices of the global church (see Ott and Netland 2006). The literature and discussions on theology of mission, much like other theological disciplines, has until recently been largely dominated by the voices of Western Christianity. There are many understandable reasons for this. But today we are fortunate that voices from majority world churches can be heard, and many of these voices are speaking about mission and mission-related concerns.

These voices provide fresh and often challenging perspectives to more traditional approaches. To use Vanhoozer's term, a "Pentecostal plurality," that is, a plurality of voices from various cultural perspectives, is needed to help us overcome our cultural limitations and bring us closer to an accurate and true interpretation of scripture (1998, 419). Wilbert R. Shenk has argued that "a dynamic theology of mission develops where there is vigorous engagement of culture by the Gospel, accompanied by critical reflection on that process"; therefore, "we must look to the evolving Christian movement in Asia, Africa, and Latin America to discern defining themes" (2001, 98). Listening to such voices is all the more important because the majority of Christians today live in Africa, Asia, and Latin America, and these churches have become a growing and powerful missionary-sending force.

THEOLOGY OF MISSION AND DIVINE DRAMA

Mission is about God's sending activity in which the church participates. This redemptive and communicative action of God goes beyond mere propositions about God and, to use Vanhoozer's (2005) metaphor, can be conceived of as *theodrama*. Theology of mission reflects on and informs the church's role in this divine drama of salvation history with a particular view to the redemptive purposes of God in the world and among the nations. Scripture provides the script and the plot of the drama; history tells us how others have interpreted and enacted the drama in the past; social sciences describe the cultural stage upon which the drama is enacted; the voices of the global church are both the critics and the new actors (no longer playing bit parts) in the drama, giving diverse perspectives on its enactment.

God the Father is the playwright and producer; Jesus Christ and his redemptive work is the message of the story; and the Holy Spirit is both the inspiration and the director guiding the actors. The mission theologian—an academic, a pastor, or a layperson—serves as the dramaturge, who carefully studies the play and helps clarify its significance and interprets the script both for the players and for the audience. In this way the drama is enacted and understood as the playwright intended (Vanhoozer 2005, 243–46). This drama is specifically missional in nature because it is played on the stage of the world, not in the confines of the church or the academy. The drama will not be complete until those from every people, nation, tribe, and tongue have beheld its glory and been taken up in its story line.

A BRIEF OVERVIEW OF HISTORICAL DEVELOPMENTS IN THEOLOGY OF MISSION

Early Developments

Though more formal theologies of mission would not be written until the Middle Ages, less formal theology of mission has always accompanied the church. As noted above, the missionaries of the New Testament, the apostles, and the authors of scripture were mission theologians. Whereas the earliest itinerant evangelists and missionary monastic movements had a theological rationale for their undertakings, they lacked an explicit, articulated theological reflection on mission (see Ohm 1962, 75–121). The early church fathers focused on apologetics and addressing the relationship between Christian faith and non-Christian philosophy.

After the sack of Rome in AD 410, Augustine developed in his later writings (e.g., Letter 199 to Hesychius, AD 418) the importance of mission beyond the boundaries of the empire and argued against the generally held view of Eusebius that the apostles had completed the Great Commission (*Hist. eccl.* 3.1). His writings on the nature of humankind, sin, and salvation were to have a great and lasting influence on theology in general and on mission in particular. By the late Middle Ages considerable thought was being given to mission; the most prolific medieval writer on mission was Raymond Lull (1235–1315), whose primary concern was the conversion of Muslims and training missionaries for that task.

The age of discovery lay to rest once and for all the view that the apostles had completed the Great Commission, and a considerable volume of literature addressing mission was produced during that period. In 1502 Christopher Columbus compiled biblical texts relating to mission in his *Libro de las Profecías*. Erasmus of Rotterdam appealed to the pope and princes to fulfill their missionary obligation by sending missionaries to save souls (*Ecclesiastae sive de ratione concionandi libri* IV, 1535). Joseph de Acosta (1540–1600), a Spanish Jesuit and missionary to the East Indies, was perhaps the most significant mission theologian of the period. In 1622 the Roman Catholic Church established the Sacred Congregation for the Propagation of the Faith to oversee the missionary efforts of the church. This organization produced the first manuals, strategies, and policies guiding mission work, making significant statements on the nature of mission and its relation to culture. However, various controversies and challenges from the mid-seventeenth century to the beginning of the nineteenth century (including the "rites controversy" in Asia, the Enlightenment, and secularization) hindered further missiological thought.

Protestant Beginnings

The Protestant Reformers were preoccupied with controversies related to the Reformation and faced extreme social instability (war, plague, etc.); thus they had little to say about mission. Many also continued to maintain that the Great Commission only applied to the original apostles. Several Dutch Reformers were among the earliest Protestant theologians who gave attention to mission. The most significant of these was Gisbertus Voetius (1588–1676), who formulated a theology of mission in his three-volume *Politica Ecclesiastica* (1663–76) and addressed mission in other writings. "Voetius attempted not only to sketch the outlines of a solid theology of missions, but he was also the first who attempted seriously to give missiology a legitimate scientific place in the whole of theology" (H. A. Van Andel, cited in Jongeneel 1991, 47). Justinian von Weltz (1621–68) pioneered German theology of mission, including vehement calls for a Protestant missionary movement. He himself eventually traveled as a missionary to South America, where he was killed by wild animals. The Reformation period, however, was in general not a fruitful period for Protestant missiological reflection.

Protestant mission efforts gradually developed in the seventeenth and eighteenth centuries under the influence of the Puritans and the Pietists. Their theological understanding of missions is more evident in popular preaching and hymns than in academic treatises. One exception was Jonathan Edwards, who balanced scriptural discernment and personal experience in his writings during the Great Awakening revival. Bosch calls Edwards's thought "the great intellectual and spiritual vein from which missionary theology in the period was mined" (1991, 277). William Carey's eighty-seven-page *An Enquiry into the Obligations of Christians to Use Means for the Conversion of the Heathens* (1792) is an outstanding example of an apologetic for Christian missions at a time when Christian leaders questioned the necessity of missions. Many of the earliest Protestant missionaries became experts in local religions and outstanding ethnographers, but few articulated a theology of mission per se.

Nineteenth and Early Twentieth Centuries

As the Protestant missionary movement came into its own in the nineteenth century, leaders began to reflect more seriously on missionary practice. For example, Henry Venn and Rufus Anderson, leaders of mission-sending agencies, are credited with coining the "three-self" formula for the autonomy of mission churches: self-propagating, self-governing, and self-supporting. According to Princeton University's 1811 original "Plan for a Theological Seminary," the institution was to be "a nursery for missionaries to the heathen," dedicated to training and qualifying youth for missionary work (Myklebust 1955, 1:146). But only in the second half of the nineteenth century did the value of the disciplined study of missions as part of missionary preparation become widely recognized. In 1849 Karl Graul, the first appointed Protestant lecturer for missions at the University of Erlangen, called for missions to be "raised out of the dimness of sentimental belief to the noon brightness of believing science" (cited in Gensichen 1971, 250). Lecturers were called and professorships were established at universities, usually occupied by former directors of mission societies.

Nevertheless, it was Gustav Warneck (1834–1910), at the University of Halle in Germany, who pioneered the first systematic study of mission. In 1874 he cofounded the journal *Allgemeine Missionszeitschrift* (Common Journal of Mission), the first of its kind. Later, in 1897, he authored the first comprehensive missiological work, *Evangelische Missionslehre* (Protestant Doctrine of Mission) with three parts in five volumes. Warneck's Roman Catholic counterpart was Joseph Schmidlin (1876–1944) of the University of Münster, who has been tagged the father of Catholic missiology. He authored *Catholic Mission Theory* (1931, German 1919) and *Catholic Mission History* (1933, German 1924), and edited the *Zeitschrift für Missionswissenschaft* (Journal for Missiology). He publicly opposed the Nazi regime, for which he was eventually executed.

The first half of the twentieth century saw remarkable progress in missiological and theological reflection as the Protestant missionary movement matured. Roland Allen (1868–1947) authored the provocative *Missionary Methods: St. Paul's or Ours?* ([1912] 1962a) challenging mission practice to radically return to the example of the apostle Paul. In 1918 the German Society for Missiology was founded to promote Catholic missiological writing and academics. The various ecumenical missionary councils and reports stirred considerable controversy over subjects such as the value of non-Christian religions and church-mission relations.

Late Twentieth Century

The third quarter of the twentieth century saw what might be considered a golden era of mission theology, during which numerous missiologists produced significant and creative theological works that are still influential today. This development was precipitated by the demise of colonialism, the tragedy of World War II, the rise of global communism, and forces of secularization. Continental missiologists such as Hendrik Kraemer, Walter Freytag, and Thomas Ohm led the way in this era. It was also a period of considerable controversy and turmoil with developments such as liberation theology (Gustavo Gutiérrez), the Church Growth Movement (Donald McGavran), and a growing rift between conciliar (groups associated with the WCC) and evangelical mission understandings.

During this era Pope John XXIII summoned the Second Vatican Council (1962–65), which produced (among other documents) the constitution *Lumen Gentium* (*LG*, 1964) and the decree *Ad Gentes* (*AG*, 1965). Later, in 1975, Pope Paul VI authored the influential *Evangelii Nuntiandi*. These documents advocated fresh and foundational understandings of mission.

Evangelical missiology advanced significantly with the establishment of missiological faculties at seminaries such as Fuller Theological Seminary and Trinity Evangelical Divinity School. Evangelical theology of mission climaxed during this quarter century with the Lausanne Congress on World Evangelization in 1974 and the formulation of the Lausanne Covenant, which was heavily influenced by John Stott. This document eloquently expressed a balanced understanding of mission, which has remained unsurpassed as a rallying point and basis of cooperation in mission among very diverse evangelical groups.

The last quarter of the twentieth century brought continued challenges and social change impacting missiology, among them social instability, anti-Westernism, and a radical return to traditional cultures including a resurgence of traditional religions. Nowhere was this more evident than in the overthrow of the shah and the establishment of a strongly anti-Western, fundamentalist Islamic state in Iran. Women's issues, human rights abuses, concerns related to globalization, and environmental stewardship increasingly occupied missiological discourse. The term *contextualization* was coined to describe serious theological engagement with culture, and contextual theologies flourished. The social sciences, such as cultural anthropology, communications, and political theory, began playing a more significant role in missiology, threatening in some cases to eclipse the theological foundations of mission.

Conciliar theology of mission continued to wrestle with questions of social justice, religious pluralism, interreligious dialogue, ecumenism, the environment, and the nature of salvation. Based on the work of Lesslie Newbigin and others, the "missional church" concept was developed, and The Gospel in Our Culture Network was formed, focusing on the need for the church's missional engagement with Western culture. The combined forces of secularization, postmodernism, and the dramatic decline of Christianity (particularly in Europe) still present enormous challenges to the Western church.

Evangelical theology of mission was not unaffected by these concerns. Its focus was nevertheless more on the relationship of evangelism and social responsibility (holistic mission), the kingdom of God and mission, religious pluralism, and spiritual power in mission. A plethora of mission strategies called for theological assessment. Various international working groups related to the Lausanne Movement have been on the evangelical forefront of producing reports and occasional papers on a wide range of mission issues of theological importance. During this period numerous majority world theologians began publishing significant works that drew international attention and brought new perspectives into the missiological discussion.

Entering the Third Millennium

With the fall of the Berlin Wall in 1989 and the end of the cold war in the early 1990s, additional dramatic impulses entered missiological thinking. Postmodern perspectives and the radical pluralism of thinkers such as Paul Knitter deeply impacted conciliar, Catholic, and some evangelical missiology. What David Barrett, Andrew Walls, and others had been predicting came to pass: the majority of Christians lived no longer in Europe and North America but in countries formerly considered "mission fields." Majority world countries also became significant missionary-sending countries. The dramatic growth of the church under oppressive circumstances in China stimulated a more optimistic spirit. Global communications were revolutionized by the Internet and other electronic media. At the same time, the gap between rich and poor widened as forces of global capitalism seemed now to be unbridled. All these developments demand a rethinking and fresh articulation of mission.

In 1990 Pope John Paul II issued the encyclical letter *Redemptoris Missio* further clarifying the Vatican's position "on the permanent validity of the Church's missionary mandate" (the subtitle of *RM*), addressing, for example, the uniqueness of Christ, the kingdom of God, the importance of the church, and interreligious dialogue.

Several dictionaries, handbooks, and reference works appeared enlarging the missiological database, making information more readily accessible to students, and enriching theology of mission (see sidebar I.3). Biblical theology of mission experienced a revival with the appearance of numerous scholarly works. On the other hand, chairs for missiology at European universities, which produced much of the rich work of the "golden era" of mission theology, are gradually being phased out of existence.

The terrorist attacks of September 11, 2001, and ensuing developments were interpreted by some as confirmation of predictions of a "clash of civilizations" (Huntington 1997). Heightened tensions between religious groups, war, and ethnic violence have continued into the twenty-first century and call more than ever for a reasoned biblical missiological response that will guide the church in its global witness and encounters with those of other faiths.

Two theologies of mission published in the post–cold war era are particularly worthy of mention. Both take a strongly historical approach and deeply reflect on these developments. Bosch's landmark *Transforming Mission* (1991) set a new standard in missiological scholarship. He examined the development of the theology of mission in terms of six historical and conceptual epochs involving paradigm shifts whereby understandings of theology and missiology have evolved. Though Bosch gave little attention to majority world theologians, women in mission, or the global growth of Pentecostalism, this work was unparalleled in its scope and scholarship. As one reviewer put it, *Transforming Mission* quickly became "the *summa missiologica* of the late 20th century. Bosch had succeeded in providing a comprehensive theoretical framework for missiology that rose above the polarities of his generation" (Roxborogh 2001).

Stephen B. Bevans and Roger P. Schroeder, both Roman Catholics, produced a similarly massive work titled *Constants in Context: A Theology of*

SIDEBAR I.3
SIGNIFICANT DICTIONARIES AND REFERENCE WORKS ON MISSION
AND THEOLOGY

Over the past two decades numerous reference works have appeared that help us better understand mission in all its facets. Each of the following works has a distinctive orientation and content focus, and for the serious student of mission all are worth owning:

- *Dictionary of Mission: Theology, History, Perspectives* (K. Müller 1997a)
- *Philosophy, Science, and Theology of Mission in the 19th and 20th Centuries: A Missiological Encyclopedia* (Jongeneel 1995–97)
- *Biographical Dictionary of Christian Missions* (G. H. Anderson 1998)
- *Evangelical Dictionary of World Missions* (Moreau 2000a)
- *World Christian Encyclopedia: A Comparative Survey of Churches and Religions in the Modern World*, 2nd ed. (Barrett, Kurian, and Johnson 2001; 1st ed. 1982)
- *Dictionary of Mission Theology: Evangelical Foundations* (Corrie 2007)

Mission for Today (2004). They too take a strongly historical perspective but with a more nuanced approach than Bosch, with greater attention devoted to Roman Catholic mission and avoiding some of Bosch's weaknesses. They trace the development of mission thinking and practice of six historical eras in terms of how six theological themes are understood: Christology, ecclesiology, eschatology, salvation, anthropology, and culture. They examine these "constants" historically as evidence of three recurring types of theology based on the work of Justo L. González and Dorothee Sölle. The types are mission as saving souls and extending the church, mission as discovery of the truth, and mission as commitment to liberation and transformation (32–72). They then propose a model of mission as "prophetic dialogue," synthesizing and giving the former models new depth and direction.

Just as historical theology traces the development of various doctrines through the ages, both Bosch and Bevans and Schroeder provide us with two versions of historical theology of mission tracing the development of missiological thought and practice through the ages. Although their insights are keen and their research voluminous, they ultimately conclude with rather tenuous understandings of mission. They have rightly helped us see how understandings of mission evolve and are influenced by history, culture, tradition, and context. But they also assume that we are prisoners of our culture and context and that there is little real hope of approaching a *true* understanding of mission. Bosch begins with the following assumption: "Ultimately, mission is undefinable; it should never be incarcerated in the narrow confines of our own predilections. The most we can hope for is to formulate some approximations of what mission is all about" (D. J. Bosch 1991, 9). Bosch himself only tentatively suggests what the next mission paradigm might be that will resolve the current crisis in mission. Bevans and Schroeder see the "constants" of mission not in how these questions have been answered but in the fact that similar questions have been continually asked (2004, 34). They affirm Bosch's warning to "beware of any attempt at delineating mission too sharply" (2004, 9; cf. D. J. Bosch 1991, 512).

In contrast, our view of scripture described above, our epistemological assumptions, and our methodological approach lead us to pursue with greater confidence a biblical understanding of God's purposes for mission. Because our knowledge remains limited and imperfect, this is a pursuit in humility. But we needn't abandon hope that we can grow in clearer biblical understanding and in more faithful practice. Such a critical realist approach allows us to progress in our understanding of God's will for mission as revealed in scripture. Though we see through a glass dimly, *we do see* (1 Cor. 13:12). Though we know in part and prophesy in part, we *can know* and *can speak* truly (1 Cor. 13:9).

We, as those before us, are influenced by our history, culture, and tradition, but we needn't remain prisoners of them. By learning from history and from the human sciences, we can come to a more complete understanding of how mission is to be lived out by the church in our time. By listening to a wide range of voices that honor Christ and his Word, we are able to see more clearly and move beyond our cultural blind spots and hermeneutical myopia. The task of this volume is to examine the various understandings, developments, and challenges of mission with scripture as our guiding authority and with history, human sciences, and multicultural perspectives as our aids, in hope of bringing us closer to a biblically faithful and practically relevant theology of mission.

PART 1

Biblical Foundations of Mission

God and the Nations
in the Old Testament

The Bible is from start to finish a missionary book, for it is the story of God himself reaching into human history to reconcile a fallen and rebellious humanity to himself and to reestablish his reign over all creation. In this sense God is a missionary God—a God who sends his emissaries, messengers, and ultimately his Son as agents in this story of salvation. This salvation will ultimately reach out to include persons of every people, nation, tribe, and tongue. It is God's initiative, and it is God who receives all glory. At first he sends primarily angels and prophets, after which he forms a people, Israel, to be sent as a witness to his righteousness and glory amid the nations. The story climaxes with the sending of his Son to purchase salvation and defeat evil at the cross. But the story then continues with the sending of a new people of God in the power of his Spirit, the church, to become his instruments and as signs of his kingdom. The story will conclude triumphantly with the return of Christ, the ultimate establishment of his kingdom, the final defeat of evil, and the universal confession that Christ is Lord.

In chapters 1 and 2, on the Bible and mission, we focus primarily on God's plan for the nations. In later chapters we examine other biblical themes of mission. Only a few representative biblical texts can be examined. We refer readers to the fine studies of Köstenberger and O'Brien (2001), Larkin and

Williams (1998), Glasser (Glasser et al. 2003), C. J. H. Wright (2006), and others for detailed examinations of this topic. As a starting point for a broader theology of mission, we must seek to capture something of the wonder and excitement of the grand panorama, even if we cannot climb every pinnacle or pause at every outlook point. We must grasp the importance, the centrality, and the glory of God's plan for the nations. What is more, we must discern our privileged location in salvation history and the role God has assigned us to play in it.

There are many themes of mission that can be investigated in a biblical theology of mission. In *Salvation to the Ends of the Earth: A Biblical Theology of Mission*, Andreas J. Köstenberger and Peter T. O'Brien examine the scriptural teaching on mission, expecting to see "an underlying logic and unity in the biblical message on this subject. For Scripture is united by one primary pervading purpose: the tracing of God's unfolding plan of redemption" (2001, 20). However, they give relatively little attention to other possible themes. Arthur F. Glasser (Glasser et al. 2003) sees the kingdom of God as the uniting theme of mission in the Bible. Others trace themes such as unity and plurality (Legrand 1990) or the universal and the particular (Bauckham 2003). These themes are not mutually exclusive but reflect different nuances and emphases unfolding various dimensions of the biblical message. Because of the great diversity in the Bible itself with its many narratives, literary genres, and historical and cultural contexts, one must be cautious about reducing the rich diversity of the Bible too narrowly to a single theme or motif. Yet within this diversity broad unifying contours stand out.

For our purposes this chapter and the next one will focus primarily on the theme of God's relationship to the nations in the unfolding of salvation history. This chapter begins with an overview and then an examination of the Old Testament. In the next chapter, we will move to the teaching of the New Testament. What will be immediately apparent is that mission does not begin with the Great Commission at the end of the Gospels in the New Testament. Rather, God's plan for the nations is a theme running throughout the entire Bible. In the Old Testament this theme emerges from time to time in significant places, remaining an underlying motif in God's election of Israel and the unfolding of salvation history. In the New Testament God's plan for the nations bursts into full realization.

GOD AND THE NATIONS IN SALVATION HISTORICAL OVERVIEW

Where is history headed in respect to God's purposes and, in particular, to God's relationship to the nations? At creation all is good, and there is harmony between God and among God's creatures (Gen. 1–2). As sin enters, the relationships of God's creatures with God and those between men and women become estranged. Creation itself is impacted by the results of human rebellion against God's reign, and the consequences are devastating (Gen. 3). But at the consummation, when God brings history to a close, his reign will be fully restored over men and women, over all nations (Ps. 96:10, 13; Isa. 2:4; Rev. 19:15), and over creation (Rom. 8:19–22), and his kingdom will be established in glory as the heavenly voices proclaim: "The kingdom of the world has become the kingdom of our Lord and of his Christ, and he will reign for ever and ever" (Rev. 11:15b; cf. 12:10).

In this time between creation and consummation, God is at work in the story of redemption, drawing peoples from all nations to himself and re-establishing his reign. Not only will the nations be brought into submission to the reign of the messianic king, but John's vision in the book of Revelation gives us a further glimpse of what God's completed plan for the nations will look like. First, we see that the work of redemption by the Lamb of God has been proclaimed and received by people from all nations and from every background:

> And they sang a new song:
>
>> "You are worthy to take the scroll
>>> and to open its seals,
>> because you were slain,
>>> and with your blood you purchased men for God
>>> from every tribe and language and people and nation.
>> You have made them to be a kingdom and priests to serve our God,
>>> and they will reign on the earth." (Rev. 5:9–10)

Shortly thereafter a similar vision of heavenly worship is described:

> After this I looked and there before me was a great multitude that no one could count, from every nation, tribe, people and language, standing before the throne and in front of the Lamb. They were wearing white robes and were holding palm branches in their hands. And they cried out in a loud voice:
>
>> "Salvation belongs to our God,
>> who sits on the throne,
>> and to the Lamb." (Rev. 7:9–10)

These verses pile up the terms to describe the variety of peoples who will be included in the eschatological worship of God: nation, tribe, people, and language. However humans might be socially categorized, representatives from every group will be included. In the words of Charles H. H. Scobie, the biblical canon from Genesis 11 (describing the scattering of the nations) to Revelation (describing the gathering of the nations) "forms a grand envelope structure framing the entire story of Scripture" (1992, 285). We now trace the biblical story of God's accomplishing this grand goal in the Old Testament.

BEGINNINGS AND THE ORIGIN OF THE NATIONS

As we have noted, at creation there was perfect harmony between God and humanity. Adam and Eve's sin was a matter of distrusting God's goodness and rebelling against his loving authority over their lives. If the purpose of man and woman is to love and glorify God, the heart of sin is the rejection of such a relationship with God. If the kingdom of God consists in essence of living under God's righteous and loving reign, then sin is the rebellion against that reign. The immediate result is shame as Adam and Eve's eyes are opened. They attempt to hide from God (Gen. 3:7–8). And here already the story of God's mission begins.

God takes the initiative in restoring the broken relationship in several ways. First, God himself searches for Adam and Eve: "But the LORD God called to the man, 'Where are you?'" (Gen. 3:9). These haunting words reveal the heart of God: he seeks lost men and women. He does not leave them hiding. He does not immediately execute the death sentence. He seeks them out, calls them to account, and speaks with them.

Second, God pronounces a series of curses (Gen. 3:14–19). Yet embedded in these curses is a promise, the so-called *protoevangelium*, a veiled pre-announcement of the gospel. To the serpent he says: "And I will put enmity between you and the woman, and between your offspring and hers; he will crush your head, and you will strike his heel" (Gen. 3:15). One day a descendent of Eve, though injured himself, will ultimately defeat Satan and the evil that he represents.

Third, before banishing them from Paradise, God provides them with clothes made of skins, not of fig leaves (Gen. 3:21, cf. v. 7). The covering of their shame comes through the shedding of blood, provided for by God himself. This is a foreshadowing of God's ultimate provision to cover our sin with the shed blood of his Son.

The devastating effects of sin become evident in the ensuing chapters of Genesis, climaxing in the destruction of all but Noah and his family in Genesis 6–9. But not long after Noah emerges from the ark, having entered a new covenant with God, sin is painfully manifested in a hideous act of sensuality (Gen. 9:20–27).

Chapter 11 of Genesis opens with the unity of humankind: "Now the whole world had one language and a common speech." But this episode ends with the failure of human religion, typified in the Tower of Babel, the confusion of languages, and the scattering of the peoples throughout the earth (Gen. 11:7–9). The unity of the human family is shattered and ethnic rivalries soon develop.

The utter failure of human efforts to restore the broken relationship with God and overcome the effects of sin is manifest in these opening narratives. But just at this point when all appears most dismal and hopeless—sin reigning, humanity in disarray, and the nations scattered—God reveals his plan for the nations, a plan to be realized through the creation of a kingdom people.

THE CREATION OF A KINGDOM PEOPLE

The Patriarchs: The Promise of Blessing to the Nations

Following the primal history of the scattering of the peoples and the table of nations in Genesis 11 comes the call of Abram in Genesis 12, "God's response to the problem of the nations of humanity" (C. Wright 1996, 39). Whereas Genesis 1–11 describes a universal history of God's dealing with humankind and humanity's efforts leading to disaster, Genesis 12 begins God's particular call of a man to become the father of a people of God's special choosing, leading to blessing. Much of the remainder of the Old Testament is the story of God's dealing with this chosen people. But embedded in this particular call is also a universal intention that includes all nations. This theme will resurface repeatedly in the unfolding of God's dealings with Israel.

Here we encounter one of the most significant promises in scripture relating to salvation history and God's plan for the nations. Genesis 12:1–3 reads:

The LORD had said to Abram, "Leave your country, your people and your father's household and go to the land I will show you.

"I will make you into a great nation
    and I will bless you;
I will make your name great,
    and you will be a blessing.
I will bless those who bless you,
    and whoever curses you I will curse;
and all peoples on earth
    will be blessed through you."[1]

On the one hand, God singles out Abram (later to be renamed Abraham), whom he will uniquely bless and from whom he will create a great nation. This is God's particular call. Yet with this particular call is also a universal intention: through Abraham God will bring blessing to *all* families of the earth. "Families" comes from the Hebrew term *mishpāhâ*, which can also mean nation, tribe, or species. This last phrase is the climax and ultimate intent of the promise. God's blessing on Abraham is not for Abraham alone.

---

1. For a brief discussion of the alternate translation "bless themselves," see Bauckham (2003, 29n3) and Köstenberger and O'Brien (2001, 30–31, including n. 13).

The promise is repeated to Abraham, then later to Isaac and Jacob in Genesis 18:18; 22:18; 26:3–4; 28:14, using in the first three passages the Hebrew term *gôy* (in place of *mishpāhâ*), which normally refers to non-Jewish people or nations.

The statement that those who bless Abram will be blessed and those who curse him will be cursed indicates that Abram (and his descendents) will be God's particular representative and mediator of grace. How one responds to him reflects how one responds to God. One must pause to ponder the magnitude of this statement: The curse or the blessing of *all people* hinges on their relationship to Abraham and his descendents. But the emphasis clearly lies with the blessing in the final phrase, predicting blessing to the nations as an assured fact.

Just how this blessing is to be experienced by the nations is not yet revealed. But as the promise to Abraham is repeated in Genesis 22:18, we are given a hint: "Through your offspring all nations on earth will be blessed, because you have obeyed me." The New Testament interprets this passage as a reference to Christ. Peter quotes it in Acts 3:25, then Paul in Galatians 3:13–16:

> Christ redeemed us from the curse of the law by becoming a curse for us, for it is written: "Cursed is everyone who is hung on a tree." He redeemed us in order that the blessing given to Abraham might come to the Gentiles through Christ Jesus, so that by faith we might receive the promise of the Spirit.
>
> Brothers, let me take an example from everyday life. Just as no one can set aside or add to a human covenant that has been duly established, so it is in this case. The promises were spoken to Abraham and to his seed. The Scripture does not say "and to seeds," meaning many people, but "and to your seed," meaning one person, who is Christ.

From Abraham will come the nation Israel, and from the nation Israel will come the Messiah, whose redeeming death and resurrection will be the source of blessing for people of all nations. Through Christ people of every nation partake in the Abrahamic blessing.

Though the blessing to the nations will reemerge in the Old Testament writings only occasionally, that fact does not diminish the profound significance of the teaching. Here the very purpose of Abraham's (and thereby Israel's) calling is linked to the well-being of the nations.

The Law: A People Who Manifest the Glory and Righteousness of the Lord among the Nations

With the exodus God begins a new era in the formation of his kingdom people. After the deliverance from Egypt and Pharaoh's army and the entry into the wilderness of Sinai, the first words that Moses then receives from the Lord are recorded in Exodus 19:5–6: "'Now if you obey me fully and keep my covenant, then out of all nations you will be my treasured possession. Although the whole earth is mine, you will be for me a kingdom of priests and a holy nation.' These are the words you are to speak to the Israelites."

Note that these words explaining the covenantal relationship and the calling of Israel are received after the Israelites have experienced deliverance but *before* God gives the law. Once again we see God's particular calling for the people of Israel to be his unique possession from among the nations. In the same breath God's universal claim over the whole earth is made. Significant here for God's missionary purposes is that Israel is not a kingdom *with* priests, but the nation itself is a kingdom *of* priests. The role of priest is that of mediation; thus Israel mediates between God and the nations (see Blauw 1962, 24; Schultz 1996; Kaiser 2000).[2] That Israel has

> *Election sets Israel apart from the nations, so that she might in a special way serve God and reveal his glory and lordship on earth and in the end bring the whole world to God. . . . Election has no goal in itself, but only the Kingdom of God.*
>
> Theodorus Christiaan Vriezen
> (cited in Blauw 1962, 23)

a priestly function among the nations seems evident in the explicit singling out of Israel as God's particular possession from among all the peoples. We also read these exact words in the New Testament applied to the new people of God, the church, in an explicitly missionary context:

> But you are a chosen people, a royal priesthood, a holy nation, a people belonging to God, that you may declare the praises of him who called you out of darkness into his wonderful light. (1 Pet. 2:9)

Walter Kaiser has called this text "Israel's missionary call" (1999). However, Israel's priestly role of mediation was more likely to be played out in its unique relationship to the Lord and in an exemplary lifestyle, and not in actually going to the nations to preach.

Israel's priestly role is closely linked with it being a holy nation. Living as a people consecrated to the Lord is essential to being a witness before the nations: "And the LORD has declared this day that you are his people, his treasured possession as he promised, and that you are to keep all his commands. He has declared that he will set you in praise, fame and honor high above all the nations he has made and that you will be a people holy to the LORD your God, as he promised" (Deut. 26:18–19). As Israel lives in obedience to the law of God, that is to say the Israelites live as people under the

---

2. A different interpretation sees "kingdom of priests" referring to Israel's relationship to and trust in God as only a priest could have, or possibly meaning that all Israelites should have access to JHWH (e.g., Schnabel 2004, 71).

reign of God, they manifest God's kingdom and are a holy nation. This in turn glorifies God among the nations and draws the nations to inquire about God: "Observe them [God's laws] carefully, for this will show your wisdom and understanding to the nations, who will hear about all these decrees and say, 'Surely this great nation is a wise and understanding people.' What other nation is so great as to have their gods near them the way the LORD our God is near us whenever we pray to him?" (Deut. 4:6–7). James Chukwuma Okoye calls this "community-in-mission" (2006, 11). "Israel would be the covenant community that is meant to manifest the nature of Yahweh and the benefits of life under Yahweh. Election would in this case be intimately connected with mission" (3–4).

Archaeological discoveries from the ancient Near East demonstrate by contrast just how substantially different the righteousness of the law of Moses was and how attractive such a lifestyle would have been. Yet even when Israel fails, God's judgment on Israel for its disobedience will be a witness to the nations:

> All the nations will ask: "Why has the LORD done this to this land? Why this fierce, burning anger?"
>
> And the answer will be: "It is because this people abandoned the covenant of the LORD, the God of their fathers, the covenant he made with them when he brought them out of Egypt. They went off and worshiped other gods and bowed down to them, gods they did not know, gods he had not given them." (Deut. 29:24–26; cf. 30:1)

Israel's relationship to the resident alien is also of significance. The resident alien, or sojourner (Heb. *gēr*), was a non-Israelite who lived in Israel and was thus subject to oppression and abuse. The law of Moses gave resident aliens certain rights and benefits, protecting them from abuse (e.g., Lev. 23:22; Deut. 14:29; 24:14–22; 27:19). No double standard was allowed. Rather, the same law applied to both aliens and the Israelites (Num. 9:14; 15:14–16, 29–30). Aliens too are the objects of God's compassion; therefore, Israel should show them compassion: "For the LORD your God is God of gods and Lord of lords, the great God, mighty and awesome, who shows no partiality and accepts no bribes. He defends the cause of the fatherless and the widow, and loves the alien, giving him food and clothing. And you are to love those who are aliens, for you yourselves were aliens in Egypt" (Deut. 10:17–19).

Yet even more significantly, aliens were to be taught the law of God and come to fear the Lord: "Assemble the people—men, women and children, and the aliens living in your towns—so they can listen and learn to fear the LORD your God and follow carefully all the words of this law. Their children, who do not know this law, must hear it and learn to fear the LORD your God as long as you live in the land you are crossing the Jordan to possess" (Deut. 31:12–13).

Thus God's kingdom people, Israel, was to demonstrate God's righteousness and treat the alien with justice and compassion. In this way the alien should come to know the fear of the Lord.

Psalms: God Who Is Worthy of the Worship of the Nations

Before examining the Psalms, we note several important texts from the historical books that originate in or describe the same approximate time frame as the Psalms. First Chronicles 16 records David's bringing of the ark of the covenant to Jerusalem. The song of thanksgiving (which is echoed in several psalms) calls Israel to make known the works of the Lord among the peoples (v. 8), to sing to the earth and proclaim his salvation (v. 23), and to tell of his glory among the nations (v. 24). The earth is to fear God (v. 30), and the nations are to know that the Lord reigns (v. 31).

When Solomon dedicates the temple, his prayer reflects the understanding of Israel's drawing the nations to God:

> As for the foreigner who does not belong to your people Israel but has come from a distant land because of your name—for men will hear of your great name and your mighty hand and your outstretched arm—when he comes and prays toward this temple, then hear from heaven, your dwelling place, and do whatever the foreigner asks of you, so that all the peoples of the earth may know your name and fear you, as do your own people Israel, and may know that this house I have built bears your Name. (1 Kings 8:41–43)

It is assumed that foreigners, that is, Gentiles, will come to pray in the temple. Answered prayers from the temple should further cause the nations to fear God (cf. Isa. 56:7). First Kings 10:1–13 recounts the queen of Sheba coming to Solomon, seeking his wisdom, and both blessing God and giving great gifts. Second Kings 5 relates the story of the Aramean army captain Naaman, who experiences healing and acknowledges the universal reign of Israel's God (v. 15). These might be considered types or forerunners of the Gentiles being attracted to Israel and recognizing the greatness of Israel's God.

The Psalms provide us with the hymnbook of the Old Testament. Here we discover the glory and greatness of the Lord in relation to the nations. God is sovereign over all peoples and nations (e.g., Pss. 22:28; 47:8; 82:8), his glory extends "to the ends of the world" (19:4), and all the peoples have seen it (97:6). Numerous prayers call for God to manifest his glory in all the earth (e.g., Pss. 57:5, 11; 72:19; 108:5).

The Psalms pick up the theme of the Abrahamic blessing to the nations. In Psalm 67, God is called upon to bless Israel with the intention that the blessing be passed on. Israel becomes the means of blessing the nations. God's election and blessing of Israel clearly has the nations in view. Note the structure of this psalm.

11

> [1]May God be gracious to us and bless us
> and make his face shine upon us, *Selah*
>
> [2]that your ways may be known on earth,
> your salvation among all nations.
>
> > [3]May the peoples praise you, O God;
> > may all the peoples praise you.
> >
> > > [4]May the nations be glad and sing for joy,
> > > for you rule the peoples justly
> > > and guide the nations of the earth. *Selah*
> >
> > [5]May the peoples praise you, O God;
> > may all the peoples praise you.
>
> [6]Then the land will yield its harvest,
> and God, our God, will bless us.
>
> [7]God will bless us,
> and all the ends of the earth will fear him. (vv. 1–7)

The opening and closing verses repeat the theme of invoking blessing in order to become a blessing to "all nations" so that "the ends of the earth may fear him." Verses 3 and 5 sound a call for the peoples to worship God. The central verse 4 calls the nations to be glad and joyfully sing, because God will judge the peoples and guide the nations. The anticipation of judgment is not normally occasion for joy. But this is possible because the judgment will be just and because the salvation of the Lord has been made known (v. 2b).

Psalm 72 is a messianic psalm of particular significance. This psalm of Solomon invokes blessing upon the king, praying, "In his days may the righteous flourish, and abundance of peace till the moon is no more. May he also rule from sea to sea and from the River to the ends of the earth" (vv. 7–8 NASB). These words clearly look beyond the reign of Solomon to anticipate the universal reign of the messianic King. The prayer continues, "And let all kings bow down before him, all nations serve him" (v. 11 NASB). The king is praised for his acts of compassion and deliverance (9:12–16). Then verse 17 (NASB) reads, "May his name endure forever; may his name increase as long as the sun shines; and let men bless themselves by him; let all nations call him blessed." The Abrahamic promise of blessing for the nations will come through the line of David and ultimately through the messianic King.

Israel is called to declare God's deeds, glory, and salvation among the nations:

> Sing praises to the LORD, enthroned in Zion;
> proclaim among the nations what he has done. (Ps. 9:11)

Give thanks to the Lord, call on his name;
    make known among the nations what he has done. (Ps. 105:1)

The Psalms also express an eschatological vision of the day when all nations will in fact recognize the glory of the Lord and worship him.

All the ends of the earth
    will remember and turn to the Lord,
and all the families of the nations
    will bow down before him,
for dominion belongs to the Lord
    and he rules over the nations.

All the rich of the earth will feast and worship;
    all who go down to the dust will kneel before him—
    those who cannot keep themselves alive. (Ps. 22:27–29)

All the nations you have made
    will come and worship before you, O Lord;
    they will bring glory to your name.
For you are great and do marvelous deeds;
    you alone are God. (Ps. 86:9–10)

With this in mind, the Psalms repeatedly call the nations to acknowledge God as Lord and to come and worship him and him alone.

Sing to the Lord a new song;
    sing to the Lord, all the earth.
Sing to the Lord, praise his name;
    proclaim his salvation day after day.
Declare his glory among the nations,
    his marvelous deeds among all peoples.

For great is the Lord and most worthy of praise;
    he is to be feared above all gods.
For all the gods of the nations are idols,
    but the Lord made the heavens.
Splendor and majesty are before him;
    strength and glory are in his sanctuary.

Ascribe to the Lord, O families of nations,
    ascribe to the Lord glory and strength.
Ascribe to the Lord the glory due his name;
    bring an offering and come into his courts.
Worship the Lord in the splendor of his holiness;
    tremble before him, all the earth.
Say among the nations, "The Lord reigns."

13

> The world is firmly established, it cannot be moved;
> he will judge the peoples with equity. (Ps. 96:1–10)

> Praise the LORD, all you nations;
>   extol him, all you peoples.
> For great is his love toward us,
>   and the faithfulness of the LORD endures forever.
>
> Praise the LORD. (Ps. 117)

> The LORD reigns,
>   let the nations tremble;
> he sits enthroned between the cherubim,
>   let the earth shake.
> Great is the LORD in Zion;
>   he is exalted over all the nations.
> Let them praise your great and awesome name—
>   he is holy. (Ps. 99:1–3)

Prophets: The Eschatological Hope for the Nations

In the Prophets, God's redemptive plan for the nations is further unfolded. The prophet Isaiah's message is particularly rich regarding God's relationship to the nations. Isaiah's central concern is the future of Zion (Seitz 1991; Dumbrell 1985; Schultz 1996, 48). The people of Israel, though judged, will be restored. God will provide salvation through a true servant. The rule of the Lord will be manifest over all nations, and ultimately the nations will recognize God and come to Zion to worship. The book closes with one of the most remarkable statements regarding the Gentile nations in the entire Old Testament.

Already in chapter 2, Isaiah reveals one of his key themes in an eschatological vision of the nations coming to Zion to worship and learn from the Lord:

> In the last days
>
> the mountain of the LORD's temple will be established
>   as chief among the mountains;
> it will be raised above the hills,
>   and all nations will stream to it.
>
> Many peoples will come and say,
>
> "Come, let us go up to the mountain of the LORD,
>   to the house of the God of Jacob.
> He will teach us his ways,
>   so that we may walk in his paths."
> The law will go out from Zion,
>   the word of the LORD from Jerusalem. (Isa. 2:2–3)

God will judge the nations. They are accountable before him. All other gods are false gods and idols. But the nations will be drawn to the exalted Lord in Zion. What is more, the Lord will establish his kingdom of peace:

> He will judge between the nations
>   and will settle disputes for many peoples.
> They will beat their swords into plowshares
>   and their spears into pruning hooks.
> Nation will not take up sword against nation,
>   nor will they train for war anymore. (Isa. 2:4)

This motif recurs throughout the book (e.g., 14:26; 19:23–25; 24:13–16; 34:1–2). Isaiah also foresees the day when Israel will experience the salvation of the Lord and make this known to the nations:

> With joy you will draw water
>   from the wells of salvation.
>
> In that day you will say:
>
> "Give thanks to the LORD, call on his name;
>   make known among the nations what he has done,
>   and proclaim that his name is exalted.
> Sing to the LORD, for he has done glorious things;
>   let this be known to all the world. (Isa. 12:3–5)

In chapter 11, Isaiah indicates that the Messiah will fill the earth with the knowledge of the Lord (v. 9), and the nations will rally to him (v. 10). One day Egypt and Assyria will be drawn to the Lord and included with Israel in God's blessing as God's people: "In that day Israel will be the third, along with Egypt and Assyria, a blessing on the earth. The LORD Almighty will bless them, saying, 'Blessed be Egypt my people, Assyria my handiwork, and Israel my inheritance'" (19:24–25).

As Christopher J. H. Wright observes, "The identity of Israel will be merged with that of Egypt and Assyria, such that the Abrahamic promise is not only fulfilled *in* them but *through* them" (2006, 236).

Isaiah's teaching regarding the servant of the Lord brings a new dimension in the progress of revelation. On the one hand, Israel is identified as the servant of the Lord (20:3; 41:8–9; 44:1–2, 21; 45:4; 48:20; 49:3). The ideal servant is described in chapter 42:

> Here is my servant, whom I uphold,
>   my chosen one in whom I delight;
> I will put my Spirit on him
>   and he will bring justice to the nations.
> . . . .

> I, the LORD, have called you in righteousness;
> I will take hold of your hand.
> I will keep you and will make you
> to be a covenant for the people
> and a light for the Gentiles,
> to open eyes that are blind,
> to free captives from prison
> and to release from the dungeon those who sit in darkness. (vv. 1, 6–7)

The servant is one chosen by the Lord to be his Spirit-filled messenger and bring justice, light, and deliverance to the nations. At this new thing the Lord is declaring that (v. 9) the nations are to rejoice in worship: "Sing to the LORD a new song, his praise from the ends of the earth, you who go down to the sea, and all that is in it, you islands, and all who live in them" (v. 10).

Yet only a few verses later we read, "Who is blind but my servant, and deaf like the messenger I send? Who is blind like the one committed to me, blind like the servant of the LORD?" (42:19). Israel clearly fails to live up to its calling as the servant of the Lord. In chapter 43 we read that the servant is to be a witness to the nations:

> All the nations gather together
> and the peoples assemble.
> Which of them foretold this
> and proclaimed to us the former things?
> Let them bring in their witnesses to prove they were right,
> so that others may hear and say, "It is true."
> "You are my witnesses," declares the LORD,
> "and my servant whom I have chosen,
> so that you may know and believe me
> and understand that I am he.
> Before me no god was formed,
> nor will there be one after me.
> I, even I, am the LORD,
> and apart from me there is no savior." (vv. 9–11)

The remainder of chapter 43 makes clear again Israel's failure. Nevertheless, God remains faithful and promises the coming of the true servant. In chapter 49 the description of the servant shifts to describe the ideal servant who will restore Israel. But "the restoration of Israel is not a sufficiently great task for the servant" (Young 1972, 274); he is to be a light to the Gentile nations making God's salvation known to all: "He says: 'It is too small a thing for you to be my servant to restore the tribes of Jacob and bring back those of Israel I have kept. I will also make you a light for the Gentiles, that you may bring my salvation to the ends of the earth'" (49:6). Only through the true servant will the salvation of the Lord at last be made known to all nations.

The New Testament applies the description "light to the Gentiles" directly to Christ (Luke 2:32; cf. John 8:12; 9:5) and the church (Acts 13:47; cf. Matt. 5:14). Then the Redeemer will receive the worship of kings and rulers (Isa. 49:7). This salvation will be made possible through the sacrificial death of the servant (53:10–12). Köstenberger and O'Brien note regarding the Servant in Isaiah, "This sequence of his ministry, namely, first to Israel that then results in blessing to the nations, suggests not only a pattern similar to the Abrahamic promises but also a partial fulfillment of them (Isa. 49:6)" (2001, 46).

Chapter 56 expresses the vision of foreigners, "others," joining themselves to the Lord, worshipping and serving the Lord in the temple, ministering to and loving the Lord. They are gathered to the Lord's holy mountain, Zion:

> Let no foreigner who has bound himself to the LORD say,
> "The LORD will surely exclude me from his people."
> . . . .
> "And foreigners who bind themselves to the LORD
>   to serve him,
> to love the name of the LORD,
>   and to worship him,
> all who keep the Sabbath without desecrating it
>   and who hold fast to my covenant—
> these I will bring to my holy mountain
>   and give them joy in my house of prayer.
> Their burnt offerings and sacrifices
>   will be accepted on my altar;
> for my house will be called
>   a house of prayer for all nations."
> The Sovereign LORD declares—
>   he who gathers the exiles of Israel:
> "I will gather still others to them
>   besides those already gathered." (vv. 3, 6–8)

Later Isaiah resumes the message of the eschatological inclusion of the nations in heretofore unprecedented grandeur. Chapter 60 paints the picture of the light and glory of the Lord drawing the nations to serve a personified Zion (vv. 1–3). Wealth will be brought to her, and nations refusing to do so will perish (vv. 11–12). The Lord will reign in peace and righteousness, and he himself will be their everlasting light and glory (vv. 17–20).

The vision climaxes with Isaiah 66, the final chapter of the book.

> "And I, because of their [the Gentiles'] actions and their imaginations, am about to come and gather all nations and tongues, and they will come and see my glory.
> "I will set a sign among them, and I will send some of those who survive to the nations—to Tarshish, to the Libyans and Lydians (famous as archers), to Tubal and Greece, and to the distant islands that have not heard of my fame or seen my

glory. They will proclaim my glory among the nations. And they will bring all your brothers, from all the nations, to my holy mountain in Jerusalem as an offering to the LORD—on horses, in chariots and wagons, and on mules and camels," says the LORD. "They will bring them, as the Israelites bring their grain offerings, to the temple of the LORD in ceremonially clean vessels. And I will select some of them also to be priests and Levites," says the LORD. (vv. 18–21)

Here no nation or language group is excluded. The Gentiles themselves become messengers (missionaries) sent by the Lord who declare the glory of the Lord to the farthest places where he had been unknown. Perhaps most remarkable in this prophecy is that Gentiles will become "priests and Levites," a position of full inclusion, of privilege and access to God. Note that it has been suggested that Isaiah 66:19 influenced Paul's missionary travel itinerary (Aus 1979; Riesner 1998, 245–53; for a discussion of difficulties with this position, see Schnabel 2004, 2:1295–97).

We turn now briefly to exemplary passages in several other prophets. Ezekiel speaks in 36:16–38 of the judgment that falls upon Israel and of the Lord scattering Israel among the nations. What is worse, the Lord says, "Wherever they went among the nations they profaned my holy name" (v. 20a). This is precisely the opposite of Israel's calling. But in the face of Israel's failure, God remains faithful. For his name's sake he will vindicate his name among the nations: "I will show the holiness of my great name, which has been profaned among the nations, the name you have profaned among them. Then the nations will know that I am the LORD, declares the Sovereign LORD, when I show myself holy through you before their eyes" (v. 23).

The manner in which this will come to pass is most astonishing. The Lord will return Israel to the land and cleanse them. "I will give you a new heart and put a new spirit in you; I will remove from you your heart of stone and give you a heart of flesh. And I will put my Spirit in you and move you to follow my decrees and be careful to keep my laws" (vv. 26–27). These words clearly anticipate the new covenant. Through the Spirit-filled obedience of God's people, the nations come to know that the Lord is God.

We also encounter an explicit reference to Israel being a blessing to the nations in the prophet Jeremiah 4:1–2. There the Lord speaks to Israel:

> "If you will return, O Israel,
>   return to me,"
>   declares the LORD.
> "If you put your detestable idols out of my sight
>   and no longer go astray,
> and if in a truthful, just and righteous way
>   you swear, 'As surely as the LORD lives,'
> then the nations will be blessed by him
>   and in him they will glory."

Richard Bauckham comments on this passage: "What is notable here is that it is Israel's fulfillment of her covenant obligations, her practice of truth, justice and righteousness, that will bring blessing to the nations (cf. Gen. 18:18–19). In order for the nations to be blessed Israel need only be faithful to YHWH. Her life with YHWH will itself draw the nations to YHWH so that they too may experience blessing" (2003, 31).

Jonah is considered the great missionary book of the Old Testament. Though numerous Old Testament prophets were given messages *for* the nations—usually of judgment—we have with Jonah the single instance where a prophet has been explicitly sent geographically *to* a Gentile nation as God's messenger. The destination, Nineveh, is one of the capital cities of the Assyrian Empire, Israel's most feared enemy. In this case the message is also one of judgment. But after the reluctant prophet has delivered his message, the entire city of Nineveh repents and calls upon God for mercy (3:1–9). God relents and holds back destruction, demonstrating that he is a God of compassion even to the most cruel of nations (3:10). His covenantal love (Heb. *ḥesed*) extends even to Gentiles (4:2).

But the book of Jonah, which is full of ironies, climaxes not with God's forgiveness of the Ninevites but with Jonah's encounter with God in the last chapter. Jonah is angry that God has shown compassion to Nineveh and is consumed with self-pity (4:1–3). After an object lesson with the vine and the worm, which only accentuates Jonah's self-centeredness, the book ends abruptly with the Lord posing a question to Jonah: "But the LORD said, 'You have been concerned about this vine, though you did not tend it or make it grow. It sprang up overnight and died overnight. But Nineveh has more than a hundred and twenty thousand people who cannot tell their right hand from their left, and many cattle as well. Should I not be concerned about that great city?'" (4:10–11).

Here the heart and character of Jonah could hardly be more dramatically contrasted with the heart and character of the Lord. While Jonah's concern is for the destruction of the heathen and his own personal comfort, the Lord's desire is to demonstrate compassion, even toward animals. The rhetorical device of leaving the closing question unanswered forces the readers to answer it: Do we identify with Jonah or with the Lord? Is not the Lord right in exercising compassion? Jonah becomes typical of Israel, or the believer, who is totally out of harmony with the intentions of God, and who has become a consumer instead of mediator of God's blessings. God's intention is to exercise compassion and grace even to the most depraved peoples who will but repent and turn to him.

The prophet Zechariah addresses Israel's relation to the nations in chapter 8 with a great message of hope. The Abrahamic promise is reiterated in verse 13, "As you have been an object of cursing among the nations, O Judah and Israel, so will I save you, and you will be a blessing. Do not be afraid, but let your hands be strong." The Lord's saving grace is contrasted to the human failings of Israel in realizing the covenant. Verses 20–23 anticipate the day of its fulfillment when people from all nations will come to Israel to worship God:

> This is what the LORD Almighty says: "Many peoples and the inhabitants of many cities will yet come, and the inhabitants of one city will go to another and say, 'Let us go at once to entreat the LORD and seek the LORD Almighty. I myself am going.' And many peoples and powerful nations will come to Jerusalem to seek the LORD Almighty and to entreat him."
>
> This is what the LORD Almighty says: "In those days ten men from all languages and nations will take firm hold of one Jew by the hem of his robe and say, 'Let us go with you, because we have heard that God is with you.'"

In chapter 9 he then describes the messianic kingdom, which will extend universal peace and righteousness to all nations.

> Rejoice greatly, O Daughter of Zion!
>   Shout, Daughter of Jerusalem!
> See, your king comes to you,
>   righteous and having salvation,
>   gentle and riding on a donkey,
>   on a colt, the foal of a donkey.
> I will take away the chariots from Ephraim
>   and the war-horses from Jerusalem,
>   and the battle bow will be broken.
> He will proclaim peace to the nations.
>   His rule will extend from sea to sea
>   and from the River to the ends of the earth. (vv. 9–10)

At first the messianic king comes in humility, on a donkey, bringing salvation. But then he is depicted as establishing a kingdom of peace over all the earth. Later Zechariah depicts the rising up of nations against Jerusalem, but with the return of the messianic king the rebellious nations will be once and for all defeated. "The LORD will be king over the whole earth. On that day there will be one LORD, and his name the only name" (14:9). The nations will bring their wealth to Jerusalem. "Then the survivors from all the nations that have attacked Jerusalem will go up year after year to worship the King, the LORD Almighty, and to celebrate the Feast of Tabernacles" (14:16). But those refusing to do so will be punished by the Lord (14:17–19).

Zechariah's vision is reiterated in other minor prophets. For example, the Lord speaks through Malachi, "'My name will be great among the nations, from the rising to the setting of the sun. In every place incense and pure offerings will be brought to my name, because my name will be great among the nations,' says the LORD Almighty" (1:11). The prophet Micah also predicts the worship of many nations in Zion (4:2), a reign of peace (4:3), the one born in Bethlehem whose "greatness will reach to the ends of the earth" (5:4), and the judgment of disobedient nations (5:15). Thus through the Messiah the kingdom of God will be established over all nations, include the worship of all nations, and extend over all the earth. In this way God's plan for the nations and God's kingdom purposes merge and come to ultimate fulfillment. A future inclusion of Gentiles in the people of God, gathering to worship the Lord in Zion, is a recurrent theme in the Old Testament. All families of the earth will one day indeed be blessed.

WAS ISRAEL'S MISSION ONE OF BEING SENT TO THE NATIONS?

To summarize, God's plan for the nations in the Old Testament is a recurring theme that emerges time and again at critical moments in the unfolding of Old Testament salvation history:

- After the fall, the promise of a savior (Gen. 3:15)
- At the call of Abraham and the patriarchs, the promise of blessing to all nations (Gen. 12:3; 18:18; 22:18; 28:14)
- After the exodus and before the giving of the law, the call of Israel to be a "kingdom of priests" (Exod. 19:5–6)
- Within the law the reminder that Israel's obedience will be a testimony to the nations (Deut. 4:6–7)
- At the return of the ark to Jerusalem (1 Chron. 16:8–36) and at the dedication of Solomon's temple (1 Kings 8:41–43; 2 Chron. 6:32–33), an invitation to the nations to worship the Lord
- During the crisis of the ensuing captivity of Israel and Judah, the promise of a greater kingdom including the Gentiles (see the passages from Isaiah noted above)
- At the restoration of the Jewish people from the Babylonian captivity, the promise of the coming messianic kingdom including the nations (cf. passages from Zechariah noted above)

From what has been discussed thus far, it is not clear whether Israel had a missionary mandate from the Lord to actually *go* to the nations (see Rowley 1944; Bright 1955; Schultz 1996; Kaiser 2000), or if Israel's missionary calling was to be a more passive witness of God's righteousness and glory in the midst of the nations, attracting the nations to *come* and worship God (see Blauw 1962; Köstenberger and O'Brien 2001; Schnabel 2004; C. J. H. Wright 2006).

A few passages could be interpreted as indicating that Israel was commanded to go to the nations. For example, various psalms call Israel to "declare his glory among the nations, his marvelous deeds among all peoples" (Ps. 96:3;

see also, e.g., 9:11b and 105:1b). Such passages could, however, be understood poetically. Or the manner in which Israel communicates may be more that of attraction and example than of overt going to preach among the nations. In this case Israel's mission was to serve the Lord faithfully as his covenant people in the *midst* of the nations. In so doing they were to be God's instrument of manifesting his kingdom and righteousness to the nations.

The Old Testament consistently depicts the worship of the Lord as being centralized in Zion. The nations were to abandon idols, submit to God's reign, and *come*. Isaiah speaks of the Word of the Lord going out from Jerusalem, but the result will be the nations *coming* to Zion (Isa. 2:3; 12:4–5; cf. Mic. 4:2). This gathering of nations is generally placed in the distant, if not eschatological, future. Israel was to be a light to the nations (e.g., Isa. 42:6), but here again the method is not explicit. Various prophets of Israel had messages for the Gentile nations, but apart from the reluctant prophet Jonah, we have no evidence of them actually traveling to the nations to deliver the message, which was normally a message of judgment. Isaiah 66:19 speaks of an explicit sending to the nations, but this is clearly an eschatological passage looking to the distant future, and Gentiles seem to be the primary agents, not Israel.

Köstenberger and O'Brien conclude, "To contend that Israel had a missionary task and should have engaged in mission as we understand it today, goes beyond the evidence. There is no suggestion in the Old Testament that Israel should have engaged in 'cross-cultural' or foreign mission" (2001, 35). They concur with Scobie (1992) that Israel was to relate to the nations (1) *historically* in terms of incorporation, that is, receiving Gentiles into the community, and (2) *eschatologically* in terms of ingathering in the last days. Furthermore, Israel was never denounced by the prophets for failing to go to the nations. C. J. H. Wright captures the concept of the mission of Israel perhaps best when he claims that although Israel did not have a missionary mandate to go to the nations, "one might say that Israel had a missional role in the midst of the nations—implying that they had an identity and role connected to God's ultimate intention of blessing the nations" (2006, 24–25).

However we may choose to answer the question regarding Israel's role among the nations, Israel failed. Israel *neither* went to the nations, *nor* did Israel live as a holy and righteous people amid the nations. Israel repeatedly fell into idolatry, perverted justice, and, with but rare exceptions, failed to manifest the righteousness and glory of God among the nations. It failed to exemplify what it means to be a kingdom people living under the blessings of God. "The difference between Israel and all the nations lies only in the undeserved election of Israel by YHWH to be his one people for the sake of bringing blessing to all the peoples. Israel is called to be faithful to her covenant with YHWH, not for the sake of superiority but in order to model this covenant relationship as an invitation to others. Israel's ethnocentric temptation was to presume on her privilege" (Bauckham 2003, 67).

Even in the postexilic era the attitude of the Israelites tended to be one of pride and privilege, looking with condescension upon the Gentile nations. Israel attempted to retain the Abrahamic blessing for itself, refusing to become the means of blessing to the nations. In so doing, it forfeited its blessing altogether. And yet, in spite of human failure, the sovereign God would fulfill his plan to bring blessing to the nations.

FIGURE 1.1: THE CENTRIPETAL MOVEMENT OF MISSION IN THE OLD TESTAMENT

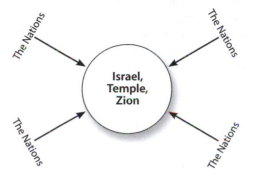

One of the most widely accepted understandings of comparing mission in the Old and New Testaments was first put forth by Bengt Sundkler (1936). He wrote to refute the argument of Adolph Harnack that a Gentile mission was nowhere in Jesus's authentic thinking or teaching. Sundkler sought to overcome the particularist-universalist dichotomy with his proposal of centripetal and centrifugal conceptions of mission (see D. T. Bosch 1969). He suggested that the Old Testament presents a *centripetal* missionary motion (drawing toward the center, see fig. 1.1), whereas the New Testament reverses this to a *centrifugal* motion (moving out from the center). The centripetal movement is that of the nations being attracted as by a magnet to the glory of the Lord manifested in Israel, the nations coming to Zion, and the centralized worship of the Lord in the temple. Johannes Blauw, for example, writes, "There is no thought of mission in the Old Testament in the centrifugal sense in which it comes to the fore in the New Testament" (1962, 35).

The centrifugal movement of mission in the New Testament marks a reversal, with God's new people being sent out to the nations, to be a witness among the nations. The nations are not to *come* to God's people in Jerusalem, but God's people are to *go* to the nations. As we shall see in the next chapter, in the age of the Spirit the transformation of mission is really more radical than the reversal of centripetal to centrifugal. Yet at the consummation and fulfillment of the Old Testament eschatological vision, the direction will reverse again, and the nations will be drawn centripetally to Zion, the new Jerusalem.

CONCLUSION

Let us summarize what we have discovered from our survey of Old Testament teachings on mission with particular reference to God and the nations:

1. God is the Creator of all and sovereign Lord over all peoples and nations.
2. Though all humans have rebelled against God's rule, God in his grace has taken initiative to provide a way of reconciliation, bringing them back into his kingdom.
3. As a result of God's call of Abraham and Israel, they were not only to be blessed but were also to become a blessing, mediating God's righteousness, glory, and salvation to the nations.
4. Israel's primary form of witness was to live righteously and worship wholeheartedly, thus manifesting the kingdom of God in the midst of the nations.
5. Israel was to proclaim the salvation of the Lord in the midst of the nations and to invite them to come and worship the Lord and worship him alone.
6. Israel failed in its mission as "light of the nations," but the Messiah would fulfill this role, create a new kingdom people, and send them as his witnesses to the nations.
7. The day would come when Gentiles from all nations would worship the Lord and be included in his kingdom people. Zion is depicted as the center point to which the nations flow.
8. God will one day judge all nations, overthrow all evil, and fully establish his kingdom of peace and righteousness over all creation.

The seeming lack of overt mission in terms of Israel being sent *to* the nations in the Old Testament should not disturb us. At first glance this may appear to be in discontinuity with the New Testament. The Bible, however, is a long story of progressive revelation in which God's concern for the nations is present from the start. God's plan of salvation unfolds in history one step at a time. The Old Testament lays a foundation for the New; seeds planted there will sprout and bear much fruit later. Both Testaments look forward to the completion of God's plan for the nations in the eschatological vision of people of every nation, tribe, and tongue worshipping God in the new Jerusalem.

The Old Testament only hints at just how the eschatological vision of the nations coming to know God will be realized. This will be revealed in the New Testament with a dramatic revolution: God's formation of a new kingdom people to bring that vision to fulfillment. It is to that part of the story we now turn.

2

God and the Nations in the New Testament

The Old Testament has given us a clear vision of God's sovereignty over the nations, his desire to bless the nations, and his ultimate inclusion of them in his kingdom. But the vision is primarily in the future. Whereas Israel as God's servant had failed to manifest the righteousness and glory of the Lord before the nations, the true Servant, the promised Messiah, would come as savior and as a light to the Gentiles. With him the Abrahamic promise of blessing to all the families of the earth comes to fulfillment (Gal. 3:13–16). The manner by which the nations will be gathered unto the Lord is manifest in the New Testament. The age of the Spirit dawns.

MISSION IN THE AGE OF THE SPIRIT

Before we examine the various teachings of specific New Testament authors and books, it is important to grasp the magnitude of transformation in mission that occurs with the completion of Christ's work of redemption, the coming of the Holy Spirit at Pentecost, and the birth of the church. This transformation affects virtually every aspect of the New Testament's depiction of mission. We noted at the end of the last chapter that the movement of mission reverses from *centripetal* in the Old Testament, Israel attracting the nations to come and worship the Lord in Zion, to *centrifugal*, an explicit sending of Christ's witnesses to the nations in the New. But the transformation of mission is really more profound than this, and the term *centrifugal* is not adequate to express that revolution.

As we have already observed, the Old Testament frequently anticipates the salvation of peoples from the farthest nations. Though the Old Testament is less clear about just *how* that would come to pass, a few passages give a glimpse of what will come to full realization in the New Testament era. The prophet Ezekiel foretells the day when God will give his people his Spirit so that they can obey him from the heart (Ezek. 36:26–27). Isaiah foresees the day when the Word of the Lord will go out from Jerusalem (Isa. 2:3; see also Mic. 4:2) and when a true servant will be a light to the nations (Isa. 42:6). Gentiles will become God's messengers to the distant coastlands, declaring God's glory among the nations (Isa. 66:19). But even this remarkable statement is embedded in a vision with Israel at the center, "And I, because of their actions and their imaginations, am about to come and gather all nations and tongues, and they will come and see my glory. . . . And they will bring all your brothers, from all the nations, to my holy mountain in Jerusalem as an offering to the LORD" (Isa. 66:18, 20a). Old Testament mission envisions the nations flowing to Zion to worship the one true God in the temple, where God's presence on earth was particularly represented.

The New Testament does not abandon this centripetal vision but in fact depicts it in even more marvelous terms. Jesus speaks of the day when Gentiles will come from east and west, from north and south to be included in the kingdom of God (Matt. 8:11–12; Luke 13:29). John's vision in Revelation describes the ultimate arrival of the kingdom, which includes a "new Jerusalem, coming down out of heaven," where God's people live and worship, where "the dwelling [tabernacle] of God is with men" (Rev. 21:2–3). Revelation 21 goes on to describe the glory and presence of the Lord in the new Jerusalem with astonishing terms, far surpassing the glory of the old Jerusalem temple: "I did not see a temple in the city, because the Lord God Almighty and the Lamb are its temple. The city does not need the sun or the moon to shine on it, for the glory of God gives it light, and the Lamb is its lamp" (vv. 22–23). The vision of the centripetal movement of the nations to worship God is fulfilled, "The nations will walk by its light, and the kings of the earth will bring their splendor into it. On no day will its gates ever be shut, for there will be no night there. The glory and honor of the nations will be brought into it" (vv. 24–26).

What we then see is a sort of expanding and contracting effect: beginning with the centralization of mission at Jerusalem in the Old Testament, then the sending out of missionaries to the nations and the decentralization of mission in the New Testament era, until the consummation, when the nations will be gathered back to the new and more glorious Jerusalem. However, the more dominant description of mission in the New Testament is that of the intervening period between the first and second comings of Christ, between the initiation of the kingdom and the full establishment of his kingdom, between the old Jerusalem and the new. That intervening period is the age of the Spirit.

Decentralization and Diffusion of New Testament Mission

Jesus's discussion with the Samaritan woman at Jacob's well is especially revealing. She raises the question about the correct place of worship, knowing that the Jews and the Samaritans differ on this issue (John 4:20). But Jesus answers that the day will soon come when the true worship of God will be geographically focused on *neither* Jerusalem *nor* anywhere else: "Jesus declared, 'Believe me, woman, a time is coming when you will worship the Father neither on this mountain nor in Jerusalem. You Samaritans worship what you do not know; we worship what we do know, for salvation is from the Jews. Yet a time is coming and has now come when the true worshipers will worship the Father in spirit and truth, for they are the kind of worshipers the Father seeks. God is spirit, and his worshipers must worship in spirit and in truth'" (John 4:21–24).

With these words Jesus decentralizes and deterritorializes the worship of God. The thought is further unfolded in the New Testament. Stephen's sermon in Acts 7 points out that God's presence is no longer tied to the Jerusalem temple (Flemming 2005, 33). The apostle Paul emphasizes that in the age of the Spirit the temple of the Lord is *his people*, independent of any geographical location. Not only are Gentiles included in the new people of God, but they themselves become a living, spiritual temple wherever they are. "Consequently, you are no longer foreigners and aliens, but fellow citizens with God's people and members of God's household, built on the foundation of the apostles and prophets, with Christ Jesus himself as the chief cornerstone. In him the whole building is joined together and rises to become a holy temple in the Lord. And in him you too are being built together to become a dwelling in which God lives by his Spirit" (Eph. 2:19–22).

A similar thought is evident in 1 Peter 2:5: "You also, like living stones, are being built into a spiritual house to be a holy priesthood, offering spiritual sacrifices acceptable to God through Jesus Christ." The Old Testament cultic language of priesthood, sacrifice, and temple is applied to the diaspora church, the community of believers themselves being the locus of God's presence wherever it finds itself.

Just as the presence of God is decentralized, so too the missionary movement is fully decentralized. Acts 1:8 depicts the disciples becoming witnesses of Christ, moving out from Jerusalem to Judea, Samaria, and the ends of the earth. This appears at first to be centrifugal, with Jerusalem still at the center. But soon mission in the New Testament evolves to have multiple centers (see fig. 2.1). Anywhere God's new people, the church, is found is a potential sending

FIGURE 2.1: THE CENTRIFUGAL, DECENTRALIZED MOVEMENT
OF MISSION IN THE NEW TESTAMENT

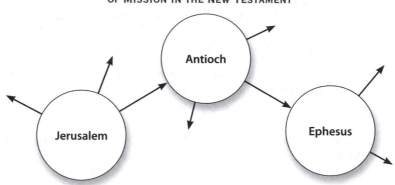

and gathering point for mission. "Jesus Christ Himself replaces Jerusalem. He is the central point around whom the nations will gather" (Blauw 1962, 92).

Even the first Christians were slow to grasp this new reality, and Jerusalem remained for some time the center of authority in the early church. But the missionary movement of the Spirit had in fact already decentralized mission. Antioch had become the sending and reporting center of the Gentile mission of Paul and Barnabas (Acts 13:1–3; 14:26–28). Ephesus later became a new center of mission from which the gospel spread to Colossae and the Lycos Valley. Through the centuries the gospel has spread from various centers: Rome, Iona (Celtic mission in the Middle Ages), Herrnhut (Zinzendorf's Moravian community from which the first major Protestant missionary movement originated), London (home of the earliest Protestant mission societies), Chicago, Nairobi, Seoul, Buenos Aires. Witnesses from these centers cross geographic, political, and cultural barriers. Furthermore, even in the early church the gospel spread not only through the ministry of the apostles. Indeed, the first Christians to take the gospel to the Gentiles in Antioch were from Cyprus and Cyrene (Acts 12:20).

Such decentralization and diffusion have never been more evident than in our own day of globalization, when many local congregations are becoming more directly involved in sending missionaries and establishing international partnerships, bypassing denominational structures and mission agencies. Wherever the church is planted a new potential sending point has been established. Whenever a new ethnic group is reached for Christ, those people become potential missionaries to yet another group. Therefore, it is better to speak of a decentralization and diffusion of mission in the New Testament than to speak of centrifugal mission. Richard Bauckham warns, "To substitute another physical centre for Jerusalem, whether Rome or Byzantium in earlier times or western Europe in the modern age of missions, was always a mistake, however understandable" (2003, 76).

28

Reframing the Kingdom of God as a Movement of the Spirit

In the Old Testament, God's kingdom is primarily associated with the nation of Israel. God is to be the ultimate king of his people, who live under his law. The people demand a human king and receive one, but this is not God's original intent (1 Sam. 8:4–22; 12:12–17). God's kingdom was to be manifest in his kingly rule through his people Israel. As a result of Israel's rejection of God as king, the nation is repeatedly conquered and oppressed by its enemies. The general expectation of the Jews in Jesus's day is that the Messiah will inaugurate a political kingdom liberated from Roman or foreign dominance. What he in fact brings is a much greater kingdom.

Jesus's teaching brings a new, unexpected emphasis on the kingdom as emanating from a spiritual center and renewal. With his coming the kingdom is at hand (Matt. 4:17). More than this, "He not only *proclaims*, but He *is* in His person the Kingdom which is at hand" (Blauw 1962, 72). As Jesus heals, casts out demons, and performs miracles, he states that these are signs that the rule of God has broken into history in a new way to overthrow evil and reverse the effects of sin; indeed the kingdom is in their midst (Matt. 12:28). He refuses to allow himself to be made king by force (John 6:15), for his kingdom is not of this world (John 18:36). When the Pharisees ask Jesus when the kingdom is coming, he answers, "The kingdom of God is not coming with signs to be observed; . . . For behold, the kingdom of God is in your midst" (Luke 17:20–21, NASB). And when his disciples ask him the same question after the resurrection, he answers by telling them that this is not for them to know, but that the Holy Spirit will come to empower them to be his witnesses (Acts 1:6–8).

The New Testament does not completely spiritualize the kingdom, but the kingdom does begin as a movement of the Holy Spirit in the spiritual dimension: "I tell you the truth, no one can see the kingdom of God unless he is born again . . . no one can enter the kingdom of God unless he is born of water and the Spirit" (John 3:3, 5), which occurs through repentance and faith (Matt. 3:2; 4:17; Mark 1:15). It is the poor in spirit, the persecuted, and the righteous to whom the kingdom belongs (Matt. 5:3, 10, 20). "For the kingdom of God is not a matter of eating and drinking, but of righteousness, peace and joy in the Holy Spirit" (Rom. 14:17).

We shall return frequently to the theme of the kingdom and its implications for understanding mission. We simply note here that the New Testament not only decentralizes mission but also denationalizes and reframes the kingdom in terms of its spiritual nature under the rule of the messianic King. The kingdom is where God reigns, not merely politically or through a national entity, but first and foremost in spirit. People must be reconciled with God to enter his kingdom, and this would be the great work that Jesus comes to earth to accomplish. Where persons repent, confess Jesus as Lord, receive forgiveness of sin, submit to the will of King Jesus, and live in the power of the Spirit, there is the kingdom of God. The kingdom will indeed have its transforming effect in all aspects of life. But it begins as a movement of the Spirit through the proclamation of the gospel of Jesus Christ, or it does not begin at all.

Transculturalization of the New Kingdom People

With the decentralization of mission in the New Testament and the reframing of the kingdom in terms of the Spirit comes also the transculturalization of the new kingdom people—the church. As the Gentiles become believers in Christ, they do not become simply Jewish proselytes. Early in the development of the church, this is a hotly debated question: Must Gentile believers become Jews? Must they be circumcised and keep the law of Moses? As the Jerusalem Christians hear of the gospel spreading to Gentiles, they repeatedly question the legitimacy of such conversions apart from the Gentiles first becoming Jews. God, however, continually demonstrates that he "does not show favoritism" (Acts 10:34). Ultimately the early church grants Gentile believers full inclusion into the new people of God (Acts 15) apart from becoming Jewish proselytes.

Paul reflects on the profound implications of this in Ephesians 2. Gentiles, once aliens to God's people (vv. 11–12), have not only been included as equals; indeed, God has created one *new* people out of the two (vv. 13–14a). Christ has broken down the wall of separation between Jew and Gentile (v. 14b). This is central to the redemptive work of Christ at Golgotha. The cross of Christ has not only purchased individual salvation but also accomplished this work of reconciliation (vv. 13, 16). It is this new people who become the new spiritual temple and dwelling place of God (Eph. 2:19–22). Elsewhere Paul writes, "There is neither Jew nor Greek, slave nor free, male nor female, for you are all one in Christ Jesus. If you belong to Christ, then you are Abraham's seed, and heirs according to the promise" (Gal. 3:28–29). Colossians 3:10–11 speaks of this new unity being rooted in the new creation of regeneration whereby the divine image is renewed in the believer: "And [you] have put on the new self, which is being renewed in knowledge in the image of its Creator. Here there is no Greek or Jew, circumcised or uncircumcised, barbarian, Scythian, slave or free, but Christ is all, and is in all."

Barbarians are included, a general term for non-Greeks. The Scythian is particularly noted because the Scythian was considered "the most barbarian of barbarians" (Bauckham 2003, 69), a spiritually and socially repugnant person to both the Jew and the Greek. Thus virtually every distinction dividing humans is transcended in the new kingdom community: religious background, social standing, ethnic heritage, gender, economic status. Belonging to Christ is the defining and unifying moment.

As the new people of God emerges and moves beyond the bounds of Jewish culture, Jewish culture is not replaced with some kind of new unified Christian culture. Rather, the church becomes genuinely multicultural. This, among other things, significantly distinguishes Christianity from Islam. Islam seeks to create an Islamic monoculture based on the Qur'an legislating a uniform social order and culture in great detail. The Qur'an itself (written in Arabic) is, strictly speaking, not even to be translated into vernacular languages.

The New Testament depicts a cultural universalization of the church in terms of inclusiveness, but not a cultural homogenization in the process. Various cultural expressions of Christian life are legitimate within this broader unity to the extent that they embody the values of the kingdom of God living out the gospel. The Jerusalem church continues to express itself in Jewish forms, such as zeal for the law and participation in temple rites (Acts 21:20–26). While the churches in Gentile contexts are expected to retain the ethical standards of the Old Testament and adopt the Jewish practice of weekly meetings (unknown to other social groups in the Roman world), they are free from the ceremonial and cultural identity of Judaism and can develop unique expressions of the one faith. This is what Andrew Walls has called the "indigenous principle" of the church (1982).

And yet even these contextual expressions of faith are conditional; they are not ultimately defining. Christian identity and "citizenship" are ultimately "in heaven" (Phil. 3:20). Peter speaks of the church as "God's elect, strangers in the world" (1 Pet. 1:1). The faithful Christian community will always represent a counterculture because the values of the kingdom will inevitably collide with and challenge the values of any contemporary culture. This is what Walls calls the "pilgrim principle" of the church (1982). For this reason we prefer to speak of a transculturalization of mission, as opposed to merely a multiculturalization of mission in the New Testament.

> *Christianity affects cultures by moving them to a position short of the absolute, and it does this by placing God at the centre. The point of departure for the church in mission . . . . is Pentecost, with Christianity triumphing by relinquishing Jerusalem or any fixed universal centre, be it geographical, linguistic or cultural, and with the result of there being a proliferation of centres, languages and cultures within the church. Christian ecumenism is a pluralism of the periphery with only God at the centre. Consequently all cultural expressions remain at the periphery of truth, all equal in terms of access, but all equally inadequate in terms of what is ultimate and final.*
>
> Lamin Sanneh (1995, 61)

31

One further remarkable fact, which might be easily overlooked, is that the New Testament is written in Greek. With the exception of a few impressive phrases (e.g., Mark 14:36; 15:34), the New Testament does not even recount the teachings of Jesus in his original language, Aramaic. As Lamin Sanneh (1989) has pointed out, the message of the gospel is translatable, the New Testament itself being a translation of Jesus's own teaching. And as the message is translated, it acquires a new dynamic. This fact is a powerful reminder that neither Jewish culture, nor the language and culture of Jesus, nor the cultures of the early church are to be absolutized and made binding for Christians everywhere. The authoritative message of the New Testament—our only written witness of the Savior's life and teaching—is already a contextualized message (see Flemming 2005).

We shall address in the next chapter Jesus's understanding of his sending into the world by the Father. The remainder of this chapter will limit our examination to God's relation to the nations in the unfolding of salvation history.

JESUS AND THE NATIONS: THE GOSPELS

From the very inception of Jesus's life and ministry, the nations are in view. Simeon's prayer at the presentation of the infant Jesus in the temple points to his messianic role in relation to the Gentiles by quoting Isaiah 49:6:

> For my eyes have seen your salvation,
>   which you have prepared in the sight of all people,
> a light for revelation to the Gentiles
>   and for glory to your people Israel. (Luke 2:30–32)

John the Baptist quotes from Isa. 40:3–5, announcing that now "all mankind will see God's salvation" (Luke 3:6). Jesus opens his public ministry in the Nazareth synagogue with the reading from Isaiah 61:1–2, identifying himself as the fulfillment of the Old Testament messianic hope (Luke 4:18–20). Matthew notes Jesus's citation of Isaiah 42:1–4, claiming to be the servant who brings justice and hope to the Gentiles (Matt. 12:18–21). Thus the Gospels clearly portray Jesus's coming as the fulfillment of the Isaianic anticipation of mission to the nations.

But regarding his earthly ministry, Jesus repeatedly indicates that he has come first to the people of Israel and that ministry to the Gentiles remains secondary (Matt. 15:24; Mark 7:26–27). This is in continuity with the Old Testament vision of blessing beginning with and through Israel. Jesus's sending of the disciples is also initially limited to the house of Israel (Matt. 10:5–6). Only after Jesus has completed the work of redemption on the cross will mission to the Gentiles be fully launched. The sad irony that the Gospel writers do not miss is that Jesus "came to His own, and those who were His own did not receive Him" (John 1:11 NASB). On the contrary, Gentiles often respond in faith to Jesus:

- The worship of the magi from the East (Matt. 2:1–11)[1]
- The Roman centurion (Matt. 8:1–13)
- The Syrophoenician woman (Matt. 15:22–28; Mark 7:25–30)
- The Samaritan woman at Jacob's well (John 4:7–29)
- Another Roman centurion at the cross who confesses, "Truly this man was the Son of God!" (Mark 15:39 NASB)

In the Sermon on the Mount, Jesus calls his disciples the salt of the earth and the light of the world (Matt. 5:13–16), perhaps an echo of the Isaianic servant being a light to the nations (Isa. 42:6; 49:6). As Jesus cleanses the temple, he recalls the vision of Isaiah 56:7: "Is it not written: 'My house will be called a house of prayer for all nations?' But you have made it 'a den of robbers'" (Mark 11:17). The citation from Isaiah is embedded in the eschatological vision of the nations coming to Zion to worship.

Jesus generally places the inclusion of Gentiles and bringing the gospel to the nations in the future. He states, "I have other sheep that are not of this sheep pen. I must bring them also. They too will listen to my voice, and there shall be one flock and one shepherd" (John 10:16). In so doing he indicates that those outside the flock of Israel are to be included in God's people, as one flock (cf. Morris 1971, 512). He looks forward to the day when people will come from "east and west" to be included alongside Abraham, Isaac, and Jacob in the kingdom of heaven (Matt. 8:11).

Speaking of the last days, in the Olivet Discourse Jesus makes the remarkable statement, "And this gospel of the kingdom will be preached in the whole world as a testimony to all nations, and then the end will come" (Matt. 24:14; cf. Mark 13:10). These words are the clearest indication that the movement of mission will be reversed, and the gospel will be bought *to* the nations. This is in fact a condition to be fulfilled prior to Christ's return and the ultimate coming of the kingdom. The same thought is indirectly referred to in Matthew 26:13, where Jesus says, "I tell you the truth, wherever this gospel is preached throughout the world, what she has done will also be told, in memory of her." The gospel *will* be preached among all the nations of the earth.

In summary, Jesus's own ministry, his teaching, and the initial ministry of his disciples continues to minister under the Old Testament economy focusing primarily on Israel. But it also envisions a future intentional mission to the nations. Jesus's positive response to the faith of Gentiles and his teachings

---

1. The gifts of gold and frankincense and myrrh (Matt. 2:11) may recall the Old Testament prophecies of the nations bringing gifts to Zion, for example, Isa. 60:6b, "And all from Sheba will come, bearing gold and incense and proclaiming the praise of the LORD."

foreshadow that mission to be inaugurated with the completion of redemption and the coming of the Spirit.

The Nations and the Kingdom

As described above, the kingdom of God in Jesus's teaching takes on a new spiritual dimension and emphasis that is no longer centered on geography or nationality. Here we note additional significant features regarding the kingdom in Jesus's teachings as it relates to mission.

UPSIDE-DOWN KINGDOM

The Sermon on the Mount evidences how dramatically Jesus's understanding of the kingdom shifts away from conformity to outward forms to inward transformation. The values comprising the essence of the kingdom are fully contrary to the values of worldly kingdoms. Meekness, humility, servanthood, and nonretaliation characterize those who are great in God's kingdom. Donald B. Kraybill has aptly called this the "upside-down kingdom" (2003). But as Kraybill points out, this does not mean that the kingdom is a matter of merely privatized values or otherworldly concerns. Kingdom values transform people, relationships, and society. The new kingdom people are to model these values in a particular way for the world to observe.

THE SIGNS OF THE KINGDOM

In Jesus's ministry, his miracles, healings, raising of the dead, and casting out of demons are signs that the kingdom is in the midst of his hearers (Matt. 12:28). These acts boldly demonstrate that the forces of evil, bondage, and suffering are subject to this messianic king. Demonic powers are those in direct opposition to God and his rule. Sickness, blindness, and death are results of the fall. But these powers are dramatically broken. Jesus then commissions his disciples to go and do the same as signs that the kingdom is near (Luke 10:8–11). Though the kingdom of God is present in the ministry of Jesus, he clearly indicates that a future kingdom in fullness is yet to come. In this sense Jesus *inaugurates* the kingdom in his earthly life but does not fully realize it, nor does he anticipate its full realization until his return.

THE PARABLES OF THE KINGDOM

The kingdom parables of Matthew 13 are especially instructive. The parable of the sower teaches that the spread of the kingdom is linked to the spread of the Word of God, though reception of the Word will be mixed, encountering at times satanic opposition and persecution (vv. 18–23). The next parable speaks of wheat growing up alongside tares (vv. 24–30). Thus in this age the kingdom will not be received by all, good and evil will coexist, and only at the end of the age will final separation and judgment occur (vv. 36–43). Similarly the kingdom is like a dragnet, which brings up both good and bad, so on the last day good and evil persons will be separated and the evil judged (vv. 47–50). These parables remind us that the kingdom, though inaugurated in Christ's earthly ministry, will not be consummated until the final day.

The parable of the mustard seed demonstrates that the kingdom will grow far beyond its seemingly insignificant beginnings (Matt. 13:31–32). The parable of yeast speaks of the almost imperceptible but ultimately pervasive influence of the kingdom (v. 33). The parables of the hidden treasure and the pearl of great price emphasize the surpassing value of the kingdom, which takes priority over all else (vv. 44–46).

Taken together these parables show that the spread and realization of the kingdom of God will be a process moving toward a day of judgment. Until that day good and evil will coexist, and the kingdom will be received by some and violently opposed by others. The spread of the kingdom in this age will not occur with the cataclysmic or violent overthrow of evil powers. Its influence and spread will be subtle but nonetheless pervasive. The imagery of growth implicitly reminds us that the advancement of the kingdom is the work of God and not human effort (cf. 1 Cor. 3:6–7). Entering the kingdom may come at great price, but at a price that is gladly paid. The end of the age will one day arrive, at which time evil will be finally judged and the righteous rewarded. It is only at the consummation that the kingdom will be realized in fullness.

GENTILES AND THE KINGDOM

Jesus anticipates the day when others will come from east and west, from north and south, and be included in the kingdom (Matt. 8:11–12; Luke 13:29), an unmistakable reference to the inclusion of Gentiles. The kingdom will no longer be bound to the people of Israel, but rather will be composed of people of faith in Jesus regardless of their ethnic background.

Luke 14 recounts an incident whereby someone comments to Jesus, "Blessed is the man who will eat at the feast in the kingdom of God" (v. 15). Jesus replies by telling a parable of a great banquet (representing the kingdom). The invited guests all have excuses not to come, so the host sends his servants to go to the highways and compel others to come (vv. 16–24). T. W. Manson comments, "This is doubtless meant to suggest a mission beyond the borders of Israel to the Gentiles" (cited in Geldenhuys 1977, 396). Matthew's parable of the wicked tenants conveys a similar message concluding, "Therefore I tell you that the kingdom of God will be taken away from you and given to a people who will produce its fruit" (Matt. 21:43).

The Great Commission

Only after Jesus has accomplished redemption through his death and resurrection does he give the disciples the explicit command to bring the gospel to the nations with the Great Commission. Only then are the conditions met to usher in the new age of the Spirit. We examine some of the unique features of the various formulations of the Great Commission in the four Gospels.

MATTHEW

Matthew's formulation of the Great Commission, which concludes his Gospel, must be understood together with the opening of his Gospel. The opening verses of Matthew begin the genealogy of Jesus with Abraham and David. Abraham's call is the beginning of God's particularistic work through a particular people, which had a universal intention. But Matthew concludes his Gospel with the commission to make disciples of all nations. The particularistic work of redemption completed by Christ makes possible the fulfillment of the universal intention that the good news is brought to the nations. Reference to Abraham in chapter 1 and reference to all nations in chapter 28 form bookends of this Gospel, framing the entire ministry of Jesus in this light. Indeed, numerous New Testament scholars see Matthew 28:18–20 as the key to understanding the entire book (see Köstenberger and O'Brien 2001, 87n4).

The Authority of the Great Commission

Matthew begins with Jesus's words, "All authority in heaven and on earth has been given to me" (Matt. 28:18). The universal Lord gives a universal commission. These words no doubt recall the prophet Daniel's words regarding the "Son of Man" (Jesus's favorite self-description): "He was given authority, glory and sovereign power; all peoples, nations and *men of every* language worshiped him. His dominion is an everlasting dominion that will not pass away, and his kingdom is one that will never be destroyed" (Dan. 7:14, emphasis added).

The Task of the Great Commission

At the center of the commission is the command to make disciples. Grammatically this is the main verb imperative; the terms "go," "baptize," and "teach" are participles describing and having imperative force linked with the imperative "make disciples." The command encompasses more than mere proclamation. "Go" stresses that the task includes *intentionally* bringing the message to the nations. Baptism (accompanied by repentance and faith) is the means by which one is publicly initiated into the new kingdom community. Teaching to obey all that Jesus has commanded emphasizes that nominal adherence to a creed or superficial membership in a religious organization is inadequate. Teaching is not merely a transfer of knowledge but a transformation of life in obedience. *All* of Jesus's teaching is binding for the disciple; one does not have the option to pick and choose from Jesus's teaching. Clearly, making disciples involves calling people to acknowledge Jesus as Lord, submitting every aspect of their lives to his lordship.

The Scope of the Great Commission

The centripetal mission of the Old Testament is now explicitly reversed. "Go" launches the centrifugal movement of mission *to* the nations. The mandate is not just to make disciples of individual persons. Rather, it is to disciple *nations*, indeed *all* nations. This is a truly staggering proposition that would verge on the ridiculous were it not for the accompanying authority and promise of the risen Christ, who gives the commission.

The Promise of the Great Commission

The commission, and Matthew's Gospel itself, concludes with the comforting and forward-looking promise of Jesus's enduring presence (28:20). The same Jesus to whom all authority is given promises to accompany the disciples on this daunting mission—they neither go on their own authority, nor do they go alone. One can hardly overlook the comprehensiveness of Matthew's formulation: *all* authority, *all* nations, *all* that Jesus commanded, who is *always* with them.

The Duration of the Great Commission

The promise linked to the commission is "to the very end of the age." This clearly indicates that the commission is to continue until Christ's return and this eon comes to an end. The promise does not end with the death of the first-generation disciples, nor does the commission. The commission fills the time between Christ's comings, ushering in the completion of salvation history. Only when the gospel has been preached to every nation will the end come (Matt. 24:14).

MARK

The Gravity of the Great Commission

Mark's unique emphasis lies in the gravity of the Great Commission. His formulation is complicated by the questionable integrity of 16:9–20. Though probably not part of Mark's original manuscript, these verses represent at least a reliable tradition consistent with the record of other authoritative New Testament teaching.

Mark emphasizes proclamation accompanied by confirming signs. His formulation adds a note of urgency not present in the other Gospels: "He who has believed and has been baptized shall be saved; but he who has disbelieved shall be condemned" (v. 16 NASB). Faith and baptism are the conditions for salvation. Rejection, however, leads to condemnation. Response to gospel preaching is a matter of eternal consequence.

Jesus's Example and the Great Commmission

Lucien Legrand (1990, 72) points out that Mark's Great Commission parallels the opening verses of the Gospel:

1:14: Jesus went into Galilee, proclaiming the good news of God.	16:15: Go into all the world and preach the good news to all creation.
1:15: The kingdom of God is near. Repent and believe the good news!	16:16: Whoever believes and is baptized will be saved, but whoever does not believe will be condemned.
1:23–28: Exorcisms	16:17b: In my name they will drive out demons;
1:29–34: Healings	16:18b: They will place their hands on sick people, and they will get well.
1:38: Let us go somewhere else—to the nearby villages—so I can preach there also. That is why I have come.	16:20: Then the disciples went out and preached everywhere.

This parallelism points to "a fundamental correspondence between the mission embraced by Jesus and the one entrusted by the Risen One to his own" (Legrand 1990, 72).

LUKE

The Salvation-Historical Significance of the Great Commission

Luke's account (24:46–47) is embedded in a resurrection appearance narrative. First, Jesus links the preaching of the gospel with salvation history by recounting how "Moses, the Prophets and the Psalms" (i.e., the Old Testament) bear witness to him (v. 44). He then leads into this version of the Great Commission with the words, "Thus it is written" (v. 46a NASB), indicating that the work of salvation and the preaching to all nations is in continuity with scriptural revelation.

The Message of the Great Commission

Jesus continues, "The Christ will suffer and rise from the dead on the third day, and repentance and forgiveness of sins will be preached in his name to all nations, beginning at Jerusalem" (vv. 46b–47). Whereas the disciples have previously been commissioned to preach that "the kingdom of heaven is near" (Luke 10:9), now forgiveness of sins becomes the heart of their message. The work of salvation is complete, and the salvific work of Christ is central to the message that the disciples are to take to the world. This is evidenced in the apostolic proclamation recounted in Acts (2:38; 5:31; 10:43; 13:38; 26:18). "Beginning at Jerusalem" accentuates the reversal of the missionary movement from centripetal to centrifugal, as indicated in Acts 1:8. Jesus adds, "You are witnesses of these things" (Luke 24:48), which also serves as a bridge to Luke's second volume, where the role of the disciples as witnesses is resumed (Acts 1:8).

The Power of the Great Commission

Also unique to Luke is Jesus's instruction to wait in Jerusalem until the Father has clothed the disciples in power (24:49). He makes clear that the mere giving of the command does not constitute immediate marching orders. Rather, the disciples are to wait for the coming of the Spirit. Only after they have received power will the age of the Spirit be fully initiated and the spread of the gospel to the nations begin in earnest. This too will be a prominent theme in Acts, where the promise of the power of the Holy Spirit is reiterated (Acts 1:8), the receiving of the Spirit at Pentecost launches New Testament mission (Acts 2), and the spread of the gospel to the nations is continually driven by movements of the Spirit. With the reception of the Spirit in power, mission begins to move out from Jerusalem.

JOHN

John's Gospel is clearly intended to be evangelistic and is thus missionary, with the stated purpose "these are written that you may believe that Jesus is the Christ, the Son of God, and that by believing you may have life in his name" (20:31). The idea of sending plays a significant role in John's Gospel.

Mission: Being Sent as Jesus Was Sent

John's version of the Great Commission sheds a profound new light on the mandate with the words: "As the Father has sent me, I am sending you" (20:21b). Whereas the formulation in the other Gospels emphasizes proclamation, John's formulation is broader and in some ways more fundamental. This wording is also found in Jesus's high priestly prayer in John 17:18, where Jesus explicitly speaks of sending the disciples "into the world." His prayer is not only for the original disciples but also for those who will believe through their message (17:20). Their unity should convince the world to believe that Jesus was sent by the Father (17:21).

Andreas J. Köstenberger concludes his study of mission in the fourth Gospel: "The fourth evangelist conceived of the mission of the Christian community as ultimately the mission of *the exalted Jesus* carried out through his followers" (1998a, 210). Jesus had told the disciples that after his departure they would perform greater works than his own (14:12). This is probably not a reference to miracles that the disciples might perform; rather, the "greater works" are a result of Jesus's completed work of salvation. Because of their place in salvation history, the disciples will have a greater message to proclaim, and that message will reach farther than Jesus's earthly ministry (cf. Köstenberger 1998a, 171–75). With the receiving of the Spirit, the disciples will become witnesses of Jesus (15:26–27). So equipped the disciples are sent to carry on Jesus's ministry in the world.

Matthew's commission to make disciples of all nations has generally been considered the most forthright description of mission (e.g., Verkuyl 1978, 106). But in recent years others have understood John's words to be the more crucial form of the Great Commission (e.g., Stott 1975, 23). We shall return to the implications of such thinking in the following chapters.

Mission as Mediation

The next verses also expand upon the Synoptic versions of the Great Commission with the words: "And with that he breathed on them and said, 'Receive the Holy Spirit. If you forgive anyone his sins, they are forgiven; if you do not forgive them, they are not forgiven'" (John 20:22–23).

As in Luke, Jesus indicates that the disciples will need the Holy Spirit to fulfill their mandate. The words of verses 22–23 have been cause for considerable controversy in the history of the church. Suffice it to say that however one might interpret the words, the disciples become mediators of God's forgiveness. Forgiveness was accomplished through the cross of Christ. But it will be the disciples and the church, as it continues their message and ministry (so Morris 1971, 847–50), that in the power of the Spirit mediate this forgiveness to the world.

SUMMARY

Though each of the formulations of the Great Commission has particular emphases, there are striking commonalities from which a profound and harmonious picture emerges:

- In each instance Christ himself gives the mandate. The missionary mandate is based on his work and his Word.
- The Great Commission in each case involves a sending into the world, to all nations, or to all creation. Mission moves out from Jerusalem, beyond the "lost sheep of Israel" (Matt. 10:6). The mission of the church is clearly oriented to others, to those yet outside the kingdom. It is a mission in the world and to the world, extending to every people, nation, and tongue.
- Each occurrence is in a postresurrection appearance of the Lord. Had Jesus remained in the grave, there would have been no good news to proclaim, no victory over the power of sin and death. But with the resurrection the work of salvation has been accomplished, and the age of the Spirit can soon begin.
- Christ himself is at the center of each formulation. Be it his sending (John); his authority, teaching, and presence (Matthew); his work of redemption and forgiveness (Luke); or his name, in which signs are performed (Mark), the message and the work of the Great Commission are inseparably bound to the person of Christ.
- The Holy Spirit (or in Matthew's version, Jesus's abiding presence) is the enabler in each instance. The mandate should not and cannot be undertaken with human energy or wisdom. God himself will provide the power through his own presence.
- In each formulation the disciples take up the ministry that Jesus initiated. We concur with Legrand that "mission has all the dimensions and scope

of Jesus' own ministry" (1990, 74). They will not die a substitutionary death for sin (this was the unique work of Christ at Golgotha). But they will become mediators of this salvation in new and more marvelous ways. They will preach good news in *all* the world and make disciples of *all* nations, they will perform works *greater* than those that Jesus performed on earth, and they will minister in power proclaiming the *completed* work of salvation and forgiveness.

As a final observation, the intimate connection between Christ's life and work and the Great Commission makes inescapable the conclusion that the missionary mandate is not simply one among many good things that the church should do. It is more than just another "program." It is the integration point of the church's entire calling. Nor can any good work be considered mission, irrespective of its relationship to Christ's work. This mandate is the climax of Jesus's teaching, a logical consequence of his redemptive work, his marching orders for the church, and his parting words at the threshold of a new era in salvation history.

Thus the joyful-earnest task falls to Christ's followers to take up where he left off in his earthly ministry, to become his agents of forgiveness and kingdom transformation in the power of the Spirit. Such an understanding of the missionary mandate must at once fill us with deep wonder, evoke a sense of great privilege, and convey a burning urgency.

THE GOSPEL TO THE NATIONS AND THE CREATION OF A NEW KINGDOM PEOPLE

Acts

Acts 1:8 depicts the great reversal of mission movement. Whereas the eschatological vision of the Old Testament saw the nations coming *to* Jerusalem, Luke depicts the gospel going out to the nations *from* Jerusalem. Many commentators have suggested that the progression of the spread of the gospel here provides an outline of the entire book of Acts.

- Acts 1–7, the gospel in Jerusalem
- Acts 8–9, the gospel in Judea and Samaria
- Acts 10–28, to the ends of the earth

In the words of Mbachu Hilary, "the whole Acts is dotted with *ta dogmata* on inculturation. The whole book is a narrative on how the gospel message is gradually but progressively inserted first into the Jewish cultural milieu (chaps. 1–12; 15) and later into the Gentile environment (chaps. 13–14; 16–28)" (1995, 73).

FIGURE 2.2: SALVATION-HISTORICAL OVERVIEW

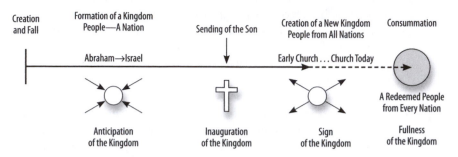

The disciples' expectation of the coming kingdom is expressed as they ask, "Lord, are you at this time going to restore the kingdom to Israel?" (Acts 1:6). Israel, in their eyes, would remain at the center of God's kingdom. Their concern regards the timing. Jesus does not deny that a kingdom on earth will one day come, but that time is not yet; it will be of another epoch. "He said to them: 'It is not for you to know the times or dates the Father has set by his own authority'" (Acts 1:7). Far from the end being near, the most exciting days of human history are about to dawn. In the intervening time mission is to proceed in the unexpected, upside-down kind of way that Jesus has previously indicated. "But you will receive power when the Holy Spirit comes on you; and you will be my witnesses in Jerusalem, and in all Judea and Samaria, and to the ends of the earth" (Acts 1:8).

Mission anticipating the fullness of the kingdom will be a mission of power, not of human, coercive power, but of spiritual power. The book of Acts makes evident that apart from the Spirit, the disciples would probably never have moved outside Jerusalem, gone to the Gentiles, accepted Gentile believers, nor convinced any hearers. Acts demonstrates that the mission of the disciples and of the church is in fact God's mission being realized through them, and at times in spite of them. It is God in the person of the Holy Spirit who initiates, motivates, empowers, and completes the progress of the gospel from Jerusalem to the nations, bringing persons of diverse cultures into his people and creating communities of the kingdom around the Savior-King, Jesus Christ (see fig. 2.2).

> *Witnesses must be faithful not only to the bare facts of the Christ-event, but also to their meaning. That is, modern witnesses are summoned to speak of the life, death and resurrection of Christ in such a way that the intrinsic divine significance of these events is brought to light.*
>
> Allison A. Trites (1977, 229–30)

MISSION AS WITNESS

The witness of the disciples—personally and publicly testifying to what they have learned, seen, and experienced with Jesus firsthand—is the primary method by which the Spirit's power will work. This recalls Isaiah's description of the servant of the Lord in terms of being "witnesses" (43:10, 12; 44:8) and the Davidic Messiah as "a witness to the peoples" (Isa. 55:4). This role is now taken up by the church. Because the claims of Christ and the first Christians are contested, Luke uses the language of the courtroom, making "witness" a particularly prominent metaphor in Acts (Trites 1977, 128). The Greek term *martus*, "witness" (including *diamarturomai*, "solemnly testify") occurs thirty-nine times in Acts, in contrast to only three times in Luke's Gospel. (The terms also figure prominently in the Gospel of John.) The role of the Christian in the "courtroom" is not that of the lawyer, judge, or jury. Bauckham describes the Christian witness as follows: "Witness is non-coercive. It has no power but the convincingness of the truth to which it witnesses. Witnesses are not expected, like lawyers, to persuade by the rhetorical power of their speeches, but simply to testify to the truth for which they are qualified to give evidence. But to be an adequate witness to the truth of God and the world, witnesses must be a lived witness involving the whole of life and even death" (2003, 99).

The disciples are not to be witnesses of an abstract dogma, nor of a religious institution, nor of a political movement. They will be witnesses of a *person*, of Jesus Christ the crucified and risen Lord. The first disciples are indeed eyewitnesses of the teaching and, in particular, of the resurrection of Jesus Christ (Acts 4:33). The sermons recorded in Acts are consistently christocentric. As Paul later writes, "For we do not preach ourselves, but Jesus Christ as Lord" (2 Cor. 4:5a). Not only does the Spirit empower the witness of the disciples (Acts 1:8), but the Spirit himself also bears witness to Christ (Acts 5:32; cf. John 15:26).

Witness to the End of the Earth

In Acts 1:8, Luke uses the phrase "ends of the earth" (Gk. *eschatou tēs gēs*) to indicate the scope of the spread of the witness. This echoes the Old Testament language of Isaiah regarding the role of Israel and later of the messianic Servant as a light for the Gentiles. Luke recounts Paul quoting Isaiah 49:9, describing his mission and the mission of the church: "For this is what the Lord has commanded us: 'I have made you a light for the Gentiles, that you may bring salvation to the ends of the earth'" (Acts 13:47, Gk. *eschatou tēs gēs*; also LXX of Isa. 45:22; 49:6).

This language also recalls the Old Testament teaching of the testimony of the heavens to God's glory extending "into all the earth" (Ps. 19:4; LXX *oikoumenē*). Bauckham (2003, 103–9) sees a parallel between the decree of Caesar Augustus to take a census "of the entire Roman world" (Luke 2:1, Gk. *oikoumenēn*), representing the grandiose claims of the Roman Empire to attain a universal reign, to Luke's depiction of the influence of the kingdom of God extending to all the earth. But the expansion of the kingdom of God will be by means of humble witness. In Acts 17:6, Luke records the statement made by Paul's opponents that Christians have already upset the whole world (*oikoumenēn*; similarly in Acts 24:5). The disciples "do not suggest that the kingdom of God is merely a more powerful or more successful version of the imperial powers. Their witness is to an altogether different kind of rule" (Bauckham 2003, 104). But the day will come when God will judge the whole world (*oikoumenēn*; Acts 17:31).

The miracle of Pentecost, whereby the disciples preach the gospel in the unlearned languages of their hearers (Acts 2), not only signals the birth of the church and the inauguration of the age of the Spirit but also forcefully demonstrates that the curse of Babel is to be overcome. The Jewish Pentecost pilgrims know Hebrew, Aramaic, or perhaps Greek or Latin, thus the miracle of tongues is for these listeners in one sense unnecessary. The miracle indicates something greater. The Abrahamic promise of blessings to the nations (following the Babel story) is on the way to fulfillment. No longer must the Gentile learn the language of the Jew, but the message of God is soon to be brought to the Gentiles in their own languages.

The Gradual Launching of Mission to the Nations

We must be cautious about overidealizing the early church. The launching of mission to the Gentiles had in some regards a slow start—due to unexpected events—and at times faced opposition. We might suppose that reception of the Holy Spirit at Pentecost would have quickly moved the apostles out of Jerusalem on their mission to the nations, but an examination of the chronology of events reveals that this was not the case.

- Pentecost: AD 30
- Samarian mission: AD 31–32
- Paul in Arabia: AD 32–33
- Paul's mission in Cilicia and Syria: AD 33–42
- Peter's mission to the coastal region (Lydda, Sharon, Joppa): AD 34
- Conversion of Cornelius: ca. AD 37–41
- Persecution and diaspora leading to the first predominantly Gentile church in Antioch: AD 41
- Possible departure of the twelve apostles from Jerusalem into the world: AD 41–42
- Paul and Barnabas's first missionary journey: AD 45–47
- Jerusalem council: AD 48 (chronology according to Schnabel 2004, 51–52, and 2008, 66–67).

The initial belief was that Christianity was an extension of Judaism, and if Gentiles were to be received into the community at all, it would be by becoming Jewish proselytes. Charles H. H. Scobie describes the mind-set of many early Jewish believers: "Their thinking followed the lines of *incorporation*: only through circumcision and acceptance of the full obligations of the Torah, that is, only by becoming a proselyte and naturalized Jew could a Gentile enter the Christian community" (1992, 295).

Over a period of time God orchestrates various circumstances and moves through various persons to propel the gospel outward from Jerusalem:

- Following the persecution of Stephen, "all except the apostles were scattered throughout Judea and Samaria" (Acts 8:1).
- The gospel enters Samaria through Philip, a Hellenistic (i.e., Greek-speaking) Jew (8:4–8). Later in the chapter it is again Philip who explains the gospel to the Ethiopian eunuch, who becomes the first African Christian (8:26–40).
- The "apostle to the Gentiles" is not one of the original twelve, but Saul of Tarsus, a former persecutor of the church (9:15).
- Peter is willing to enter the house of the Gentile centurion Cornelius only after a supernatural vision is thrice repeated (10:9–11:18). Others criticize Peter for his behavior (11:1–2), and only after hearing Peter's remarkable story do they glorify God, saying, "So then, God has granted even the Gentiles repentance unto life" (11:18)—something apparently unexpected.
- As the persecuted Christians reach Phoenicia, Cyprus, and Antioch, the thought of a Gentile mission is still far from their minds; they were still "telling the message only to Jews" (11:19b). But then believers from Cypress and Cyrene (not even from Judea), who apparently didn't know any better, become instrumental in the formation of the first predominantly Gentile church (11:20–21). The Jerusalem church is initially skeptical of the development and sends Barnabas to investigate the integrity of the movement (11:22–23).
- The predominantly Gentile church of Antioch becomes the first church to intentionally send Barnabas and Paul as missionaries to the Gentile world and remains the primary sending base (13:1–3; 14:26–28; 15:35).
- In AD 48 (some eighteen years after Pentecost), the Jerusalem council convenes to determine the place of the Old Testament law in the church and resolve the tension between Jewish and Gentile believers (Acts 15). Opposition to the inclusion of uncircumcised Gentiles in the church is officially rejected. Acts 15 is sometimes called the "emancipation proclamation" for the Gentile mission, as Gentiles can now become Christians without first becoming Jewish. The progress of the gospel is not only liberated from the law of Moses but also from any specific culture.

45

Thus the full implications of mission to the nations develop over time in the early church, and not without suspicion and opposition. God continually intervenes in often unexpected and dramatic ways, mobilizing the church into missionary action and demonstrating his inclusion of Gentiles in his new people. There will be setbacks, but ultimately God's mission will prevail. Christ will build his church (Matt. 16:18). Luke expresses this, describing the growth of the church in terms of how the Word of God "spread" (Acts 6:7; 13:49), continues to "grow and be multiplied" (12:24 NASB), and "growing mightily and prevailing" (19:20 NASB). The Word of God takes on a self-dynamic, making the ministry of the disciples almost incidental. Mission is completely God's mission!

Pauline Epistles

Acts provides us with a historical look at the creation of the new people of God as the gospel advanced from Jerusalem to the nations. But the Epistles provide us with an internal look at the life of these new kingdom communities—the churches. Paul's letters also reveal much about his own sense of calling and ministry as the missionary par excellence. We noted above that Paul envisioned the church composed of Jew and Gentile in one new people, and that his understanding of the kingdom emphasized the spiritual and ethical renewal of its members. We look now at Paul's self-understanding as the apostle to the Gentiles and the question of the Great Commission (or lack thereof) in Paul's writings.

PAUL, APOSTLE TO THE GENTILES

Paul called himself the apostle to the Gentiles (Rom. 11:13; Gal. 2:8). His own calling and ministry dovetail with God's salvation purposes for the nations. From the time of his conversion, this was revealed to him as his special calling (Acts 9:15; 22:21; Rom. 1:5; Gal. 1:15–16; Eph. 3:1–10). Paul's frequent allusions to the Isaianic servant evidence his understanding of his calling, and the calling of the church, as being in continuity with the servant's role as light to the nations (see O'Brien 1995, 7 and n. 19). Romans is particularly rich with passages revealing Paul's self-understanding as missionary in the story of God's purposes. His apostleship is "to call people from among all the Gentiles to the obedience that comes from faith" (1:5). The wording "obedience that comes from faith" indicates that his mandate is not accomplished with a superficial conversion of Gentiles but includes their growth to maturity in Christ (O'Brien 1995, 34). Reference to obedience of faith among the nations is repeated in the concluding words of the letter (16:26), thus serving as bookends and indicating the importance of the theme to the entire book.

The gospel is God's power for salvation, "first for the Jew, then for the Gentile" (1:16). This is literally reflected in Paul's practice as described in Acts, of first preaching in the synagogue, and usually after rejection there moving on to preach to Gentiles. Jew and Gentile alike have sinned and failed to live up to the light that they have been given; thus all are equally culpable and dependent upon God's saving grace manifest in Christ and appropriated by faith (Rom. 1–3). God has in fact demonstrated his mercy to both Jew and Gentile (9:23–24), indeed, "for there is no difference between Jew and Gentile—the same Lord is Lord of all and richly blesses all who call on him, for, 'Everyone who calls on the name of the Lord will be saved'" (10:12–13).

This immediately raises a series of questions, which Paul uses rhetorically to press home the urgency of mission: "How, then, can they call on the one they have not believed in? And how can they believe in the one of whom they have not heard? And how can they hear without someone preaching to them? And how can they preach unless they are sent?" (10:14–15a). The logic is irresistible: Only as messengers are sent will people (everywhere) be able to call upon the Lord and be saved. As Paul and Barnabas were sent out by the church of Antioch (Acts 13:1–3), so the need remains for sent ones, that is, missionaries, to bring the message of good news to those who have not heard.

As Paul draws Romans to a close, he returns explicitly to the theme of his calling and mission. Daniel Jong Sang Chae (1997) has argued persuasively that Romans 15:14–21 and Paul's self-awareness as apostle to the Gentiles are the keys to understanding the entire book. Paul is called "to be a minister of Christ Jesus to the Gentiles with the priestly duty of proclaiming the gospel of God, so that the Gentiles might become an offering acceptable to God, sanctified by the Holy Spirit" (15:16). Because Paul couches his mission in terms of priestly ministry and offering, mission to the nations itself is raised to an act of worship.[2] Mission is more than an obligation of obedience. What greater gift of worship, what more profound offering can the believer lift up to God than those who once were far away but have been brought near, sanctified by the blood of the Lamb (Eph. 2:13), and have become his worshippers also!

Paul then makes an astonishing claim that reveals his missionary strategy. God has worked through him in the power of the Spirit, such that Paul can assert, "From Jerusalem and round about as far as Illyricum I have fully preached the gospel of Christ" (15:19 NASB). Later he states that there is no further place for him in these regions (15:23). Obviously Paul has not preached in every city or village; much less has every person in this region from Jerusalem to Illyricum (today the Balkan states) heard the gospel. What does he mean then by "fully preached" and the statement that he is no longer needed? Many commentators believe these passages mean that having planted churches in key cities, Paul has established a beachhead for the gospel in the region, and

---

2. Some see this as a reference to the financial offering of the Gentile churches that Paul brought to Jerusalem, though such offerings may be symbolic of the Gentiles themselves (e.g., O'Brien 1995, 50–51; Howell 1998, 113).

he is confident that the newly established churches will multiply and reach the entire region with the gospel. His pioneering work is complete.

Ferdinand Hahn, for example, writes, "Paul was content on each occasion to carry the gospel to the centres of a district and to trust that the message would spread out from there" (1965, 16). And indeed this was often enough the case as the gospel spread from churches such as Pisidian Antioch (Acts 13:49), Thessalonica (1 Thess. 1:8), and Ephesus (Acts 19:20; 1 Cor. 16:9) to impact the entire region. Thus neither the conversion of individuals alone nor even the planting of individual churches was the goal of the Pauline mission. Rather, he viewed his work in a region completed only when reproducing congregations had been established.

Paul continues, "It has always been my ambition to preach the gospel where Christ was not known, so that I would not be building on someone else's foundation" (Rom. 15:20). He anticipates reaching as far as Spain (15:24, 28), the end of the earth in the ancient world's eyes. Paul's pioneering aim is to continue reaching out to yet unreached peoples and establish additional multiplying churches. Some writers suggest that this Pauline strategy is the very "essence of missions" (e.g., Piper 1993, 212n39).

Finally, Paul evidences flexibility and adaptability in his missionary methods and lifestyle as epitomized in his oft-quoted maxim in 1 Corinthians 9:19–23.

> Though I am free and belong to no man, I make myself a slave to everyone, to win as many as possible. To the Jews I became like a Jew, to win the Jews. To those under the law I became like one under the law (though I myself am not under the law), so as to win those under the law. To those not having the law I became like one not having the law (though I am not free from God's law but am under Christ's law), so as to win those not having the law. To the weak I became weak, to win the weak. I have become all things to all men so that by all possible means I might save some. I do all this for the sake of the gospel, that I may share in its blessings.

One must discern between what is essential and what is nonessential—and therefore adaptable. For Paul there is no question: the highest good is to win others for Christ. "[Winning] cannot refer only to their conversion, since in verse 22 he speaks of his aim of winning the 'weak.' . . . Paul's goals of winning Jews, Gentiles and weak Christians has to do with their full maturity in Christ and thus signifies *winning them completely*" (Köstenberger and O'Brien 2001, 181). All else becomes subordinate to this goal. In so doing he is prepared to surrender his personal rights in order to "share in its blessing." Only in so doing will he win the highest prize (vv. 24–27).

THE PAULINE GREAT COMMISSION

Given the explicit mandate and commands in the Gospels to evangelize and disciple the nations, and given the passion for mission that is apparent in Paul's own life and ministry, the absence in Paul's letters of any explicit exhortation to evangelize or undertake mission demands explanation. Paul seems to take for granted that the very logic of the gospel and the moving of the Holy Spirit compel the church to undertake mission apart from further explicit commands.

We summarize here arguments by Peter T. O'Brien (1995), Robert Plummer (2006), and others that taken together comprise a sort of Pauline Great Commission.

- The expected multiplication of once-established churches (noted in the above discussion of Rom. 15:19) presumes that the churches were in fact active in the propagation of the faith. The churches apparently understood their responsibility for mission.

- Romans 10:14–15 speaks explicitly of the necessity of messengers being sent to preach the gospel to those who haven't heard.

- Paul concludes his discussion of the ministry of reconciliation in 2 Corinthians 5:20: "We are therefore Christ's ambassadors, as though God were making his appeal through us. We implore you on Christ's behalf: Be reconciled to God." The "we" indirectly includes believers in general who are willing to be ministers of reconciliation.

- Paul presents himself as an example to the believers. This would naturally include his concern for evangelism and mission (1 Cor. 4:16; 11:1; Eph. 5:1; 1 Thess. 1:6; 2:14; 2 Thess. 3:7).

- In Philippians 1:14–18, Paul speaks of unnamed persons who as a result of his imprisonment "have been encouraged to speak the word of God more courageously and fearlessly" (v. 14). Though some are preaching Christ from malicious motives, Paul rejoices all the same that Christ is proclaimed.

- The Philippian "partnership in the gospel" (Phil. 1:5), "contending as one man for the faith of the gospel" (1:27; cf. v. 30), and their charge to "hold out the word of life" (2:16) include active proclamation of the gospel.

- In Paul's discussion of spiritual warfare in Ephesians 6:10–17, he speaks of putting on the shoes of the gospel of peace and of taking up the sword of the Spirit, which is the Word of God. Verse 15 is translated in the NRSV, "As shoes for your feet put on whatever will make you ready to proclaim the gospel of peace." The picture is one not merely of a defensive but also of an offensive posture. The believer is to be ready to present the gospel confidently and in the power of the Spirit.

- In Colossians 4:5–6 Paul exhorts, "Be wise in the way you act toward outsiders; make the most of every opportunity. Let your conversation be always full of grace, seasoned with salt, so that you may know how to answer everyone."

O'Brien concludes, "There may be fewer instances of evangelistic outreach in the Pauline letters than we would expect. But the reason for this . . . lies in Paul's preference for speaking about the dynamic progress of the gospel" (1995, 127; e.g., Eph. 6:19; Col. 4:3–4; 1 Thess. 1:8; 2 Thess. 3:1). Wolf-Henning Ollrog's study of Paul's coworkers shows that the churches Paul planted were not merely recipients of the apostolic mission, but through the sending of coworkers they assisted in the Pauline mission and became active partners in it (1979, 129). It was taken for granted that the churches would participate in this way, and an examination of Paul's missionary coworkers demonstrates that nearly every church Paul planted is represented.

Paul clearly writes as a missionary to mission churches, often addressing a dysfunction or challenge that the young churches faced. His concern is that they grow as communities reflecting kingdom values. These letters serve less as an overt call to mission and more as witnesses to what kingdom communities can and should look like. Through such communities the gospel will both be embodied and progress to the ends of the earth.

General Epistles

We limit our comment on the general epistles to two passages from 1 Peter. In the words of P. J. Robinson, "1 Peter is an excellent missionary document which deals with the most basic question about the church in the world namely its existence in society as a new and distinct community with a totally new lifestyle" (1989, 177). The recipients of this letter were Christians facing opposition. But opposition is no occasion to retreat from witness. In the face of suffering and slander Peter exhorts the believer, "But even if you should suffer for what is right, you are blessed. 'Do not fear what they fear; do not be frightened.' But in your hearts set apart Christ as Lord. Always be prepared to give an answer to everyone who asks you to give the reason for the hope that you have" (1 Pet. 3:14–15a). The lifestyle of the church gives credibility to the witness of the church. But the nonverbal example must be accompanied by the verbal witness and explanation.

More significant for the self-understanding of the church in relation to mission is 1 Peter 2:1–11. The nature and calling of the new people of God is framed in Old Testament categories, indicating continuity of Old and New Testament concepts of mission (Köstenberger 1998b, 202–3). As noted earlier, verse 5 teaches that this new people of God is a spiritual house, for a holy priesthood to offer spiritual sacrifices through Christ. Acceptance or rejection of him divides people into two groups: those destined for doom, and those who become a stone in this spiritual house.

Peter then weaves into his description of the church quotations from Exodus 9:5–6 (see discussion in chapter 1), Isaiah 43:21, and Hosea 1:9, 2:23 to more explicitly describe the calling and mission of the new people of God: "But you are a chosen people, a royal priesthood, a holy nation, a people belonging to God, that you may declare the praises of him who called you out of darkness into his wonderful light. Once you were not a people, but now you are the people of God; once you had not received mercy, but now you have received mercy" (1 Pet. 2:9–10).

The calling and mission of the church is in continuity with Israel's priestly calling in Exodus 19:5–6, but realizes it in a more glorious manner. The four-fold description of the church in verse 9 is especially profound considering the salvation-historical location of the verse:

A *chosen race*—Humanity is no longer divided between the Jew and the Gentile, between races or ethnic groups or rivalries. For the redeemed there is one *new race* that transcends all others, a race of God's own choosing and creation.

A *royal priesthood*—In God's new community humanity is not divided into priests and non-priests. Rather, all who belong to this spiritual house have as priests both direct access to God and the obligation to mediate between humans and God. The community as a whole functions in this priestly manner.

A *holy nation*—The term takes on new significance in view of the command to make disciples of all nations (*panta ta ethnē*), who become in Christ one new, holy nation (*ethnos hagiov*).

A *people for God's own possession*—This people has a unique relationship to God. Being God's possession is a position not only of privilege but also of service to become God's instruments in accomplishing his will in salvation history.

Peter explicitly indicates that the purpose of this calling is proclamation of the excellencies of God. He quotes Isaiah 43:21, a passage describing the eschatological restoration of God's people. The term used for "proclaim" (*exangeilēte*) is used only here in the New Testament and can have the sense of "proclaim far and wide" God's wonderful deeds of mercy (Schniewind, cited in P. J. Robinson 1989, 183). As the church lives out this calling of God, true to its identity in Christ, it becomes both living and verbal witness to God's mercy and glory. To miss this is to miss God's intention for his people. Neither the call of Israel nor the call of the church is intended to be an end in itself. Rather, it is the call of privilege to be God's channel of blessing to others, which will ultimately result in the glorification of God. This is also consistent with the Abrahamic promise of blessing in order to become a blessing to the nations. God's calling and grace are the foundation of mission. The mercy we have received is both motivation and the content of the proclamation.

Leading into his next section, in verse 11 Peter addresses his hearers as "aliens and strangers." This is a reminder that the people of God are not at home in the value systems of this fallen world. Their ultimate citizenship and loyalty is in the kingdom.

THE CHURCH TODAY—LIVING IN THE MISSIONAL TRAJECTORY OF THE NEW TESTAMENT

The book of Acts ends abruptly. There is no conclusion or summary statement. The reader is simply left with Paul preaching the gospel under house arrest in Rome. Köstenberger and O'Brien reflect on this: "Finally, the open-ended conclusion of the book seeks to draw the readers in to identify with the powerful advance of the gospel of salvation, and to include them in the continuing task of spreading this word. The apostolic testimony did not reach the ends of the earth with Paul's arrival in Rome. This open-endedness is a reminder of the unfinished task and encouragement to all of us as readers to be committed to the ongoing *missio Dei*" (2001, 157).

The Gospels, Acts, and the Epistles do not spell out in detail an exact methodology for mission. Rather, we find a variety of methods by which the gospel is preached and churches are established. We must be cautious about making the book of Acts into a step-by-step handbook for mission to be replicated in detail. This was not Luke's intent. As Bauckham states, "The Bible does not map out for us the path from Pentecost to the kingdom. It invites our trust in God rather than mastery of calculation of history. . . . As we should certainly have learned from the biblical story, there will be both shocks and surprises" (2003, 92).

What we have is a picture of a movement of God's Spirit centered in the person, work, and message of Jesus Christ. We find recurrent themes, discover underlying values, and observe a trajectory of how God was moving in and through the church into the world. The church today is to live in that trajectory of mission. This means continuing to live in that movement from Pentecost to Christ's return; from creation to new creation; from Jerusalem to the ends of the earth to the new Jerusalem; from the mustard seed to the tree; from a handful of Jewish disciples to a people from every nation. It means to continue to live under the authority of the apostolic teaching, living as a kingdom people in a hostile world, suffering if necessary, being salt and light. It means serving in the power and creative guidance of the Spirit, never failing to be surprised by what God is doing. It means resisting "mission entropy" and instead pioneering the frontiers and not resting until the good news has reached the farthest corner of the earth and the lordship of Christ is acknowledged among every people.

CONSUMMATION

It is fitting that the New Testament should close with a book that not only pulls back the curtain on the stage of history, revealing the end of the story, but is also preeminently a book of worship. At the center of this worship is Christ, the Lamb of God, surrounded by angelic beings and by those who have been redeemed by the blood of the Lamb. As one song of worship reads, "You were slain, and with your blood you purchased men for God from every tribe and language and people and nation" (Rev. 5:9). The work of redemption on the cross will not have been in vain. The promise of blessing and salvation reaching the nations will come to pass. The next verse echoes Exodus 19:6 and 1 Peter 2:9, "You have made them to be a kingdom and priests to serve our God, and they will reign on the earth" (Rev. 5:10). This is the culmination of the work of Christ, for which he will be worshipped in all eternity.

Revelation also graphically depicts the ultimate victory of God over all evil and the establishment of the kingdom in fullness. In Revelation the witnesses of Christ's kingdom are depicted in conflict with the kingdom of this world, Babylon. To the end, Christ's witnesses refuse coercion or violence but rather suffer violent persecution. It is not until the arrival of Christ himself, as final judge and almighty King, that the powers of evil are once and for all over-thrown. Tragically, men and women who have chosen to worship the beast and reject Christ and his kingdom will share the fate of eternal punishment in the lake of fire (Rev. 19:20; 20:10–15). The response of people to the message of Christ's witnesses is of eternal consequence. This lends a weight of urgency and finality to the mission of the church.

The closing pages of the Bible depict the new Jerusalem appearing as the center of the kingdom in the new creation, a place of infinite glory and worship in the immediate presence of the living God (Rev. 21–22). The centripetal mission of the Old Testament, which became centrifugal and decentralized in the New, now becomes once again centripetal in the consummation. The Old Testament eschatological vision of the nations coming to a new Zion is now fulfilled, but it could not have been realized without the decentralized and diffused mission to the nations of the New Testament era.

CONCLUSION

Our survey of God's plan for the nations in the Old and New Testaments has revealed more continuity than is often assumed. God's universal intention of bringing fallen humanity back into his fellowship and under his reign has un-folded through the particular calling of individuals and peoples. These people became God's mediators of blessing, which extends to all nations. Israel's specific mission was more centripetal, to live as God's kingdom people in the midst of the nations and thus draw them to become worshippers of the Lord. God had revealed that he would in the future include the nations as part of his people and would one day send messengers to the farthest places and gather people from every nation to himself in Zion. Israel failed as the servant of the Lord, but the Messiah would come as a light to the nations and accomplish redemption.

With the New Testament this vision was inaugurated in an unexpected way. Not only was Jesus of Nazareth the promised Messiah who purchased salvation on the cross, but he began a movement of the Spirit that reversed the missionary direction, sending his people to the ends of the earth, calling people everywhere to repent, be reconciled to God through Christ, and enter the kingdom. This was to be a new people of his choosing who would be composed of persons from every nation. His people would become a spiritual temple as a dwelling place of the Spirit, manifesting his kingdom in word and deed. The church continued in continuity with Israel's calling as a true servant of the Lord and a light to the nations. Though faced with persecution and spiritual opposition, Christ will build his church until the gospel has been preached among every people. Then he will return victoriously to finally judge all evil and gather his people from all nations to worship him for all eternity in the new Jerusalem. The eschatological vision will be realized, and God will be glorified in all creation.

3

The Justification of Mission

Missio Dei

The very existence of Christian mission has throughout history been continually challenged. In the first century the challenge came from the Jewish community on one side and the imperial cult on the other. In the Middle Ages it was the challenge of Islam. In the seventeenth century it was the challenge of the Enlightenment, and in the twentieth century it was the challenge of secularism, the failure of two world wars between "Christian" nations, and the horror of the Holocaust in the land of the Reformation. Today a host of arguments opposing the very concept of mission can be named:

- *Socioreligious*—Religious pluralism abounds, whereby conflicting religious views not only coexist in a society, but any attempt to convert a person from one religious conviction to another is considered arrogant, bigoted, or intolerant.
- *Epistemological*—The rejection of any kind of universal truth claim that is valid for all people and all times.
- *Historical*—Christian missions have been associated with colonialism and viewed as instruments of Western imperialism, capitalism, or even the CIA.

- *Anthropological*—Missionaries are accused of destroying traditional cultures.
- *Ethical*—Genocide, violence, and war in seemingly Christian lands such as Northern Ireland, Rwanda, and the Balkans cast doubt on any suggestion of the ethical superiority of Christianity. In the name of religion wars have been fought; even acts of terrorism have been committed. Missionary work only fans the flames of religious conflict and the resulting human suffering—it is, bluntly put, immoral.
- *Psychological*—People fear any kind of religious "fundamentalism" and stigmatize strong religious convictions as extremist, oppressive, and dangerous. Evangelistic messages that include warnings about eternal judgment are considered both offensive and manipulative.
- *Pragmatic*—Today Christians are in nearly every country of the world; thus there is no longer any need for foreign missionaries. Mission work should at best be reduced to compassionate assistance and economic development.

> *The central premise of missionary preaching is the reality of God: Creator, Sustainer, Judge, and Redeemer.*
>
> Lamin Sanneh (1989, 158)

In light of these objections, can mission be justified in the eyes of reasonable people (see the case study at the end of the chapter)?

Christian mission calls men and women from every cultural, religious, and social background to confess that "Jesus is Lord," thus embracing Jesus of Nazareth as Christ and Savior, placing all of life under his authority, and preparing for his kingdom. This is a call to the most radical personal change, ultimately impacting every aspect of life. But what right do Christians have to call others to such commitment? Not only critics of Christianity but also sincere Christians wrestle with such questions. Unless they are answered adequately, the mission of the church will lack authority and confidence and be threatened at its very core.

Some of these specific questions will be discussed in later chapters. Here we address the fundamental justification of mission. Lesslie Newbigin rightly frames the issue in terms of ultimate authority and commitment: "The question of authority is not to be answered by trying to demonstrate the usefulness of missions for some purpose that can be accepted apart from the ultimate commitment upon which the missionary enterprise rests" ([1978] 1995, 14). What, then, is that ultimate commitment?

THE UNIVERSAL GOD WITH A UNIVERSAL PLAN

The justification of mission must start with the very person, plan, and character of God himself as revealed in the scriptures. The Bible begins with God as the Creator of all that is, and all that he creates is good, because God himself is good. He is utterly unique in comparison to other gods or idols. God is frequently referred to as the God of heaven and earth, and of all nations, a universal God. Here are but a few examples:

- "Acknowledge and take to heart this day that the LORD is God in heaven above and on the earth below. There is no other." (Deut. 4:39)
- "To the LORD your God belong the heavens, even the highest heavens, the earth and everything in it." (Deut. 10:14)
- "O LORD, God of Israel, enthroned between the cherubim, you alone are God over all the kingdoms of the earth. You have made heaven and earth." (2 Kings 19:15b; cf. Isa. 37:16)
- "O LORD, God of our fathers, are you not the God who is in heaven? You rule over all the kingdoms of the nations. Power and might are in your hand, and no one can withstand you." (2 Chron. 20:6)
- "You alone are the LORD. You made the heavens, even the highest heavens, and all their starry host, the earth and all that is on it, the seas and all that is in them. You give life to everything, and the multitudes of heaven worship you." (Neh. 9:6)
- "Rise up, O God, judge the earth, for all the nations are your inheritance." (Ps. 82:8)

One of the most pervasive themes of the Bible, particularly the Old Testament, is the vanity of worshipping idols and the folly of following false gods. Repeatedly Israel's idolatry incurs the judgment of God. The prophets of Israel continually denounce false gods and exalt the God of Israel as incomparable to other gods (e.g., 2 Sam. 7:22; 1 Kings 8:23, 60; Ps. 86:8, 10; Isa. 46:9; see C. J. H. Wright 2006, 75–104, and 136–88). The Lord alone is God and worthy of worship—not only in Israel but among all peoples.

> Declare his glory among the nations,
>   his marvelous deeds among all peoples.
>
> For great is the LORD and most worthy of praise;
>   he is to be feared above all gods.
> For all the gods of the nations are idols,
>   but the LORD made the heavens.
> Splendor and majesty are before him;
>   strength and glory are in his sanctuary.
>
> Ascribe to the LORD, O families of nations,
>   ascribe to the LORD glory and strength. (Ps. 96:3–7)

The first two commandments, along with numerous other biblical teachings, leave no room for doubt: God is a jealous God, he alone is worthy of worship, and all other gods are false gods. The denunciation of idols is unparalleled in contemporary Canaanite religion (C. J. H. Wright 2006, 159). The God of Israel is not limited to a geographical, national, or ethnic sphere (as are some of the gods of Israel's neighbors). In more contemporary terms God cannot be reduced to a private god of a person's individualized, customized faith. The God of the Bible is universal in his creatorship, in his reign, in his claims upon women and men, in his lordship over all nations and the earth, in his supremacy over all other spiritual powers, and in his redemptive plan. Paul argues in the opening chapters of Romans that both Jew and Gentile are culpable and accountable before this God. "Is God the God of Jews only? Is he not the God of Gentiles too? Yes, of Gentiles too" (Rom. 3:29).

The Bible also speaks of God having a universal will and plan for his creation. He reveals himself, seeks fellowship, and communicates with personal beings he has created. Man and woman are placed at the climax of his creation, bearing the divine image. All men and women bear this image (albeit marred by the fall) and are thus objects of God's love and subject to his lordship. Though all have rebelled against God and are thus worthy of eternal punishment, God has a universal plan to restore that relationship, to ultimately renew the fallen creation and bring all things under his lordship, thus establishing his universal kingdom. This offer of salvation and this message of the kingdom are to be extended to people of every nation and of every ethnic or linguistic group, to all ages, to men and to women, to rich and to poor. This is the universal plan of the universal God, and it is the ultimate justification of the universal scope of mission.

Apart from this understanding of God, it is impossible to understand and justify mission. The Great Commission as formulated in Matthew 28:18–20 begins with Jesus's utterly astonishing universal claim, "All authority in heaven and on earth has been given to me. Therefore go . . ." There is no person, society, nation, or realm that is beyond the authority of Christ. Such a conviction stands in contrast to postmodern approaches to truth that not only affirm the validity of competing views of God but also reject any proposal of a grand narrative that attempts to explain a universal purpose or plan for life.

God's authority over all creation is invested in the Son, Jesus Christ, and it is this Christ who commissions the church to be his witnesses and calls men and women of every people, nation, and tongue to submit to his lordship. If we are to take the straightforward teaching of the Bible seriously, we can confidently maintain the validity of God's universal claims upon men and women, indeed, upon all creation. For this reason Christian mission—insofar as it is in harmony with God's own mission—has universal legitimacy. The Great Commission is universal in its scope: "all nations" (Matt. 28:19), "to the very end of the age" (Matt. 28:20), "all creation" (Mark 16:15), "all nations" (Luke 24:47), "to the ends of the earth" (Acts 1:8).

Count Nicholas Ludwig von Zinzendorf, leader of the Moravians, who launched the first significant Protestant missionary movement, justified mission on the basis of the lordship of Christ (Vicedom 1965, 12). He spoke of Christ as the Creator-Savior, the ultimate originator of mission, whose work of redemption, like his work of creation, pertains to the entire world (Bintz 1979, 22). There is no more fundamental justification for mission than this. The kingdom of darkness questions the universal reign of God, and its denial is the root of sin and evil—beginning in the garden and extending throughout history.

The conviction of God's universal lordship is no reason for pride or condescending attitudes and is most certainly no pretext for coercion. The spirit of the gospel obliges Christians to respect the freedom of conscience and religious convictions of others who may reject our beliefs. Indeed, Christians are called to love their enemies and persecutors (Matt. 5:43–48).

THE UNIVERSAL GOD BECOMES PARTICULAR

At the same time, God's universality is played out within history in particularity. This is unquestionably the greatest wonder and miracle of the Christian faith. Not only has the universal God worked in particular circumstances of space and time in human history, for example, through redemptive activity, by performing miracles, and by answering prayers. Not only has the universal God called a particular man, Abraham, to become the father of a particular nation, Israel, through whom one day his universal plan to bless *all* nations would be realized. Not only has the universal God anointed a particular king, David, through whom the universal King of kings would come. Not only has the universal God spoken through particular angels and prophets making his universal will known, but as the author of Hebrews states, "In the past God spoke to our forefathers through the prophets at many times and in various ways, but in these last days he has spoken to us by his Son, whom he appointed heir of all things, and through whom he made the universe" (1:1–2).

The universal God *himself* became particular in the incarnation of the Son; the Second Person of the Triune Godhead became a man, born in a particular place, on a particular night, under particular circumstances of Roman rule, in a particular Jewish environment. "The Word became flesh and made his dwelling among us. We have seen his glory, the glory of the One and Only, who came from the Father, full of grace and truth" (John 1:14).

Because God himself has entered history in the person of Christ, human history takes on eternal significance. The language of the New Testament unmistakably identifies Jesus of Nazareth with YHWH of the Old Testament (see C. J. H. Wright 2006, 105–35). Human history can no longer be considered accidental or arbitrary; it takes on a meaning beyond itself. "Therefore, this material and physical and historical world is not just a pale reflection of some universal essence beyond time. It is a part of God's great salvation and eschatological future" (Roxburgh 2000, 187). Mission brings this story into the story of each people and each individual person, giving each particular story eternal significance by connecting each particular story with the universal plan of the eternal God.

The Christian faith is not an abstract philosophy or speculative ideology. The truth of biblical faith is anchored in historical events. God's love and plan for salvation become visible, concrete, physical: "But God demonstrates his own love for us in this: While we were still sinners, Christ died for us" (Rom. 5:8). "This is how God showed his love among us: He sent his one and only Son into the world that we might live through him" (1 John 4:9). It is through this historical person of Jesus the Christ that God has made salvation available to all. Through the second coming of Jesus Christ, God will ultimately fulfill his plan to establish his universal kingdom on earth. This singular, astounding fact makes the question concerning the person of Jesus Christ the most central and essential question facing all humanity. All else is secondary.

Many Christians understand the confession "Jesus is Lord" individually— "Jesus is *my personal* Lord." But for the early Christians this confession meant much more. As one familiar with the challenges of religious pluralism in South Asia, Vinoth Ramachandra observes, "The earliest Christian profession, 'Jesus is Lord,' was never merely a statement of personal devotion but a claim to universal validity. Christian mission made sense only on the premise that the crucified Jesus had been enthroned as the true Lord of the whole world, and thus claiming allegiance of the whole world" (1996, 226).

For the Jewish believer this confession identified Jesus of Nazareth with YHWH, Lord of the Old Testament. For the Gentile believer it meant that the confession "Caesar is Lord" could not stand next to the confession "Jesus is Lord"—and this potentially at the cost of life. Today in a pluralistic world the confession "Jesus is Lord" must rule out the validity of other competing religious options with other lords. It places Jesus Christ above all others; he is "Lord of all" (Acts 10:36). The confession is not merely "Christ is Lord," but "*Jesus* is Lord," emphasizing the particularity of God's saving activity through the historical Jesus. We are confessing not a vague, "cosmic," ethereal Christ known by other names but God in the particularity and specificity of Jesus of Nazareth; "Salvation is found in no one else, for there is no other name under heaven given to men by which we must be saved" (Acts 4:12). This leads Paul to write,

> And being found in appearance as a man,
>   he humbled himself
>   and became obedient to death—
>   even death on a cross!

> Therefore God exalted him to the highest place
> > and gave him the name that is above every name,
> that at the name of Jesus every knee should bow,
> > in heaven and on earth and under the earth,
> and every tongue confess that Jesus Christ is Lord,
> > to the glory of God the Father. (Phil. 2:8–11)

Thus the biblical story moves from the universality of the Father's creation, to the particularity of the Son's incarnation, death, and resurrection, and then again to the universal of the Spirit sending God's people into the entire world to proclaim the message of salvation and the coming kingdom of God. In the words of Richard Bauckham, "Mission takes place on the way from the particularity of God's action in the story of Jesus to the universal coming of God's kingdom. It happens as particular people called by God go forth from here to there and live for God here and there for the sake of all people" (2003, 10).

The church empowered by the Holy Spirit now brings this universal message of God's particular love and universal reign to all peoples. Because of the diversity of peoples—be it their language, ethnicity, history, or culture that sets them apart—the presentation of God's universal message and the realization of God's life in them will (or should) take a particular expression among each people. This is the biblical story of God's mission and the church's participation in that mission.

MISSION AS GOD'S MISSION—MISSIO DEI

Mission as a Divine Prerogative

Mission has often been justified in terms of compassion for the lost or the biblical mandate to preach the gospel and make disciples of all nations. The command of the Bible as the inspired and trustworthy Word of God is authority enough to justify mission. But such approaches tend to emphasize mission as a human initiative in response to God's command and acts of salvation. Justifying mission solely on the basis of explicit commands in the Bible makes mission a human act of obedience, easily separated from God's overarching purposes in history and failing to see mission as central to the entire story of the Bible. As Georg F. Vicedom has argued, "The mission to the nations would be legitimate even if Jesus had not given the Great Commission" (1965, 38) because it is part of the whole story of the Bible.

> *Mission has its origin in the heart of God. God is a fountain of sending love. This is the deepest source of mission. It is impossible to penetrate deeper still; there is mission because God loves people.*
>
> David J. Bosch (1991, 392)

61

In the mid-twentieth century a Copernican revolution took place in the understanding of mission. Mission came to be understood as *God's mission* (Latin *missio Dei*), that is to say, mission is rooted in divine initiative and character. In the Bible "we confront a God who in his very essence is the basis for mission today. Mission begins with God himself, not merely because he is the God of mission but because his very character is mission" (Gnanakan 1989, 67).

Mission is God's own undertaking, and the mission of the church is participation in God's mission. God is a missionary God, and mission is rooted in the sending activity of the Triune God—Father, Son, and Holy Spirit. Jesus's statement to his disciples, "As the Father has sent me, I am sending you" (John 20:21b), is the most explicit biblical basis for this understanding. As the sending will of God was realized in the sending of the Son, so Jesus now sends the church. Through God's sending of the Spirit, the church is empowered to become his agents of mission. Indeed, the whole story of the Bible can be understood in terms of God's sending activity.

Rightly understood, grounding mission in the *missio Dei* does not reduce the importance of scriptural commands, nor does it excuse Christians from the joyful and sacrificial obligation of mission work. Rather, it reframes our understanding of mission in terms of God's own character and prerogative. The mission of the church is embedded in the great drama of God's mission.

Development of the Concept of Missio Dei

Though the grounding of mission in the sending activity of God did not become prominent until the second half of the twentieth century, similar concepts can be found in earlier thinkers. A theology of "divine missions" describing the Father's sending of the Son, and the Father and the Son sending the Spirit, was developed by Augustine and later by Scholastics such as Thomas Aquinas (see Bevans and Schroeder 2004, 289). But no parallel was drawn to the sending of the church.

In the eighteenth century Zinzendorf did not describe mission as an action of the church, but rather considered Christ "the Lord of Mission," who in his sovereignty inaugurates the age of mission through the Holy Spirit (Beyreuther 1960, 74). In 1889 the mission spokesman A. T. Pierson wrote of mission as a work of God as well as a work with God (see Forman 1977, 87–88). Early in the twentieth century, Gustav Warneck described the most "fundamental doctrine of mission" in these terms: "Not only subjective obedience to mission, but also the entire objective *existence* of mission is rooted in the certainty that God is the origin of mission. The same divine authority that mothered the very thought of mission is also the only power that can drive the will for missionary service (John 10:16; 1 Cor. 9:16ff.; Rom. 1:14; Gal. 1:16) and offer the sure foundation and guaranty for the success of mission" (Warneck 1897,

1:66). But divine initiative was not the centerpiece of these thinkers' theology of mission.

In 1932 the influential Swiss theologian Karl Barth called for the grounding of mission not in ecclesiology, soteriology, or comparative religion, but in the activity of God himself. He recalled that the term *mission* was first used in the ancient church to describe the sending activity of the Trinity. Karl Hartenstein (then director of the Basel Mission), influenced by Barth, built on this idea in 1934.

But it was at the International Missionary Conference at Willingen, Germany, in 1952 that the concept of *missio Dei* began to reshape missiological thinking, even though the term *missio Dei* itself was not used at the conference. Rather, it appeared in Hartenstein's conference report (see Richelbächer 2003; Günther 2003; and Sundermeier 2003).

The historical setting of this conference was significant. It took place in the wake of two world wars between "Christian" nations and the horror of the Holocaust. With what credibility could the church attempt to speak to the non-Christian world? The Western colonial system, which had facilitated mission work, was collapsing. What would become of mission work in the former colonial countries? Even worse, a communist government under Mao Tse-tung had come to power in China, the world's largest "mission field," and missionaries were being expelled. Could human governments stop the spread of the gospel? Mission was facing perhaps its greatest crisis since the Islamic threat of the Middle Ages. As a result the missionary enterprise had become unsure of itself, having seemingly lost its confidence, credibility, and legitimacy. Willingen was called by some an "orgy of self-criticism" (Günther 2003, 529).

The solution was found in the Copernican revolution of mission: God's character and initiative displaced humanity's as the center of mission. Or, to shift metaphors, the house of mission could not be built on the shifting sands of human intentions, obedience, and efforts, but rather on the bedrock of divine will. "Willingen 1952 was the first time that mission was so comprehensively anchored in the doctrine of God" (Sundermeier 2003, 560). Hartenstein wrote in the conference report that "the sending of the Son to reconcile the universe through the power of the Spirit is the foundation and purpose of mission. The *missio ecclesiae* comes from the *missio Dei* alone. Thus, mission is placed within the broadest imaginable framework of salvation history and God's plan for salvation" (cited in Richelbächer 2003, 589–90). This understanding seemed to promise a way out of the crisis that mission was facing.

But attempts to unfold the practical meaning and implications of *missio Dei* proved problematic. The understandings of *missio Dei* moved in three different directions (Günther 2003, 528–29):

1. The Germans, represented by Hartenstein and Walter Freytag, took an eschatological, salvation-historical approach. Mission is God's activ-

ity in history between the two comings of Christ. When the gospel is preached to all nations, Christ will return to establish his kingdom in fullness.

2. The Dutch, represented by J. C. Hoekendijk, saw God's mission as the fulfillment of kingdom promises within history. Mission is God's activity *in* the world to *serve* the world.

3. The Americans, who were still heavily influenced by the social gospel, argued that the church responds to God's dynamic activity in the present situation and aims for personal and social transformation. The American report to Willingen claimed that the central element of the missionary task is not saving souls but rather the "sensitive and total response of the church to what the triune God has done and is doing in the world" (quoted in Forman 1977, 109).

Vicedom gave the most systematic presentation of the concept in his book titled *Missio Dei* (1958; translated as *The Mission of God*, 1965). He offered the following definition: "The MISSIO DEI is the work of God through which everything that He has in mind for man's salvation—the complete fullness of His Kingdom of redemption—is offered to men through those whom He has sent, so that men, freed from sin and removed from the other kingdom, can again fully come into His fellowship" (Vicedom 1965, 45).

With the untimely deaths of Hartenstein (1952) and Freytag (1959), the Dutch and American interpretations prevailed in conciliar theology of mission. This led increasingly to social and political understandings of mission as participation in God's acts of liberation in human societies. For Hoekendijk and others the church became one means among many that God may use to accomplish his mission in the world. God could accomplish his purposes apart from either the church or the gospel. The missionary task, according to this view, is to look for God's work in the world (sometimes called "signs of the times"). This was usually defined in terms of the struggle for justice and participation in such movements. Because the church serves the world, the world sets the agenda for the church. Such views were especially influential at the WCC Assembly at Uppsala in 1968. This understanding, reflected in liberation theologies, reached its zenith at the Commission on World Mission and Evangelism (CWME) Conference of 1972–73 in Bangkok.

At the time the Germans, given their recent history with the Third Reich and the "German Christians," were all too aware of the dangers of associating God's will with human efforts and political movements. Thus they opposed such a secularization of the *missio Dei* and emphasized the ultimate hope of the kingdom in Christ's return, maintaining the provisional nature of mission in this age as a sign of the coming kingdom. The church is to play a prophetic role in relation to sociopolitical movements. Evangelical critiques of the views articulated at Uppsala and Bangkok were not lacking (e.g., Winter 1973; Beyerhaus 1974; Johnston 1978) and caused heightened tensions between conciliar and evangelical missiologists.

The debate raises these questions: Does the *missio Dei* remain bound to the *donum Dei* (gift of God) in Jesus Christ and the need for grace, forgiveness, and reconciliation with God? Or is the *missio Dei* more to be understood in terms of God's general concern for the whole creation, *missio Dei mundo* (mission of God in the world)? Attempts have been made to harmonize these two views, seeing God's concern for sustenance of creation and humanity, while at the same time recognizing the need for spiritual salvation. For example, a statement by the Lutheran World Federation, *Mission in Context* (2004, 2.1.1–3), speaks of God's mission as Creator (Father), God's mission as Redeemer (Son), and God's mission as Sanctifier (Spirit). Such approaches are similar to the "two mandates" view that proposes God has given a creation mandate and a gospel mandate (discussed in chap. 6).

Wolfgang Günther (2003, 530) notes in retrospect two major criticisms of the *missio Dei* concept. First, it was alleged to have led to a triumphalism in mission and allowed mission to move on too quickly to "business as usual." Second, it was felt that *missio Dei* was so vague that it could accommodate virtually any conception of mission. It became a "shopping cart" term—one could put in or take out whatever one wanted. *Missio Dei* became a "Trojan horse" in the theology of mission (Rosin, cited in D. J. Bosch 1991, 392)—with the term one could smuggle into "mission" *any* pet theory or activity. On the other hand, *missio Dei* could remain so nebulous that it could simply mean all that God wants done in the world. Also it could be critiqued that for some *missio Dei* led to an almost passive view of the role of the church (e.g., Aring 1971). James A. Scherer summarizes well: "In the decade of the 1960s, *Missio Dei* was to become the plaything of armchair theologians with little more than an academic interest in the practical mission of the church but with a considerable penchant for theological speculation and mischief making" (1993, 85).

Though the terminology of *missio Dei* was nearly abandoned due to such criticisms, it has nevertheless retained a certain power in expressing the theological foundation of mission and continues to be used. Virtually all branches of Christianity—conciliar Protestant, evangelical, Roman Catholic, and Eastern Orthodox—have embraced the term, albeit with differing nuances (D. J. Bosch 1991, 390–91). God is indeed a missionary God, and a biblical examination of God's sending activity as the Triune God will lead us to a sound understanding of the mission of the church in the world today.

A TRINITARIAN GROUNDING OF MISSION

Recognition of the work of the Trinity in mission is not new and was articulated in early nineteenth-century Protestant thought (see Chaney 1976, 217). But

> Trinitarian Affirmation of Mission:
> *We commit ourselves to a renewed
> emphasis on God-centered missiology.
> This invites a new study of the opera-
> tion of the Trinity in the redemption
> of the human race and the whole of
> creation, as well as to understand the
> particular roles of Father, Son, and
> Spirit in mission to this fallen world.*
>
> Iguassu Affirmation
> (W. D. Taylor 2000a, 19)

more concerted reflection rooting the mission of the church in the mission of the Trinity developed following Willingen. In 1963 Newbigin wrote a small but classic work, *Trinitarian Doctrine for Today's Mission*. Later he wrote, "The mission of the church is to be understood, can only be rightly understood, in terms of the trinitarian model" (1989, 118). The Roman Catholic document *Ad Gentes*, which emerged from Vatican II in 1965, also took a trinitarian approach to mission. The Orthodox document on mission *Go Forth in Peace* (Bria 1986) also placed the Trinity at the center of mission. The Brazilian theologian Leonardo Boff (1988) developed a trinitarian theology of liberation. The World Evangelical Fellowship's (WEF) Missiological Consultation held in Iguassu, Brazil, in 1999 featured four Bible studies by Sri Lankan evangelist and theologian Ajith Fernando on "biblical trinitarianism and mission," and the Iguassu Affirmation included a "Trinitarian Affirmation of Mission."

We limit our discussion here primarily to biblical statements regarding the sending activity of the Father, the Son, and the Holy Spirit and consider some of the implications for the sending of the church.

Sending by the Father

We established above that God, the Father, is the universal Lord, Creator, Judge, and Lover of humanity. The Father's character of holiness demands justice and righteousness. But his character of love and compassion moves him to provide a way of redemption and reconciliation that fallen people might reenter fellowship with him and receive the gifts of his kingdom.

The Father's sending activity is rooted in his character. He sends various messengers and events to bridge the gap, to reveal himself, to communicate his will, and to accomplish his purposes with humanity in history. These acts of sending are usually linked to purposes of grace and the restoration of his relationship with his people, though he at times also sends in order to judge and demonstrate his holiness.

The Old Testament repeatedly speaks of God sending prophets, through whom he speaks, though the people seldom listen (Jer. 7:25–26; 25:4; 29:19; 35:15; 44:4–5). The Chronicler writes, for example, "The LORD, the God of their fathers, sent word to them through his messengers again and again, because he had pity on his people and on his dwelling place" (2 Chron. 36:15; see also

Judg. 6:8; 1 Sam. 15:1; 2 Sam. 12:1; 2 Kings 2:2–6; 17:13; 2 Chron. 25:15; Isa. 48:16; Jer. 19:14; 25:4, 17; 26:12, 15; 28:1; 29:19; 42:21; 43:1; Hag. 1:12; Zech. 6:15; 7:12; Mal. 4:5).

Through the prophets God sends his Word, which will accomplish his sovereign purposes:

> As the rain and the snow
> come down from heaven,
> and do not return to it
> without watering the earth
> and making it bud and flour-
> ish,
> so that it yields seed for the
> sower and bread for the
> eater,
> so is my word that goes out
> from my mouth:
> It will not return to me
> empty,
> but will accomplish what I desire
> and achieve the purpose for which I sent it. (Isa. 55:10–11)

> *The missionary movement of which we are part has its source in the Triune God Himself. Out of the depths of his love for us, the Father has sent forth His own beloved Son to reconcile all things to himself. . . . On the foundation of this accomplished work God has sent forth His Spirit, the Spirit of Jesus. . . . We who have been chosen by Christ . . . are by these very facts committed to full participation in His redeeming mission to the world.*
>
> Final Statement from the International Missionary Conference, Willingen, 1952 (cited in Günther 2003, 529–30)

God sends Joseph to Egypt to save his family (Gen. 45:5–8). God sends Moses to deliver his people (Exod. 3:12–15; 7:16; Num. 16:28; 1 Sam. 12:8). He sends judges to deliver and rule Israel (Judg. 6:14), and he sends King Saul on a mission of destruction (1 Sam. 15:18, 20).

God also sends angels to accomplish his purposes, including guidance, protection, revelation, and destruction (e.g., Gen. 19:13; 24:7; 1 Chron. 21:15; 2 Chron. 32:21; Dan. 6:22; Luke 1:19, 26; Acts 12:11; Rev. 22:6). He sent theophanies (divine appearances), sometimes called "the angel of the Lord" (e.g., Judg. 13:6–9). God's sovereignty is evident in that he sends thunder, hail, and fire (Exod. 9:23; 1 Sam. 12:18); serpents (Num. 21:6); hornets (Deut. 7:20); pestilence (2 Sam. 24:15; 1 Chron. 21:14); lions (2 Kings 17:25); and disease (Isa. 10:16; see also McDaniel 1998).

God the Father's sending is always purposeful. The very idea of sending emphasizes that God has taken initiative. From the time of the fall, humans have sought to hide from God, to escape him, and to deny him. But he has exercised grace and mercy in order to reconcile lost women and men to himself. He sends John the Baptizer to prepare the coming of his Son (Matt. 11:10; Mark 1:2; Luke 7:27), with which the sending and saving activity of God climaxes.

Sending of the Son

The New Testament is replete with statements describing the sending of the Son into the world. We begin with statements found in the Gospels, especially those from Jesus himself. Our examination will not be limited to instances where specifically the word *send* is used but will also include statements regarding the purpose of his coming, such as when Jesus says, "I have come that . . ." This is especially important in John's Gospel; as Köstenberger notes, "While references to the purposes of Jesus' mission are rare in connection with sending terminology, they are more common with terms of 'coming'" (1998a, 91).

THE SENDING OF JESUS IN THE SYNOPTIC GOSPELS

Jesus's sending by the Father means that he was the immediate representative of the Father on earth: "He who receives you receives me, and he who receives me receives the one who sent me" (Matt. 10:40; cf. Mark 9:37; Luke 9:48). Explicit statements regarding Jesus being sent are relatively few in the Synoptic Gospels. Yet like the tip of an iceberg, they reflect broad themes in Jesus's ministry.

- Jesus was *sent to preach the kingdom*: Jesus said, "I must preach the good news of the kingdom of God to the other towns also, because that is why I was sent" (Luke 4:43b). To preach the kingdom is to call for repentance and proclaim that the kingdom of God is near (Matt. 4:17). Such preaching was often accompanied by miracles and deliverance from demons, which evidenced the healing and liberating power of God's presence (e.g., Matt. 4:23; 9:35; 12:28).
- Jesus was *sent to Israel*: "I was sent only to the lost sheep of Israel" (Matt. 15:24). Though Jesus often received Gentiles who sought him out, his ministry was primarily to Israel. The Gentile mission would be launched only after his death and resurrection and the sending of the Spirit.

When we examine statements in which Jesus says, "I came . . . ," a range of purposes emerge.

Jesus came *to fulfill the law*: Jesus says in the Sermon on the Mount, "Do not think that I have come to abolish the Law or the Prophets; I have not come to abolish them but to fulfill them" (Matt. 5:17). This statement is best understood as realizing the Old Testament messianic promises (cf. Luke 24:44) and perhaps also as fulfilling the righteous demands of the Old Testament law (Rom. 10:4; see Carson 1984, 141–46). Jesus's self-understanding was in full continuity with salvation history.

Jesus came *to create division*: As people become followers of Jesus, even families will be divided because of him. "I have come to bring fire on the earth, and how I wish it were already kindled! . . . Do you think I came to bring peace on earth? No, I tell you, but division" (Luke 12:49, 51; cf. Matt. 10:34–35). In the interim period until Jesus returns, the contours dividing good and evil will be heightened, and Jesus himself will be the watershed.

Jesus came *to seek and to save the lost*: When Jesus is criticized for calling the tax collector Levi to become his follower, he replies, "I have not come to call the righteous, but sinners to repentance" (Luke 5:32). When similarly criticized for having table fellowship with the tax collector Zacchaeus, he replies, "For the Son of Man came to seek and to save what was lost." As James and John want to call fire upon Samaritans who would not welcome Jesus, he forbids them, "for the Son of Man did not come to destroy men's lives, but to save them" (Luke 9:56). The same intention is evidenced in the parables of the lost coin, the lost sheep, and the lost son, which were also told in response to criticism of Jesus's association with tax collectors and sinners (Luke 15).

Jesus came *to give his life as a ransom*: "The Son of Man did not come to be served, but to serve, and to give his life as a ransom for many" (Matt. 20:28; Mark 10:45). Here we see the means by which Jesus would save the lost: he came to give his life as a substitutionary ransom to purchase the freedom of men and women from the bondage of sin. The price would be the shedding of his blood for forgiveness of sins (Matt. 26:28). This would be the ultimate service and the ultimate sacrifice.

One of the most crucial passages to the interpretation of Jesus's mission is Luke 4. As Jesus begins his public ministry, he reads in the Nazareth synagogue from the prophet Isaiah (61:1–2). Luke reports the occasion:

> "The Spirit of the Lord is on me,
>   because he has anointed me
>   to preach good news to the poor.
> He has sent me to proclaim freedom for the prisoners
>   and recovery of sight for the blind,
> to release the oppressed,
>   to proclaim the year of the Lord's favor."
>
> Then he rolled up the scroll, gave it back to the attendant and sat down. The eyes of everyone in the synagogue were fastened on him, and he began by saying to them, "Today this scripture is fulfilled in your hearing." (Luke 4:18–21)

According to Luke, Jesus stops short of completing the citation from Isaiah, which reads, "to proclaim the year of the Lord's favor and the day of vengeance of our God, to comfort all who mourn," apparently indicating that the element of judgment is not part of his purpose in coming.

The passage has been variously interpreted with views falling along the spectrum between a largely spiritual to a more literal and political understanding of the passage. If we are sent as Jesus was sent, does this mean that the struggle for social justice should be a high priority in mission? We shall return in a later chapter to discuss in more detail the interpretation of this passage and its implications for mission.

However we may choose to interpret Luke 4, Luke's Gospel repeatedly emphasizes Jesus's concern for the poor, for outcasts such as tax collectors and lepers, and for other marginalized people. Jesus indeed cared for the whole person. Moreover, his miracles, healings, casting out of demons, and acceptance of the rejected were powerful signs that the kingdom had come near and that the power of sin and the bondage of evil were to be defeated in the person of Jesus. This victory was not limited to the spiritual realm but reached into people's daily lives.

The Sending of Jesus in the Gospel of John

No other Gospel speaks of Jesus being sent by the Father as frequently as John. Andreas J. Köstenberger and Peter T. O'Brien observe that "the Fourth Gospel's primary focus is the mission of Jesus: he is the one who comes into the world, accomplishes his work and returns to the Father; he is the one who descended from heaven and ascends again; he is the Sent One, who, in complete dependence and perfect obedience to his sender, fulfils the purpose for which the Father sent him" (2001, 203). John's Gospel is built from the very beginning around the understanding that Jesus is the eternal Logos, the Word become man, sent into the world to manifest God's presence, to do the will of the Father, and to save the world (1:1, 14).

Jesus repeatedly speaks of having been sent by the Father (e.g., John 5:23; 6:29; 7:18; 8:16; 10:36; 11:42; 12:45; 17:18; and 20:21a). "I proceeded forth and have come from God, for I have not even come on My own initiative, but He sent Me" (NASB 8:42b; cf. 7:28). He preexisted before the incarnation and would return to the Father after his work on earth was accomplished (7:33; 16:28).

- Jesus was sent *to do the will and work of the Father,* not his own. "For I have come down from heaven not to do my will but to do the will of him who sent me" (John 6:38; see also 4:34; 5:30; 8:29; 9:4).
- Jesus came *to teach the truth*. "In fact, for this reason I was born, and for this I came into the world, to testify to the truth" (18:37b). "For I did not speak of my own accord, but the Father who sent me commanded me what to say and how to say it" (12:49; see also 3:34; 7:16; 12:46).
- Jesus came to *give fullness of life*. "I have come that they may have life, and have it to the full" (10:10b; see also 6:33, 57).
- Above all, it was the will of the Father that Jesus *complete the work of salvation*. "For God so loved the world that he gave his one and only

70

Son, that whoever believes in him shall not perish but have eternal life. For God did not send his Son into the world to condemn the world, but to save the world through him" (3:16–17; see also 6:39; 12:47b).

Köstenberger summarizes the basic characteristics of sending in John's Gospel: (1) bringing glory and honor to the sender; (2) doing the sender's will, working his works, and speaking his words; (3) witnessing to the sender and representing him accurately; and (4) knowing the sender intimately, living in close relationship with the sender, and following his example (1998a, 191). To these we would add: (5) accomplishing the work of redemption so that salvation and eternal life might be available to all who believe.

PAUL'S UNDERSTANDING OF JESUS'S SENDING

Paul interprets the sending of the Son as primarily for the purpose of redemption. With the sending of the Son, God's salvation is sent to the Jew and the Gentile (Acts 13:26; 28:28).

> For what the law was powerless to do in that it was weakened by the sinful nature, God did by sending his own Son in the likeness of sinful man to be a sin offering. And so he condemned sin in sinful man, in order that the righteous requirements of the law might be fully met in us, who do not live according to the sinful nature but according to the Spirit. (Rom. 8:3–4)

> But when the time had fully come, God sent his Son, born of a woman, born under law, to redeem those under law, that we might receive the full rights of sons. Because you are sons, God sent the Spirit of his Son into our hearts, the Spirit who calls out, "*Abba*, Father." (Gal. 4:4–6)

In Galatians Paul emphasizes the historical nature ("of a woman") and religious context ("under the law") of the incarnation. Redemption leads to a new relationship with God, namely, that of being adopted as sons (i.e., no longer servants or mere subjects). Moreover, with adoption comes also the gift of the Holy Spirit, who brings the believer into an intimate relation with the Father. Here again we see the Trinity active in redemption and sending. The Father sends the Son for redemption. Then the Spirit is sent to empower the believer and convict the world. This leads us to the sending of the Spirit.

Sending of the Spirit

The sending of the Holy Spirit by the Father and the Son continues the one time sending of the Son through the ministry of the disciples (Vicedom 1965, 55). The sending of the Spirit in John is related to the ministry of the disciples in the world. This begins with the teaching ministry of the Spirit: "But the Counselor, the Holy Spirit, whom the Father will send in my name, will teach you all things and will remind you of everything I have said to you" (John 14:26).

The ministry of the Spirit continues with the Spirit bearing witness to Jesus Christ through the disciples: "When the Counselor comes, whom I will send to you from the Father, the Spirit of truth who goes out from the Father, he will testify about me. And you also must testify, for you have been with me from the beginning" (John 15:26–27). When the Spirit is sent, he will also have a ministry in the world, convicting the world regarding sin, righteousness, and judgment, which are related to the person of Christ (John 16:7–11).

We note parallels in John's Gospel between the purpose of the sending of the Spirit and the purpose of Jesus's sending, in particular to bear witness to the truth. Luke's treatment of the sending of the Spirit is directly linked to the reception of the Spirit by the disciples. They are not to leave Jerusalem until they receive the Spirit (Luke 24:49). When they have received the Spirit, they will be empowered to be witnesses of Jesus to the ends of the earth (Acts 1:8).

As the Spirit is sent, the gospel is spread in new power and conviction. When we survey the book of Acts, it is apparent that nearly every time believers are filled with the Spirit, some form of proclamation occurs. Paul repeatedly makes reference to the fact that he preached the gospel not in word only, but in the power and conviction of the Holy Spirit (Rom. 15:19; 1 Cor. 2:4; 1 Thess. 1:5). Through the sending of the Spirit at work in the church, the gospel spreads and transforms.

The Sending of the Church

JESUS'S SENDING OF THE DISCIPLES

The purpose of Jesus's calling of the disciples is to send them: "He appointed twelve—designating them apostles—that they might be with him and that he might send them out to preach" (Mark 3:14). On two occasions Jesus sends the disciples on ministry tours: first the twelve (Matt. 10:1–42; Mark 6:7–13; Luke 9:1–6), then the seventy (Luke 10:1–20). The following is the account in Matthew 10:

- They are given authority to heal, cast out demons, and even raise the dead (vv. 1, 8).
- They are to go to Israel only (vv. 5–6).
- They are to go preaching, "The kingdom of heaven is at hand" (v. 7 NASB).
- They serve in full dependence on the Father's provision (vv. 9–11).
- Response to their message will lead to peace or judgment (vv. 12–15).
- Their demeanor is as sheep among wolves (v. 16).

- They will face opposition (vv. 17–23).
- The Spirit will speak through them (10:20).

In short, the ministry of the disciples was to imitate the ministry of Jesus. As John Harvey summarizes, their authority, activities, message, target group, and results were the same as those of Jesus (1998, 43). This was but a preparation for the much greater ministry that would follow Pentecost as recorded in Acts. The sending of the Twelve and of the seventy as recorded in the Gospels are sendings of limited duration and authority—one time sendings. The disciples are given explicit instructions, they return to resume following Jesus, and they do not undertake such tours again on their own initiative; "thus, they did not have an independent assignment as long as the Lord remained on earth" (Vicedom 1965, 57). Only after the resurrection and the receiving of the Spirit would their sending take on a fully new dimension. They are instructed not to leave Jerusalem until receiving the Spirit (Luke 24:49), emphasizing that the post-Easter sending will be of a qualitatively different nature.

The apostle Paul, though not one of the original Twelve, described his sending by recounting these words of the risen Christ to him in Acts 26:16–18: "Now get up and stand on your feet. I have appeared to you to appoint you as a servant and as a witness of what you have seen of me and what I will show you. I will rescue you from your own people and from the Gentiles. I am sending you to them to open their eyes and turn them from darkness to light, and from the power of Satan to God, so that they may receive forgiveness of sins and a place among those who are sanctified by faith in me."

THE SENDING OF THE CHURCH TODAY

After the death and resurrection of Jesus Christ came Pentecost, and the church, the new people of God, was born. The resurrected Christ sends the disciples into the world with the giving of the Great Commission and the sending of the Holy Spirit. The *scope* of their sending is enlarged as they are sent as Christ's witnesses not merely to Israel but to the ends of the earth. With the sending of the Spirit, the ministry initiated by Jesus and the original disciples explodes across the globe. The *duration* of their sending is extended until the end of the age (Matt. 28:20). Also, the *message* of their sending is expanded to include forgiveness of sin, now that Christ has completed the work of redemption. Finally, the *power* for their sending is granted as they receive the fullness of the Holy Spirit. The church today continues on this trajectory of mission.

The sending of the church is intimately linked to the sending activity of the Trinity. It is not by human authority, but through the authority of the Triune God, who as Father sends, as Son redeems, and as Spirit empowers. It is in the name of this Triune God that believers are baptized (Matt. 28:19). The Triune God is at work in the Father adopting believers as children through the redeeming work of the Son and by sending his Spirit into our hearts (Gal. 4:4–6). The Father opens doors for the gospel (1 Cor. 16:9; 2 Cor. 2:12; Col. 4:3a), so that the mystery of the Son can be spoken (Col. 4:3b), and the Spirit can confirm the message and convince the hearers (Rom. 15:19; 1 Cor. 2:4; 1 Thess. 1:5). Apart from messengers being *sent*, the universal invitation of salvation to all who call upon the name of the Lord cannot be preached, heard, and thus believed (Rom. 10:11–15).

The sending of the church is most evident in Jesus's commissioning word in John 20:21b: "As the Father has sent me, I am sending you." But in just what way are we sent as Jesus was sent? John has earlier reported that being sent by Jesus makes one Jesus's representative, which in turn makes one indirectly a representative of the Father: "I tell you the truth, whoever accepts anyone I send accepts me; and whoever accepts me accepts the one who sent me" (John 13:20).

Above we noted Köstenberger's summary of Jesus's sending in John's Gospel as (1) glorifying the sender, (2) doing the sender's will and speaking his words, (3) witnessing to the sender, and (4) knowing the sender intimately. "All these aspects of what one sent is required to be and do, are applicable to the disciples as they are sent by Jesus" (Köstenberger 1998a, 91). The immediate context of John 20:22 emphasizes that this commission is closely linked to the ministry of forgiveness of sin. Köstenberger and O'Brien summarize: "As Jesus did his Father's will, they have to do *Jesus'* will. As Jesus did his Father's works, they have to do *Jesus'* works. As Jesus spoke the words of his Father, they have to speak *Jesus'* words. Their relationship to their sender, Jesus, is to reflect Jesus' relationship with *his* sender" (2001, 222).

Summary

Without the sending activity of the Trinity, there is no mission, for there is no gospel. The core of the gospel is that God the Father so loved the world that he gave—that is, he *sent*—his one and only Son into the world. The same Spirit of God, who moved over the surface of the waters at creation (Gen. 1:2) now moves the church to all peoples and nations as witnesses to Jesus Christ (Acts 1:8). This Spirit will convict the world concerning sin, righteousness, and judgment (John 16:8).

Newbigin summarizes well the importance of a trinitarian understanding of mission: "Thus even in the most elementary form the preaching of the Gospel must presuppose an understanding of the triune nature of God. It is not, as we have sometimes seemed to say, a kind of intellectual cap-stone which can be put on to the top of the arch at the very end; it is, on the contrary, what Athanasius called it, the *arche*, the presupposition without which the preaching of the Gospel in a pagan world cannot begin" (Newbigin [1963] 1998, 36).

PRACTICAL IMPLICATIONS

The foregoing discussion has several practical implications for the biblical justification of mission.

Assurance That Mission Is God's Prerogative and Undertaking

The foregoing discussion not only justifies mission but relieves the church of the sense that the success of mission depends on human efforts and strategies. "Mission is the work that belongs to God. This is the first implication of *missio Dei*" (Vicedom 1965, 5). This does not excuse the church from sacrificially committing itself to God's mission, but it does give the church a deep sense of privilege and confidence that it is part of something bigger than itself—it is God's instrument in the progress of salvation history. "We are not engaged in an enterprise of our own choosing or devising. We are invited to participate in an activity of God which is the central meaning of creation itself. We are invited to become, through the presence of the Holy Spirit, participants in the Son's loving obedience to the Father" (Newbigin [1963] 1998, 83).

We Can Confidently Proclaim the Gospel to All People

In a pluralistic society where multiple truth claims and religious convictions coexist, the charge is often leveled that the Christian faith cannot have universal validity. Furthermore, the attempt to convert persons from other faiths to Christianity is condemned as intolerant, bigoted, or imperialistic.

But the mission of the church flows directly from the missionary will of God, who is the universal Creator of heaven and earth, and before whom all will give account. His love seeks to embrace all people. This moves the church to proclaim the gospel in bold humility and justifies the validity of biblical truth for every man and woman of every nation, culture, or ethnic group. We can confidently say with Paul, "I am not ashamed of the gospel, because it is the power of God for the salvation of everyone who believes: first for the Jew, then for the Gentile" (Rom. 1:16).

The Person of Jesus Christ Must Remain Central to Both the Method and the Message of Mission

We are sent as Jesus was sent. We are not left to our own inventiveness or cleverness to determine the nature of mission. In essence mission is continuing the ministry of Jesus. In a sense it is even more. Since the death and resurrection of Jesus, we have a yet fuller message of forgiveness, salvation, and reconciliation. The commission is about more than doing good in the world. "The mission can be nothing else than the continuation of the saving activity of God through the publication of the deeds of salvation" (Vicedom 1965, 9).

> Missionaries and nationals are agreed, "that the world's evangelization is a divine enterprise, that the Spirit of God is the great Missioner, and that only as he dominates the work and workers can we hope for success in the undertaking to carry the knowledge of Christ to all people. They believe that he gave the missionary impulse to the early church, and that today all true mission work must be inaugurated, directed and sustained by Him."
>
> John R. Mott, 1910 (cited in Stott 1992, 396)

Mission Must Be Undertaken in Dependency on the Power of the Holy Spirit

The power of mission is the enabling power of the Holy Spirit. God, the Spirit, himself is at work empowering witness, convicting hearers, performing signs, transforming lives, creating kingdom communities, and gifting for service. The very thought of Jesus's original disciples, floundering and fearful as they were, boldly bringing the gospel to the ends of the earth in the face of persecution is absurd apart from the transforming and enabling power of the Holy Spirit. The church today has grown and has manifold resources unimaginable to the first Christians. Nevertheless, the thought is no less absurd that we should be able to advance the kingdom one millimeter apart from God's enabling power. Jesus appointed us as his disciples to go and bear much fruit that will remain (John 15:16), but he could not have stated the importance of our total dependence on him more clearly: "apart from me you can do nothing" (John 15:5b).

We Can Be Encouraged and Inspired to Renew Our Commitment to Mission

Involvement in mission is participation in the purposes of God. To quote Newbigin again, "The truth that the church is itself something sent into the world, the continuation of Christ's mission from the Father, something which is not so much an institution as an expedition sent to the ends of the earth in Christ's name, has been grasped with new vividness" ([1963] 1998, 12). Have we in fact grasped this?

Whereas the simple truth "Jesus loves me" gives our lives infinite value in time and eternity, by becoming God's vehicles of mission in this age our lives take on significance within history. For this we dare not become proud. Immediate success is not promised to the church, for many will enter the kingdom by suffering, and in the world we will face tribulation. But ultimate success is assured for the purposes of God, because Christ has overcome the world (John 16:33).

God's plan for the nations is moving through the landscape of history like a great locomotive empowered by the Spirit, riding on the tracks of his revealed will in scripture, until its final destination is reached: the worship of the nations in his everlasting kingdom of righteousness and glory. The forces of evil cannot stop it. This mission will not fail. The assurance of this truth, the wonder of the privilege of participation, and the sweetness of his fellowship in service should propel us as his people today to gladly commit ourselves anew and with total abandon to God's mission.

CASE STUDY: "MISSION IS IMMORAL!"

Since early childhood Amber had been fascinated by missionaries visiting her Sunday school. She had the highest respect for them. Last summer she participated in a mission trip to Jamaica, and just yesterday she had discussed the possibility of long-term missionary service with her pastor. As she sat in the cafeteria of State University pondering over her lunch, she suddenly said almost in spite of herself to her roommate Shelia, "I think God may be calling me to be a missionary."

Shelia was stopped cold, fork in midair. "You can't be serious!" Though Shelia occasionally attended church, she found Amber's thought as strange as if she had announced that she would become a Martian. "Aren't there already enough Christians around the world? Why should you sacrifice everything you've worked for to go off to Africa or someplace? If you want to help, I think it would be better just to send money. You know, Americans aren't really liked very much around the world these days."

As Amber was attempting to answer Shelia's concerns, Paul joined them at the table and chimed into the conversation. "Missionary? Do you mean handing out blankets at a refugee camp or something?" Amber sheepishly

attempted to explain that she was actually more interested in evangelism among teenagers. "You mean that you are actually going to try and convert people from their religion to become Christians?" retorted Paul in disbelief. "What gives you the right to think that your religion is any better than theirs?" Paul's tone was noticeably irritated.

Just as Amber was beginning to feel attacked and regretting that she had brought up the subject, a student sitting behind them leaned over and interjected, "Say, I've been overhearing your conversation. You know, of course, that missionaries are culture destroyers. They have no respect for people's beliefs or customs. They do stupid things like making the native women wear bras!" Though the others thought the comment a bit rude, they couldn't help but laugh out loud. Amber's shoulders were beginning to slump.

The eavesdropper continued, "And by the way, if you would read history, you'd know that missionaries not only tried to 'civilize the poor savages,' but they supported colonial governments. Some people believe that naive missionaries are being used by Western governments to undermine the traditional values of third world countries. There may even be something to accusations that some missionaries are really CIA informants."

After a thoughtful pause Shelia reentered the conversation. "Sometimes I get the feeling that religion is at the root of a whole lot of human conflict in the world. Just look at Northern Ireland, the Israeli-Palestinian conflict, or Muslim terrorists. Weren't there riots recently in Indonesia between Christians and Muslims?" To which Paul added, "Yea, and what about the genocide in Rwanda? They were supposed to all be Christians. See how much good that did!"

In a desperate attempt to escape the embarrassment and shame, Amber changed the subject, "Did any of you see the basketball game last night?"

But as if to hammer the last nail to the coffin of Amber's dream, the eavesdropper interrupted once again, saying out loud what everyone but Amber was thinking, "If you want to know what I think, mission work is downright arrogant and immoral."

Amber was so confused and upset she quickly excused herself from the table and returned to her room. She had never heard such accusations against missionaries and assaults on mission work. Maybe missionaries weren't heroes after all. Maybe the days of foreign missions really were past.

After gathering her thoughts she called Charlotte, her best friend at church. Charlotte had recently attended a seminar on world missions. Amber rehearsed the conversation with Charlotte, concluding with the question, "What should I say to all this? In light of all of that they said, can missionary work really be justified?"

REFLECTION AND DISCUSSION

1. If you were Charlotte, how would you answer Amber?

4

The Purpose and Nature of Mission

Having established that the mission of the church is the mission of a universal God, we now turn to more carefully define the purpose and nature of that mission. We noted in the introduction that some contemporary missiologists assume that mission is indefinable and that only broad approximations can be hoped for. Others have suggested that mission or the *missio Dei* includes simply everything that God sends the church to do (e.g., Stott 1975, 30; Kirk 2000, 24). But such definitions are hardly helpful. Stephen Neill is often quoted in this regard: "If everything is mission, nothing is mission. If everything the church does is to be classed as 'mission,' we shall need to find another term for the church's particular responsibility for 'the heathen,' those who have never yet heard the Name of Christ" (1959, 81).

How we define mission is of the greatest practical importance if the church is to focus its efforts on being a truly missional church. In the following discussion we differentiate between the purpose of mission and the task of missions. When we speak of the *purpose of mission*, we are speaking of the broad, comprehensive goal of mission, that is, that which is ultimately to be accomplished, that to which all tasks contribute, the overall framing and spirit of mission. In the following chapters we will address the *task of missions*, which describes the specific activities and undertakings central to fulfilling the ultimate purpose of mission. Of course, how one defines the purpose of mission will have much to do with how one defines the task of missions.

We will examine the purpose and nature of mission as follows:

- *Doxology*, the glorification of God, as the highest and most overarching *purpose* of mission to which all others flow
- *Redemption* as the *foundation* of mission
- *The kingdom of God* as the *center* of mission
- *Eschatology* as the *hope* of mission
- *The nations* as the *scope* of mission
- *Reconciliation* as the *fruit* of mission
- *Incarnation* as the *character* of mission

In chapter 10 we will discuss the Holy Spirit as the power of mission.

DOXOLOGY AS THE PURPOSE OF MISSION

If there is any overarching purpose of mission it is this: God's glory should be magnified in all the earth and before all creation. Scripture teaches that God's glory is manifest in many ways, for example, in creation (e.g., Ps. 19:1–6). But in a much more wonderful way, God's glory is manifest in his specific acts of salvation. As God fulfills his mission in history, his glory, his righteousness, and his love become undeniably evident. This glory is echoed back to him in the praises of his redeemed people.

Salvation history climaxes as the glory of God is marvelously revealed in the sending of the Son into the world to purchase our salvation and defeat the powers of sin, death, and evil. "The Word became flesh and made his dwelling among us. We have seen his glory, the glory of the One and Only, who came from the Father, full of grace and truth" (John 1:14). Doxology is christological in that Christ is not only the author of salvation, but "all things were created by him and for him" (Col. 1:16b). The ministry of the Holy Spirit is to glorify Christ (John 16:14). The book of Revelation is full of Christ-exalting worship (e.g., Rev. 1:17; 5:6–14; 7:9–10). As men and women hear the message of Christ, receive forgiveness, and live under Christ's lordship, they glorify God with their lives and become worshippers of God in the fullest sense of the term. God is most greatly glorified.

As we have already seen, numerous scriptures point to this with particular reference to the nations and the role of God's people in the midst of the nations. The nations are repeatedly called to acknowledge the greatness of the Lord and become his glad worshippers, for example, Psalm 67:3–4a, "May the peoples praise you, O God; may all the peoples praise you. May the nations be glad and sing for joy." The Old Testament eschatological vision foresees the nations in worship, for example, Psalm 22:27, "All the ends of the earth will remember and turn to the LORD, and all the families of the nations will bow down before him," or Psalm 86:9, "All the nations you have made will come and worship before you, O Lord; they will bring glory to your name." The fact that God's glory and salvation inspire the worship of people from the most diverse nationalities, ethnic backgrounds, and social standings serves to further magnify the universal praiseworthiness of God.

Jesus himself glorifies the Father (John 7:18; 17:1) and is the radiance of his glory (Heb. 1:3). He summarizes his earthly ministry praying, "I have brought you glory on earth by completing the work you gave me to do" (John 17:4). He sends the Holy Spirit to the believer to be a witness and to glorify Christ (John 15:26–27; 16:14). Jesus is glorified in his disciples (John 17:9–10) and exhorts his followers, "In the same way, let your light shine before men, that they may see your good deeds and praise your Father in heaven" (Matt. 5:16). The church is called three times in Ephesians 1:5–14 to live to the praise of God's glory. It is to manifest his wisdom (Eph. 3:10) and proclaim his excellencies (1 Pet. 2:9). All that we do is to be to God's glory (1 Cor. 10:31).

> *For from him and through him and to him are all things. To him be the glory forever! Amen.*
> Romans 11:36

Sin is described as falling short of the glory of God (Rom. 3:23), and idolatry is a corruption of God's glory (Rom. 1:23). On the other hand, faith (Rom. 4:20), repentance (Rev. 16:9), obedience (2 Cor. 9:13), and steadfastness in trials (1 Pet. 1:7; 2:12) glorify God. The very essence of conversion is captured in the example of the Thessalonian believers who "turned to God from idols to serve the living and true God" (1 Thess. 1:9). As the grace of God spreads to more people, the glory of God is multiplied (2 Cor. 4:15). The glory of God as manifest in Christ is a recurrent and prominent theme in Pauline literature (see Little 2005, 52–73).

In Romans 15, the apostle Paul employs the language of worship to describe his pioneering mission work among the Gentiles. The proclamation of the gospel is a "priestly duty" whereby the Gentile believers become "an offering" (v. 16). This is undoubtedly a reference to Isaiah's vision of messengers who go to the nations and "to the distant islands that have not heard of my fame or seen my glory. They will proclaim my glory among the nations. And they will bring all your brothers, from all the nations, to my holy mountain in Jerusalem as an offering to the LORD" (Isa. 66:19–20). Paul then continues, "Therefore I glory in Christ Jesus in my service to God" (Rom. 15:17). Not only is God's glory the ultimate goal of mission, but the practical work of mission is one of proclaiming God's glory and is in itself a priestly act of worship.

Finally, the New Testament eschatological vision reveals the worship of the redeemed from "every tribe and language and people and nation" (Rev. 5:9; 7:9). Here the Lamb of God is glorified with songs of worship by the heavenly host because his work of redemption has not been in vain but has in fact reached and been embraced by those from every people. The book of Revelation is full of the worship and glory of the Lord.

This understanding of mission was present in the earliest Protestant missiology. In the mid-seventeenth century, Gisbertus Voetius formulated a threefold purpose of mission as the conversion of the heathen, the planting of the church, and the glorification and manifestation of divine grace (see Bavinck 1960, 155; Jongeneel 1991). Jan Jongeneel, however, considers this threefold goal a modern restriction of Voetius's original sevenfold goal given in *Politica Ecclesiastica*, which included conversion and church planting but also a variety of activities such as regathering persecuted believers, reformation of deficient churches, reunification of divided churches, and financial support (1991, 63–64).

The glory of God is the crowning purpose to which conversion and church planting contribute. For Voetius, mission is explicitly an expression of the will of God in predestination (eternal decree), and missionary sending is the means of fulfilling this decree. God is thus the first cause of mission, the church the secondary active cause. The glory of God is the *ultimate* end of mission; conversion and church planting are *penultimate*. Even the kingdom of God is subordinate to God's glory. "God is not only the first cause but also the ultimate goal of missions" (Jongeneel 1991, 68). J. H. Bavinck builds on Voetius's understanding, devoting a whole chapter to "The Threefold Aim" concluding, "The aim of missions is thus preoccupied with God, with his glory, with his kingdom" (1960, 158).

In the Calvinistic tradition God's glory was the "taproot" of mission among the early Puritans (Beaver 1968a, 121). Jonathan Edwards saw God's work of redemption as his greatest and most glorious work, for which all other works exist. "Church participation in the work of redemption is the most glorious of all the works of the Church. For in that participation, the work of redemption is completed, and that work perfected which brings the most glory to God" (Chaney 1976, 225). "For the glory of God and His kingdom!" was the slogan of the late eighteenth-century Dutch pioneer missionary Johannes Theodorus Van der Kemp (Enklaar 1978, 284). But by the early nineteenth century, *gloria Dei* had disappeared from missionary sermons and promotion. Personal, individual conversion became increasingly prominent.

The second of "seven indispensable basic elements of mission" listed in the evangelical *Frankfurt Declaration on the Fundamental Crisis in Mission* (1970) states, "The first and supreme goal of mission is the glorification of the name of the one God throughout the entire world and the proclamation of the lordship of Jesus Christ, his Son." According to Peter Beyerhaus, principle author of the Frankfurt Declaration, the primary vision of biblical revelation is not the meeting of human need per se, neither bodily nor spiritual, but it is a vision of God himself as the almighty Creator and Redeemer. "The sending of the church into the world serves first and foremost the glorification of the triune God in the world. If our theology of mission is to be biblically oriented the *doxological* motive must be primary" (Beyerhaus 1996, 269). Christopher R.

SIDEBAR 4.1
DOXOLOGY IN EASTERN ORTHODOX THEOLOGY OF MISSION

The theology of mission as understood in the tradition of Eastern Orthodoxy also focuses on doxology. James J. Stamoolis summarizes the general Orthodox view: "The ultimate aim of mission is to restore all of humanity to a right relationship with God, which would issue in all of humankind correctly praising the trinity" (2000, 715). Beyond this, "if the ultimate purpose of God's mission is the revelation of his glory, then God's purpose in calling humankind is for humans to be partakers of the divine glory" (Stamoolis 1986, 51).

Ion Bria speaks for Orthodoxy in *Go Forth in Peace: Orthodox Perspectives on Mission*: "Evangelistic witness is a call to salvation, which means restoration of the relationship of God and humanity, as understood in the Orthodox teaching of theosis" (1986, 30). The goal of evangelistic witness is conversion to a life characterized by the restored image of God. This divine image in turn reflects God's glory.

For Orthodoxy the liturgical expression of the church becomes a method of outreach, with the Eucharist playing a central role:

> Although the eucharist is the most perfect access to the economy of salvation, it is the goal—and also the springboard—of mission, rather than the means of mission. The eucharist reveals the iconic function of the church. The church as institution points to the eucharistic assembly as its sole genuine image, as the transparent icon of Christ. (Bria 1986, 19)

Verbal proclamation is important, especially for believers, but proclamation also occurs in the celebration of the Eucharist. The Eucharist forms the very source and center of Christian life and witness. Though partaking of the Eucharist is reserved for members of the church, the Eucharist proclaims the death and resurrection of the Lord until he comes again—and this proclamation is intended for non-Christians as well as for nominal Christians (Bria 1986, 29).

"Liturgy after the liturgy" is the continued engagement in the world—liturgy is not withdrawal from the world but rather sends the believer into the world for service. Works of love are witness to the coming kingdom of God. This witness will involve the struggle against poverty and oppression, healing, and liberation. With the words of dismissal after the Eucharist, "Go forth in peace," the congregation is to live as witness to the coming kingdom in their communities.

REFLECTION AND DISCUSSION

1. What Bible passages might affirm or challenge this view of mission?
2. Describe your view of the relationship between worship, liturgy, Eucharist, and mission.

Little concurs: "A doxological orientation enables the church to safeguard itself from any humanization or horizontalization process in mission" (2005, 51). In popular terms, ultimately mission is not about us, it's about God.

Such views may risk artificially separating the glorification of God and service to humanity, for both are inseparable expressions of love for God (e.g., 1 John 4:20–21). Nevertheless, this vertical purpose keeps all horizontal undertaking of mission in proper perspective.

John Piper has popularized the worship of God as the purpose of mission in his *Let the Nations Be Glad!* (1993; 2003). "Missions is not the ultimate goal of the church. Worship is. Missions exists because worship doesn't. . . . Worship, therefore, is the fuel and goal of missions" (1993, 11). He explains further, "All of history is moving toward one great goal, the white hot worship of God and his Son among all the peoples of the earth. Missions is not that goal. It is the means. And for that reason it is the second greatest human activity in the world" (1993, 15). Piper clarifies that by "worship" he does not mean merely singing or a particular worship style. Worship for Piper is a spiritual experience characterized by being satisfied with God (2003, 223).

There can be little disagreement that God's glory and the worship of the nations for all eternity are the ultimate end to which mission works. These will remain when all else has passed away and mission as such has ceased. Christopher J. H. Wright adds that worship is not only the goal but the source of mission: "But in another equally biblical sense we could say that mission exists because praise does. The praise of the church is what energizes and characterizes it for mission, and also serves as the constant reminder that we so much need, that all our mission flows as obedient response to and participation in the prior mission of God—just as all our praise is in response to the prior reality and action of God" (2006, 134).

Both the personal and the corporate encounter with God in worship give mission its passion, power, and authenticity. As Ken Christoph Miyamoto asserts, "Mission ceases to be Christian when it is separated from worship" (2008, 158). Mission and worship are in fact inextricably linked. "If worship, in the narrower cultic sense, thus enables mission to keep its divine source constantly before it, mission in its turn enables worship to be truly authentic" (Davies 1966, 18).

Mission flows *from* and then back again *to* God's glory. Doxology gives all other activities and elements of mission their ultimate purpose. "The true purpose of mission is not then the growth of the church, the saving of souls, or the humanization of society, but an acted-out doxology. It is that God may be glorified on earth as in heaven" (Greene 2002, 69).

REDEMPTION AS THE FOUNDATION OF MISSION

If doxology is the ultimate purpose of mission, then the work of redemption is the foundation of mission, for as Edwards argued, God is most glorified in his work of redemption. Satan and his demonic host rebelled against God and led humanity into sin, and creation was impacted. The Bible is the wonderful story of God restoring his rule over all creation and, in particular, of reaching out to redeem fallen humanity from the curse of sin, Satan, and death. Through the work of redemption, God restores fallen men and women to his fellowship, triumphing over both mundane and cosmic forces of evil. Ultimately all creation will be redeemed.

This work of redemption begins with the promise of the *protevangelium* in Genesis 3:15 and then moves through the provision of the sacrificial system in the law of Moses. God acts throughout history: sending prophets, performing miracles, bringing judgment and deliverance. But God's redemptive work reaches its climax in the sending of his Son, Jesus Christ, who became man, lived, died on the cross, and rose again for the forgiveness of sin. He has ascended to the right hand of God where he intercedes for us (Rom. 8:34).

Sin is humanity's greatest problem, for it separates us from God and poisons human nature. This separation from God bears the bitter fruit of conflict, war, injustice, hate, egoism, and everything that creates suffering and evil in human relations. With the fall men and women not only fell into spiritual death but also fell subject to the power of the prince of evil, Satan (Eph. 2:1–2; Col. 1:13). Nature itself suffers under the weight of the fall (Gen. 3:17–18; Rom. 8:20). Until the question of human sinfulness and guilt before God is resolved, there can be no talk of entering the kingdom of God. There can be only superficial change, there is no hope of life after death, and there is no power to confront the forces of evil.

But this is the heart of the good news of the kingdom. Christ came to give his life as a ransom for many (Mark 10:45). He came to make us alive to God, forgiving our sin, canceling the debt, nailing it to the cross, and disarming rulers and authorities (Col. 2:13–15). "For he has rescued us from the dominion of darkness and brought us into the kingdom of the Son he loves, in whom we have redemption, the forgiveness of sins" (Col. 1:13–14). It is at the cross that one enters the kingdom. Satan will ultimately be defeated, and creation will be renewed (Rom. 8:19–21; 2 Pet. 3:13; Rev. 21:1). For this reason the cross and resurrection are the "fulcrum of history" (Braaten 2008, 130).

The biblical authors use a wide range of terminology and metaphors to describe this work of Christ: salvation, redemption, atonement, forgiveness, reconciliation, regeneration, propitiation, adoption, liberation, cleansing, and so on. In this manner the message speaks to the widest range of human experiences, worldviews, and felt needs, but always bringing the hearer back to the cross and the empty grave as God's ultimate act of salvation and demonstration of love.

God's saving act in Christ is the foundation of the gospel and thus the foundation of mission. Paul could say, "For I resolved to know nothing while I was with you except Jesus Christ and him crucified" (1 Cor. 2:2). He defines the gospel: "For what I received I passed on to you as of first importance: that Christ died for our sins according to the Scriptures, that he was buried, that he was raised on the third day according to the Scriptures" (1 Cor. 15:3–4). This gospel is the power of God to save all who believe, whatever their ethnicity, nationality, or social standing (Rom. 1:16). Apart from faith in this Christ remains only judgment (John 3:18–19; Acts 4:12).

Many contemporary theologies of mission move too quickly to the message of the kingdom and its social implications, emphasizing church planting or compassion, and speaking of holistic ministry. The saving work of Christ in the life of the believer and in the Christian community will have far-reaching implications for all these concerns. But we dare not move too quickly to these issues and pass over the cross. For apart from Christ's work of redemption, all these considerations are without power and without foundation in God's own saving and transforming work. We remain dead in our trespasses (Eph. 2:1).

The purpose of mission must always be tethered to the cross of Christ. We cannot speak of Christ as *merely* a moral teacher, prophet, religious radical, social reformer, compassionate healer, or example of selfless love. Although he was all these things, he was also much more. He was first and foremost *Savior*. "Christ Jesus came into the world to save sinners" (1 Tim. 1:15b). Without the confession of Christ as Lord and Savior, we cannot speak of Christian mission.

THE KINGDOM OF GOD AS THE CENTER OF MISSION

The kingdom of God is the center of mission in the sense that it is the orientation point of mission. From this center all mission activity and understanding emanates. The concept of the kingdom of God captures in a single phrase the divine intent to bring all things under his rule, to reconcile all things to himself, to restore that which is fallen and corrupted, and to overthrow all powers in opposition to him and his reign of peace, joy, and righteousness.

> *What is the ultimate goal of the* missio Dei? *The answer is easy to find: in both the Old Testament and the New, God by both his words and deeds claims that he is intent on bringing the kingdom of God to expression and restoring his liberating domain of authority.*
>
> Johannes Verkuyl (1978, 197)

The kingdom of God is a concept spanning the full flow of salvation history and encompassing all realms of life. In the Old Testament the kingdom was closely linked to the nation of Israel. The kingdom was central to the teachings of Jesus. In the New Testament a new spiritual dimension becomes prominent to the kingdom, transcending ethnic, national, social, and gender barriers, beyond the nation of Israel. Yet throughout, the core concept to the kingdom remains God's rule. As George Eldon Ladd writes, "The kingdom of God is first of all the divine redemptive rule manifested in Christ, and it is secondly the realm of sphere in which the blessings of the divine rule may be experienced" ([1959] 1992, 114).

God's rule was rejected by Satan and his demonic hosts, by humankind with the fall, and all creation groans under the effects of sin. But God's plan in history is to reestablish his glorious and righteous rule over all creation and particularly over all nations. His rule is one in which grace and justice meet. God's justice is manifest in his righteous standards revealed in his Word and his unwavering holiness. The scriptures assure us that a final day of reckoning will occur when evil and unrighteousness will be judged once and for all—goodness and righteousness will ultimately prevail. But God's grace is manifest in the cross of Christ, where grace and justice meet, opening the way for his kingdom to be established through forgiveness, reconciliation, and transformation in the power of the Spirit. The gospel itself is called the "gospel of the kingdom" because it is the good news that God's kingdom has been inaugurated with Christ's coming (Matt. 4:23; 9:35; 24:14; Luke 16:16; Acts 8:12).

> *Thus the mission of the church is not only that of employing the keys of the Kingdom to open to both Jew and Gentile the door into the eternal life which is the gift of God's Kingdom; it is also the instrument of God's dynamic rule in the world to oppose evil and the powers of Satan in every form of their manifestation.*
>
> George Eldon Ladd
> ([1959] 1992, 121)

As we have just argued, the redemptive work of Christ laid the foundation of the kingdom. Thus as men and women are reconciled to God through faith in Christ, the most fundamental condition for entering God's kingdom is met. To enter the kingdom, people must be born again, born of the Spirit, through childlike faith in the Son of God (Matt. 18:3; John 3:3–5). For this to occur, people must hear the gospel (Rom. 10:13–15).

God creates a new kingdom people of the redeemed, the church. The church is not that kingdom. But as people of the kingdom living in the power of the Spirit, they become a living *sign* of the kingdom and an *instrument* of that kingdom, which is yet to come in all fullness with Christ's return. Bondage to sin is broken, lies are exposed by truth, relationships are restored and healed, the compassion of God is lived out, and a prophetic voice is sounded challenging the injustices of human kingdoms and pointing the way to a better one:

- The kingdom is not a nation, but will be composed of people from all nations.
- The kingdom is not a religious institution, though it is manifest in the church.

- The kingdom is not a culture, though it purifies and transforms cultures.
- The kingdom is not a moral or ethical code, though it calls all thought and action to submit to the righteousness of Christ.
- The kingdom is not an ideology, though it challenges every human ideology.
- The kingdom is not a political movement, though it confronts political power structures.
- The kingdom is not an economic system, though it addresses the dangers of greed and the evils of poverty and exploitation.
- The kingdom is not coercive, though it is persuasive in love.

The kingdom is a great mystery, yet it is as real as the wood of the cross upon which Jesus was nailed (see sidebar 4.2). It cannot be reduced to a formula or bottled for sale, yet it is as near as the neighbor in need or the sinner's cry for forgiveness.

However, the concept of the kingdom of God is so broad and comprehensive that its usefulness in defining the purpose of mission is limited. The concept of the kingdom runs the same risk that the concept *missio Dei* faced: it can—and has—become a catchall to justify any good work, any spiritual ministry, any economic or political agenda, any new strategy as "mission." Biblically unpacking just what the kingdom means for mission is complex.

Again we return to the most basic and profound confession of the kingdom: "Jesus is Lord." With this confession, rightly understood, all of life is placed under Christ's lordship. Christ's all-embracing lordship is rightly the center of mission, and in this sense we can speak of the kingdom of God as the center of mission.

SIDEBAR 4.2
MYSTERIES OF THE KINGDOM

Howard A. Snyder (1991, 16–17) notes the following six mysteries relating to the kingdom. Read the accompanying Bible passages and reflect on how your understanding of the kingdom is enriched and challenged.

1. Present versus future (Mark 1:15; Matt. 6:10)
2. Individual versus social (Matt. 13:44; Luke 12:32; John 3:3; Luke 13:29)
3. Spirit versus matter (1 Cor. 15:50; John 18:36; Luke 4:18–21; Rev. 5:10)
4. Gradual versus climactic (Mark 4:26–28; Matt. 25:1–6)
5. Divine versus human action (Luke 19:11–27; Ps. 99:1–2; Matt. 6:33; Col. 4:11)
6. The church as identified with the kingdom versus the church as different from the kingdom (Matt. 16:19; 7:21)

ESCHATOLOGY AS THE HOPE OF MISSION

The impression is sometimes given that if we were to only diligently enough preach the gospel, plant the church, live as prophetic witnesses, and confront evil in all its forms, we could usher in the kingdom of God. The Bible, however, presents a more sober picture of the forces of good and evil leading up to the end of this age. The church will not realize the kingdom in fullness but will be a witness to the kingdom as a light shining in the midst of darkness until the great day of dawning occurs. In fact, the contours of good and evil will only sharpen, and God's people will face persecution. For this reason we must place our understanding of the kingdom and with it our understanding of mission in eschatological perspective. The hope of mission is not in the success of human efforts but in the final intervention of God himself with Christ's return and the fullness of the kingdom. At the same time, we are to live as a sign of the kingdom, pointing to that coming day, and drawing our hope and strength from the promise of the new creation.

> *Mission then involves the declaration of God's purposes for the establishing of his Kingdom by a people who in an anticipatory sense actualise this Kingdom. This infers a total involvement of the Church in God's total mission. If we are to take the Lordship of Christ seriously we must recognize the totality of the scope of mission in its concern for God's ultimate purposes. The Church in its mission today must break out of its own small horizon and discover the implications of God's Kingdom horizon. It is then that the reality of the Kingdom of God can become the very dynamic for mission.*
>
> Ken R. Gnanakan (1989, 119–20)

When the disciples encountered the risen Christ, they were concerned about when the kingdom would come in fullness. Jesus responded that this was not for them to know. Rather, they were to receive the power of the Holy Spirit and become his witnesses to the ends of the earth. Upon saying this, he ascended to heaven, from whence he will one day return (Acts 1:6–11). The implication is clear: in the time between Christ's ascension and his return, the task of the church is to be his witness in all the earth. This is also implied in Matthew's account of the Great Commission. After commanding his followers to make disciples of all nations, Christ promises his presence to the end of the age (Matt. 28:19–20). His presence is linked with his commission, which will not end until this age ends. This is consistent with Jesus's earlier teaching in the Olivet Discourse: "And this gospel of the kingdom will be preached in the whole world as a testimony to all nations, and then the end will come" (Matt. 24:14; cf. Mark 13:10). The spread of the gospel to all nations is the assignment of the church to be fulfilled before and in anticipation of Christ's return.

Unfortunately, breathtakingly speculative interpretations of "signs of the end times," setting dates for Christ's return, and unedifying debates and divisions within the church over eschatological positions have made the discussion of eschatology distasteful and accordingly avoided. Nevertheless, eschatology is central to our understanding of the biblical story. Throughout the history of the church, eschatology has played a profound role in understanding mission (see Weidenmann 1965; Peskett 1997; and Chaney 1976, 269–80). A recent issue of *International Bulletin of Missionary Research* (33:3, July 2009) has reopened the discussion from various perspectives. Our understanding of mission must be framed eschatologically. Such an approach has less to do with speculations about end times or theological systems. Rather, it concerns the very meaning given to history and the goal toward which it is proceeding.

According to the worldview of many peoples, time (and life in general) is understood as cyclical—an endless repetition of life and death, day and night and seasons, victories and defeats, defilement and cleansing, and so on. In contrast, the biblical view of time is more linear. History is understood as progressing from creation to consummation, with a starting point and an end point. We live in that in-between period progressing toward the end. This understanding of time and teleology gives history purpose and meaning. Life will not simply repeat itself in an endless cycle, subject to the whims of unseen powers or the flawed schemes of humankind. There is a God of purpose who created and who will bring the course of history to his intended goal.

But the God of the Bible is not the God of deism, who passively observes creation as history takes its natural course. Nor is he an abstract God of philosophy or an esoteric higher power removed from the human experience. The God of the Bible is active within history. God's ultimate intent and purpose for history will be an eternal kingdom of peace and righteousness, more glorious than the garden of Eden (Rev. 21). Until then God has chosen to work primarily through his people, the church, to accomplish his mission within history.

Oscar Cullmann's salvation-historical approach to eschatology (1950; 1961) remains helpful. He emphasizes the purpose of mission as preparation for Christ's return and as a *Vorzeichen* (anticipatory sign) of the coming kingdom. Cullmann stresses that mission remains God's work, and human effort cannot hasten Christ's return. He also argues that in 2 Thessalonians 2:6 "*That which restrains*" the coming of the Antichrist is the preaching of the gospel to all nations (1961, 51–52). This, he believes, is apparent with reference to Mark 13:10–14 and Matthew 24:13–15, where the preaching of the gospel to all nations precedes the end and thus the coming of the Antichrist. A similar view is held by Peter Beyerhaus (1996, 706, 709) and C. Timothy Carriker (1993).

Karl Hartenstein made eschatology the very center of mission: "Mission is the obedient witness of the confessing church . . . in anticipation of the kingdom of God" (1933, 13). Although baptism and church planting are necessary tasks of missions, they are not ultimate and must be understood as witness to the final goal of mission: the coming eschatological kingdom to be fully established only at Christ's return. This eschatological kingdom is the final goal of all missionary work (39).

David J. Bosch, who studied under Cullmann, reflects in his early work a similar understanding. "Mission is in essence witness to the reign of God which *has come* in Christ to the one *yet coming*. The missionary proclamation of the church gives the time between the resurrection and parousia of Christ its salvation-historical meaning" (1959, 197). Bosch maintains also in his later writing that the salvation-historical approach remains the "soundest base for an understanding of the eschatological nature of mission from a postmodern perspective" (1991, 504).

The mission of the church, as participation in God's mission, gives history its meaning in the time between the comings of Christ, because mission is that process of inviting persons from every people to enter God's kingdom and become his glad servants and worshippers. As this task is completed, this age will have fulfilled its purpose, and the kingdom will come in all fullness. On the one hand, we look back to Christ's first coming, whereby he inaugurated his kingdom, establishing at the cross the conditions for entering his kingdom. On the other hand, we look forward to his return, when he will finally defeat all forces of evil, judge the unrighteous, and establish his kingdom of peace.

During this interim age the forces of evil—the kingdom of this world— continue to rebel, deceive, and pervert justice. God's people as witnesses to truth and righteousness will be targets of the wrath of such forces. Jesus's call for his people to be the salt of the earth and the light of the world comes in the very context of opposition and persecution (Matt. 5:11–16). Thus he does not allow the church the option of retreat or otherworldliness. Mission is a call to engage the world, not by using the means of the world, but rather by following the example of King Jesus himself in bold meekness—as witnesses, not as warriors.

Such an understanding of eschatology and mission is not shared by all mission theologians. Already at the International Missionary Conference (IMC) meetings in Tambaram (1938) concerns were expressed that mission was becoming a this-worldly undertaking with little reference to the transcendent. The German delegation advocated that only an eschatological framing of mission could save mission from secularization (Scherer 1990, 406). When the WCC met in Evanston (1954) under the theme "Christ—The Hope of the World," eschatology continued to play a role. The conference report reads, "It is thus of the very nature of the Church that it has a mission to the whole world. That mission is our participation in the work of God which takes place between the coming of Jesus Christ to inaugurate God's Kingdom on earth, and His coming again in glory to bring that Kingdom to its consummation. . . .

The Church's mission is thus the most important thing that is happening in history" (cited in Scherer 1990, 404).

However, in the 1960s humanization and liberation became the dominant themes in conciliar theology. Cullmann's salvation-historical eschatology fell out of favor, and a realized eschatology became dominant. Mission is to work toward the realization of the kingdom within history through human institutions and the struggle for justice. This overshadowed the hope of a future kingdom to be established at Christ's return.

In 1974 at the International Congress on World Evangelization in Lausanne, Switzerland, evangelicals affirmed an eschatological framing of mission. The Lausanne Covenant reads: "We believe that the interim period between Christ's ascension and return is to be filled with the mission of the people of God, who have no liberty to stop before the end" (Article 15). The second major Lausanne Committee for World Evangelization (LCWE) gathering in Manila (1989) took place under the motto "Proclaim Christ until He Comes." However, eschatology as such was hardly addressed.

The church today lives in the tension between living as kingdom people in this world and hoping for a future kingdom in the next. Some evangelicals so emphasize the fallenness of this world and Christ's return as the only hope that they reject all efforts to work toward the kingdom within history. On the other hand, ecumenical groups in particular have tended to work as if there were no hope apart from this world, and that human effort could usher in near utopia. Bosch writes of "mission as action in hope" (D. J. Bosch 1991, 498), seeking to find a balance whereby mission is "both future-directed and oriented to the here and now" (508). However, he leaves the tension largely unresolved.

Theology of mission must return to an eschatological perspective to maintain balance in this tension. The church lives as a sign of the kingdom in this age, which entails living as kingdom people within the Christian community and advocating values of the kingdom in the society at large. Yet because scripture reminds us of human frailty and fallenness, we dare not associate the kingdom with any particular political ideology, economic system, or moral agenda. Because the world will remain hostile toward the kingdom, the church does not entertain the illusion that the kingdom can be realized within history. We ultimately live in the hope that the kingdom will be fully realized only at Christ's return. But mission is an anticipation of that kingdom; a foretaste of life under the lordship of the King is made manifest. The church living under Christ's lordship becomes not only a sign of the kingdom, but in the words of George Florovsky, "The church is 'anticipated eschatology'" anticipating in part the kingdom yet to come in fullness (cited in Braaten 2000, 306). Mission is also an urgent invitation for others to enter and adopt the hope of salvation and the coming kingdom knowing that a day of final judgment will come.

THE NATIONS AS THE SCOPE OF MISSION

Our survey of the biblical teaching on God and the nations in chapters 1 and 2 revealed that since the formation of the nations following Babel, God has had a plan to bless the nations. Universal blessing would come through the particular call and election of Abraham, then through Israel, through whom the Redeemer would come. The Prophets foretold a day when the Gentile nations would be included in God's people and become his worshippers. With Christ's work of redemption completed and with the creation of his new kingdom people through the Holy Spirit, the message of salvation and blessing is to be brought to the nations. This is the end toward which history is moving, and it is the end toward which mission must also move. Indeed, only when the gospel has been preached to every nation will the end come (Matt. 24:14). Not only does Jesus send the church into the world (John 17:18), but he sends it to the *ends* of the earth (Acts 1:8). The church is heir to the mandate to make disciples of *all* nations (Matt. 28:19).

The purpose of mission must therefore include bringing the gospel to the ends of the earth and bringing people from every nation to Christ. Though there has been considerable debate about the precise meaning of "all nations" (*panta ta ethnē*) and related formulations in Matthew 28:19 and 24:14, the language of Revelation 5:9 and 7:9 is unmistakably comprehensive. The terms are piled up: *phulē* (ethnic group, tribe), *glôssēs* (tongue, language group), *laos* (people, nation, crowd), *ethnos* (nation, people, Gentiles). Clearly no matter how the human family might be categorized, divided, or related, people from all categories or groupings will be reached, and some from each will become part of the new people of God.

The phrase "ends of the earth" in Acts 1:8 and other passages clearly indicate a geographic aspect to the scope of mission (see Bauckham 2003, 55–81). Until the twentieth century, thinking about the missionary task tended to focus almost exclusively on geography and bringing the gospel to Africa, Asia, and Latin America. To be a missionary one had to "cross salt water." Not only do the majority of Christians now live in those lands formerly considered "mission fields," but such a conceptualization of the scope of mission misses the more fundamental biblical understanding of "all nations" and "ends of the earth." For example, hundreds of diverse linguistic and ethnic groups live within the modern nation-state of India. Though churches have been planted within the geopolitical boundaries of India, those churches may be relatively confined to specific ethnic groups, while others remain unreached. Discipling every nation cannot be considered completed as long as there remain ethnic groups without a witness for Christ and from which none have yet come to faith in Christ.

Furthermore, today large populations of diverse ethnic groups live in traditionally Christian North Atlantic countries, for example, Kurds living in Berlin, Germany, or Hmong living in St. Paul, Minnesota, in the United States. To the extent that such peoples have no intelligible and intentional witness to the risen Christ, they cannot be considered "reached," even though they live in geographic proximity to Christians of other ethnicity and may have citizenship in a nominally Christian nation. Such peoples are sometimes called "hidden peoples" because they are easily overlooked and do not live in traditional "mission fields." It is often incorrectly assumed that they could be easily reached by other nearby Christians (underestimating cultural, social, or linguistic barriers that separate them).

The scope of mission mandates that *all* must be reached irrespective of geography, nationality, or ethnicity. Ralph Winter and the "frontier missions" movement have tirelessly reminded the church of this task. Piper has argued at length that the task of missions is not merely to win the greatest number of individuals for Christ but rather to win individuals from *all* the people groups of the world (1993, 167–218).

Contemporary emphases on the kingdom of God as the primary focus of mission have often overlooked the bringing of the gospel to the nations. Advocates of the "missional church" have rightly emphasized that the Western church must understand itself as on mission in its own post-Christian society. But this does not excuse the church from its obligation of bringing the gospel to every yet-unreached people.

Piper has eloquently described how reaching the nations dovetails with the doxological purpose. "There is something about God that is so universally praiseworthy and so profoundly beautiful, and so comprehensively worthy and so deeply satisfying that God will find passionate admirers in every diverse people group in the world" (1993, 222; see also sidebar 4.3). God does not inspire the service and worship of a select group of humanity; rather, there are members of every people group who acknowledge him as worthy of worship and who gladly enter his kingdom. The acknowledgment of God's greatness and lordship is not a matter of culture, upbringing, or personal taste.

SIDEBAR 4.3
SAVING MORE INDIVIDUALS OR REACHING MORE NATIONS?

Discuss how you agree or disagree with these statements by John Piper (2003, 157):

> The task of missions may not be merely to win as many individuals as possible from the most responsive people groups of the world but rather to win individuals from *all* the people groups of the world. . . .
>
> [Missions] *cannot* be defined in terms of crossing cultures to maximize the total number of individuals saved. Rather, God's will for missions is that every people group be reached . . . and that a people be called out for his name from all the nations.

When the gospel is communicated in an understandable manner, people from all walks of life, from all nations, from all classes of people will be found who respond with repentance, faith, and worship. They abandon false gods, idols, and ideologies and turn to serve the living and true God (1 Thess. 1:9). God inspires the deepest commitment, adoration, and sacrifice—even unto martyrdom—from people of the most diverse cultures and backgrounds.

As we saw in chapter 3, the Lord is not just the God of Israel nor the God of Western culture. He is the God of *all* peoples. He is the Creator of heaven and earth. He is able to save and satisfy *all and any* who call upon his name. In this diversity of worship, a many-colored tapestry is woven to God's glory. A full orchestra of ethnic diversity produces a symphony to his honor. And this is happening in our day. Thus the purpose of mission must include the nations, indeed *every* nation, as the scope of its vision.

RECONCILIATION AS THE FRUIT OF MISSION

Broken human relationships at every level—among individuals, families, classes, ethnic groups, and nations—is perhaps the bitterest and bloodiest earthly curse of sin. Deep wounds of injustice and hatred exist between many peoples of the world. "Ethnic cleansing," genocide, civil war, religious hostilities, class divisions, racial tension, and domestic violence are daily the subject of news headlines. If the church is to be a sign of the kingdom, then reconciliation between individuals and peoples, *horizontal reconciliation*, must be evident in the fellowship of the church.

Though horizontal reconciliation was hardly spoken of in any way central to the purpose of mission until the late twentieth century, reconciliation has now become increasingly a subject of deep concern in missiology. Recent civil wars, racism, religious persecutions, and ethnic strife in places such as the Balkans, Central Asia, and Africa during the years following the collapse of global communism heightened awareness of the depth and urgency of the problem. Intentional planting of multiethnic churches has also become a high priority in many North American denominations.

The 2004 LCWE Forum for World Evangelization in Pattaya included an issue group on reconciliation that produced the Lausanne Occasional Paper no. 51, titled "Reconciliation as the Mission of God." The document advocates that "Christians participate with God's mission by being transformed into ambassadors of reconciliation." The theme of the WCC Commission on World Mission and Evangelism (CWME) in Athens in 2005 was "Come Holy Spirit, Heal and Reconcile." Robert J. Schreiter, a leading Roman Catholic missiologist, suggested in a preparatory paper for that conference that reconciliation and healing provide a new paradigm for mission (2005).

Where genuine reconciliation between hostile groups occurs as a fruit of mission, the power of the gospel is evident, and God is greatly glorified. Jesus himself said that love will mark us as his disciples and unity will convince the world that Jesus is from God (John 13:35; 17:20–23). But where reconciliation fails and animosity or hostility prevails, the name of Christ is dishonored.

Before speaking to horizontal reconciliation, however, we must address *vertical reconciliation*, that is, reconciliation with God. This is both theologically and experientially necessary. Only as people are reconciled with their Maker, experiencing the forgiveness of God offered in Christ, do they find the power to forgive and reconcile human relations at the deepest level, forgiving one another as Christ has forgiven them (Eph. 4:32). We have argued that redemption is the foundation of mission. It is also the door to reconciliation. The roots of strife and conflict between humans lie in the fall, conflict, and separation from God. The ultimate solution to human conflict will also be found in the solution to the human-divine conflict by reconciliation with God through Christ.

Paul sees his mission as a ministry of reconciliation, for he writes in 2 Corinthians 5:18–20: "All this is from God, who reconciled us to himself through Christ and gave us the ministry of reconciliation: that God was reconciling the world to himself in Christ, not counting men's sins against them. And he has committed to us the message of reconciliation. We are therefore Christ's ambassadors, as though God were making his appeal through us. We implore you on Christ's behalf: Be reconciled to God."

As the gospel is preached and the message is accepted, the first fruit of mission is reconciliation with God. One of the greatest strivings of the manifold religions of humanity is to find peace with God, the gods, or the unseen powers. Sacrificial systems, ritual washings, pilgrimages, ascetic practices, and cultic rites are all used in attempts to attain this. For others life has lost significance because there is no significant relationship to the source of all meaning, the living God.

The gospel is a tremendous message of grace and freedom that God has done for us what we could not do for ourselves. The human-divine relationship, once characterized by hostility, fear, or indifference, is transformed into one of harmony, peace, and love through Christ's work. Where there was once shame, guilt, or purposelessness, there is now honor, forgiveness, and significance. This is possible because it pleased the Father through Christ,

> and through him to reconcile to himself all things, whether things on earth or things in heaven, by making peace through his blood, shed on the cross.
>
> Once you were alienated from God and were enemies in your minds because of your evil behavior. But now he has reconciled you by Christ's physical body through death to present you holy in his sight, without blemish and free from accusation. (Col. 1:20–22)

Once again we see the centrality of the work of Christ on the cross to mission. What greater gift can there be to men and women than this: to become friends with God, to experience no shame before God, to live in harmony with God, and to anticipate an eternity of fellowship with God, our Maker! This is the great gift of God in Christ, and mission delivers this gift to the world. Contemporary discussions of reconciliation that emphasize the horizontal while overlooking the primacy of the vertical focus on the fruit apart from the root (see Engelsviken 2005; Matthey 2005; N. E. Thomas 2005, 456).

On the basis of vertical reconciliation, horizontal reconciliation becomes possible in the most profound way. The vertical and horizontal dimensions of Christ's work of reconciliation are inseparably related (Willmer 2007). Paul describes the reconciliation between Jew and Gentile in this way:

> But now in Christ Jesus you who once were far away have been brought near through the blood of Christ.
>
> For he himself is our peace, who has made the two one and has destroyed the barrier, the dividing wall of hostility, by abolishing in his flesh the law with its commandments and regulations. His purpose was to create in himself one new man out of the two, thus making peace, and in this one body to reconcile both of them to God through the cross, by which he put to death their hostility. He came and preached peace to you who were far away and peace to those who were near. For through him we both have access to the Father by one Spirit. (Eph. 2:13–18)

The peace with God created by the blood of Christ also creates peace between peoples by creating a new humanity. This new humanity is no longer divided by race, ethnicity, social standing, or gender (Gal. 3:28). This new humanity finds its identity not in lineage, ethnicity, clan, nationality, or social standing, but rather in relationship to Christ. We have been adopted into a new family of God (Eph. 1:5), and our primary citizenship is now in heaven (Phil. 3:20). This family of God does not exist in the abstract. It exists in kingdom communities, in local churches composed of real people. Because our sanctification is not complete, horizontal reconciliation is a process, often long, costly, and incomplete this side of Christ's return.

Because vertical reconciliation is so foundational to horizontal reconciliation, to evangelism, to church planting, to philanthropy, and to justice, we maintain that reconciliation is more than merely a task of missions; it is central to the overarching purpose and nature of mission. The restored relationship with God, and its attendant restored human relations, is central to the message of the gospel. The kingdom of God is characterized not merely by an absence of evil, injustice, or alienation, but positively by the restoration of harmony and fullness in both the vertical and the horizontal dimension of the human experience.

INCARNATION AS THE CHARACTER OF MISSION

Christ's incarnation has become one of the most widely used motifs in conceptualizing mission. John 1:14 speaks of the Word becoming flesh and dwelling among us. The Son of God became fully man, surrendering his divine position, adopting the Jewish culture, lifestyle, and language, and ultimately emptying himself in death on the cross (Phil. 2:6–8). Some missiologists advocate that the incarnation *is* mission and the *only* model or definition of mission. For example:

- "The incarnation . . . *is* mission. . . . The incarnational mission of Christ is thus the only model of mission" (WCC preparation paper for San Antonio 1989, cited in Guder 1994, 419).
- "True mission should always be incarnational" (Manila Manifesto [MM], section A.4).
- "Indeed, all authentic mission is incarnational mission" (Stott 1992, 358).

Missionary identification, holistic ministry, liberation, contextualization, inculturation of the church, and manifestation of the life of Christ have all been argued for on the basis of the incarnation. Evangelical, conciliar, Roman Catholic, and Orthodox theologians alike have crafted incarnational missiologies (for a detailed overview, see Langmead 2004).

The Incarnation as a Model for Mediating the Life of Christ

Incarnating the gospel in this sense means becoming Christ to the people one serves. Though the incarnation was used to describe social ethics in nineteenth-century Anglican theology (Ramsey 1960, 30–43), John Mackay, former president of Princeton Theological Seminary and founding president of the WCC, has been credited with being the first to develop the concept of the incarnation in connection with mission, in 1964. Just as Christ's life revealed in word and deed what God is like, so too the Christian witness's pattern of living must reveal what God is like and be commensurate with the gospel. This includes identifying with the hearer's environment and being sensitive to people's needs. The witness gives "concrete expression by word, act, and disposition to the reality of love, of Christian *agape*, mediating thereby the love of God in Christ Jesus" (Mackay, cited in Guder 1994, 422).

Though the Christian can in no way embody divinity as Christ did, scripture makes clear that believers can become mediators of Christ's love and life to others. The apostle Paul could say,

- "I have been crucified with Christ and I no longer live, but Christ lives in me" (Gal. 2:20a).
- "Follow my example, as I follow the example of Christ" (1 Cor. 11:1).
- "We always carry around in our body the death of Jesus, so that the life of Jesus may also be revealed in our body" (2 Cor. 4:10).

These verses illustrate a parallel between the incarnate Christ's manifestation of the Father (John 14:9) and the believer's life manifesting Christ. First Peter 2:21 reads, "To this you were called, because Christ suffered for you, leaving you an example, that you should follow in his steps." Alan Neely makes this the very heart of mission when he writes, "In essence therefore this is the mission of Jesus' followers, to walk in Jesus' steps" (2000, 474). This occurs not only individually but also collectively as the church. The church is the body of Christ and visibly manifests Christ in its corporate life (e.g., 1 Cor. 14:25b).

The Incarnation as a Model for Holistic Ministry

Daryl Guder (1994) argues that the incarnation serves an integrative function in theology of mission, bringing together the being, doing, and saying of witness. Just as Christ lived out the gospel in all that he said and did, so too being sent as Christ was sent, the church must live out the gospel in word and deed. For Guder this means that the struggle for justice cannot be separated from proclamation of the message of salvation.

Liberation theologians have taken the implications of the incarnation a step farther. Christ's incarnation is understood as identifying not merely with humanity in general but particularly with the poor, oppressed, and marginalized of society. Jon Sobrino calls evangelizers to "recapitulate Jesus' own incarnation" by identifying with and sharing the pain of the poor (1985, 136). The first chapter of Orlando E. Costas's book *Christ Outside the Gate* is titled "Contextualization and Incarnation: Communicating Christ amid the Oppressed." He writes, "To incarnate Christ in our world is to manifest the transforming presence of God's kingdom among the victims of sin and evil. It is to make possible a process of transformation from personal and corporate evil to personal and collective freedom, justice, and wellbeing" (1982, 16). The Manila Manifesto reflects this approach: "True mission should always be incarnational. It necessitates entering humbly into other people's worlds, identifying with their social reality, their sorrow and suffering, and their struggles for justice against oppressive powers. This cannot be done without personal sacrifices" (MM A.4).

We will reserve our assessment of holistic ministry and liberation theology for later chapters. But we can surely agree that to minister as Christ ministered will mean living out the gospel in word and deed, caring for people as whole people. God did not just send a message; he sent his Son. It will never be adequate to simply deliver a message in an isolated or disengaged manner, disregarding the needs of the hearers. Paul could write to the Thessalonians, "We were delighted to share with you not only the gospel of God but our lives as well, because you had become so dear to us" (1 Thess. 2:8b).

The Incarnation as a Model of Cultural Identification

It has been argued that in the same manner that Jesus identified with humanity, fully adopting the culture of the Jewish people, so too the missionary should fully adopt the culture of the people he or she is serving. The 1978 Lausanne Consultation on Gospel and Culture Willowbank Report (LOP no. 2, 1978) includes a section titled "The Incarnation as a Model for Christian Witness" and calls the incarnation "the most spectacular instance of cultural identification in the history of mankind." The report understands identification in terms of missionaries "mastering their language, immersing [themselves] in their [i.e., the host] culture, learning to think as they think, feel as they feel, do as they do," and may go further to adapting one's standard of living.

Darrell Whiteman adopts a similar approach, rejecting the extremes of "going native" but advocating the following:

> In the same way in which God entered Jewish culture in the person of Jesus, we must be willing to enter the culture of the people among whom we serve, to speak their language, to adjust our lifestyle to theirs, to understand their worldview and religious values, and to laugh and weep with them. . . .
>
> The same process of Incarnation, of God becoming a human being, occurs every time the gospel crosses a new cultural, linguistic, or religious frontier. (2003, 408)

More radical approaches such as those of Jonathan Bonk (1991) and Tom and Betty Sue Brewster (1982) have called missionaries to *fully* identify by adjusting their lifestyle, living if necessary in poverty; adopting the local diet, housing, and clothing; surrendering privileges of being an expatriate; and seeking full acceptance as an insider of the culture.

Although it is surely commendable for missionaries to identify with the host culture, such radical approaches to incarnational identification are questionable for several reasons:

- No missionary can ever "incarnate" into a culture as thoroughly as Jesus did simply because Jesus, unlike the expatriate missionary, was *born* into his new environment as an insider.
- *Total* identification is practically speaking impossible and unrealistic. No matter how hard the missionary tries, identification will never be perfect. The radical identification approach can place a weight of unnecessary guilt and stress on the missionary who feels obligated to do the impossible (D. M. Howard 2004).
- Missionary attempts at total identification are not always helpful or appreciated, and may be misunderstood or viewed as foolish, deceptive, lacking integrity, or downright silly by local people. The missionary may in so doing also sacrifice his or her health or the well-being of their family (see examples in Hill 1990, 1993; Baker 2002).

- Preoccupation with surface-level identification, such as clothing or diet, may well detract or become a substitute for deeper-level identification, such as empathy or obtaining an insider worldview (McElhanon 1991, 391; Hiebert 1982b).
- Certain missionary roles, such as that of change agent, are often better performed by outsiders.

At a more fundamental level we must ask, is the incarnation of Christ really a model of cultural identification at all? The parallel between missionary identification and Jesus's becoming a man founders in so many ways that using the term *incarnational* borders on trivializing the incarnation. Jesus was the third person of the Trinity, the eternal God, who became human. The gulf he bridged was that of heaven and earth, time and eternity, transcendence and immanence. Such can hardly be compared with a missionary moving from the United States to Angola or from Korea to Kazakhstan. The missionary remains but as a human reaching fellow humans. Jesus's identification with humanity through the incarnation was qualitatively different.

Nevertheless, with the incarnation Jesus *did* identify with humanity (Phil. 2:5–8; Heb. 2:14–15; 4:15). This spirit should indeed characterize the servant of Christ. *Total* identification may be unnecessary and impossible for the missionary, but this does not mean that *no* identification is necessary or possible. Learning the language and culture of a people, shedding ethnocentrism, demonstrating solidarity, valuing a people's lifestyle, selflessly serving, adjusting one's standard of living, understanding their world, and seeking to empathize with their hurts, fears, joys, and hopes are evidence of love and a Christlike spirit. These are traits that are too little taught to and too little evidenced by missionaries. In scripture we see the example of Paul:

> Though I am free and belong to no man, I make myself a slave to everyone, to win as many as possible. To the Jews I became like a Jew, to win the Jews. To those under the law I became like one under the law (though I myself am not under the law), so as to win those under the law. To those not having the law I became like one not having the law (though I am not free from God's law but am under Christ's law), so as to win those not having the law. To the weak I became weak, to win the weak. I have become all things to all men so that by all possible means I might save some. I do all this for the sake of the gospel, that I may share in its blessings. (1 Cor. 9:19–23)

Paul was prepared to alter his lifestyle for the sake of people to whom he ministered. This no doubt meant adopting practices that were personally offensive to him given his strict Jewish upbringing. He did so in order to win others for Christ, whatever the price. Paul repeatedly suffered for the sake of those he was seeking to serve (2 Cor. 4:12; Eph. 3:13; 2 Tim. 2:10).

The Incarnation as a Model for Contextualization or Inculturation

The incarnation has also served as a model for contextualizing both the message of the gospel and the life of the church in specific cultures. Karl Müller summarizes: "Just as the Logos took on a concrete human nature and this concrete human being was a revelation of God, so should the message be 'incarnated' in every culture" (1997b, 199). Darrell Whiteman sees the incarnation as a model for contextualization (1997, 6). Dean Gilliland speaks of the incarnation as a "matrix for appropriate theologies" (2005, 493). This approach has been most clearly advocated by the Roman Catholic Church. The Second Vatican decree, *Ad Gentes*, speaks of the incarnation as a model for inculturation of the church in this way: "The Church, in order to be able to offer all [people] the mystery of salvation and the life brought by God, must implant herself into these groups for the same motive which led Christ to bind Himself, in virtue of His Incarnation, to certain social and cultural conditions of those human beings among whom He dwelt" (*AG* 10).

Churches are to be inculturated as the divine word takes root in a culture "in harmony with the economy of the Incarnation" (*AG* 22). Pope John Paul II expanded upon this approach in *Redemptoris Missio*, which devotes an entire section to "Incarnating the gospel in peoples' culture" (*RM* 52). Theresa Okure applies this concept to the church in Africa: "Our understanding of the mystery of the Incarnation should serve as the solid foundation for understanding inculturation. . . . Inculturation functions as the process by which Christ becomes 'native to or incarnated in' particular African cultures. Without it Christ remains an outsider or a foreigner to a culture, he does not become a citizen; and then the culture itself cannot be redeemed by him" (cited in Bate 1994, 95–96).

Assessment of Incarnational Understandings of Mission

What are we to make of these various understandings of incarnational mission? We can biblically affirm the importance of mediating Christ's life, of ministering in word and deed, of identifying with people, and of contextualizing the message of the gospel and the life of the church. But is the incarnation of Christ an appropriate model for justifying or expressing these values?

Some, such as Ross Langmead, see the incarnation as essential to understanding mission in the most comprehensive sense. "God's incarnating nature and its expression in the incarnation of Jesus Christ together provide the basis for mission, the motivation and enabling power for mission, and the model for mission" (2004, 34). Langmead adds, "Our understanding of God's incarnating activity throughout history and in Jesus Christ leads us to (1) the pattern of mission, (2) the ability to engage in mission, and (3) the whole framework for mission" (58).

Others reject the model altogether as theologically and exegetically inappropriate (e.g., Köstenberger 1998a, 212–17; Schnabel 2004, 1574–75; Hesselgrave 2005, 141–63). They argue that the point of comparison between Jesus's sending and the sending of the church in John 17:18 and 20:21 is not the incarnation or identification, but rather the relationship between the sent one and the sender. The incarnation of Jesus is entirely unique and cannot in any way be replicated or imitated by Christians. The focus of Jesus's ministry in John's Gospel is not "service to humankind" (as some incarnational mission models advocate) but rather the work of redemption and forgiveness. Andreas J. Köstenberger concludes, "Not the way in which Jesus came into the world (i.e., the incarnation), but *the nature of Jesus' relationship with his sender* (i.e., one of obedience and utter dependence), is presented in the Fourth Gospel as the model for the disciples' mission" (1998a, 217).

Erhard Berneburg argues that the incarnational model of mission is a "functionalization" of the biblical doctrine of the incarnation (1997, 354). The incarnation becomes a methodological model for evangelism and ethics and can thereby lose its unique redemptive meaning. David Hesselgrave (2005, 141–63) and Christopher Little (2005) argue that while we can clearly learn from Jesus's example, Paul's ministry is the more appropriate model for missionary practice today.

Incarnational Mission as Humble, Selfless Service

Concerns about the interpretation of John 20:21 may be well taken. But another passage in scripture *explicitly* holds forth the incarnation to all believers (not only missionaries) as a model for character and service:

> Do nothing out of selfish ambition or vain conceit, but in humility consider others better than yourselves. Each of you should look not only to your own interests, but also to the interests of others.
> Your attitude should be the same as that of Christ Jesus:
>
>> Who, being in very nature God,
>>> did not consider equality with God something to be grasped,
>> but made himself nothing,
>>> taking the very nature of a servant,
>>> being made in human likeness.
>> And being found in appearance as a man,
>>> he humbled himself and became obedient to death—even death on a
>>> cross! (Phil. 2:3–8)

Here the point of comparison between the incarnation of Christ and the life and ministry of a Christian is *humility*, *selflessness*, and *surrendering one's rights for the sake of others*. This attitude should most certainly characterize believers in general and every missionary in particular. Such an attitude will lead to most of the incarnational understandings of mission described above. This is consistent with other passages holding forth Christ's life and death as an example of sacrificial service and love to be followed by believers (e.g., 1 Pet. 2:21).

The broader context of Paul's statement of identification in 1 Corinthians 9 is an argument for surrendering one's rights. Paul surrendered his right to earn a living from ministry (9:1–18), and he surrendered his preferred lifestyle to win others for Christ (9:19–23). John R. W. Stott explains the implications of incarnational mission in this way: "It tells us that mission involves being under the authority of Christ (we are sent, we did not volunteer); renouncing privilege, safety, comfort and aloofness, as we actually enter other people's worlds, as he entered ours; humbling ourselves to become servants, as he did" (1992, 265).

To summarize, we affirm an incarnational model of mission understood as humble self-renunciation for the sake of others whereby the life and love of Christ become manifest to others. Mission in the spirit of Christ is an undertaking of selfless love, a surrender of rights and privileges, in order to serve and identify with others for the sake of the gospel. Incarnational mission profoundly defines the *character* of mission, which in turn impacts our understanding, our method, and our commitment in mission.

This understanding of mission should give us pause when we consider various popular developments in mission today that seem to emphasize quick results and shallow commitments (see sidebar 4.4). The church must never cease to learn the value of ministry shaped by the attitude of Christ and guided by the Pauline principle of "all things to all men, that I may by all means win some."

SIDEBAR 4.4
MAKING IT PRACTICAL

Read John 20:21, Philippians 2:3–8, and 1 Corinthians 9:1–23 and formulate your own definition of incarnational mission in light of these questions:

- How does an incarnational understanding of mission challenge your present thinking about mission and missionaries?
- How can or should an incarnational understanding of mission impact short-term mission efforts?
- In what ways do globalization and the widespread use of the English language negatively affect an incarnational attitude in mission?
- Realizing that total missionary identification is impossible, what *are* some of the rights or privileges that missionaries should be prepared to surrender for the sake of the gospel and to manifest Christ's love?

CONCLUSION

In this chapter we have argued that *doxology is the highest purpose of mission*: God is drawing people from every nation to himself who declare his glory and become his worshippers. This worship will endure for all eternity. *Redemption is the foundation of mission* in that God himself has reached out in grace to fallen humans by the sending of his Son, Jesus Christ. The work of redemption through his death and resurrection was at the heart of Christ's coming to earth. He thereby provided the way of forgiveness and restoration of the God-human relationship. This was at the heart of the gospel message and the core of the apostolic preaching.

The kingdom of God is at the center of mission in that the work of redemption results not only in personal salvation but in the restoration of God's reign over his redeemed people and through the redeemed community. The new kingdom people, the church, become a living sign of the kingdom in this age as they live under Christ's lordship and work for the cause of holiness, righteousness, and justice in all their relationships and in the world. *Eschatology is the hope of mission* because we know that the kingdom will one day come in fullness when Christ returns. In this age the church lives in anticipation of that kingdom by bringing the gospel of the kingdom to the nations. This is done in the confidence that the promise of the Lord will be fulfilled: not only will the gospel be preached to every nation, but from every nation there will be those who embrace the Savior and enter the kingdom. For this reason *the nations are the scope of mission*. As revealed in the scriptures, God has a plan to draw the nations to himself. Mission cannot rest until the gospel of the kingdom has been brought to people of every nation, ethnic group, language, and social standing.

Reconciliation is the fruit of mission because mission brings the message of reconciliation to an alienated world. This reconciliation begins with the restored relationship with God and moves outward to restore human relationships, becoming one of the most fundamental signs of the kingdom and evidencing genuine *shalom*. This too is in anticipation of the fullness of the restoration of all things upon Christ's return. Finally, the *incarnation is the character of mission*. Everything the church undertakes in the cause of mission must be characterized by a spirit of humility, selflessness, and sacrifice, for these traits characterized Christ's sending. This is the fruit of the Holy Spirit, who both empowers and transforms for mission.

We conclude by defining mission in this way: Mission is the sending activity of God with the purpose of reconciling to himself and bringing into his kingdom fallen men and women from every people and nation to his glory. Mission is a sign of the kingdom and an invitation to the nations to enter the kingdom and share the hope of the kingdom promised in Christ's return.

5

The Task of Missions

Convictions and Controversy

Having defined the purpose and nature of mission, we can now more specifically describe the task of missions. The task of *missions* (plural), as opposed to the purpose of *mission* (singular), describes the specific undertakings of the church in the world to fulfill its mission. It includes particular efforts, projects, and the tasks for which missionaries are commissioned by the church.

We will examine how Christians have defined the task of missions historically and then evaluate these biblically. Space constrains us to limit our discussion primarily to developments since the Reformation. The historical development of these views reveals how others have wrestled with similar questions that we may assume are unique to our day. We can also see more clearly the potential consequences of the various approaches. Finally, we become humbly aware of the fact that the way we interpret the Bible, and even the questions we ask, is influenced by traditions and issues we have inherited.

The following motifs are seldom found in their most extreme forms. These tasks should not be understood as mutually exclusive, though in the heat of debate they have often been presented as such. In both theory and practice there is usually considerable overlap in the various approaches.

PROCLAMATION AND CONVERSION AS THE TASK OF MISSIONS

Historical Development

The earliest Protestant mission efforts were inspired by the Puritan and Pietist traditions that were intertwined with each other. They began as reform movements within the established churches of England and Germany. The first missionary society, the Company for Propagating the Gospel in New England and Parts Adjacent in North America, founded in England in 1649, supported the Puritan John Eliot (1604–90), who worked among Native Americans. Pietists Bartholomew Ziegenbalg (1687–1719) and Henry Plütschau (1676–1747) are also considered to be among the first Protestant missionaries.

Early founders of British missions, such as Thomas Bray, who helped found the Society for Promoting Christian Knowledge (SPCK) and the Society for the Propagation of the Gospel (SPG), were concerned for the salvation and the conversion of indigenous peoples in the British colonies (Van den Berg 1956). Though Puritan missionaries to Native Americans in the seventeenth century, such as Eliot, included spreading civilization in the task of their mission, preaching of the gospel was the primary method for doing so (Knapp 1998). Sidney Rooy concludes his study of Puritan theology of missions by noting, "The soteriological consideration that men must be brought to personal conversion dominates the Puritan message" (1965, 310). This grew out of the conviction of the utter lostness of humanity apart from divine grace. Furthermore, "to a great extent the goal of mission was simply the conversion of souls. No matter was greater since this was God's concern in sending his Son" (316). The Puritans engaged in various humanitarian efforts and in the advancement of justice, especially for the Native Americans. "The humanitarian motive, however, was not permitted to eclipse the soteriological one" (317). They sought to glorify God by being his instrument of bringing redemption to the nations. Nothing less than the conversion of the world was their goal (Chaney 1976, 241–51).

The first truly dynamic Protestant missionary movement emerged in the mid-eighteenth century from the Moravian Brethren, who were deeply rooted in German Pietism. German Protestant missions into the nineteenth century has been called the "child of Pietism" (Oehler 1949, 110). Moravian Pietism also profoundly influenced John Wesley and British Methodism. In the words of Johannes Van den Berg, "Zinzendorf rocked the cradle of the Methodist movement" (1956, 75).

At home German Pietists emphasized the need for personal conversion and discipleship in the life of the individual Christian as a response to what they felt was a cold formalism and lack of spiritual commitment in Lutheran orthodoxy. Church reform—not church planting—was the goal, and this reform was to come through spiritual renewal of the individual. As such, groups began sending missionaries whose primary focus was on individual conversion. The first Pietist missionaries, Ziegenbalg and Plütschau, expanded their mission agenda to include education, medical, and social work, but mission leaders in Europe admonished them to simply preach (Verkuyl 1978, 177).

Count Nicholas Ludwig von Zinzendorf (1700–1760), leader of the Moravian Brethren, spoke of missions as "gathering souls for the coming kingdom." He had a fundamental aversion to organized church structures, calling the church the "donkey, hospital, and refuge for uneasy souls," a "branch of the mother city," a temporary "village of the Lord" waiting for his return (cited in Hoekendijk 1967, 48–49). He even forbade the Moravian missionaries to formally establish churches. Mass conversion was not expected. Zinzendorf wrote, "We seek the first fruits of the nations, and when we have two to four of them we will commend them to the Savior and what he wants to do through them" (cited in Schomerus 1935, 291). A larger ingathering of souls would come only later, at which time the founding of churches would be necessary. But for now, so Zinzendorf, the goal of mission was the gathering of saved individuals into small fellowships (*ecclesiolae*) as the firstfruits of the coming kingdom harvest to take place upon the Lord's return (Hoekendijk 1967, 54–59). David J. Bosch summarizes, "Both the Pietists and the Moravians were primarily concerned about *conversio gentilium*, without clarity about what would happen to the people once they were converted. The 'planting of the Church' was not a goal of mission. . . . The entire emphasis fell on conversion. All missionary activities were merely aids serving this overriding primary goal" (1980, 131).

Not only Pietism and Puritanism but later revivalism as manifest in the two Great Awakenings (mid-eighteenth and early nineteenth century) played a great role in shaping mission understanding as the Protestant mission movement emerged (Van den Berg 1956, 91). Emphasis clearly lay on the importance of personal conversion, and mission was primarily a matter of proclamation (Forman 1977, 77). This was typified in the preaching of John Wesley, George Whitefield, and in later generations Charles G. Finney, Dwight L. Moody, and Billy Graham. Conversion came to be understood in terms of a personal decision of faith, usually with some form of public confession.

One factor contributing to the single-minded emphasis on proclamation was concern for Christian unity. For example, the interdenominational London Missionary Society (LMS) expressed a remarkable ecumenical spirit. Founding member David Bogue stated in 1795, "We are called together this evening to the *funeral of bigotry*" (cited in Van den Berg 1956, 129). In 1776 a fundamental principle stated, "Our design is not to send Presbyterian, Independency, Episcopacy or any other form of Church Order and Government, . . . but the glorious gospel of the blessed God to the Heathen" (130).

The evangelization of the world could be achieved only if Christians would lay aside their confessional and denominational loyalties and cooperate with one another for the sake of the gospel. Interdenominational mission societies downplayed church planting, which would only raise ecclesial and doctrinal controversies. But simple evangelism was a task upon which virtually all could agree.

Most foundational to this understanding of mission, however, is the conviction that the individual sinner is destined for God's judgment and that only by repentance and faith in Christ can one be saved from eternal damnation. Thus hearing the gospel is every human's deepest need, and proclaiming the gospel the most urgent missionary task. The very thought of thousands perishing without Christ created a great sense of urgency. Leaders such as Hudson Taylor of the China Inland Mission could passionately speak of a Niagara Falls of thousands of souls perishing daily without hearing the gospel. Nothing should distract missionaries from getting the gospel as quickly as possible to as many people as possible. The Student Volunteer Movement and later student mission movements promoted the evangelization of "the world in this generation." Leaders such as Arthur T. Pierson and John R. Mott sought to guard against charges of superficial or hurried evangelization (Forman 1977, 88). But the general tenor was one of extreme urgency.

Generally speaking, evangelism was understood as the central task of missions by most Protestant mission agencies throughout the nineteenth century. Historian Stephen Neill observes, "Protestant missionaries have gone out with the earnest desire to win souls for Christ, but with little idea of what is to happen to the souls when they have been won" (cited in W. R. Shenk 2001, 151).

Until the late nineteenth century most missionaries shared the basic conviction of the necessity of hearing the gospel for salvation. Though Gustav Warneck, the father of modern missiology, was an advocate of church planting and Christianization as the task of mission, he strongly affirmed the centrality of proclamation and conversion as the essential starting point of mission. In 1891 he wrote, "Jesus' sending is for the salvation of souls. The salvation of souls is and remains everywhere the essential core work of Christ's messenger. When this core work is displaced from its central role, a clouding of the sending task has begun. . . . Conversion of a people must begin with individual conversions, and these individual conversions must compose a long *phase* of the mission period" (cited in Hoekendijk 1967, 90).

However, alternative understandings of salvation, the valuing of non-Christian religions, and the questioning of biblical authority began to undermine the centrality of proclamation in mission. By the early twentieth century in North America, the fundamentalist-modernist debate had polarized division between advocates of mission as proclamation and advocates of mission as social action. Though evangelism never disappeared from the agenda of the WCC, as we will see below, the conciliar movement redefined evangelism, and verbal proclamation lost its priority. Johannes Verkuyl warns, "A genuine interest in the salvation of individual souls may never be absent in mission work"

(1978, 180), and the WCC has more recently reaffirmed the importance of evangelism and a call to personal conversion (Werner 2008). But there remains little clarity regarding the universal truth of the gospel and the nature of its proclamation (e.g., WCC 1985; 2000, §17, 63–67).

The Lausanne Congress on World Evangelization (1974) was an evangelical high watermark in response to the conciliar movement's redefinition of mission and evangelism. It focused on effective world evangelization under this definition: "To evangelize is to spread the good news that Jesus Christ died for our sins and was raised from the dead according to the Scriptures, and that as the reigning Lord he now offers the forgiveness of sins and the liberating gifts of the Spirit to all who repent and believe" (Lausanne Covenant §4). The LCWE has continued to sponsor working groups and conferences related to world evangelization, though it has broadened its concerns beyond mere proclamation.

Assessment

Proclamation is clearly central to the New Testament understanding of mission. Both the Lukan and the Markan form of the Great Commission emphasize proclamation. Wherever the apostles and early missionaries traveled, they proclaimed the gospel and called for people to become committed followers of Jesus Christ (see sidebar 5.1). The message was adapted to the hearers, but the offense of the cross was never compromised, no matter how dangerous for the messenger or how foolish it seemed to the hearers. The early Christians were convinced regarding Christ that "salvation is found in no one else, for there is no other name under heaven given to men by which we must be saved" (Acts 4:12). The emphasis on proclamation is rooted in Paul's link between proclamation and soteriology:

> For, "Everyone who calls on the name of the Lord will be saved."
> How, then, can they call on the one they have not believed in? And how can they believe in the one of whom they have not heard? And how can they hear without someone preaching to them? (Rom. 10:13–14)

To remove explicit communication of the saving acts of God in Christ from missions is to remove the very core and climax of salvation history and the only message that can bring eternal salvation from judgment and reconciliation with God to sinful men and women. Whatever might be added to the task of missions, proclamation cannot be eliminated from it.

While maintaining the centrality of proclamation and personal conversion, a one-sided emphasis on evangelism to the exclusion or neglect of other aspects of the missionary task must be avoided. Several dangers may be noted.

First, *emphasis on rapid communication of the gospel can lead to superficial understanding of the gospel and shallow conversions.* Popular mottos such as, "no one should hear the gospel twice until everyone has heard it once," have a certain persuasive logic. For example, Arthur T. Pierson, who is associated with the Student Volunteer Movement of the late nineteenth century, said of evangelism, "To stop or linger anywhere, even to repeat the rejected message, so long as there are souls beyond that have never heard it, is at least unjust to those who are still in absolute darkness" (cited in Robert 2003, 200).

But what does it mean to "hear the gospel"? The task of clearly communicating the gospel across cultures is complex. The worldview, the felt needs, potential misunderstandings, the decision-making process of a people must all be taken into consideration to ensure that the hearer genuinely understands the gospel message. Even Paul and Barnabas faced the challenge of being misunderstood by their hearers (Acts 14:8–18). Strategies of rapid world evangelization may produce impressive reports and statistics of persons who have heard the gospel and numbers of "decisions" registered. But the longer-term fruit of such efforts is often questionable. Nominalism is a widespread problem in churches everywhere. Syncretism, immorality, failure to comprehend basic biblical teachings,

---

SIDEBAR 5.1
THE EVANGELISTIC PROCLAMATION OF THE APOSTLE PAUL

Though Paul adapted his message to the audience, consistent themes can be discerned by examining his evangelistic preaching in the book of Acts and writing in 1 Thessalonians (see also Schnabel 2008, 126–30, 155–208):

1. There is only one true and living God, Creator of heaven and earth (Acts 14:15–17; 17:24–28).
2. God is holy and righteous and will judge all evil (Acts 17:30–31; 1 Thess. 4:6b).
3. Men and women are accountable before God and must turn from serving idols and false gods to serve the one true God (Acts 14:15; 17:29–31; 1 Thess. 1:9).
4. Jesus Christ is the promised messianic Redeemer, the Son of God, who through his life, death, and resurrection delivers us from sin and God's wrath (Acts 13:26–38; 17:2–3; 1 Thess. 1:10).
5. Repentance and faith in Christ are necessary to receive forgiveness and eternal life (Acts 13:39–41, 48; 16:30–31; 17:30; 20:21; 26:20; 1 Thess. 2:13).
6. Encouraging hearers to live worthy of God, who calls us into his kingdom (Acts 14:22; 19:8; 20:25; 28:23, 31; 1 Thess. 2:12; 4:1, 7).

REFLECTION AND DISCUSSION

1. What elements of Paul's evangelistic message are emphasized in evangelism today? What elements are missing or underemphasized?
2. Are all the above points equally essential for an unbeliever to rightly understand the gospel?
3. Are there aspects of the gospel that need to be more emphasized or more carefully explained for contemporary audiences? Explain your answer.

or a "Sunday only" Christianity is often the result of hurried or superficial proclamation. This does not bring glory to God or advance his kingdom.

Second, *proclamation apart from discipleship, church planting, and kingdom concerns truncates the Great Commission.* The Markan and Lukan versions of the Great Commission emphasize proclamation and witness. However, Matthew explicitly defines mission in terms of making disciples who obey all that Jesus has taught us (Matt. 28:19–20). John speaks of being sent as Jesus was sent, which entails much more than mere preaching (John 20:21). The apostle Paul not only proclaimed the gospel but also gave considerable effort to the ongoing development of the believers and their churches. Proclamation alone cannot be considered fulfillment of the Great Commission.

Third, *proclamation that emphasizes a "decision" apart from the lordship of Christ misunderstands biblical conversion.* Clearly the apostles called their listeners to repentance and faith in Christ. Proclamation was an urgent call to decision. But it is a decision for a life in fellowship with God and under his lordship. True conversion is not merely acceptance of the gift of eternal salvation, though it surely begins there. "Conversion is . . . a change in allegiance in which Christ is accepted as Lord and center of one's life" (D. J. Bosch 1991, 488). True evangelism calls people not only to receive forgiveness in Christ but also to radical discipleship as followers of Christ. As such, it will inevitably impact the whole life and community.

Fourth, and finally, *one-sided emphasis on individual decisions does not adequately take community into account.* Wilbert Shenk observes of the nineteenth century: "Ecclesiology played no significant role in the development of mission theology, except marginal Tractarian influence in Great Britain" (2001, 150). Warneck was one of the first to theologically argue against an overly individualized understanding of mission in his *Evangelische Missionslehre* (1897–1905). The relationship between soteriology and ecclesiology must be established in the theology and practice of mission. Western culture has been deeply affected by values of personal freedom and individual choice. Many other cultures are more group oriented; thus identity and decision making are influenced by group processes. Overly individualized approaches to proclamation and conversion neglect such factors.

Jesus taught that one must be prepared to leave family to become his disciple (Matt. 10:37; Luke 14:26). *But* those who follow him receive a new family (Matt. 19:29; Mark 10:29–30). The New Testament reports not only individual conversions but also conversions of large numbers of people and whole households (Acts 2:41; 16:33–34). As these people became Christians, churches were formed where faith was nurtured and lived out in community. This is the biblical norm. The formation of healthy churches will not occur automatically by simply preaching the gospel.

Although proclamation alone cannot be seen as an adequate definition of the missionary task, it certainly is the necessary starting point of mission. The explicit statements of the Great Commission, the example of the apostles, and the logic of the gospel make proclamation fundamental. Mission that does not explicitly bring the good news of God's salvation in Jesus Christ to the world cannot be considered biblical mission.

CHURCH PLANTING AND GROWTH AS THE TASK OF MISSIONS

Historical Development

The Roman Catholic Church has long made *plantatio ecclesiae* (church planting) a central task of missions (see sidebar 5.2). This was in part due to the doctrine formulated by Cyprian in the first half of the third century: *extra ecclesiam nulla salus,* there is no salvation outside the church. The Reformers generally affirmed this view but, with the exception of the Dutch colonial mission, Protestants were reticent to place the church at the center of mission (Kärkkäinen 2003, 71–77; Gensichen 1971, 130).

Church planting was stated as a missionary motive during the seventeenth-century Second Reformation in Holland. "Missionary activity was necessary, not only because perishing souls had to be saved or because the coming Kingdom had to be prepared, but also because the Church in which the Kingdom became partly made manifest had to expand to the ends of the earth" (Van den Berg 1956, 184). Gisbertus Voetius declared proclamation, church planting, and doxology as the purposes of missions. But views emphasizing proclamation dominated the early practice of Protestant missions.

Early Protestant mission growing out of Puritanism, Pietism, and revivalism initially emphasized church renewal through conversion, not church planting. Though early Puritans in North America viewed the establishment of the church as a part of missions, the actual establishment of churches for Native Americans was largely unsuccessful (Rooy 1965, 321–22). Many early North American mission leaders identified the church with the kingdom of God. Thus planting the church, as a fellowship of truly converted souls, in all lands was essential to the great goal of bringing all creation under Christ's rule (Chaney 1976, 246–48).

As noted above, Pietism had no articulated ecclesiology. As the local people became Christians, they were by necessity gathered into churches. "Yet the idea of *plantatio ecclesiae* was certainly not the main stimulus of the missionary awakening: the Evangelicals went out 'to save souls,' and the formation of the church on the mission-field was a corollary of their labours, but not necessarily their prime target" (Van den Berg 1956, 159). Only as more church-based, confessional mission agencies were formed did church planting become a more explicit task of Protestant missions.

The experience of planting churches, especially with often nonliterate new believers in strange cultures, was a new one that had not always been carefully

SIDEBAR 5.2
PLANTATIO ECCLESIAE IN ROMAN CATHOLIC THEOLOGY OF MISSION

The planting of the church where it does not yet exist has long held an important place in Roman Catholic understandings of mission. Since Cyprian's famous statement in the first half of the third century, *extra ecclesiam nulla salus* (there is no salvation outside the church), the church has been understood as central to salvation and mission. This doctrine became official teaching in 1215 at the Fourth Lateran Council (Canon 1; see Ohm 1962). By the end of the nineteenth century, Catholic theologians discussed the possibility of salvation for persons outside the church through "implicit faith" (Shorter 1988, 93–94), a view later affirmed by Vatican II (*LG* 16; *AG* 7).

In the twentieth century two Catholic schools of thought regarding church planting developed (see Brechter 1969, 118; Ferguson 1984; Oborji 2006). Joseph Schmidlin (1876–1944), the father of Roman Catholic missiology, represents the older Münster School. He placed primacy on salvation of souls, describing the stages of missionary work as:

1. The proclamation of the gospel, the Christian faith, among the heathen
2. The internal conversion, the change of heart, and the external conversion, the incorporation into the church, and reception of baptism
3. The organization of the church from the simple formation of communities to the establishment of full hierarchy. (K. Müller 1987, 37)

The Louvain School, represented by Pierre Charles (1883–1954), placed primacy on church planting over individual salvation, the purpose of mission being "to plant the visible Church wherever it is not yet planted, that is to bring salvation (faith and the sacraments) within reach of all souls of good will" (cited in K. Müller 1987, 76–77). The church should be seen not as merely a means of salvation, but as "the one point of contact where the whole work of the Creator returns to its Savior" (ibid.).

Vatican II sought to synthesize the Louvain and Münster schools, applying a new, broader conception of the church as the people of God. As noted above, a broader view of salvation was affirmed, and the language of *extra ecclesiam* was not used. Yet it also affirmed that "the proper purpose of this missionary activity is evangelization, and the planting of the Church among those peoples and groups where it has not yet taken root" (*AG* 6). On the one hand, proclamation and conversion must lead to the planting of churches in the hierarchical and sacramental sense; on the other hand, apart from faith and conversion the formal establishment of a church would be utopian (Brechter 1969, 118–19).

Karl Müller (1918–2001) has stated that today "the one-sidedness of the so-called Louvain School is abandoned practically everywhere." Yet he goes on to affirm that "'the founding of new communities of the people of God' is a theologically accurate way to paraphrase the concept of mission" (1987, 34).

Some, such as Walbert Bühlmann (1982, 248), hold that the church has already been planted wherever possible and mission now consists in the ongoing evangelistic activity (in a very broad sense) of those churches. Nevertheless, in 1990 Pope John Paul II wrote:

> The mission *ad gentes* has this objective: to found Christian communities and develop Churches to their full maturity. This is a central and determining goal of missionary activity, so much so that the mission is not completed until it succeeds in building a new particular Church which functions normally in its local setting. (*RM* 48)

REFLECTION AND DISCUSSION

1. How would you assess and resolve the tension between the Louvain and the Münster schools of thought?

2. What aspects of Protestant theology and ecclesiology impact how Protestant theology of mission should view the place of church planting in mission?

3. To what extent do you believe that Protestant understandings of salvation are overly individualistic, neglecting the importance of identification with the church?

considered. William Carey was a notable exception. He published a "Form of Agreement" in 1806 with his coworkers, which indicated "winning of individuals" along with "founding of churches and organizing schools" as central purposes of their mission (Verkuyl 1978, 179). The agreement also explicitly stated that the churches should be entrusted to national pastors. The missionary should then superintend these churches and "direct his efforts continually to the planting of new churches in other places, and to the spread of the gospel in his district to the utmost of his power" (cited in Stanley 1992, 381).

Among the first Protestant mission leaders to formulate the task of missions in terms of planting indigenous churches were the American Rufus Anderson (1796–1880), foreign secretary of the American Board of Commissioners for Foreign Missions, and Englishman Henry Venn (1796–1873), secretary of the Church Missionary Society. They are credited with formulating—initially independent of each other—the famous "three-self" definition of indigenous churches as *self-propagating*, *self-governing*, and *self-supporting*. They observed that missionaries often remained in one location indefinitely because the churches planted were so dependent on foreign leadership and funds. Venn and Anderson advocated that by planting three-self churches, missionaries would be freed to pioneer new fields, and national believers would take up responsibility for evangelizing their own and neighboring people.

Anderson also reacted to the pietistic emphasis on individual conversion to the neglect of developing truly indigenous churches. He said, "Missions are initiated for the spread of a scriptural, self-propagating Christianity" (cited in Verkuyl 1978, 65). Four aspects were to be kept in view: (1) conversion, (2) organizing converts into churches, (3) giving the ministry of the churches over to the nationals, and (4) conducing them to independence and self-propagation. Throughout the nineteenth century the three-self formula became the generally accepted mission strategy, though it was seldom practiced with consistency (Beaver 1968a, 116). The churches that were planted were generally patterned after the missionaries' sending churches, and missionaries were usually reluctant to entrust local believers with leadership in the churches.

Warneck advocated in the very first sentence of his multivolume *Evangelische Missionslehre*, "By Christian mission we mean the entire endeavor of Christianity to plant and organize Christian churches among non-Christian peoples" (1897, 1:1). For him the task of missions builds on individual conversion but must lead to the founding of churches: "The task of Christian mission is the expansion of Christianity, i.e., the planting of the Christian church in the entire world. This planting should not take place through random or sporadic proclamation of the Christian message of salvation to individual souls, but demands an *ordered undertaking* that leads to the founding, nurture, and organization of a national Christian community, a church" (1897, 1:4). Churches are not to be merely a collection of individual converts but form an indigenous community under local leadership able to impact the whole society. This he called christianization—the final goal of the missionary task.

Numerous other mission leaders and theologians advocated church planting as central to the task of mission. These include, among others, Robert Speer (1902, 39–40), Roland Allen ([1912] 1962a, 81), H. W. Schomerus (1935), Hendrik Kraemer (1938, 287), Walter Freytag (1961, 2:184), and David Hesselgrave (1980, 29, 33). Georg Vicedom concluded, "The goal of mission is the proclamation of the message to all mankind and gathering them into the church" (1965, 103).

Under the influence of Johannes Christiaan Hoekendijk, conciliar mission understanding moved in the 1960s and 1970s to a radical rejection of any kind of church-centered mission. However, more moderate positions have since been taken. For example, the WCC document *Mission and Evangelism: An Ecumenical Affirmation* states, "It is at the heart of Christian mission to foster the multiplication of local congregations in every human community" (WCC 1982, §25).

In the 1960s Donald A. McGavran and the Church Growth Movement began having wide influence on mission thinking. McGavran was firmly convinced that true mission must result in growing churches. He defined mission as *"an enterprise devoted to proclaiming the Good News of Jesus Christ, and to persuading men to become His disciples and dependable members of His church"* ([1970] 1980, 26). "Today's supreme task is effective multiplication of churches in the receptive societies of earth" (41). For McGavran church growth is not merely a matter of increasing numbers, as is often alleged, but rather church membership is viewed as the best outward sign that disciples are being made. As a missionary in India he observed that extensive social work, education, orphanages, and the like were having little impact on leading people to become Christians and responsible church members. The eternal salvation of these people was his foremost concern.

He argued further that only by planting churches could social improvement ultimately be achieved. "Whenever missions have planted churches successfully, improvements in the areas of health, education, agriculture, justice, and freedom have followed. The church is the most powerful instrument known for the alleviation of social ills" (Glasser and McGavran 1983, 28–29). He summarizes in his seminal work *Understanding Church Growth*: "Nothing will advance the cause of world evangelization more than for church leaders and missionaries to cease thinking exclusively in terms of good work of one kind or another and begin thinking of *the central task* in terms of incorporating responsible converts in ongoing congregations and multiplying these in natural social units" ([1970] 1980, 455–56).

Other spokesmen of the Church Growth Movement emphasized the practical importance of church planting in fulfilling the Great Commission. C. Peter Wagner, for example, is famously quoted, "The single most effective evangelistic method is planting new churches" (1990a, 11). Ralph Winter argues, "Even if an agency specializes in medical work, or orphan work, or radio work, or whatever, it must be aware of, and concerned about, the interface between that activity and the church-planting function" (1974, 135). The evangelical Congress on the Church's Worldwide Mission at Wheaton (1966), influenced by the Church Growth Movement, concluded in the Wheaton Declaration that "church planting has the priority among all other missionary activities, necessary and helpful though they may be" (1966, 17).

Though Article 4 of the Lausanne Covenant states, "The results of evangelism include obedience to Christ, incorporation into his church and responsible service in the world," church planting did not figure prominently at Lausanne I. However, presentations by leaders such as Winter and Howard A. Snyder made strong cases for church planting in missions. Snyder, for example, contended: "To do justice to the biblical understanding of evangelism, we must go a step further and say that the goal of evangelism is the formation of the Christian community. It is making disciples and further forming these disciples into living cells of the Body of Christ—new expressions of the community of God's people" (1975, 331).

The Manila Manifesto that emerged from Lausanne II has only one reference relating to church planting, stating that when the church spreads the gospel "the gospel creates the church which spreads the gospel which creates more churches in a continuous chain reaction" (MM II, B, §8).

Church planting and growth as the task of missions has never regained the prominence it had during the mid-twentieth century in the theology of mission. But in mission *practice* several evangelical movements have given fresh impetus to church planting. Winter's "unreached peoples" strategy and "frontier missions" emphasized the importance of an indigenous church for every distinct social or ethnic group (e.g., Winter 1975 and Wood 1995). Only when such churches have been planted can a people be considered "reached." This philosophy was behind the AD2000 and Beyond Movement, which sponsored the Global Consultations on World Evangelization in Seoul, Korea (1995), and in Pretoria, South Africa (1997; see Bush 2000 and 2003). Discipling a Whole Nation (Montgomery 1980, and www.dawnministries.org) and the Alliance for Saturation Church Planting (www.alliancescp.org) have also advanced the strategy that world evangelization is best achieved through planting churches within the reach of every person.

John Piper presents the most articulate and biblically reasoned case for the unreached peoples' understanding of missions in his immensely popular *Let the Nations Be Glad!* (1993, 2003). He unequivocally states,

> Missions exists to plant Christ-purchased, God exalting worshipping communities of the redeemed in all the peoples of the world.
>
> The passion of a missionary—as distinct from that of an evangelist—is to plant a worshipping community of Christians in a people group who has no access to the gospel because of language or cultural barriers. (2003, 208)

Recently, two authors have specifically discussed the place of church planting in mission from an evangelical perspective. Stuart Murray (2001) has argued for subsuming the task of church planting to the *missio Dei* and the advance of the kingdom of God. Richard Hibbert has responded making a strong case "that the planting of new churches is the primary way God's mission is accomplished, and that without it the other goals of mission cannot be achieved" (2009, 331).

Assessment

The planting, establishing, and growth of churches are central to the flow of salvation history and the expressed will of Jesus Christ. Throughout salvation history God has chosen to work through a people. In the Old Testament that people was primarily Israel, and in the New it is the church. Church planting and growth are Christ's own work, for he has said, "I will build my church" (Matt. 16:18b). Jesus's work of redemption was not merely to save individuals, but he "gave himself for us to redeem us from all wickedness and to purify for himself a people that are his very own, eager to do what is good" (Titus 2:14).

The New Testament knows little of an individualized faith separated from Christian community. If we speak of evangelism, we must also speak of the church. In the book of Acts, we see God himself "adding" new believers to the church (Acts 2:41, 47; 5:14). One cannot read Acts without noting that nearly everywhere the gospel was preached, communities of believers are formed. Evangelism led to the establishment of churches under a local spiritual leadership and interrelated with other churches. To belong to Christ is also to belong to Christ's people (1 Cor. 12:13). Conversion "is the summoning of men and women into a visible fellowship with a view to carrying out God's will in the world" (Newbigin 1969, 97). This is in part because "the New Testament knows nothing of a relationship with Christ which is purely mental and spiritual, unembodied in any of the structures of human relationship" (106).

The church remains God's primary agent to accomplish his purposes in this age. The planting and growth of Christ-centered, Bible-believing, Spirit-filled churches is God's chosen way to multiply a witness to his kingdom on earth. God has surely used individuals, even godless kings and potentates to accomplish his purposes. But the church remains the only community that is uniquely called to live out the values of the kingdom (1 Pet. 2:9). Even Lesslie Newbigin, who takes issue with the Church Growth Movement, writes: "It is futile to talk of the church as agent of liberation—in whatever terms we understand that task—unless we also pay attention to the ways in which the church in any place comes into being and grows. . . . The calling of men and women to be converted, to follow Jesus, and to be part of his community is and must always be at the center of mission" ([1978] 1995, 121).

The command to baptize is an indirect command to form communities. Though there is no command to plant churches, there is the command to baptize (Matt. 28:19–20). Baptism is a sign not only of repentance, forgiveness, and new life (Rom. 6:3–4) but also of enfolding into the body of Christ (1 Cor. 12:13) and identification with the new community of faith.

The planting and healthy development of churches were central to Paul's mission. He was not only concerned about evangelism. Recent New Testament studies have emphasized the importance of church planting and nurture in the ministry of Paul (e.g., O'Brien 1995, 43; Haas 1971, 69; Wedderburn 1988, 97). This is a key to understanding Romans 15:18–25. Paul could only consider his work in a region completed when reproducing churches had been planted and commended to local leaders. Andreas J. Köstenberger and Peter T. O'Brien conclude that "the activities in which Paul engaged as he sought to fulfill his missionary commission included not only primarily evangelism through which men and women were converted, but the founding of churches and the bringing of believers to full maturity in Christ" (2001, 184).

Church planting should not be understood merely pragmatically as an effective means of evangelism. The church is the bride of Christ. He gave himself for her and is sanctifying her to present her to himself in all purity, beauty, and glory (Eph. 5:25–27). Thus, to plant and build up the church in love and holiness is to beautify the bride of Christ.

We conclude from this that church planting and development must indeed be considered central to the task of missions. However, we must consider not only the activity of church planting but also the *kind* of church planting that occurs. And here is where legitimate concerns must also be voiced.

Church planting cannot be understood as the advancement of a particular religious institution, denomination, or organization. Unfortunately, the work

119

of church planting can easily become a matter of denominational flag raising, sheep stealing, number counting, or ecclesial kingdom building. None of this has anything to do with a biblical understanding of the church and mission. Hoekendijk, the sharpest critic of "ecclesiocentric" mission, often overstated his case. But he was correct in pointing out that the church does not exist to serve itself, and any self-serving ecclesial goals of mission are inconsistent with the spirit of Christ and the gospel. Missions dare not be preoccupied with church-centered and largely church-internal issues becoming "a veritable merry-go-round around the Church" (Hoekendijk 1952, 324).

In the New Testament, church planting was a result of evangelism and discipleship. New churches were formed as people came to faith in Jesus Christ. These churches were not isolated but interrelated with other churches. The consistent concern of Paul in his letters to the churches was that they not merely exist, hold meetings, or perform some religious function. Rather, his concern was that they grow in Christ, in holiness, and in love. If church planting does not result in communities of believers who are a corporate sign of the kingdom seeking to honor the King of kings in every aspect of life, then church planting can become a dubious undertaking.

CIVILIZATION AND MORAL IMPROVEMENT AS THE TASK OF MISSIONS

Historical Development

Civilization has throughout most of mission history been considered important if not central to mission work. By "civilization" we mean the intentional attempt by missionaries to bring not only the gospel but the culture of their sending church to non-Christian peoples. It was viewed a moral obligation, if not a practical necessity, to raise "heathen savages" from their depravity by civilizing them. During a millennium of Christian mission after Christianity became the official religion of the Roman Empire, becoming a Christian was generally equated by the Western Church with becoming Roman. There was relatively little accommodation to local culture or expression. In the Western church the languages of the cross (Hebrew, Greek, and Latin) were the only languages allowed for the liturgy. A common practice among early Roman Catholic as well as Protestant missionaries was to gather new believers into Christian communities, often forming towns, and proceeding to teach Western customs, lifestyles, morals, and manners. There were of course exceptions, but the general assumption was that Western culture is Christian culture.

From the perspective in the twenty-first century, the mixture of Western culture and the gospel is readily condemned along with the ills of colonialism and ethnocentrism. But for earlier generations the very idea of separating religious belief from cultural expression was difficult to imagine. To fail to "civilize" the indigenous people would have been considered morally negligent or to regard them as less than equally human.

An explicit link between missions and civilizing was articulated by the brilliant humanist Desiderius Erasmus (1466–1536), who saw missionary work as a taming of wild peoples. The Enlightenment thinker Gottfried Wilhelm Leibniz (1646–1716), who did not believe in eternal judgment, viewed not soteriology but rather the cultural expansion of Christianity as a motive for mission. For him the kingdom of God was a *vernünftig-sittliche Weltordnung* (a rational-moral world order), grace being a matter of moral evolution, not salvation. In 1697 Leibniz called Protestants to take up mission in the name of civilizing the world. True to Enlightenment ideals, human rationality was seen as the key to overcoming superstition and solving human problems. Such views regarded mission as a matter more of education than of conversion (Van den Berg 1956, 13–17; Zangger 1973; Merkel 1920). Leibniz's view of culture was, however, nuanced. He believed for example that Europe should bring Christianity and science to China, but China should in turn teach Europe natural religion and ethics (Collani 2006, 219). The early Pietist leader August Herman Franke read Leibniz and corresponded with him. The Enlightenment ideal of inevitable progress through rationality and Western-style education exercised a powerful influence on missions.

The Puritan vision of wedding evangelism and civilization was rooted in the conviction of the unity of humanity. "They were holistic in mission in that they believed that every part of every culture must be transformed to be like the heavenly kingdom" (J. B. Carpenter 2002, 525). Unfortunately, the vision of the heavenly kingdom was hardly discernible from genteel European culture with biblical morality. Most missionaries until the twentieth century considered it an act of compassion not only spiritually but also socially to bring the "savages" out of their darkness and to share with them the fruits of Western civility and culture.

In early North American mission thinking, social and moral reform was, along with evangelism and church planting, part of the overarching goal of bringing all things under Christ's reign—the Puritan theocratic vision. "Behind all this stood the dream of a Christian empire which would extend itself to the ends of the world" (Van den Berg 1956, 22). Social transformation was thus not a secondary goal, though only achievable as a result of the preaching of the gospel and conversion (Chaney 1976, 248).

Many believed that civilizing was a precondition to the conversion of "primitive" peoples. For example, John Eliot worked primarily for the conversion of Native Americans, but he was convinced that lasting conversion could only be accomplished if the Native Americans abandoned their nomadic lifestyle and became civilized. In this sense colonization was a means of evangelization and sanctification. To this end he isolated converts in "praying towns" governed by biblical standards and the English manner of life. Henry Knapp, however, argues that Eliot "did not seek to destroy the Indian culture for political or economic reasons," that he sought to uphold their freedom, and that he did not impose a British model of government on the Praying Towns (1998, 123).

By 1674 Eliot had established fourteen villages with four thousand converts. This pattern became quite typical of mission work in many places. The Puritan Cotton Mather expressed this conviction: "Wherefore, may the people of New-England . . . be encouraged still to prosecute, first, the *civilizing*, and then the *Christianizing* of the barbarians in their neighbourhood; and may the New-Englanders . . . make a *mission* of the gospel unto the mighty nations of the Western Indians" (cited in Rooy 1965, 284).

Until the mid-eighteenth century the civilizing motive was subsumed under spiritual motives, for "the religious context was strong enough to prevent the cultural motive from becoming an independent factor in the missionary development" (Van den Berg 1956, 61). In the second half of that century, the cultural motive began to assume prominence as Enlightenment ideals and rejection of "religious enthusiasm" became more powerful. Such ideals combined later with the concepts of "manifest destiny" as powerful motives.

During the colonial era and the early formation of the United States, missionaries were viewed by governments as the most prudent and efficient way to civilize Native Americans (Beaver 1968a, 118–19, 133). This was evident in the Civilization Fund Act enacted by the U.S. Congress in 1819. Missionaries proved the best agents of the plan, with various mission societies creating schools that educated some 239,000 Native Americans (Noel 2002, 21).

The ideal of mission as education was taken especially seriously by the SPCK, which established libraries, literature, and schools as the instruments of mission (Van den Berg 1956, 45). The Pietist Danish-Halle Mission in Tranquebar (India) came under the guidance of the SPCK and was eventually so influenced by rationalism that mission work was nearly entirely secondary to civilizing. The opinion was loudly voiced especially in German universities that the only realistic approach to mission would be to first civilize the people, which would then lead naturally and logically to a major turn to Christianity. This notion eventually killed the Halle-Pietist missionary movement (Richter 1928, 138; Wellenreuther 2004).

William Carey, clearly a conversionist, expressed the sentiments of the time when he wrote in his *Enquiry*, "Can we hear that they are without the gospel, without government, without laws, and without arts and sciences; and not exert ourselves to introduce amongst them the sentiments of men, and of Christians? Would not the spread of the gospel be the most effectual mean of their civilization? Would not that make them useful members of society?" (Carey 1961, 70). The clear (and from our perspective utterly astonishing) assumption is that people without the gospel and Western civilization are without any form of respectable culture, or even law and government, and are thus without the "sentiments of men," and are not useful members of society.

As numerous mission agencies were founded in the early nineteenth century, it was not unusual for civilization to be explicitly included in the goals of the mission work. For example, the stated purpose for the founding of the Basel Mission in 1816 included raising up missionaries for cooperation with English and Dutch mission societies as "spreaders of charitable civilization and as preachers of the gospel" (cited in Schlatter 1916, 28). Founders of the Rhine Mission Society believed that mission work could only succeed when the indigenous people were first colonized. This led to the development of significant commercial undertakings as part of the mission effort (Braun 1992, 41). At the end of the nineteenth century, the Neukirchen Mission epitomized the spirit with the slogan *Kolonisieren heißt Missionieren* ("colonization is mission"; see Brandl 1998, 283).

Such convictions persisted throughout the "great century." As late as the early twentieth century, C. F. Andrews, missionary to India at St. Andrews College in Delhi, could write, "Christian civilisation is in one sense the embodiment of the Christian faith, and this Christian civilisation must be given to India, as well as the Christian message, if the message is to become intelligible" (cited in M. M. Thomas [1972] 2002, 93).

The missionary task of civilizing often went hand in hand with colonialism. Colonialism was sometimes viewed as the path to civilizing, which would in turn prepare the way for the gospel. The association of Christian mission and colonialism, including all its attendant evils, was inevitable. However, contrary to popular critiques, missionaries were often the first to fight for the rights of the indigenous people in opposition to colonial policy, though often enough they also saw collaboration with colonial powers as the only way to eradicate some of the more extreme local practices.

Popular rhetoric and blanket condemnation of missionary collaboration with colonialism fail to recognize the complex relationship in a more nuanced light (see Neill 1966; Robert 2008). Missionaries, often at great personal sacrifice, fought the evils of colonialism such as slavery. Indeed, one comprehensive study of the historical record from the early nineteenth to the mid-twentieth century demonstrates that "when missionaries were independent of state control, they moderated, not exacerbated, the negative effects of colonialism" (Woodberry 2006, 3; 2004).

Not only missionaries but also leading theologians linked mission with cultural expansion. Friedrich Schleiermacher (1768–1834), sometimes called the father of modern Protestant theology, argued that "mission was primarily a cultural enterprise and accompanied a general transfer of culture. Mission involves cultural extension" (Verkuyl 1978, 171). Ernst Troeltsch (1865–1923) viewed Christianity and mission as a stage on the way to a higher world religion and civilization. In the period of 1890 to 1918, numerous books appeared praising the social improvements accomplished by missionaries, thus fueling the civilization motif in popular opinion. The most famous was James S. Dennis's three-volume *Christian Mission and Social Progress* (1897–1906). Charles W. Forman writes, "'Civilizing' was only a secondary and subordinate methodology in American thought. But by the end of the nineteenth century the broad cultural impact of missions received so much recognition that from then on it was often considered an independent and parallel methodology" (1977, 113).

There were also critical voices. Venn and Anderson flatly rejected civilizing as an approach to mission (W. R. Shenk 2001, 39–41; C. P. Williams 1990, 4). Warneck pleaded that civilization not be used as a means of Christianization (1874, 285). Some missiologists in the early twentieth century, such as Bruno Guttmann, who studied under the pioneer of cultural psychology Wilhelm Wundt, argued vigorously for the value and protection of local cultures. Roland Allen, writing in 1912, was far ahead of his time in rejecting civilization and social reform as legitimate mission undertakings ([1912] 1962a; see also Sanneh 2008, 218–34).

As Lamin Sanneh has pointed out, by translating the gospel into the vernacular, even the most ethnocentric missionaries planted the seeds of a truly indigenous church that would grow and take expressions unimagined by the missionaries. God would overrule the cultural blindness of missions, for the majority world church by the late twentieth century would numerically overshadow the Western church in what Sanneh calls "post-Western Christianity" (1989 and 2008).

But ethnocentric attitudes and the ideal of civilization stubbornly persisted until the mid-twentieth century and in some cases persist to the present day. William Hocking's writings and the Laymen's Foreign Missionary Enquiry summary report "Rethinking Mission" (1932) continued to speak of preparing the way for a coming world civilization to replace the traditional task of missions. As Forman observes, "The immediate post-war [World War I] years still carried much of the high idealism that had been preached during the war and interpreters of missions linked mission work to the hopes for world-wide democracy and a new international order." A case was presented "for missions as the necessary vehicle to carry forward the higher purposes of the war" (1977, 95). The ultimate failure of Western civilization and culture in the atrocities of World War II finally lay to rest any serious advocacy of civilization as a task of missions. Growing awareness of anthropology and ethnography also contributed to this change. However, more subtle forms of the civilization motif continue to accompany missions today as a result of cultural naïveté, ethnocentrism, and views equating free-market capitalism and Jeffersonian democracy with Christianity.

Assessment

We must guard against self-righteous condemnation of the civilization model. From the vantage point of the twenty-first century, it is easy to condescendingly reject the civilizing approach to mission as sheer ethnocentrism, arrogance, and cultural dominance. But our presumed superiority to those of the past can blind us to genuinely learning from them today. Consider the times and the realities that the missionaries often faced. Particularly in the nineteenth century, the Industrial Revolution and scientific discoveries of the West created a great sense of Western superiority over nonindustrialized cultures.

Missionaries encountered not only what appeared to be primitive lifestyles but often brutal traditions and customs, including widow burning, cannibalism, the killing of twins, foot binding, ethnic warfare, and harmful initiation rites. Certainly the extreme practices were often overplayed in the promotion of missions. But such conditions nevertheless called for action. The dividing line between insensitive cultural imposition and genuine concern for justice and human betterment is not always easy to discern. Stereotypes of culture-destroying missionaries must thus be nuanced; as Ryan Dunch writes, "The popular image of the finger-wagging missionary condemning a host culture wholesale and seeking to replace it in its entirety is, to say the least, implausible as a general type; such a person would soon have proved useless as a missionary and been recalled" (2002, 322).

The trading companies might have been content to leave the local people unchanged in their misery or inhumane practices so as not to disturb commerce. But missionaries could not remain idle. They sought to do what they felt to be the most compassionate thing and share the fruits of Western civilization, which unfortunately too often went beyond the abolition of extreme practices to include the niceties of Victorian mores. They knew few alternatives. Missionaries invested their lives often at great personal sacrifice in what they believed to be the betterment of the people they loved and served. History has demonstrated that these efforts were not in vain (see Woodberry 2006).

Missionaries were influenced by the spirit of their times and often looked condescendingly upon other cultures. But as Robert Woodberry (2006) has argued, they resisted prevalent views of "scientific racism," which claimed that dark-skinned people were fundamentally inferior to whites and unable to be civilized. Missionaries were criticized by their contemporaries for viewing indigenous peoples too highly. In the words of Harvard historian William Hutchinson, "If deficient from a modern point of view in sensitivity to foreign cultures, they were measurably superior in that regard to most contemporaries at home or abroad" (cited in Woodberry 2006, 5).

Ironically, in spite of its generally low regard for local cultures, the mission movement contributed significantly to independence movements in the colonial states and to their cultural identity. Missionaries who opposed abuses of colonialism and fought for the rights of indigenous peoples set an example (see Warren 1967; Goodall 1964; Woodberry 2006). Sanneh has argued that through translation of the Bible, missionaries (at times unintentionally) contributed both to the preservation of culture and to the empowerment of local people

(1989). Many of the hospitals, schools, and universities established under the principle of civilization remain as cherished institutions today.

The negative effects of ethnocentrism and "civilizing" on missions should not be underestimated. Its practical outworkings have indeed been the source of some of the bitterest fruit of the missionary movement throughout history. The association of mission with imperialism has dramatically impacted perceptions of the gospel from China to Latin America. Although he overstates his case, Liberian Christian leader Burgess Carr expresses the depth of offense felt by many who were not from the West in the 1970s: "Mission boards and missionary societies are perpetrators of structural violence at the deepest level of our humanity in the so-called younger churches" (cited in Escobar and Driver 1978, 11).

Ethnocentrism and cultural superiority prevail in missions today in a variety of new ways. The missionary task can easily become one of condescendingly helping the "poor natives," who seem by Western standards so backward. There is a fine line between this and compassionate serving and sharing as equals. In what ways has the short-term mission movement seriously taken culture into account? The tsunami of over one and a half million Americans annually traveling internationally in the name of Christ has staggering implications. It should also give us pause when we consider models of mission being advocated today that make the development of business and the promotion of free-market capitalism the handmaids of mission or even the centerpiece of mission strategy.

Has a Western superiority in entrepreneurial savvy or technological gadgetry compromised the missionary task? How do such strategies differ fundamentally from the civilization model? Civil religion that unquestioningly equates the American way, democracy, and individual freedom with Christian values is alive and well within American evangelicalism. We are naive if we assume that such developments have no impact on our missionary efforts. Just as missionaries of earlier generations who honored Christ and the Bible became entangled in the well-intended but oft ill-fated task of civilization, we are no less in danger of similar entanglement today.

Understanding the task of missions in terms of civilization and social betterment encumbers the faithful transmission of the gospel. Although the gospel surely addresses human need in social as well as spiritual dimensions, it dare not become confused with or bound to a specific cultural expression or social ideology. Inherent in the very nature of the gospel is its ability to transcend specific cultural expressions and ethnic boundaries and to plant itself anew in the most diverse settings. Linking the gospel with civilization or social uplift (by whose definition?) not only culturally imprisons and disguises the gospel but also diffuses missionary efforts. Sanneh summarizes the problem as recognized by Roland Allen: "Allen noted that the civilization mandate saddled missions with a distracting message and a crushing burden. . . . Missions stretched their resources to cover medical, educational, and social work as forms of preaching the gospel. Social uplift became the goal and rationale of the gospel. The work of Christ was constructed as lifting people out of poverty and backwardness" (Sanneh 2008, 226).

A biblical understanding of culture is the necessary corrective. A fair reading of the New Testament reveals a remarkable degree of cultural sensitivity, creativity, and respect for local cultures in the early church as the gospel spread outside the religious and cultural confines of Judaism (see Flemming 2005). These breakthroughs in mission theology, attitudes, and practice did not come without conflict and pain in the New Testament, nor will they today. The Bible also demonstrates that both good and evil are to be found in every culture. Culture change will be inevitable when the gospel takes root among a people. The gospel does not impose a particular monolithic culture upon any people but will transform the culture of every people group that embraces it.

We must remember the complex and changing nature of culture. No culture is static; rather, all cultures are in the process of change for good and for bad. This is especially true in today's age of globalization. Cultures are not museum pieces to be preserved at any price. Cultures embody human lives, lives that are entitled to change so long as the people directly affected are the ones who guide that change in an informed manner. Many cultural changes introduced by missionaries have been welcomed. Furthermore, blanket "blasting" of Western culture and naive idealizing of majority world cultures are not appropriate responses to the evils of colonialism or the woes of its victims. Western culture is not a monolithic entity—good or evil. Majority world cultures are not necessarily more honorable. The persistent concept of the "noble savage" must be laid to rest. Conversely, using the label "cultural imperialism" as a sledgehammer to critique the entire missionary enterprise fits neither the historical realities nor the complex nature of culture change and the missionary impact on it (see Dunch 2002).

The gospel challenges and changes every culture. The gospel transforms human cultures, uprooting evil and advancing justice and righteousness. This transformation is not to be equated with westernization or modernity. We needn't apologize for missionaries who fought for the education of women or against the slave trade. Much wisdom is needed to discern the difference between gospel transformation and foreign cultural imposition. The safest approach enables local believers to read the scriptures for themselves and apply them to their life situations. Christ changes lives, and changed lives lead to changed cultures. As people of compassion, missionaries and local Christians alike can play a part in social change, sharing with each other their wisdom, knowledge, resources, and technologies in responsible ways. Compassion will mean working to introduce change to alleviate suffering and injustice, which may at times resemble "civilizing." This leads us to the next approach to the task of missions.

PHILANTHROPY, HUMANIZATION, AND LIBERATION AS THE TASK OF MISSIONS

Historical Development

In the early period of Protestant mission, philanthropy was a common feature of the missionary task. Though it may appear at times similar to civilization and is not always free from condescension, philanthropy is in its general tenor quite different. Its goal is to alleviate suffering, demonstrate compassion, and help people reach their full human potential. This latter aspect is termed humanization. Mission as liberation is a particular form of humanization that is more focused on alleviating social injustice and breaking the bonds of poverty, usually through systemic political, social, or economic change.

Starting with the earliest Protestant missionaries, hospitals, schools, orphanages, literacy programs, leprosaria, and other institutions of compassion were established. Nigerian theologian Yusufu Turaki writes of Africa: "Christian missions have done more to bring about social, religious, and human development and change than any other human agent in Africa south of the Sahara. . . . They made substantial contributions to nation-state building and to modernizing African societies" (2000, 275). Indeed, in many countries missionaries can receive visas only if they provide philanthropic or development services.

The notion that philanthropy is ancillary to evangelism in mission work began to change at the close of the nineteenth century. Around 1890 the conviction that people who had not heard of Christ were lost for eternity began to erode in many circles. Missionary concern in such groups came to be increasingly focused on alleviating human need in this life (Forman 1977, 112).

In the late nineteenth century, Walter Rauschenbusch (1861–1918), Henry Emerson Fosdick (1878–1970), and others began promoting the social gospel, which defined sin in social terms and advocated realization of the kingdom of God on earth through social action and change, a christianization of the social order. It must be noted that Rauschenbusch believed in the necessity of evangelism and personal conversion but rejected what he regarded as one-sided premillennial views that undermined work for social progress (Fishburn 2004, 235).

Christianization was, however, unwittingly assumed to be the American way of life (Verkuyl 1978, 196). In 1912 Rauschenbusch believed that the United States was almost christianized (Fishburn 2004, 236). Though World War I was a setback to such optimism, the fundamentalist-modernist debate in America filled the sagging sails of the social gospel with fresh wind. Hopes were also high that the world could be made safe for democracy. In the years following World War I, more liberal American missions increased emphasis on social action: adult education, literacy, agriculture, and so on (Forman 1977, 96). Social evil was attacked at the microstructural level (individual aid, education, and employment). Only later would liberation theologies seek to alter society at the macrostructural level (i.e., economic and political systems).

Evangelicals rejected the social gospel and thus shied away from any social agenda whatsoever for church and mission. The fundamentalist-modernist debate polarized the positions further, impacting mission work and theology. Modernists tended to increasingly emphasize mission as democratization and improvement of living standards. Hospitals and schools were no longer seen as *means* or *partners* of evangelism, but as *ends* in themselves. At the IMC in Jerusalem (1928) the shift in conciliar thinking was evident. Newbigin summarized the meeting: "The preaching of the Gospel and the service of men's needs are equally authentic and essential parts of the Church's responsibility" (cited in Bassham 1979, 342). The missionary came to be viewed more and more as philanthropist, explorer, or development worker. Non-Christian religions were no longer viewed as inherently false or evil. The Laymen's Foreign Missionary Enquiry report *Rethinking Missions* (1932) advocated that social service should not be subordinated or necessarily linked to proclamation but should be done for its own sake.

By the mid-1930s the dark clouds of National Socialism and fascism were gathering over Europe. German missiologists protested the secularization of mission. Freytag was typical of the Germans who initially resisted any political or secular agenda for mission. "[Missions] is not to bring in new circumstances nor to create and develop programs of a political, cultural, social or even confessional nature. It has this one mandate alone, that the message of God will be believed" (Freytag 1940, 306). By the 1940s American evangelicals such as Samuel M. Zwemer, Robert H. Glover, and Harold Lindsell were writing reactive theologies aimed at returning to more biblically based missiology, emphasizing a high view of scripture and the biblical mandate for missions.

But in conciliar missions the more socially oriented voices were to prevail. Evangelism was being redefined as good news in the form of good works. The American J. Merle Davis, serving on the IMC, wrote in 1947, "Evangelism is cure of sick bodies, of broken down, inefficient, and eroded farms, of illiteracy, of insufficient and unbalanced diet, unsanitary homes, impure drinking water" (cited in Forman 1977, 97).

One of the most significant voices to emerge in the mid-twentieth century was that of Johannes Christiaan Hoekendijk (1912–75), secretary of the Netherlands Missionary Council. As noted above, he energetically opposed "ecclesiocentric" goals of mission such as church planting and growth. "Church-centric missionary thinking is bound to go astray, because it revolves around an illegitimate center" (Hoekendijk 1952, 332). The sending of the church is a sending to serve the world. He defined the kingdom of God largely in terms of justice for the poor and oppressed and argued that this should be the center of mission. From this viewpoint came the controversial watchword, "The world sets the agenda for the church." According to Hoekendijk the church is only one means among many that God uses to establish his kingdom: "There is a stubborn tradition in our midst that interprets the aim of evangelism as the planting of the church (or even the extension of the church). . . . [But] the church is (nothing more and nothing less!) a means in God's hand to establish shalom in this world" (1966, 23–25).

The church should thus participate in political or other movements that work for justice in the world, be they explicitly Christian or not, because these are signs of God's work in the world for his kingdom. Though numerous missiologists within the conciliar movement rejected Hoekendijk's radicalization, the tenor of his approach prevailed. The Swiss missiologist Ludwig Rütti was the Roman Catholic counterpart of Hoekendijk and proposed a similar secularization of mission.

Thomas Kramm (1979) describes this development as a fundamental split in eschatological thinking at the time. On the one hand was a salvation-historical, ecclesiological model, distinguishing between the church and the world, held by the Germans and the evangelicals. On the other hand was a historical-eschatological model identifying salvation history with human history, whereby the role of the church is ambiguous. The latter view became the dominant theme within conciliar theology of mission. By the time of the third plenary meeting of the WCC in New Delhi (1961), salvation history was viewed as being increasingly realized in the course of human history. Mission as participation in God's work in the secular world dominated the WCC General Assembly in Uppsala (1968), with the world setting the agenda of mission. "Everything became mission at Uppsala: health and welfare services, youth projects, work with political interest groups, constructive use of violence, the protection of human rights" (D. J. Bosch 1980, 190). Europeans preferred the term *shalom* as the goal of mission; Americans preferred the term *humanization*.

The report from Uppsala states, "We have lifted up humanization as the goal of mission because we believe that more than others it communicates in our period of history the meaning of the messianic goal." Of the earlier views of mission as spiritual redemption the report continues, "It was assuming that the purpose of mission was Christianization, bringing man to God through Christ and his church. Today the fundamental question is much more that of *true* man, and the dominant concern of the missionary congregation must therefore be to point to the humanity in Christ as the goal of mission" (cited in D. J. Bosch 1991, 383).

This trend climaxed at the CWME meeting Bangkok (1972/73) under the theme of "Salvation Today," whereby salvation was understood primarily in sociopolitical terms. Indian lay theologian and then moderator of the WCC (1968–75) M. M. Thomas was a vocal advocate of the humanization view. In his address at Bangkok he stated, "Herein lies the mission of the church: to participate in the movements of human liberation in our time in such a way as to witness to Jesus Christ as the Source, the Judge and Redeemer of the human spirituality and its orientation which are at work in these movements, and therefore the Savior of man today" ([1972] 2002, 87). "Salvation itself could be defined as humanisation in a total eschatological sense. And all our struggles on earth for the fragmentary realization of man's humanity point to this eschatological humanisation as their judgement and fulfilment" (95).

This draws attention to a parallel and related theological development that has deeply impacted conciliar mission thinking: liberation theology. Liberation theology was initially influenced by the political theologies of Jürgen Moltmann and Johann Baptist Metz. Latin American liberation theologians such as Gustavo Gutiérrez were particularly concerned about social change at the macro level that would alleviate poverty and empower the oppressed. Social analysis became essential to theology, and many of these theologies were strongly Marxist in orientation. Praxis and identification with the oppressed were to precede and shape theological reflection. According to Gutiérrez, the theologian "will be someone who is personally and vitally engaged in historical realities with specific times and places. . . . In the last analysis, the true interpretation of the meaning revealed by theology is achieved only in historical praxis" (1973, 13). By discerning the "signs of the times," the church could identify movements of God's mission for justice within history. Various other liberation theologies developed addressing injustices in Asia, Africa, and among African Americans.

Such theologies generally share the conviction that the kingdom of God is realized within history through the struggle for justice and the liberation of the oppressed. Mission becomes linked with this struggle. Even the Maoist revolution in China was viewed as an instrument of the kingdom heralding a new era of salvation history (see Sanneh 2008, 251–55). The failure of many hopeful reform movements and the global collapse of communism in 1990 have led to reassessment in liberation theologies. They nevertheless remain a powerful voice within conciliar missions.

Such theological developments further deepened the breach between evangelical and conciliar missions. Evangelical missiologists such as Donald McGavran, Peter Beyerhaus, Arthur Johnstone, and David Hesselgrave argued for the spiritual agenda of mission through evangelism and church planting, often to the exclusion of any social agenda whatsoever. Social change might be a fruit but was certainly not the root of Christian mission. On the other hand, as we shall see in the next chapter, other evangelicals began to reassess their rejection of a social agenda for mission.

Following Bangkok, the WCC General Assembly held in Nairobi (1975) began to distance itself from radical politicizing of mission and started to recover a place for evangelism without abandoning the social agenda. Section Report I from Nairobi, "Confessing Christ Today," reads, "The gospel includes: the announcement of God's kingdom and love through Jesus Christ, the offer of grace and forgiveness of sins, the invitation to repentance and faith in him, the summons to fellowship in God's church, the command to witness to God's saving words and deeds, the responsibility to participate in the struggle for justice and human dignity, the obligation to denounce all that hinders human wholeness, and a commitment to risk life itself" (Paton 1975, 52).

At the CWME in Melbourne (1980), one spoke more of "holistic mission" and returned to viewing the church as God's primary instrument of mission. Following Lausanne (1974) many evangelicals began to argue for social action as a part of mission (to be discussed in the following chapter). Attempts were made at the CWME in San Antonio (1989) to bridge gaps between the WCC and evangelicals, but these efforts bore meager fruit. Conciliar mission thinking remained too ambiguous in matters relating not only to social action but also to the value of non-Christian religions and the uniqueness of Christ. This has made genuine rapprochement between evangelical and conciliar mission difficult. Beyerhaus (1996, 14) rightly notes that the differences are of a fundamental theological nature and should not be merely glossed over with pragmatic solutions to the tension.

Assessment

We have traced a long road in mission thinking from a basic compassionate concern for the practical needs of people, but which is subordinate to spiritual and eternal needs, to a view that places social and economic needs at the very center of mission, to the exclusion of conversion or spiritual needs. Though most in the conciliar movement have moderated, moving away from the more extreme positions, the fundamental concern for a realized kingdom within history in the form of justice and humanization remains central to much conciliar missiology. We assess here the conciliar approach. Evangelical approaches to social action and holistic mission will be dealt with in the next chapter.

Humanization and liberation understandings have taken seriously the plight of the poor, oppressed, and marginalized. Approaches to mission that declare simplistic spiritual answers for all humanity's problems without also addressing the sociopolitical roots of those problems are neither credible nor in the spirit of the gospel. God's concern for the plight of the poor and disenfranchised is well attested in the Old Testament, in the life of Jesus, and in the early church. "The righteous care about justice for the poor, but the wicked have no such concern" (Prov. 29:7). The question is not whether the church *should* be concerned about the poor and the economic systems that contribute to poverty and oppression; rather, the question is *how* such issues should be addressed and how such concerns relate to the overall task of missions.

Mission as humanization and liberation is based on a secularized understanding of mission. Evangelism is often redefined in terms of alleviating physical, social, and economic need. Eschatology becomes an inner-historical hope based primarily on the power of social change. Bosch comments on this development, "Mission became an umbrella term for health and welfare services, youth projects, activities of political interest groups, projects for economic and social development, the constructive application of violence, etc." (1991, 383). Indeed, *mission* and *missionary* become shorthand for the discharge of societal responsibilities, and the gospel becomes merely social ethics (507). Such extreme views made the church expendable and were naively optimistic, making disappointment inevitable. W. A. Visser 't Hooft at the WCC assembly in Uppsala voiced a concern for balance: "A Christianity which has lost its vertical dimension has lost its salt, and is not only insipid in itself, but useless to the world. But a Christianity which would use the vertical dimension as a means to escape from responsibility for and in the common life of men is a denial of the incarnation of God's life for the world manifested in Christ" (cited in Hoffman 1975, 698).

Humanization and liberation downplay the spiritual needs of men and women. The depth of human sinfulness and the need for life-transforming spiritual renewal in Christ are underestimated. Can mission be considered *Christian* if the spiritual state of the people involved is considered secondary? Did not Jesus himself say, "Do not be afraid of those who kill the body but cannot kill the soul. Rather, be afraid of the One who can destroy both soul and body in hell" (Matt. 10:28), and "What good is it for a man to gain the whole world, yet forfeit his soul?" (Mark 8:36). Mission must take seriously not only the temporal needs but especially the eternal needs of lost men and women.

Surely a view of mission as an exclusively inner-historical realization of the kingdom strictly in terms of liberation and justice must be rejected as unbiblical. Newbigin, while affirming the need for social change as a part of mission ([1978] 1995, 109), reminds that this must be placed in a larger perspective on the missionary task: "The demand for unity among the churches and the demand for justice and peace among the nations, if they are not rooted in what God has done for all the world in Jesus Christ, can themselves become new forms of domination. There cannot be any greater task, or any deeper joy than to tell the world what God has done for us in Jesus Christ and to enable others to know, love, and serve him as Lord and Savior" (1997, 52).

Mission as humanization and justice has a deficient theology of the cross. Jesus becomes in many such theologies merely an example of a social reformer, an innocent sufferer, or a friend of the oppressed. Redemption is understood in this-worldly terms, and Christ's work is one of mere inspiration and identification. The cross is emptied of its redemptive power. Such an understanding of mission is surely very distant from that of the apostle Paul, who could say, "I resolved to know nothing while I was with you except Jesus Christ and him crucified" (1 Cor. 2:2). There can be no kingdom without Jesus, the cross, and the act of repentance and faith that brings men and women into the kingdom as new creatures in Christ (John 3:3; 2 Cor. 5:17). Newbigin asks, "How does one interpret the cross in relation to the (perfectly legitimate) aspirations of the Jews of Jesus' time for political liberation?" ([1978] 1995, 101). Jesus was not a political revolutionary in the usual sense of the term, and he clearly disappointed such expectations.

Humanization and liberation give little attention to the mandate to disciple the nations. Matthew's Great Commission calls the church to make disciples of all nations (Matt. 28:19–20). The Matthean commission is not merely relegated to a secondary place, but it is entirely absent from most approaches to mission as humanization. McGavran's question at Uppsala, "what about the two billion unevangelized?" has yet to be taken seriously in postwar conciliar missiology. Once evangelism has been redefined in more social and material terms and the soteriological efficacy of non-Christian religions has also been elevated, the need to bring the gospel as a message of eternal salvation to the yet-unreached peoples of the world is virtually irrelevant. The vision of people from *every* nation worshipping the Lamb of God (Rev. 5:9; 7:9) is absent from this vision of the kingdom.

Making political or economic agendas central to mission risks making mission the handmaid of human agendas and political ideologies. The current political and economic ideology (be it Marxism, democracy, or free-market capitalism) is easily identified with the kingdom of God or as a movement of God. D. J. Bosch (1991, 492) notes that the church has been notorious in misreading the signs of the times, hailing everything from National Socialism to apartheid to Marxism as God's work in history. Christians tend to sacralize the dominant sociological forces of history. Beyerhaus (1996, 267) warns that there is no universally recognized standard for social reform. Indeed, these standards change rapidly with the latest social theories and definitions of political correctness. Mission history is replete with examples of mission having been compromised by human agendas such as the crusades, the conquistadores, and colonial imperialism. The agenda of mission must hold tightly to the divine mandate revealed in scripture. The church is to communicate and live out the values of the kingdom, remembering that these can never be too closely confused with specific human institutions and movements.

Conciliar understandings of mission have led to dramatic decline in foreign mission efforts. For example, the number of missionaries sent by WCC-related mainline denominations dropped from 80 percent in 1900 to only 6 percent of all North American missionaries by the end of the century. Alone from 1952 to 1996, the number of missionaries from conciliar churches dropped from 8,800 to 2,900. Numerous major denominations eliminated their foreign mission boards altogether or subordinated them to other national ministries. There are various reasons for this, which Paul E. Pierson has outlined (2003), but most fundamental was the redefinition of mission as all that the church does in the world. The spiritual needs of people apart from Christ were no longer central. Pierson draws lessons from developments in conciliar missions: "First, it is clear that mission can go forward only if based on an adequate biblical

---

SIDEBAR 5.3
"GOD'S PREFERENTIAL OPTION FOR THE POOR"

Since the 1970s one of the most controversial phrases in theology of mission has been "God's preferential option for the poor." Though used more widely by conciliar and Roman Catholic theologians, many evangelicals—particularly those in the majority world—have also adopted this language (see Walker 1992). God "opts" for the poor and disadvantaged by being their defender. He sides with them not by loving them more than others but by exercising righteousness and justice on their behalf. His love for them is evidence of his love for all. It is thus argued that the church is obligated to become an advocate and defender of the poor by not merely alleviating their poverty but also by working toward the transformation of oppressive social and economic structures. Moreover, "the poor are not to be seen as objects of mercy, but as people who are particularly gifted by God to represent his justice to the rest of the world" (Moreau 2000c, 711).

REFLECTION AND DISCUSSION

Read these Bible passages and consider what you believe to be the appropriate response of Christian mission to the problem of poverty and addressing the needs of the poor.

1. Exodus 23:3, 6; Leviticus 19:15
2. Psalm 35:10; 82:3–4; 140:12
3. Proverbs 10:4; 19:17; 20:13; 21:13
4. Isaiah 10:1–2; 25:4; 58:6–8
5. Matthew 19:21; Luke 4:18–19

---

and theological foundation. . . . I am convinced that the center, though not the totality, of mission must always involve calling men and women to faith in Jesus Christ, gathering them into worshipping and witnessing communities" (2003, 81).

Though the secularization of mission in political movements, humanization, and social ethics must be rejected as betrayal of the very core of the gospel, the concerns are legitimate. God is concerned for the plight of the poor, the oppressed, and the marginalized. This is a recurrent theme in the prophets and in Luke's Gospel. Although these concerns alone cannot comprise the central task of missions, they do represent genuine needs that the gospel addresses (see sidebar 5.3).

CONCLUSION

Protestant understandings of the task of missions developed from a broad consensus focusing primarily on evangelism accompanied by works of compassion and development to quite divergent emphases driven by opposing convictions regarding the very foundations of mission. During the second half of the twentieth century, considerable tension and polarization about these questions grew between conciliar and evangelical wings of Protestantism.

The foregoing discussion has demonstrated that the various approaches and emphases each have their strengths and weaknesses when biblically assessed. So what then is the place of philanthropy and humanization in a biblical understanding of the task of missions? What is the role of the church and church planting in mission? How does evangelism relate to social action in the missionary endeavor? To these questions we now turn.

6

The Task of Missions

Convergence and Conclusions

The story of theology of mission, as described in the previous chapter, developed well into the 1970s somewhat tumultuously with great controversy and divisions. Only toward the end of the twentieth century has there been moderation in the positions and some rapprochement between evangelical and conciliar missiologists. Meanwhile, within evangelical theology of mission, positions began to emerge giving greater attention to social action as a part of mission.

Various evangelical theologies have emerged defining themselves as holistic (sometimes spelled wholistic) because they seek to understand mission in terms of ministry to the whole person. Other terms used for similar positions include *integral mission* or *transformative mission.* These approaches represent attempts to achieve a convergence of the traditional evangelical concern for proclamation and church planting with a more comprehensive view of mission including social action and compassion ministries.

In some ways the evangelical debate regarding the relationship of evangelism and social action has been unfruitful. Charles Ringma notes two reasons for this: "The first is that the biblical story reflects God's concern for the whole person, the community, and the created order. . . . Second, in the long history of the Christian church there is no *major* tradition not affirming that love of

God involves love of neighbor and not teaching that the church has a missional, prophetic and transformative role in the world" (2004, 434).

Nevertheless, the debate has emerged from various legitimate theological, historical, and practical concerns. Before proposing our approach to integrating these concerns, we briefly examine the evangelical discussion thus far.

EVANGELICALS, SOCIAL ACTION, AND HOLISTIC MISSION

True followers of Christ have always been people of compassion and concern for the plight of the poor and underprivileged. This concern was characteristic of Jesus, of the early Christians, and of the church and missionaries throughout history. However, toward the end of the nineteenth century various theological developments served to polarize approaches to mission. On the one hand, liberal groups relativized the message of the Bible and questioned the necessity of evangelism. The postmillennial social gospel emphasized inner-worldly improvements to usher in the kingdom of God (Fishburn 2004). On the other hand, premillennialism became more prominent among evangelicals, and the urgency of evangelism increased with the belief in Christ's immanent return and ensuing judgment. World evangelization, not social programs, would hasten Christ's return. Improvement of this world prior to Christ's return was viewed by some as futile. The North American modernist-fundamentalist debate in the early twentieth century heightened the divisions. Conciliar groups tended more toward social service; fundamentalists and evangelicals tended to emphasize evangelism (see Patterson 1990).

> *Social action is that set of activities whose primary goal is improving the physical, socio-economic and political well-being of people through relief, development, and structural change.*
>
> Ron Sider (1993, 165)

In the wake of this debate, evangelical missions did not cease to be compassionate, as they are sometimes caricatured, and continued to operate hospitals, schools, and orphanages. But such works were considered subordinate to evangelism and church planting. In 1902 Robert E. Speer termed the proposal that foreign missions reorganize the social fabric "a mischievous doctrine." He argued that missions should implant the life of Christ in the hearts of all people and leave the results to God (cited in Peters 1972, 171). Efforts to change social, political, or economic structures were viewed with considerable suspicion as a compromise to the social gospel.

The appearance of Carl F. H. Henry's *Uneasy Conscience of Modern Fundamentalism* in 1947 signaled an early shift in evangelical social ethics, reclaiming social action as a legitimate biblical concern. When radical conciliar views of mission as humanization and liberation emerged in the 1960s and 1970s, the polarization in mission circles was heightened. But already in 1966 a gradual change in evangelical thinking was apparent at the World Congress on Evangelism in Berlin, where social dimensions of the gospel were explored in several papers. Also in 1966 the Congress on the Church's Worldwide Mission was held at Wheaton. The resulting Wheaton Declaration recognized evangelical failures in biblically addressing various social problems and called for evangelical social action and concern for justice. Such action, wherever possible, was to be accompanied by verbal witness to the gospel (Wheaton Declaration 1966, 13, 24).

In 1973 the Workshop on Evangelicals and Social Concern held in Chicago produced the Chicago Declaration of Evangelical Social Concern and birthed Evangelicals for Social Action (ESA). One of the stated core values of ESA reads, "The CHURCH is called to be a model of the Kingdom of God as it points to the person of Jesus Christ and works towards God's vision of a just society. Evangelism and social transformation are indivisible in the work of the kingdom" (ESA n.d.).

Numerous evangelical theologians from the majority world began to express impatience with a missiology that was perceived to dichotomize the spiritual and the material needs of people. At the Lausanne Congress on World Evangelization in 1974, several papers were presented addressing social responsibility and mission (Douglas 1975). An ad hoc group also formed to draft a paper titled "Theology and Implications of Radical Discipleship" (1975) advocating a bolder stance on the importance of social action in mission. The Lausanne Covenant reflects this concern in Article 5, "Christian Social Responsibility," which reads in part, "Although reconciliation with other people is not reconciliation with God, nor is social action evangelism, nor is political liberation salvation, nevertheless we affirm that evangelism and socio-political involvement are both part of our Christian duty. . . . When people receive Christ they are born again into his kingdom and must seek not only to exhibit but also to spread its righteousness in the midst of an unrighteous world." Conciliar efforts to define mission as social action and salvation as political liberation are explicitly rejected, and a distinction between evangelism and social action is retained. But both are regarded as a Christian duty.

In 1975 John R. W. Stott released his *Christian Mission in the Modern World*, marking a shift in his thinking. He had come to view the Johannine version of the Great Commission in John 17:18 and 20:21—to be sent as Jesus was sent—as the most crucial formulation, taking precedence over the Matthean formulation (to make disciples). He viewed social action as an equal though independent partner of evangelism, while retaining the primacy of evangelism over other activities that may rightly be called mission. This development was especially significant due to Stott's leadership within the Lausanne movement and his general acceptance as one of evangelicalism's most respected mission statesmen. In a later book, *The Contemporary Christian* (1992), Stott devoted an entire chapter to "Holistic Mission" (337–55).

Numerous other evangelicals also began to link John 20:21 with Luke 4:18–19, arguing that to be sent as Jesus was sent means proclaiming good news to the poor and setting the captives free in a literal sense. Mission so conceived has a social-ethical obligation, and discipling the nations is viewed as just one aspect of mission. Jesus's ministry became the paradigm for mission, replacing the example of the early apostolic mission described in Acts. In the words of Samuel Escobar, "Jesus was sent by God the Father and was God's best missionary, the true model for Christian mission" (2003, 99).

By the 1980s the evangelical missiological discussion was in full swing with numerous publications and consultations seeking to clarify an evangelical position regarding the place of social action in mission and its relationship to evangelism. Perhaps the most significant was the LCWE-sponsored international Consultation on the Relationship between Evangelism and Social Responsibility (CRESR, 1982) in Grand Rapids, Michigan. Participants represented a balance of geographical regions, denominational backgrounds, and evangelical viewpoints. The resulting report, Lausanne Occasional Paper (LOP) 21 (LCWE 1982), concluded that social action is a *consequence of, a bridge to, and a partner of evangelism.*

> Evangelism, even when it does not have a primarily social intention, nevertheless has a social dimension, while social responsibility, even when it does not have a primarily evangelistic intention, nevertheless has an evangelistic dimension.
>
> Thus, evangelism and social responsibility, while distinct from one another, are integrally related in our proclamation of and obedience to the gospel. The partnership is, in reality, a marriage. (LOP 21, C)

It maintained that evangelism has a "certain priority":

> Seldom if ever should we have to choose between satisfying physical hunger and spiritual hunger, or between healing bodies and saving souls, since an authentic love for our neighbour will lead us to serve him or her as a whole person. Nevertheless, if we must choose, then we have to say that the supreme and ultimate need of all humankind is the saving grace of Jesus Christ, and that therefore a person's eternal, spiritual salvation is of greater importance than his or her temporal and material well-being (cf. 2 Cor. 4:16–18). (LOP 21, D)

Considerable attention was given to the nature of the kingdom of God and signs of the kingdom. Eschatology was addressed, concluding that utopian visions of human accomplishment must be rejected and that ultimate hope must remain in the work of God. A helpful distinction between social service (relieving human need, philanthropy, etc.) and social action (removing causes of human need, political activity, structural social change, etc.) was made. Overall, the report was balanced and irenic, providing a helpful basis for evangelical consensus. Some felt that the statement did not go far enough. But even René Padilla, one of the more ardent advocates of social action, would later comment that the CRESR statement could hardly be improved upon (2002, 55).

In 1983 the World Evangelical Fellowship sponsored the Consultation on the Church in Response to Human Need at Wheaton. In the third track of this consultation, evangelicals not only embraced social responsibility but began with greater boldness to speak of holistic mission. For example, Edward R. Dayton, then vice president of World Vision, wrote in his paper, "And what is social transformation for the Christian? Is it not the entire business that God is about, namely, the redemption of the world?

> *Looking at proclamation and demonstration in making known the Kingdom of God we need to see them constituting one whole. . . . Not merely parts held together, not even priorities maintained, but our primary concern is for a submission to God as representatives of his Kingdom so that his purposes will be accomplished through the obedience of his people. Mission will be incomplete unless seen from the whole horizon of the Kingdom.*
>
> Ken Gnanakan (1989, 206)

And is not the *mission* of the church social transformation in every dimension?" (Dayton 1987, 54). The consultation statement called the church to promote not merely "development" but "transformation" directed at structural social and economic change (Samuel and Sugden 1987, 256–58).

During these years evangelicals produced a sizable body of literature advocating holistic mission and calling for social action (e.g., Costas 1974, 1979, 1982; Escobar and Driver 1978; Dyrness 1983; Padilla 1985). Advocates of holistic mission sought to biblically ground their position in several ways. Some, as noted above, focused on Jesus, who ministered to the whole person, as the model for mission. Others emphasized the expansion of the kingdom of God as the most comprehensive way to define mission, moving away from narrowly defined tasks such as evangelism or specific social projects: "The demands of the kingdom do not encompass only personal and ecclesial affairs, but also social and institutional issues. This new order is not limited to the community of faith. Instead it embraces all of history and the universe, and it is the task of the ecclesial community to witness to that all-encompassing reality" (Costas 1982, 93; see also Kirk 1983, 16, 55; Gnanakan 1989).

Another approach defined salvation in terms of the whole person and not merely as forgiveness of sin and eternal life. David J. Bosch observes, "One's theology of mission is always closely dependent on one's theology of salvation; it would therefore be correct to say that the scope of salvation—however we define salvation—determines the scope of the missionary enterprise" (1991, 393). For example, at Lausanne, Padilla pleaded for "a concept of salvation that includes the whole man and cannot be reduced to the simple forgiveness of sins and assurance of unending life with God in heaven. A comprehensive mission corresponds to a comprehensive view of salvation. Salvation is whole-ness. Salvation is total humanization" (Padilla 1975, 130).

Ronald J. Sider (1993, 29) relates holistic ministry to a holistic anthropology and holistic understanding of salvation. Proponents such as Ken R. Gnanakan (1989) reject any attempt to prioritize evangelism or social action.

Costas described the comprehensiveness of the missionary mandate: "No dichotomies here: not a vertical vs. horizontal emphasis of mission; not re-demption vs. humanization—but a holistic vision of God's mission to the world and the church's role in it" (1974, 309).

Responses to Evangelical Holistic Mission

Evangelical advocates of holistic mission have not been without their critics. Early along Harold Lindsell argued that social ministries should be undertaken only insofar as they "pragmatically" contribute to evangelism and the higher goals of mission (1955, 189).

Donald A. McGavran, as we have seen, argued for the primacy of evange-lism and church planting in mission over all else that the church undertakes. Indeed, all other activities of the church "must contribute to, and not crowd out, maximum reconciliation of men with God in the Church of Jesus Christ" ([1970] 1980, 43). His primary line of reasoning was that only personal conver-sion and church planting would lead to personal and social change. Though he himself had directed a leprosarium, he was convinced that "salvation granted to those who believe in Jesus Christ is still the supreme need of man, and all other human good flows from that prior reconciliation to God" (ibid.). Over time "social lift" will occur as people adopt biblical priorities in life (297–98). He further argued that it is not the place of *missions* to foment social activ-ism, for missionaries are guests in a land. Rather, it is the responsibility of the *church* to work for social change, for it is composed of local citizens (292). "*When churches multiply in a non-Christian population*, they will bring God's purposes to bear on the particular part of the social order which they can influence" (293). Thus, he continues, there should be no tension between advocates of mission and advocates of social action. Both are necessary, but both are not the responsibility of missions. This reflects the traditional dis-tinction between the work of a local church and the work of missions as that of missionaries advancing the gospel among the unreached.

McGavran and the Church Growth Movement received considerable cri-tique from advocates of holistic mission (e.g., Costas 1974). C. Peter Wagner, a popular spokesperson of the movement, responded with his book *Church Growth and the Whole Gospel* in 1981, calling himself a believer in holistic mission (91) while maintaining the priority of evangelism. Similar posi-tions were taken by German missiologists Peter Beyerhaus (1974) and Erhard Berneburg (1997, 360–64).

David Hesselgrave has been one of the most ardent critics of holistic definitions of mission. Based in part on Andreas J. Köstenberger's (1998a) interpretation of John 20:21, he argues that holistic mission has an inadequate biblical basis. He claims that the Matthean formulation of the Great Commission is the "final and most complete statement on the subject" (1999, 281; also 1990). He advocates with Little (2005) that the apostle Paul is the best model for mission (Hesselgrave 2005, 141–65). He promotes what he calls the traditional view of "prioritism" (in contrast to holism), which doesn't rule out the place of social action in mission but gives clear priority to evangelism and church planting (2005, 117–39).

Complicating Factors in the Holistic Mission Debate

Though the CRESR report in 1982 offered a minimal basis of evangelical consensus to move the discussion forward, some tension within the evangelical movement over the relationship of evangelism and social action remains to the present. The debate is complicated and problematic in at least two ways.

First, within evangelicalism much of the discussion reflects a polarization emerging from the differing historical and contextual backgrounds of the discussion partners. Many opponents of holistic mission fear that evangelical missiology will develop in the direction of conciliar missiology, which redefined mission and in some cases jettisoned evangelism and church planting altogether. They fear that mission may be hijacked by a particular social agenda. Hesselgrave notes, for example, that by the end of the twentieth century only 6 percent of all missionaries from North America were from mainline denominations, whereas 70 percent were from evangelical agencies (2005, 317). "The missionary endeavor was marginalized in part because the ecumenical vision of mission was gradually broadened by the W.C.C. to include everything the church does in the world—and even what God does outside the church. The effort to carry out *missio Dei* came to be divorced from obedience to the Great commission" (323).

On the other hand, advocates of holistic mission often come from contexts where poverty and injustice are deeply pressing concerns (see Chapman 2009). They view strictly spiritual solutions as inadequate. They argue that the gospel lacks credibility and is compromised where compassion and social action are not intentionally combined with proclamation. They are impatient with a status quo mentality regarding structural injustice, which has often characterized the church and mission work.

Many of the arguments on both sides of the debate are attempted correctives to real or perceived extreme positions. As Sri Lankan theologian Ajith Fernando says, "The church is notorious for its course corrections" (2007, 40). It lays in the nature of course corrections to state positions in extreme terms, which often leads to positions that are again out of balance.

143

Second, the positions are often not as far apart in practice as they are in the rhetoric. Virtually all evangelical critics of the holistic approach *do* advocate that Christians should exercise compassion and to some extent work against unjust social systems. They simply believe that such activities should be subordinate to evangelism. On the other hand, all evangelical advocates of holistic mission emphasize the importance of proclamation, many even making proclamation a priority. Thus the debate seemingly revolves more around terminology than substance.

A Brief Assessment

Without question the gospel calls men and women to repentance that brings all aspects of life under Christ's lordship. Spiritual life, forgiveness of sin, the reconciled relationship with God, and the power to live righteously begin with repentance and faith in Jesus Christ. There can be no substitute for this, and there can be no farther-reaching decision than this extending into eternity. However, rightly understood and received the gospel leads to transformation at both the personal and the social level in this life. We cannot be satisfied with superficial conversions or nominal church membership. As Tite Tiénou has argued, "Evangelism cannot be privatized or interiorized: it has social effects" (1987, 178). Lives transformed by the Holy Spirit will be lives that not only share the gospel message with others in word but that also manifest in deed the love of God and his concern for the poor and oppressed. Sin affects not only personal but also corporate life, and Christians are called to resist sin in whatever form it appears.

> *The preaching of the Gospel and the service of men's need are equally authentic and essential parts of the church's responsibility. But neither is a substitute for the other. No amount of service, however expert and however generous, is a substitute for the explicit testimony to Jesus Christ. No human deed can of itself take the place of the one deed by which the world is redeemed and to which we must direct men's eyes. There is no equivalent to the Name of Jesus. But equally, the preaching of that Name will be empty, if he who speaks it is not willing to deal honestly and realistically with the issues that his hearers have to face. An escapist preaching which refuses this involvement is no true witness to the Kingdom. We are not to be reporters only, but also signs of the Resurrection, and that means that we are living out in our flesh the experience of victory over the powers of evil. . . . The true relation between the word and the deed is that both must be visibly rooted in the same reality; namely in that new community which is created and indwelt by the Holy Spirit.*
>
> Lesslie Newbigin (1965, 422)

*Verbal witness to the gospel cannot be separated from practical demon-
strations of love and action addressing human need.* To do so would be to
undermine the credibility of the gospel and to be a living denial of the very
message we proclaim. The Bible is abundantly clear on this. We are admonished by our Lord, "In the same way, let your light shine before men, that they
may see your good deeds and praise your Father in heaven" (Matt. 5:16). Paul
speaks of imparting to the Thessalonians not only the gospel but also his very
life (1 Thess. 2:8). Faith apart from works is dead (James 2:14–26). Speaking
about God's love without practicing it is hypocrisy (1 John 3:17–18). Lesslie
Newbigin speaks of an almost inseparable link between preaching the gospel
and action for God's justice, for "again and again the simple logic of the gospel
itself has drawn [those who would emphasize proclamation] irresistibly into
some work of education, healing the sick, feeding the hungry, helping the
helpless" ([1978] 1995, 91–92).

*Scripture clearly teaches God's concern for the poor and oppressed, and
he expects his people to share that concern.* We cite here but a few exemplary
passages. The Lord loves righteousness and justice (e.g., Pss. 11:7; 33:5; 36:6;
89:14; 103:6). The ordinances of the law of Moses protected the poor, the widow,
the orphan, and the alien (e.g., Exod. 23:1–9; Lev. 19:9–15). To pervert justice
would forfeit God's blessing (e.g., Deut. 27:19). The exercise of justice, setting
the oppressed free, feeding the hungry, and clothing the naked, is a condition
for answered prayer and joy in the Lord (Isa. 58:1–14). The prophets repeatedly
denounced injustice and oppression of the poor (e.g., Amos 5:11–12). Scripture
calls God's people to work for the cause of justice and compassion.

> Defend the cause of the weak and fatherless;
>   maintain the rights of the poor and oppressed.
> Rescue the weak and needy;
>   deliver them from the hand of the wicked. (Ps. 82:3–4)

> Learn to do right!
> Seek justice,
>   encourage the oppressed.
> Defend the cause of the fatherless,
>   plead the case of the widow. (Isa. 1:17)

> He has showed you, O man, what is good
> And what does the LORD require of you?
> To act justly and to love mercy
>   and to walk humbly with your God. (Mic. 6:8)

Religion that God our Father accepts as pure and faultless is this: to look after
orphans and widows in their distress and to keep oneself from being polluted by
the world. (James 1:27)

Whether we choose to call this concern a task of missions or to simply call it an ethical mandate, Christians are obligated to demonstrate love and compassion as well as work toward justice for all as a sign of the kingdom and a reflection of God's character.

Though meeting spiritual, physical, psychological, and social needs can hardly be separated in practice, spiritual needs do have greater weight. We affirm the CRESR statement on this point. As demonstrated above, God is indeed concerned about the needs of people as whole persons. However, the attempt to entirely erase the distinction between "vertical" and "horizontal" needs is both unbiblical and misguided. Jesus taught, "Do not be afraid of those who kill the body but cannot kill the soul. Rather, be afraid of the One who can destroy both soul and body in hell" (Matt. 10:28), and, "What good is it for a man to gain the whole world, yet forfeit his soul?" (Mark 8:36). J. Robertson McQuilkin comments, "If all people on earth could prosper and be given a college education, full employment prevailed, all injustice and warfare ceased, and perfect health prevailed, but people remained alienated from God, his father heart would still be broken. His priority for alienated human beings is reconciliation to himself" (1993, 177).

> *The tendency among some evangelicals to downplay verbal proclamation—including persuading people to receive Christ's salvation—demands a fresh call for evangelicals to emphasize the urgency of proactive evangelism. And if talk of priority will help the church to a fresh commitment, then so be it.*
>
> Ajith Fernando (2007, 44)

In light of scripture's clear and repeated teaching on the eternal consequences of one's spiritual state—forgiveness and eternal life versus judgment and eternal condemnation—we must maintain that the spiritual and temporal needs of people cannot be placed on an equal plane.

Fernando, who heartily endorses holistic mission, observes a neglect of proclamation by some advocates of holistic mission. Though uncomfortable with the language of priority, he calls for "a fresh commitment to proactive evangelism" (2007, 41).

Lamin Sanneh (2008, 217–42) has argued persuasively in the spirit of Roland Allen ([1912] 1962a) and Vincent Donovan (1978) for a return to the apostolic approach to mission. There is no greater transforming power than the translation of the gospel message and entrusting that message to the work of the Holy Spirit in the local people. Even the best-intended missionary efforts at social development can smack of colonialism and culturally taint or even emasculate the gospel. But as, so to speak, the lion of the gospel is set loose among a people, then personal, ecclesial, and community change occurs in dramatic and unexpected ways.

146

Rather than using the word *priority* (with its potential confusion; see sidebar 6.1), it may be more helpful to speak of the ultimacy, the added weight or the center of gravity placed by the New Testament on the spiritual dimensions of the missionary task in this age. The task of missions should address the most diverse of human needs, but the ministry of spiritual redemption and transformation remains uniquely central in both method and spirit.

This understanding is reflected in the practice and statistics of North American mission agencies: 61.2 percent of mission agencies, 87.6 percent of missionary personnel, and 45.1 percent of budgets are devoted primarily to evangelism and discipleship, whereas 12.2 percent of agencies, 4.9 percent of workers, and 49.1 percent of budgets are devoted primarily to relief and development (Moreau 2007; Jaffarian 2008, 37).

Jesus's and Paul's ministry serve as complementary paradigms for mission. Attempts to dichotomize these two models (if the term *model* is even appropriate) are unnecessary. Jesus is an example for us in his character, compassion, humble service, and suffering (see John 13:15; 1 Cor. 11:1; Eph. 5:1–2; Phil. 2:5–8; 1 Thess. 1:4; 1 Tim. 1:16; and 1 Pet. 2:21). The redemptive goal of Jesus's mission becomes the foundation of the mission of the church, and the incarnation of Christ models the character of Christian mission (see chap. 4). However, Jesus's ministry must be understood in its salvation-historical context, which did not include an intentional Gentile mission (see chap. 2).

SIDEBAR 6.1
FIVE WAYS THE PRIMACY OF EVANGELISM MIGHT BE UNDERSTOOD

(adapted from Ronald Sider 1993, 167–68)

1. A logical question: Can you have Christian social responsibility without first having Christians?
2. An ontological question: Is anything (or indeed everything) in this world as important as a living relationship with the living God that leads to eternal life?
3. A vocational question: Are not different Christians gifted with different callings, and do they not therefore properly allocate their time very differently?
4. A temporal question: Does not the immediate circumstance (e.g., a devastating flood) influence what in particular situations one does first?
5. A resources question: How do we allocate scarce resources of time, personnel, and money?

REFLECTION AND DISCUSSION

1. What biblical teaching or examples might support the various points listed above?
2. Describe a situation where evangelism would take priority over social responsibility.
3. Describe a situation where social action might take priority over evangelism.

This would be realized in the post-Pentecost ministry of the apostles, exemplified in the work of the apostle Paul. We should thus see both paradigms as complementary: Jesus demonstrating the character of mission, and Paul demonstrating mission to the nations in the age of the Spirit.

Luke 4:18–19 is an unquestionably central passage to understanding the mission of Jesus. With his coming the kingdom of God breaks into history, and this kingdom ultimately brings liberation to all aspects of life. This was demonstrated in the signs of Jesus's earthly ministry, though he did not literally set prisoners free and rejected attempts to make him into a political liberator (e.g., John 6:15). Numerous New Testament scholars argue that "the poor" in Luke 4:18 is best understood metaphorically as "the pious poor" or "the poor in spirit" (see Köstenberger and O'Brien 2001, 115–18, and J. B. Green 1994). Yet if the church is to live as a sign of the kingdom, then it cannot neglect attention to liberation from all aspects of human suffering and sin.

We may choose to make John 20:21 the more central expression of the church's mission, but linking it exclusively to Luke 4:18–19 is incomplete. Our understanding of John 20:21 must be informed also by other sayings of Jesus and the example given to us in the sending of the apostles as described in Acts. With Paul, a pioneering evangelistic and church-planting ministry was most prominent. But we should not overlook the fact that even Paul's ministry was one whereby he imparted "not only the gospel of God but our lives as well" (1 Thess. 2:8). Paul's "planting ministry" was complemented by "watering ministries" of coworkers such as Apollos (e.g., 1 Cor. 3:6).

The church is to be a sign of the kingdom of God, but equating the kingdom with any and all good in the world is misguided. The kingdom of God is characterized by God's reign of peace, justice, compassion, and redemption from all the consequences of sin. At its center is the restored relationship with God.

Political action committees, the Red Cross, and other nonconfessional charitable, humanitarian, and development organizations are worthy and good causes. Human government is a gift of God intended to uphold justice (Rom. 13:1–7). All these efforts help make the world a better place, and Christians may support them. But they are not to be confused with the kingdom of God. Certainly God can and has used even evil nations, such as the Babylonians, for his purposes (Hab. 1:5–11). But nowhere in scripture are we told that unbelievers or secular institutions are somehow contributing to or participating in God's kingdom, even when they do good things. As important as alleviation of suffering and establishment of justice are, the essence of the kingdom of God goes far beyond this. "For the kingdom of God is not a matter of eating and drinking, but of righteousness, peace and joy in the Holy Spirit" (Rom. 14:17).

Kingdom lives and kingdom communities are not characterized only by concern for the poor and oppressed. They are also characterized by personal righteousness in many other ways: "Do you not know that the wicked will not inherit the kingdom of God? Do not be deceived: Neither the sexually immoral nor idolaters nor adulterers nor male prostitutes nor homosexual offenders nor thieves nor the greedy nor drunkards nor slanderers nor swindlers will inherit the kingdom of God" (1 Cor. 6:9–10). Jesus said, "But if I drive out demons by the Spirit of God, then the kingdom of God has come upon you" (Matt. 12:28). Such passages are often overlooked in the discussion of the kingdom and mission.

The societal dimension of the kingdom is realized in this age less through human governments or agencies and more in the life of the church, where God transforms his people. The church is not the kingdom, but it is to be a sign of the kingdom yet to come. As the church lives under God's rule, it becomes a community of love, salt, and light in the world, preaching the good news, demonstrating compassion, advocating justice, and doing good. But the kingdom will be realized in fullness only at the consummation with Christ's return.

Because the Bible itself does not precisely define the term *mission*, we should exercise humility and grace in the ongoing discussion. Whereas the Bible defines terms such as *evangelism*, *salvation*, and *righteousness*, the term *mission* as such is not found in the Bible. The question is: should the task of missions be defined primarily in terms of the mandate of the church to bring the gospel to all nations, or should it be defined more broadly in terms of all that the church should do in relation to the world? As the Lausanne Covenant states, both evangelism and social action are Christian duties. The ongoing discussion should focus on the biblical teaching regarding both obligations in a spirit of grace, humility, and unity in the cause of the gospel.

THE TWO MANDATES AND THE TASK OF MISSIONS

One approach to understanding the responsibilities of the church in the world is in terms of two mandates: the creation mandate and the gospel mandate (see table 6.1). The source of this approach has been traced back to the Reformers, such as John Calvin and Martin Luther. Jonathan Edwards (1703–58) claimed that there were two aspects to redemption: personal conversion, sanctification, and glorification, on the one hand, and creation, history, and providence, on the other (see Chaney 1976, 217). Various missiologists such as George W. Peters (1972, 166–71), Edward C. Pentecost (1982, 37–51), Peter Wagner (1981, 12–14), and Erhard Berneburg (1997, 261–67) have adopted the concept of two mandates to describe the relationship between the two obligations of social action and evangelism. The concept has also been applied to a theology of culture (Hegeman 2004) and politics (Marshall 1985).

Framing the church's responsibility in the world in terms of the two mandates is a comprehensive way to express God's concern for the totality of human life and creation. The aforementioned debate tended to focus on

149

specific activities such as evangelism to save souls or social action to alleviate poverty and oppression.

The Creation Mandate

The creation mandate, also called the cultural mandate or the social mandate, describes the divine intent for human life and culture as it applies to all peoples. It is based on the creation order as described in Genesis 1:26–31. In the words of Arthur F. Glasser, "the totality of human existence and the physical world comes within the concern of the cultural mandate" (Glasser et al. 2003, 39). All women and men are created in God's image and thus have dignity and worth, no matter how fallen or marred this image has become. Life is sacred. Work is good. Humans are given authority to rule over creation and are stewards of the environment. Family life is the most fundamental social structure for procreation and human relationships.

The most essential elements of the creation mandate were established prior to the fall. But particularly in a fallen world, human government becomes necessary to order social life, protect basic human rights, and restrain the destructive outworking of human sinfulness (Rom. 13; 1 Pet. 2:13–14). All societies have ways of raising children, caring for the weak, providing for the elderly, governing their affairs, and coping with crises. All societies also have some form of creative expression, which may include art, music, dance, rituals, oral traditions, literature, and the like.

God's creation order does not call for uniformity in the way that these various relationships are structured. But the creation order does require maintaining underlying ethical values such as protecting human dignity, stewardship of the environment, justice, and compassion. The Ten Commandments might be viewed as the most fundamental statement of a creation ethic essential to the well-being of all people (Berneburg 1997, 268).

Because of the sinful state of all humans, all societies are fallen and fail to attain God's intention for human fulfillment, culture, and government. Christians live in the hope that one day God's rule will be restored over all creation; then all these values and relationships will be brought back into perfect alignment with the creation mandate. But Christians work in this age toward the realization of that hope as God's grace provides opportunity.

Though the creation mandate is given to all people, God's people have a particular obligation to lead the way in its fulfillment. "The cultural mandate calls Christians to responsible participation in human society, including working for social justice and the healing and compassion ministries undertaken to foster human welfare" (Bassham 1979, 343). As Christopher J. H. Wright (2006) has so thoroughly demonstrated, the Old Testament people of God, Israel, was to manifest in the midst of the nations the righteousness and reign of God spiritually, socially, and economically in all its relationships.

150

TABLE 6.1
GOD'S CONCERN FOR THE TOTALITY OF HUMAN LIFE

	Creation Mandate	Gospel Mandate
Given to and binding for…	all humanity (Christians and non-Christians alike)	Christians and the church
The purpose is…	provide for human well-being in an ordered and just society	provide for a restored relationship with God and freedom from effects of sin in all areas of life
Applies to…	human dignity, family, government, stewardship of the environment, care for the poor and weak, creative expression	spiritual life, vertical and horizontal reconciliation, bringing all aspects of life under the lordship of the King
Primary biblical basis…	Gen. 1–2; Exod. 20:1–17; Jer. 29:7; Mic. 6:8; Rom. 13; Gal. 6:10; 1 Pet. 2:13–14	Matt. 28:19–20; Acts 1:8; Eph. 2
Advocated by…	the state, institutions, action groups, philanthropic and development organizations; the church as salt and light	the church, mission agencies
Typical activities…	social action, hospitals, schools, relief efforts, economic development, family advocacy, environmental protection, etc.	evangelism, discipleship, church planting, cross-cultural mission to all peoples
God's provision…	common grace, general revelation	special grace, special revelation, the power of the Holy Spirit
Fulfilled in this age…	in part and imperfectly	in part as a sign of the kingdom yet to come

Both mandates will be perfectly fulfilled when God establishes his kingdom on earth at the consummation (Rev. 21).

Today the church is called to be a living sign of the kingdom, to fulfill the creation mandate, and to embody and advocate such values as human dignity, family, just government, environmental stewardship, and creative expression. This mandate includes advocacy of such values for all humans, at home or abroad, as missionary or local believer, as expatriate or citizen.

Most humanitarian or philanthropic work would fall under the category of the creation mandate. The church cannot depend on governments to meet these needs. We are our brother's keeper. Concerns about pollution, global warming, and other environmental issues have led some missiologists to include stewardship of the environment as part of the mission of the church (e.g., Kirk 2000, 164–83; Langmead 2002; C. J. H. Wright 2006, 397–420; Walls and Ross 2008, xiv and 84–104; for an overview, see Effa 2008).

In short, the creation mandate describes the ethical obligations of Christians and non-Christians alike in all aspects of their lives: personal, familial, social, and civil. It reflects God's concern for all aspects of life. It is expressed

151

in the social ethic of the Old Testament and is summarized by the second half of the Great Commandment: "Love your neighbor as yourself" (Matt. 22:39b). This commandment is given irrespective of the neighbor's religion, social standing, or ethnic background as illustrated in the parable of the good Samaritan (Luke 10:29–37). However, fulfillment of the creation mandate should not be confused with realization of the kingdom of God to the extent that it does not include reconciliation with God and the lordship of Christ (see Berneburg 1997, 275–78).

The Gospel Mandate

The gospel mandate, on the other hand, is given only to Christians. It is sometimes called the spiritual mandate, the new creation mandate, or the redemptive mandate. This mandate is best summarized by the Great Commission: "Therefore go and make disciples of all nations, baptizing them in the name of the Father and of the Son and of the Holy Spirit, and teaching them to obey everything I have commanded you" (Matt. 28:19–20a). The gospel mandate deals with the broken relationship with God, which is the ultimate source of human suffering and our failure to fulfill the creation mandate.

The gospel mandate is more comprehensive than mere evangelism or church planting. It represents the fullness of God's redeeming work accomplished in Christ. By bringing the message of salvation, the gospel mandate offers a restored relationship with God. The power of sin, death, and Satan is broken. Through regeneration our true humanity is restored as the image of God is renewed in us. This makes the first half of the Great Commandment possible: "Love the Lord your God with all your heart and with all your soul and with all your mind" (Matt. 22:37).

The activities that fulfill the gospel mandate include evangelism, discipleship, church planting, cross-cultural mission, and the realization of kingdom values in the church and the lives of believers. These in turn impact human relationships at all levels. Humanitarian or philanthropic work may fall under the gospel mandate when it is explicitly linked to the aforementioned activities. The gospel mandate furthermore calls the church to bring this message to every person of every standing in every nation. We have the example of the early church and the apostles being driven with great passion and at great sacrifice to fulfill this mandate, bringing the gospel to the ends of the earth and planting kingdom communities wherever the message was received.

THE RELATIONSHIP BETWEEN THE CREATION AND GOSPEL MANDATES

Some, such as Harold Mare (1973), see the gospel mandate as having priority over the creation mandate. Glasser sees the two mandates as distinct, but fusing into one fundamental task as Jesus inaugurates the kingdom of God

(Glasser et al. 2003, 39). Sunday Aigbe adds a third "prophetic mandate" that "critically challenges every dimension of the society and the state," and "creates the vital force and sets the parameters for the cultural and evangelistic mandates (1991, 38, 40). Yet, others resist altogether the idea of describing the church's obligation in terms of two (or more) mandates. According to Bosch, "The moment one regards mission as consisting of two separate components one has, in principle, conceded that each of the two has a life of its own. One is then by implication saying that it is possible to have evangelism without a social dimension. What is more, if one suggests that one component is primary and the other secondary, one implies that the one is essential, the other optional" (1991, 405).

There is indeed a sense in which we cannot dichotomize Christian life and obligation. The gospel message is not merely one of personal salvation but includes the hope of transformed relationships and values entailing social responsibility. The two mandates belong together. Neither is optional. But retaining a distinction between the mandates is useful for several reasons.

First, they represent very different kinds of activities and concerns. They represent two dimensions of human experience and need. Maintaining the distinction allows the church to be involved in both without blurring the distinctive purpose of each. As Sider correctly observes, "In fact, many good evangelistic programs (student evangelism, for example, or Billy Graham crusades) contain very little direct social action. Similarly, many very good programs of social action (e.g., Bread for the World's excellent political work for the poor) have very little direct evangelistic intent. These programs are not wrong because they are not doing both" (1993, 170).

Though the creation mandate is lived out by Christians in Christ's name, compassion is not "bait" for evangelism. As Sider maintains, "Social concern need not be pre-evangelism to be legitimate. Our doctrine of Creation tells us that it is good for all people to enjoy the bounty of the Creator during their three score years and ten. . . . If God continues to shower the good gifts of Creation on all, regardless of their faith or unbelief, then Christians too should work for physical, social, economic, and political well being for all. Simply on the basis of Creation, those tasks have validity and importance" (1993, 142–43).

Second, maintaining the distinction helps to ensure that neither aspect is neglected in the overall responsibility of the church. In conciliar mission social responsibility has tended to overshadow or redefine evangelism, and in evangelical circles the creation mandate has often been wrongly reduced to a tool of the gospel mandate.

We find the early church creating two separate structures that roughly correspond to the two mandates: apostles and elders with the responsibilities of "prayer and the ministry of the Word," and deacons who "wait on tables" providing for widows (Acts 6:1–6). Maintaining a distinction guarded the integrity

153

of both, allowed for delegation of responsibility, and helped distinguish the different challenges, resources, and gifts necessary to fulfill each mandate.

Third, fulfillment of the gospel mandate is a logical and practical condition of rightly fulfilling the creation mandate. Only as men and women are reconciled with God, are empowered by the Holy Spirit, and live out the values of the kingdom will they become salt and light in society and be able to rightly live out the creation mandate.

Fourth, retaining the distinction between the mandates also helps us to discern between the obligations of all members of the human family (the creation mandate) and the unique obligation of the church (the gospel mandate). Christians as members of the human race and as members of the church bear both obligations. Non-Christians and Christians alike can cooperate in the fight for just and fair legal systems or in catastrophic relief efforts. But only Christians know the grace of God in Jesus Christ. Only they will bring this message to the world. The gospel mandate reminds us that we live not by bread alone but by every word that proceeds from the mouth of God (Matt. 4:4) and that our ultimate hope is not in this world (1 Cor. 15:19; Col. 1:5; Titus 3:7).

FIGURE 6.1:
THE INTERDEPENDENT RELATIONSHIP OF THE TWO MANDATES

Fulfilling the gospel mandate
leads to deep-level fulfillment of
the creation mandate as a source
of God's love and values.

Creation Mandate
human dignity, family,
justice, compassion,
stewardship of creation,
creative expression

Gospel Mandate
evangelism,
discipleship,
church planting

Fulfilling the creation mandate leads
to credible fulfillment of the gospel
mandate as expression of God's love.

154

Although we can retain a distinction between the two mandates, the two are nevertheless intertwined and should rarely be separated in actual practice. They are symbiotic and interdependent (see fig. 6.1). Fulfilling the creation mandate is necessary as a genuine expression of the love of God. It lends credibility to the fulfillment of the gospel mandate. As described in the CRESR statement, it can be a preparation, partner, and fruit of the gospel mandate.

Fulfillment of the gospel mandate, on the other hand, leads to the power to fulfill the creation mandate. People experience the power of God's love in Christ and the transformation of the Holy Spirit. God's love becomes the motivation and God's revelation provides the values for fulfilling the creation mandate.

The creation mandate can only rightly be fulfilled when the relationship to God is restored. The gospel mandate can only rightly be fulfilled when Christians are a living testimony to what a restored creation order looks like, that is, an order based on love, compassion, and justice. Both are an obligation, both are necessary; one is of a more general ethical nature, the other of a more explicitly spiritual nature.

THE TWO MANDATES AND MISSION

How do the two mandates relate to the task of missions? We return to our definition of the purpose of mission from chapter 4: Mission is the sending activity of God with the purpose of reconciling to himself and bringing into his kingdom fallen men and women from every people and nation to his glory. This ultimately describes the fulfillment of both mandates.

Fulfillment of both mandates is thus included in the task of missions, but the gospel mandate is more fundamental for several reasons. First, as noted above, only through reconciliation with God can the creation mandate be fulfilled in the deepest sense. The redemptive work of Christ moves beyond individual salvation and the church and impacts the social order. Second, only the church has been given the gospel mandate. Third, Christ did not send his followers into the world merely to do good works but explicitly to be his witnesses and make disciples. Thus ethical obligations, such as being a good citizen or feeding the hungry, by themselves cannot alone rightly be considered the task of missions. The creation mandate is essential to the life and witness of the church, but by itself it is not the task of missions (see Peters 1972, 170–71).

Jesus healed the sick, fed the hungry, and cared for people's temporal needs (aspects of the creation mandate). These actions were signs of the coming kingdom. But it was the work of redemption on the cross that was foundational to that coming kingdom, apart from which there would be no kingdom. Likewise, most central to the calling of the church is the mandate to do what the world cannot do: to proclaim the message of salvation and reconciliation with God, to be a witness to the power of the risen Christ to transform life and make all things new, to be a sign of the kingdom that is not of this world.

C. J. H. Wright correctly comments that the cross of Christ is "the unavoidable center of our mission" (2006, 314), because whatever forms of evil we confront—spiritual, social, economic, physical, or mental—it is the power of the cross that disarms evil, defeats Satan, transforms sinful humans, and is the foundation of the coming kingdom of righteousness and glory. Thus the cross is central to both mandates. And yet the message of the cross is made explicit and the power of the cross released only through fulfillment of the gospel mandate.

TOWARD A DEFINITION OF THE TASK OF MISSIONS

In the foregoing discussion a variety of themes have emerged that might legitimately describe the task of missions: proclamation and conversion, church planting and growth, humanization and liberation. We have concluded that all are a Christian obligation, but that the spiritual dimension, the gospel mandate, is most foundational and central to the mission of the church.

We propose the following definition of the task of missions that integrates these various themes: *The task of missions is the creation and expansion of kingdom communities among all the peoples of the earth.* At first glance this definition may appear to be no different than church planting and growth. But by describing churches as "kingdom communities," this definition goes farther because kingdom communities fulfill both the gospel mandate and the creation mandate. Such a definition not only reflects evangelical convictions but is also consistent with the sentiment expressed in the WCC document "Mission and Evangelism: An Ecumenical Affirmation," which reads, "This task of sowing the seed needs to be continued until there is, in every human community, a cell of the kingdom, a church confessing Jesus Christ and in his name serving his people" (WCC 1982, §25).

Kingdom communities are not so much formal religious institutions as they are committed fellowships of disciples of Jesus Christ seeking to live out their faith in all biblical fullness. They are communities of those redeemed by the saving work of Christ on the cross and faith in one gospel, of which Christ is the center. They are increasingly experiencing the lordship of King Jesus over all of their individual and corporate life. As kingdom communities they live as signs of the kingdom, hope in the coming kingdom, and advocate kingdom values wherever they might have influence, as a voice of truth, righteousness, justice, and reconciliation. Kingdom communities may or may not have the formal elements of organized churches such as buildings, ordained clergy, and detailed polity or doctrinal statements. But they are fellowships committed to joyfully serving the King in the power of the Spirit and according to the Word of God. They are congregations with the following three dimensions (see fig. 6.2):

- Doxology—the Great Calling
- Evangelism and discipleship—the Great Commission
- Compassion and social concern—the Great Commandment

Just as no cube can be one-dimensional, so too true kingdom communities cannot have one dimension apart from the other two. At the same time, each of the three dimensions remains distinctive and important in its own right. Yet the cube forms a single whole, each dimension inseparably influencing the others.

The task of missions is not simply to *be* such communities—that might be considered the mission (singular) of the church. Rather, the task of missions (plural) is to *create* and *expand* such communities among *all* peoples of the earth. The nations are included in the scope of the task of missions, because kingdom communities are to be planted among all peoples of the earth. Because they are *kingdom* communities, the kingdom of God remains at the center of mission. Because the church remains God's primary vehicle to advance his kingdom in this age, the planting and expansion of churches as kingdom communities among all peoples are absolutely central to defining the task of missions.

When the task of missions is so understood, then *the means of missions can be defined as evangelism and discipleship, leading to the planting, growth, and multiplication of churches that manifest the reign of God in word and deed.* The emphasis on "word and deed" is significant. The gospel mandate emphasizes "in word." The creation mandate emphasizes "in deed." Both demonstrate submission to and restoration of the reign of God—the heart of the kingdom. Creating three-dimensional kingdom communities means that the missionary task must intentionally work in such a way that *all three*

FIGURE 6.2:
THREE DIMENSIONS OF KINGDOM COMMUNITIES

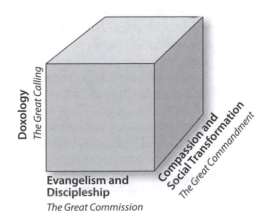

157

dimensions are continually in view. Though emphases may differ depending on context and need, none of the dimensions can be ignored in the process of creating such communities.

Let us briefly examine these three dimensions of kingdom communities and discover how they integrate the various biblical concerns of mission in a holistic manner while at the same time retaining the centrality of the gospel mandate.

Evangelism and Discipleship—The Great Commission

Here the gospel mandate is made the foundation of the missionary task. Preaching the gospel, making disciples, and gathering these believers into communities whose members are committed to one another and to God is foundational to all else. This reflects the Great Commission according to Matthew: "Therefore go and make disciples of all nations, baptizing them in the name of the Father and of the Son and of the Holy Spirit, and teaching them to obey everything I have commanded you" (Matt. 28:19–20a). This is the gospel mandate. Missions must begin here, or it does not begin. Only through evangelism, discipleship, and church planting—the Great Commission—can the Great Commandment be truly lived. The Great Commandment begins with the call to love God with all one's heart, soul, and mind, from which flows love for neighbor (Matt. 22:37–39). Only as we first experience God's love are we able to love him and others (1 John 4:19). Only by entering the kingdom through repentance and childlike faith can believers be born anew and live kingdom lives. Only through reconciliation with the Creator can the creation mandate be realized in the believing community and rightly advocated in the larger society. Only as communities are committed to the lordship of the King can they become a sign of the kingdom in this age.

Here is the heart of mission: God's deep compassion, seeking and saving the lost, freeing from sin and Satan. Here is the only hope for sinful men and women to experience forgiveness of sin, to have peace with God and the hope of eternal life. Here is the scope of mission reaching out to people of every ethnic, linguistic, social, and economic standing. Only the gospel has the power to save and redeem. Only the message of the cross has the power for true reconciliation, between God and humans and between estranged peoples.

The task of missions is to create such communities that are not content with being served, being edified, and being safe. In this dimension of kingdom communities, the purposes of mission to redeem and reconcile are addressed. True discipleship and true community in the power of the Spirit will lead to sharing the message with others and living out the Great Commandment, the second dimension of kingdom communities.

158

Compassion and Social Concern—The Great Commandment

The creation mandate calls all people, but especially God's people, to live justly and compassionately with others, to be stewards of the environment, to guard human dignity, and to nurture the image of God in men and women. The Great Commandment calls the church to love God and as an outworking of this to love neighbor—the two cannot be separated (Matt. 22:37–39; 1 John 4:20). Love is the mark of discipleship (John 13:35). Love is the fulfillment of the law of God (Rom. 13:10; Gal. 5:14). Love reflects the very character of God (1 John 4:8). Kingdom communities are characterized by loving relationships evidenced in tangible ways, beginning with the family of God and moving out to others, including enemies (Matt. 5:43–48; Rom. 12:9–21; Gal. 6:10).

Kingdom communities become instruments of God's mercy and compassion to the poor, the suffering, and the marginalized. They work not only to alleviate immediate need but also to help people to help themselves, through development, education, and provision of opportunities. Just as Christ's earthly ministry not only redeemed from spiritual evil but also confronted evil in all its manifestations (sin, sickness, injustice, the demonic), so too kingdom communities confront evil in whatever forms it is manifested: personal, familial, social, economic. This may include working to change structural evil in economic systems or in the social order that perpetuate poverty, oppress minorities, or prevent people from full realization of their human potential. The task of missions is not to do all these things but to create local communities that do them among all people.

Doxology—The Great Calling

There is no higher calling than the call to become a child of God, to worship, honor, and glorify him with all our being for all eternity. God has predestined his people, the church, "to the praise of his glorious grace" (Eph. 1:6). As the living temple of the Holy Spirit, a people purchased by the blood of Christ, we glorify God with our bodies (1 Cor. 6:20). When the Great Commission is carried out and the Great Commandment is lived out, God's glory will be magnified in all the earth. Jesus said in the Sermon on the Mount, "In the same way, let your light shine before men, that they may see your good deeds and praise your Father in heaven" (Matt. 5:16). Such communities will be living signs of God's coming kingdom. They will be living evidence of God's grace, mercy, and justice, a compelling, living invitation to others to become worshippers of the one true God.

Kingdom communities are passionate about obeying God's will with all their being, their very lives being a holy sacrifice (Rom. 12:1). Whereas reconciliation with and submission to God is the essence of the kingdom, righteousness is the character of the kingdom, and transformed lives and communities are the fruit of the kingdom, worship is the *joy* of the kingdom.

Worship the LORD with gladness;
   come before him with joyful songs. (Ps. 100:2)

Let the heavens rejoice, let the earth be glad;
   let them say among the nations, "The LORD reigns!" (1 Chron. 16:31)

Kingdom people realize that God alone is worthy of worship and that he is at the center of history, not us. To quote John Piper, "Worship is ultimate, not missions, because God is ultimate, not man" (1993, 11). And in the words of Paul, "For from him and through him and to him are all things. To him be the glory forever! Amen" (Rom. 11:36). Kingdom people seek to redeem and claim all dimensions of culture for the glory of God: work, play, the arts, and every aspect of human expression and relationships (1 Cor. 10:31; Col. 3:17, 23).

We summarize with the words of D. Zac Niringiye, "Kingdom community is both the means and the goal of the proclamation of the good news of the Kingdom of God" (2008, 18). Missions has the task of creating such communities until the heavenly vision and God's mission are fulfilled: "Who will not fear you, O Lord, and bring glory to your name? For you alone are holy. All nations will come and worship before you, for your righteous acts have been revealed" (Rev. 15:4; cf. Ps. 86:9).

CONCLUSION

In conclusion we can say that *mission* is God's sending of Christians, the church, into the world as messengers of reconciliation and renewal to bring men and women of every nation into God's kingdom. They are to live as salt and light in their communities as a sign of the coming kingdom when all things will be restored under God's rule. However, the church has not fulfilled its mission by merely *being* such a community wherever it finds itself, as great a challenge at that is. Rather such communities must be multiplied among the diverse peoples of the world, and this is the task of missions.

Thus the *task of missions* is the sending activity of the church to create and expand such kingdom communities among every people of the earth. This will be done through evangelism and church planting that is not satisfied with superficial conversion or institutional advancement. Rather, these new communities must be nurtured and challenged to manifest the reign of God in word and deed, impacting all areas of life—spiritual, social, mental, and physical—thus furthering God's mission in the world. All of these areas are illustrated in figure 6.3.

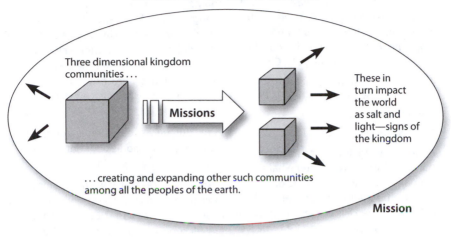

FIGURE 6.3:
MISSION AND THE TASK OF MISSIONS

Three dimensional kingdom communities . . .

Missions

These in turn impact the world as salt and light—signs of the kingdom

. . . creating and expanding other such communities among all the peoples of the earth.

Mission

CASE STUDY:
TO SUPPORT OR NOT TO SUPPORT?

(Note: The missionary and the country named are both fictional.)

Faith Church had a strong commitment to missions and supported numerous missionaries and projects. Phil, chairman of the mission committee, came with anticipation to the evening meeting. The agenda was short, so he arranged to have a few missionary prayer letters read and then to spend time praying for the various concerns.

They began by reading a letter from Jill Huntington, a missionary doctor in Islamastan. Jill's letter reported glowingly of the rural clinic where she worked. She was able to offer the only medical care within a day's journey for over fifty thousand people in the region. Countless lives had been saved, and some of her attempts to improve

hygienic practices in the region and reduce illness were finally having positive results. The people were always grateful and had great respect for Jill.

However, the strongly Islamic government began watching Jill more closely. Americans were viewed by the officials with increasing suspicion. Though Jill had a visa as a development worker, they suspected that she was really a missionary attempting to use medicine as a means to coerce people to become Christians. They found such behavior manipulative, deceptive, and a violation of Islamic law. She was sternly warned—so Jill reported in her letter—that if she were caught proselytizing or telling people in any way about Jesus, she would be expelled from the country within twenty-four hours.

"I have chosen to continue my work and to help the people of Islamastan, even if I cannot share the gospel or even do this in the name of Jesus. To do otherwise would not only jeopardize the work but be deceptive and unfitting of a Christian."

As Phil concluded reading the letter, he noted an uncharacteristic silence in the room.

Charles finally broke the silence.

CHARLES: "Evangelism is the most central thing in missions. No matter what a missionary's assignment is, he or she needs to be sharing the gospel regularly. In fact, I've been a little concerned about Jill's ministry for a while now. Maybe it's time to reconsider our support of Jill. Frankly, it may be humanitarian, but I don't think that it really qualifies as missionary work."

PAMELA: "Charles, mission is all about doing what Jesus did. Jesus didn't just preach but also fed the hungry and healed the sick. He cared for the whole person. I agree that wherever possible a missionary such as Jill should care for both the body and the soul. But in my opinion she is worthy of missionary support, even if she isn't able to share the gospel or do it in the name of Jesus."

BETH: "But the Great Commission seems pretty clear to me. It says we are to preach the gospel to every creature and to make disciples of all nations. How can you call it mission if the work cannot even be done in the name of Jesus?"

Tension in the room was evident.

PHIL (attempting to slow the discussion and calm emotions): "Why don't we take a moment to step back from Jill's particular situation and discuss more fundamentally what the role of compassion ministries are in our missions program?"

MARK: "I think that compassion is compassion, and evangelism is evangelism, and they should just be kept separate. We feed the hungry because it is the right thing to do, whether we do it in Jesus's name or not. Besides, we want to avoid creating 'rice Christians' who accept Jesus only because of what they can get in return."

BETH: "But are we really helping people if we care for their bodies but not for their souls?"

CHARLES: "That's right. If we take Pamela's logic to an extreme, any do-gooder could call himself a missionary. We may as well support the Peace Corps also!"

PHIL (with a touch of irony and humor): "Well, we wouldn't want to go to extremes would we? [pause] Seriously, I don't think that we are going to solve this issue tonight. I suggest that we pray about it and study the matter more carefully before we make a decision.

"I'd like to make one more suggestion. Sam, would you be willing to do a bit of research on this, and come to the next meeting with some biblical guidelines and a suggestion regarding our support of Jill Huntington's work in Islamastan?"

REFLECTION AND DISCUSSION

If you were Sam . . .

1. Which Bible passages would you recommend for study on this issue?
2. What other issues or principles would you recommend that the committee consider?
3. What would be your recommendation regarding the support of Jill's work in Islamastan?

PART 2

Motives and Means for Mission

7

The Motivation for Missions

The motivation for missionary work should flow out of our understandings of the purpose, nature, and task of mission. But knowing *what* we should do is not the same as understanding *why* we do it. Though we may have clarified the *reason* for mission, this may not be enough to move the *will* to undertake mission. Motivation influences the *spirit* and the *commitment* with which missionary work is conducted. Motivation reflects attitudes, and attitudes in turn impact relationships and methods in profound ways.

Our discussion thus far has focused more on the divine intent and initiative in mission. Here we consider the more human factor. Motivation for mission will have much to do with the manner in which mission is promoted, missionaries are recruited, funds raised, prayers enlisted, and projects adopted. Motivation for mission involvement comes through various channels such as Bible study, sermons, conferences, books, brochures, films, personal encounters, magazine and Internet ads, and dreams. Today motivation for missionary service often begins with participation in a short-term mission experience.

Motives for mission usually do not occur in isolation. In his study of seventeenth- and eighteenth-century missionary motives, *Constrained by Jesus' Love* (to which we will frequently refer), Johannes Van den Berg summarizes, "We conclude that no one isolated motive or single factor can explain the growth of the missionary ideal: it is through the fullness of motives that the church was thrown back upon its primary task: to proclaim the Gospel of Christ over all the earth" (1956, 187). Looking at the motivation for mission historically reveals the extent to which motives for mission have been influenced by everything from current events to popular piety. A more recent qualitative empirical study of missionary candidates confirms the overlapping and mixed nature of personal missionary motivations (K. McQuilkin 1990).

Rarely are motives for mission entirely pure; "throughout the history of the Christian mission pure and impure motives have been as mixed through each other as the clean and unclean animals of Noah's ark" (Verkuyl 1978, 163). In hindsight we are quick to identify the blind spots and other flaws in the mission motivation of past generations. It is more difficult (and certainly unpopular) to identify the mixed nature of our own motives. Some motives are clearly articulated; others are subtle and subconscious. Second-guessing the unspoken motives of our contemporaries, much less the motives of those of other ages, is a precarious undertaking.

We also must keep in mind that throughout history countless missionaries laid down their lives as they sought to serve God. The death rates of nineteenth-century missionaries to tropical West Africa were staggering. And yet new recruits were ever forthcoming. Candidates knew before leaving that the odds of death by disease before they even learned the local language were enormous. Thus we must temper our judgment of their motives when we ourselves are unwilling to make similar sacrifices.

Fortunately, God is sovereign and works through our feeble efforts and in spite of even questionable motives. Nowhere is this more evident than in the life of the unwilling and unforgiving prophet Jonah. However, it is not our place to judge the motivation of others but rather to consider our own; in Van den Berg's words, "a living confrontation with the past, which still in its many forms is so near to us, can help to reveal to us the true nature of our own motives" (1956, 214).

QUESTIONABLE MOTIVATIONS FOR MISSIONS

Motives for mission that we consider questionable are those that are either inconsistent with biblical understandings of mission or are in some way harmful to the cause of missions. Not all the motives labeled here as questionable are inherently misguided. But they can become easily mixed. Furthermore, many of these motives would not have been considered questionable by earlier generations, and indeed when seen in their historical context they can become understandable.

False or impure motives for mission have been present since the beginning of the church. Paul viewed the motives of some of his contemporaries in this way: "It is true that some preach Christ out of envy and rivalry, but others out of goodwill. . . . The former preach Christ out of selfish ambition, not sincerely, supposing that they can stir up trouble for me while I am in chains.

But what does it matter? The important thing is that in every way, whether from false motives or true, Christ is preached. And because of this I rejoice" (Phil. 1:15, 17–18). Thus even when we become aware of less than noble motives of others, we should share the same attitude as the apostle Paul, who rejoiced when the gospel was spread, whatever the motivation.

Civilization, Colonialism, and Cultural Superiority

In chapter 5 we saw that civilization and the spread of Western culture were considered a task of missions throughout much of mission history. This was especially so in the nineteenth and early twentieth centuries. The task of civilization was often considered to be a moral obligation. During much of what might be called the era of Christendom, from the fourth through the eighteenth centuries, the Western church was identified with Western culture. As the official religion of the state, imperial expansion meant also Christian expansion. Indeed, at times coercion was considered a legitimate means of christianization.

During the ages of exploration and modern colonial expansion, colonial powers often opened up lands for missionary work in places where missionaries previously had no access. Under the Roman Catholic system of patronage, the colonial rulers were charged by the church to care for the spiritual needs of the people, both natives and colonists, living in their realms. The relationship between Protestant colonizing nations and mission work was more ambivalent, but still the assumption of Western superiority remained unchallenged.

The earliest Protestant missionary efforts were often linked to the colonial interests of England and the Netherlands. Van den Berg suggests that magistrates and seafarers were Protestants desirous of "crippling Rome's power and planting the banner of Protestant Christianity even on the most distant coast. In these strivings they were backed by many of the clergy at home, especially the Puritan preachers, whose party advocated an aggressive anti-Spanish policy" (1956, 22). Anglican missions to Native Americans in the colonial era were viewed as a means of resisting Roman Catholic and French influences in the region (Rooy 1965, 284). The government considered christianization more prudent and cheaper than military action to control the Native Americans (Beaver 1968a, 118–19). After the Revolutionary War, the United States War Department enlisted mission agencies to civilize Native Americans (133). The Civilization Fund Act of 1819 financed numerous missionary schools of various denominations in this effort (Noel 2002).

However, civilization alone was rarely the primary intent of the missionaries themselves. This motive was often blended together with a genuine holistic concern for not only the souls but also the lives of the people. As we noted in chapter 5, civilization was sometimes considered a prerequisite to conversion. Furthermore, it was thought to be a moral obligation to elevate

167

"savages" to a higher standard of living, allowing them to share in the fruits of Western culture.

The Puritans shared the dream of a theocratic realm—that God's rule be extended over all of creation. Such motives might be considered less related to civilization per se and more to a realization of the *theocratic* vision. "Christianization of society was not primarily the desire of strong-willed clergymen for power; it was meant as a surrender to the universal Lordship of Christ" (Rooy 1965, 325). Theocratic dreams died with the death of Cromwell in 1658. Henceforth, church and state in Europe would be increasingly separated.

The civilizing motive was often a strange mix of both condescension and high ideals as illustrated in the example of the Puritans. They referred to Native Americans as "miserable natives" and enacted legal codes targeted at changing their native customs, civilizing them in "Praying Towns." This attitude, however, was rooted in the conviction that Native Americans were equally human and thus capable of being "civilized"—a view not shared by most Europeans, who considered them subhuman. To neglect nurturing virtues such as industriousness (a Puritan ideal of sanctification) among Indian converts would be to deny their equal humanity. The Puritans were no less critical of aspects of European culture (J. B. Carpenter 2002, 521–24). John Eliot, Jonathan Edwards, and David Brainerd defended the Native Americans against exploitation. Similar examples could be recounted throughout mission history (see Woodberry 2006).

John Williams, the famous LMS missionary to the South Pacific was not beyond appealing to colonial commercial interests in promotion of missions when he said prior to his departure in 1817, "Thus we see that the nation at large is interested, and that everyone, who is concerned to promote the commercial welfare of his country, is bound to exert himself on behalf of the missionary cause" (cited in Van den Berg 1956, 145).

A sense of "manifest destiny" was part of the air that Americans breathed and was a powerful motive from the mid-nineteenth to early twentieth centuries. The phrase was likely coined by John L. O'Sullivan, who wrote: "The far-reaching, the boundless future will be the era of American greatness. In its magnificent domain of space and time, the nation of many nations is destined to manifest to mankind the excellence of divine principles; to establish on earth the noblest temple ever dedicated to the worship of the Most High—the Sacred and the True" (1839).

God's blessings on America were understood as a great stewardship that must be employed for the sake of the world (see Beaver 1968a, 133–39). As late as 1891 the preface to Josiah Strong's best seller *Our Country* read, "As goes America so goes the world, in all that is vital to its moral welfare. . . . The future of Christianity" depends upon "the future of this country. . . . The United States [is] first and foremost the chosen seat of enterprise for the world's conversion" (cited in W. J. D. Edwards 2004, 164). The concept of progress through civilization found expression in James S. Dennis's three-volume *Christian Mission and Social Progress* (1897–1906), which credited missions with great advances of civilization in the non-Christian world. By the beginning of the twentieth century, few mission leaders were condoning imperialism and its penchant for national aggrandizement. But, as Forman observes, while "imperial aggrandizement *per se* was condemned, the door was left open for imperial domination with altruistic intention" (1977, 85).

Often enough missionaries encountered severe poverty, illiteracy, and traditional practices such as slavery, widow burning, or killing of twins that could not be ignored. Western civilization in terms of education, law, human rights, government, morals, work ethic, and way of life were seen as the only humane alternative. Popular stereotypes of cultural damage done by missionaries must be tempered by facts of the historical record. Enormous good was also accomplished through civilizing efforts. "We should not lose sight of the positive legacy of missions in the areas of racial attitudes, education, civil society, and colonial reform" (Woodberry 2006, 4). Many missionaries resisted imperialistic endeavors, exposed abuses, and fought for the rights of indigenous peoples.

Motives and attitudes of cultural superiority prevail in the missionary effort today through neocolonialism in the form of cultural and/or economic dominance. Following World War II, General Douglas MacArthur called for one thousand missionaries to be sent to Japan as a countermeasure against communism. Some today see mission work as a means of democratization or as an answer to the threat of radical Islam. Many short- and long-term missionaries view host cultures with condescension. They confuse Western culture with Christian values; promote (intentionally or unintentionally) a materialistic worldview, individualism, and competitiveness; and tenaciously defend policies of their country of origin. Western missionaries are not the only ones guilty of such attitudes. Paul's attitude must be continually rediscovered, "For I resolved to know nothing while I was with you except Jesus Christ and him crucified. I came to you in weakness and fear, and with much trembling" (1 Cor. 2:2–3).

Ecclesial Power and Denominationalism

During the first centuries of Christianity, the church was a minority movement, with minimal ecclesial structure and even less direct public influence. However, as Christianity became the official imperial religion of the Roman Empire and the church grew in structure and political influence, the understanding of the nature of the church and its mission were also changed. The church became a powerful institution linked to the state. "It can be said that much of the work of missions in the Middle Ages was undertaken for the sake of the enlargement of this-worldly power and influence of the Church. And this form of the ecclesiological missionary motive was legitimized by the fact that the empirical Church and the Kingdom of God were seen as coextensive" (Van den Berg 1956, 181).

Ecclesial power and influence have taken a different form in Protestant missions. Protestantism was not as monolithic as Roman Catholicism, nor was it linked to the state in the same way. Germans and Scandinavians were generally Lutheran, Dutch were Reformed, English Anglican, Scottish Presbyterian, and so on. There were also minority groups such as Mennonites, Baptists, Quakers, and radical Pietists. Eventually denominations emerged, initially linked to ethnic or national roots but becoming more competitive for converts and influence among other ethnic groups. The SPG in the eighteenth century was the arm of the Anglican Church seeking to establish itself in the colonies in competition with Quakers and Presbyterians and combating the Roman Catholic Church (Van den Berg 1956, 64). However, many of the earliest Protestant mission societies were nondenominational or only loosely affiliated with denominations. Even denominational societies were generally quite open and ecumenical. But by 1840 tensions began to arise between them (D. J. Bosch 1991, 330–32). Meanwhile, churches on the mission fields were given relatively little freedom for self-expression or contextualization, often becoming clones of the sending denominations. Sometimes interdenominational missions that strictly avoided denominational associations in the sending country formed fiercely denominational church associations in their countries of ministry.

In the words of Stephen Neill, "at the start Protestant missions had tumbled in higgledy-piggledy, without any plan or consultation. The resulting confusions were endless" (1964, 541). Eventually comity agreements between mission agencies were made to avoid competition and confusion. They agreed to divide a country into territories, and a single mission agency or denomination would be responsible for a given territory. Such agreements were generally respected, though in many ways they were impractical. Boundaries were often arbitrary, and a proliferation of denominations within the same country ensued.

Fortunately, in recent decades mission agencies have sought greater partnership and cooperation with national churches and with one another. Nevertheless, denominational pride, flag raising, and sheep stealing have been and continue to be a problem in mission motives. Sometimes competition for the "missionary dollar" has created pressure to report successes in areas such as evangelism and church growth. The most gifted national workers are often recruited from one group by another, a type of "shepherd stealing." Renewal groups claim that existing churches are dead or deficient. Existing churches or mission works feel threatened and become defensive.

We cannot enter into the complexities of denominationalism here, other than to say that ecclesial kingdom building in competition with others cannot be considered an appropriate motive for mission. Few question the value of churches being associated in fellowships or denominations, nor can renewal movements be condemned because they may create divisions. But competitiveness with other churches or mission organizations is entirely contrary to Jesus's prayer "that all of them may be one, Father, just as you are in me and I am in you. May they also be in us so that the world may believe that you have sent me" (John 17:21). Such a situation was also unthinkable in Paul's conception of the church (1 Cor. 1:10–13).

Condescending Pity

The line between genuine (respectful) compassion and condescending pity is a fine one. Van den Berg quotes one Christian leader at the end of the eighteenth century as claiming, "The richest fruit of our philanthropy has been a cold, ineffective pity" (1956, 99). We will discuss later the motive of compassion, but as David J. Bosch describes it,

> Compassion and solidarity had been replaced by pity and condescension. In most of the hymns, magazines, and books of the early nineteenth century, heathen life was painted in the darkest colors, as a life of permanent unrest and unhappiness, as life in the shackles of terrible sins. . . .
>
> The pagans' pitiable state became the dominant motive for mission, not the conviction that they were objects of the love of Christ. (1991, 290)

Reports of infanticide, widow burning, cannibalism, and other horrors were true enough and demanded a Christian response. However, these reports were often sensationalized in an imbalanced or dehumanizing manner.

Parallel to the sense of pity was the usually unspoken assumption that Western missionaries were the only hope for such miserable souls. Acts 16:9, recounting Paul's vision of a Macedonian begging him to "come over and help us," was frequently quoted and depicted in terms of the helpless and miserable heathen looking to the church (in the West) to come to their rescue (see fig. 7.1).

Asceticism

The ascetic motivation for mission is present "when missionary service is sought for as a means to come nearer to God along the road of self-denial, penance and sacrifice" (Van den Berg 1956, 178). Mission can thus become a means to one's own personal salvation or spirituality. Because missionary work often enough involves sacrifice and suffering, it is not surprising that ascetic motives are sometimes behind missionary service.

The monastic movements illustrate asceticism like no other. Celtic missionaries of the early Middle Ages have become a popular missionary model to be emulated (see, e.g., Hunter 2000 and Warner 2000). These culture-friendly pilgrims established communities of service, compassion, and spirituality

171

FIGURE 7.1
SEALS REPRESENTING QUESTIONABLE MOTIVATIONS FOR MISSIONS

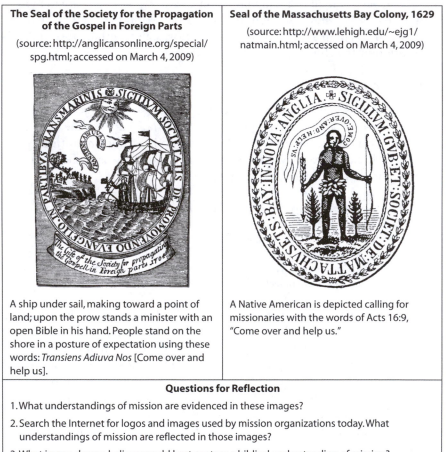

The Seal of the Society for the Propagation of the Gospel in Foreign Parts (source: http://anglicansonline.org/special/spg.html; accessed on March 4, 2009)	Seal of the Massachusetts Bay Colony, 1629 (source: http://www.lehigh.edu/~ejg1/natmain.html; accessed on March 4, 2009)
A ship under sail, making toward a point of land; upon the prow stands a minister with an open Bible in his hand. People stand on the shore in a posture of expectation using these words: *Transiens Adiuva Nos* [Come over and help us].	A Native American is depicted calling for missionaries with the words of Acts 16:9, "Come over and help us."

Questions for Reflection

1. What understandings of mission are evidenced in these images?
2. Search the Internet for logos and images used by mission organizations today. What understandings of mission are reflected in those images?
3. What image do you believe would best capture a biblical understanding of mission?

throughout Europe. Their exemplary lifestyle attracted many to become Christians. But what is less often noted about the Celtic mission is its fundamentally ascetic motive. Even compared to other religious orders, the asceticism of Irish monasticism was extreme. The purpose of the Celtic travels was not intentionally for mission, but rather

> an expression of ascetic homelessness. The monks undertook journeys to distant places as part of their discipline of penance, and for the sake of their own salvation. . . . For them *peregrinatio*, pilgrimage, became a way of pushing their renunciation to extreme limits. But the pilgrim must help others he meets on their journeys, so that the concept of pilgrimage often merged into that of mission—even if both

pilgrimage and mission remained subordinate to the spiritual perfection of the monk. (D. J. Bosch 1991, 233)

Such a pilgrimage, known as green or white martyrdom, was considered the highest form of asceticism. Green martyrdom was more penitential in motivation; white martyrdom was more service oriented. Saint Columba is an example of an ascetic-pilgrim-missionary (see also Bevans and Schroeder 2004, 121).

As a result, "pilgrimage and mission became one and the same activity" (M. Robinson 2004, 179). Idealized popularizations of Celtic Christianity are in fact "a mixed bag of orthodoxy, heterodoxy, and wishful thinking" (Meek 2000, 230). Later with the Anglo-Saxon monastic tradition, motivation shifted from renunciation to mission itself and produced missionaries such as Boniface, the apostle of Germany (D. J. Bosch 1991, 235).

Ascetic motives are also discernible among Protestant missionaries, though with different nuances. For example, the Dutch reformer Heurnius spoke of confirming one's election through service (Van den Berg 1956, 20). Traces of ascetic motives might be found in David Brainerd, who wrote in his diary, "I rejoiced in my work as a missionary; rejoiced in the necessity of self-denial and still continued to give myself up to God" (cited in Van den Berg 1956, 96). As Van den Berg points out, "Both Brainerd and [Henry] Martyn tried to realize something of the pilgrim-character of true Christianity on the hard road of self-denial which their missionary work demanded. . . . But this aspect of asceticism was subordinated to the great goal of their labours: the glorification of God through salvation of sinners" (ibid., 180).

Jonathan Edwards's disciple Samuel Hopkins greatly influenced American missionary sentiments. His idea of "universal disinterested benevolence" entailed a fully selfless service with no thought of personal benefit, neither in this world nor in the next (Forman 1977, 71; Beaver 1968a, 121). He wrote, "The best manner in which to glorify and obey God is to serve Him in a way which produces the highest good and brings the least possible personal honor and profit, and that is missionary service and support of missions" (cited in Beaver 1968a, 121). John Wesley described his motivation for going to the colonies (Georgia) in 1735: "Our end in leaving our native country was not to avoid want . . . but singly this—to save our souls, to live wholly to the glory of God" (cited in Beaver 1968a, 95). By evangelizing the Native Americans, he hoped to mortify the desires of the flesh. This motivation, however, disappeared in his later ministry. We can only speculate about the extent of ascetic motives behind those nineteenth-century missionaries headed to nearly certain death in tropical West Africa, bringing their own coffins as packing crates when they departed.

Adventure and Romantic Ideals

A common argument by early Reformers against the need for missions was built on Eusebius's idea that the Great Commission had been fulfilled by the apostles. But during the age of discovery, reports from world travelers confirmed that if the gospel had ever reached the ends of the earth, there was little evidence of it in most places in the world. This, along with the establishment of Western colonial and trading settlements, brought the reality of a world without Christ to the attention of Christians.

In the eighteenth century well-publicized accounts from Captain James Cook circulated and captured the imagination of many Christians, sparking curiosity and the romance of meeting "noble savages" in exotic and faraway places. "Christians, no less than others, shared in the sense of enlarged horizons that came with the discovery of so many hitherto unknown lands" (Neill 1964, 247). Such information stimulated the interest of key figures such as William Carey. Reports from Tahiti resulted in "innumerable" applications to the LMS for missionary service there (Van den Berg 1956, 154). Later reports from such colorful and famous figures as David Livingstone continued to whet the appetite of many for adventure or possibly even fame.

Following World War II there was a surge in evangelical mission activities as a result of the thousands of U.S. soldiers who had served overseas. After being exposed to the spiritual and physical needs of people in East Asia and Europe, many returned as missionaries. Mission agencies such as New Tribes Mission, Greater Europe Mission, and Missionary Aviation Fellowship were created (J. A. Carpenter 1997, 178–81). Since the 1980s media coverage of the Islamic revolution and terrorism have raised Christian interest in mission to Muslims. The drama of the fall of the Iron Curtain stimulated interest in mission to former communist countries.

Are these simply means that the sovereign Lord has used to raise awareness and mobilize missionaries? Or has missionary motivation become dependent on the latest news headlines—the more dramatic, the more motivating? The dream of the North American pastor who grew up in the cold war era to someday teach the Bible in Russia or China is almost breathtakingly exciting, and the opportunity to fulfill that dream has become for many a reality. Again, the motives of such people are undoubtedly sincere. But the need for teachers may be much greater elsewhere. In fact, the effectiveness of such teachers can be questioned (Livermore 2004). Thus the desire for personal fulfillment or adventure may overshadow concerns for serving where the need is greatest.

Even in today's age of media and travel, the hunger for adventure and the exotic has not abated. An Internet search of "mission adventures" will find dozens of advertisements for programs offered by the most diverse organizations. Surely there is no greater adventure than to serve God, especially in cross-cultural ministry. However, adventure seeking or personal experience in itself is a questionable motivation for mission.

Self-Realization and Edification

One of the most common and powerful motivations for missionary service today would have been thoroughly inconceivable only a few generations ago: self-realization. People interested in missionary service often look for opportunities that will give them the greatest sense of personal fulfillment. This is partly due to increased emphasis on spiritual gifts, but it is more generally related to the individualism and consumer mentality that is so much a part of Western culture. We may indeed experience fulfillment when using our gifts and talents to God's glory. But this legitimate desire can easily become secondary to a more self-interested quest for personal fulfillment.

Traditional missionaries considered themselves missionaries first and teachers, evangelists, or specialists second. By necessity they often took on tasks that were incongruent with their desires or competencies. Today it is not unusual for missionaries to insist on serving in specific roles that suit their skills and interests, and not a few have resigned from missionary service when this was not possible. According to the World Evangelical Alliance (WEA) Mission Commission's study on missionary attrition, "lack of job satisfaction" was ranked thirteenth in a list of twenty-five reasons for attrition accounting for 2.9 percent of all attrition of missionaries sent by older sending countries (W. D. Taylor 1997, 92).

Congregations and individuals are looking for opportunities that will not only meet the needs of those they go to serve but will also benefit the participants and sending congregation. This goal is frequently realized through short-term mission trips. Advertising for short-term mission trips that does not include the assurance that the participant's life will be changed or benefited in some way is rare.

Such appeals should not be rejected outright. These programs are well intended. But the motivation, especially for youth, can be very mixed indeed. Paul could speak of serving so as to become a partaker in the gospel and to receive "the prize" and a "crown that will last forever" (1 Cor. 9:23–25). Self-interest is thus not entirely absent from motivation for service. But Paul also describes his ministry as an offering of sacrifice (Phil. 2:17; 2 Tim. 4:6), notes that he has suffered for the sake of the gospel (Col. 1:24), and calls Timothy to join him in suffering for the gospel (2 Tim. 1:8). Paul's litany of selflessness, afflictions, and opposition associated with his ministry given in 2 Corinthians 6:1–10 is not necessarily something to be sought, but it reveals that the motive of missionary service cannot be limited exclusively to self gain.

Gender-Related Motives

Only in recent decades have ministry opportunities for significant spiritual leadership and pastoral care been opened to women in most Western churches. "Opportunities for worthwhile careers were limited for middle-class women in Victorian Britain (and America). Marriage and motherhood or genteel but poverty-stricken and indolent spinsterhood were the options open to many women" (Bowie 1993, 5). Missionary service proved to be an unprecedented open door for service and leadership for women. This motive is only included as questionable because it would not be adequate if it occurred in isolation. Ruth A. Tucker gives two reasons why missions so captured the commitment of women: "Opportunities for women were and are restricted in the institutionalized church at home, and mission leaders, because of their compulsion to reach a lost world for Christ, have been less restrictive than church leaders in this respect" (1988, 9).

The Holiness movement opened the way for women in ministry with such personalities as Hannah Whitall Smith and Phoebe Palmer. But foreign missionary service would prove to be an avenue for ministry from virtually all traditions. From the very beginning of the Protestant missionary movement, women played a significant role, initially as prayers, promoters, and fund-raisers (Beaver 1968b, 35). At first actual missionary service was only possible as a missionary wife. But this would eventually change with single women being sent out in large numbers as missionaries in their own right.

As the value (and potential quantity) of single female missionaries came to be recognized, their numbers skyrocketed. In fact, demand for single women missionaries exceeded supply, and recruitment of them was not easy (Swaisland 1993, 70). Such new opportunity for service came with the high price of difficult living conditions, broken health, miscarriage, loss of children, or even early death (Bowie 1993, 7–8). Thus the gender motive for missionary service should not be seen strictly in terms of personal fulfillment.

Lottie Moon in China, Amy Carmichael in India, and Mary Slessor in Calabar (Nigeria) became household names that inspired many women to consider missionary service. By 1900 there were forty-one women's mission-sending agencies in the United States and seven in Canada (Beaver 1968b, 88). In 1907, 4,710 single women were serving as foreign missionaries (McKinney Douglas 2000). By the early decades of the twentieth century, women missionaries outnumbered men by two to one (Tucker 1988, 10; P. Williams 1993, 43).

Today there is increased opportunity for women to exercise leadership roles in many churches and denominations. This factor perhaps helps explain the reduction in the number of single women missionaries as a percentage of the overall missionary workforce to about 11 percent (McKinney Douglas 2000, 880). Still, missionary service remains for women a significant option for ministry.

We now turn to motives for missions that are both biblical and conducive to effective missionary work.

APPROPRIATE MOTIVATIONS FOR MISSION

In light of the previous discussion, what are appropriate motives for mission? We will briefly examine six.

Compassion and Human Need

Compassion is a character mark of our missionary God, who "so loved the world that he gave his one and only Son" (John 3:16). We read in Matthew's Gospel this description of Jesus's compassion: "Jesus went through all the towns and villages, teaching in their synagogues, preaching the good news of the kingdom and healing every disease and sickness. When he saw the crowds, he had compassion on them, because they were harassed and helpless, like sheep without a shepherd" (Matt. 9:35–36).

Jesus was moved by both the physical and the spiritual need of the people. Paul could speak of his sufferings and afflictions for the sake of the gospel occurring "in the Holy Spirit and in sincere love" (2 Cor. 6:6). He refers to others who preach Christ out of love (Phil. 1:16). The prophet Jonah is reprimanded by the Lord not for his disobedience but for his lack of compassion toward those who faced the impending wrath of God (Jon. 4).

One of the workings of the Holy Spirit in the life of the believer is love (Rom. 5:5; Gal. 5:22). It is thus to be expected that Christians will be motivated to mission by the same compassion that motivated Christ and the apostles. This compassion has both a temporal and an eternal dimension: compassion for the physical, social, or emotional plight of people, and compassion for the spiritual lostness of people who apart from Christ face God's eternal judgment.

Such motivation has been evident throughout the history of missions. Though Erasmus had argued for civilization as the task of missions, later he wrote of "a pure desire to see souls freed from Satan's tyranny and won for the Redeemer" (Van den Berg 1956, 13). For the Dutch Reformers in the seventeenth century, "compassion with the temporal and eternal fate of the heathen" was among motivations for mission (19–20). For Lutherans and Calvinists of the Second Reformation in the eighteenth century, soteriology was not central, but rather "pity and compassion were powerful incentives to take the work of missions in hand" (29).

> But once the sediment of guilt is dredged from men's hearts so that the stream of the Holy Spirit can again flow freely, he shall again open up the springs of love, mercy and pity from which a genuine concern for mission has always arisen.
>
> Johannes Verkuyl (1978, 165)

SIDEBAR 7.1
"RESCUE THE PERISHING"

(Fanny Crosby, 1869)

Rescue the perishing, care for the dying,
Snatch them in pity from sin and the grave;
Weep o'er the erring one, lift up the fallen,
Tell them of Jesus, the mighty to save.

Refrain: Rescue the perishing,
care for the dying,
Jesus is merciful, Jesus will save.

Though they are slighting Him,
still He is waiting,
Waiting the penitent child to receive;
Plead with them earnestly,
plead with them gently;
He will forgive
if they only believe.

Refrain

Down in the human heart,
crushed by the tempter,
Feelings lie buried that grace can restore;
Touched by a loving heart,
wakened by kindness,

Chords that were broken will vibrate once
more.

Refrain

Rescue the perishing, duty demands it;
Strength for thy labor the Lord will provide;
Back to the narrow way patiently win them;
Tell the poor wand'rer a Savior has died.

Refrain

REFLECTION AND DISCUSSION

1. What motivations for mission are evident in this famous hymn?
2. What does this hymn tell us about the writer's understanding of mission and evangelism?
3. In what ways does this hymn strike you as antiquated, inappropriate, or as worthy of (re)affirmation today?

Early Puritan missionaries, such as John Elliot, and Pietists of the seventeenth and eighteenth centuries were motivated primarily by compassion and a joy to witness to the power of grace over sin (Beyreuther 1961, 39). John Wesley gave little attention to hell and judgment, in contrast to George Whitefield. But both emphasized the universal love of God. Salvation of souls was absolutely central (Van den Berg 1956, 100).

Visions of unbelievers perishing for eternity apart from Christ were not uncommon in sermons. For example, at the General Assembly of the Presbyterian Church in the USA in 1803, a sermon proclaimed, "Suppose in that dreadful day some miserable condemned pagan just ready to sink into the eternal flames should turn his despairing eyes upon you and exclaim in a voice that shall rend your heart: 'Why, why did you not warn me of this day?'" (cited in Van den Berg 1956, 101). Sermons and promotional literature emphasized great urgency in bringing the gospel to the thousands who were perishing without Christ (see sidebar 7.1). Statistics were calculated for how many were perishing by the year, month, day, hour, and minute (Beaver 1968a, 127–29).

Somewhat related to compassion was the motive of debt. Van den Berg writes, "In the Evangelical circle—though not exclusively there—the voice of the Christian conscience was heard and it found its echo in a striving towards restitution for the wrongs inflicted upon other races, by bringing them into contact with the source of life and peace" (1956, 150). He cites numerous evangelicals who denounced the evils brought to India and Africa through British colonial power. "This 'pang of sympathy' became a motive for Christian deeds, born out of a deep feeling of debt, and as the most important deed the Evangelicals considered the proclamation of the gospel" (151).

Toward the end of the nineteenth century, the conviction that people are eternally lost apart from conscious faith in Christ began to wane. Compassion in mainline missions shifted more to standard of living, ignorance, and other temporal needs. Evangelicals, on the other hand, have continued to emphasize compassion in view of the fate of the lost and their eternal destiny. John Piper succinctly summarizes this view: "If people are cut off from eternal life (Eph. 2:2–3, 12; 4:17; 5:6), and if calling on Jesus is their only hope for eternal, joyful fellowship with God . . . , then love demands missions" (2003, 155). Later he continues, "The biggest problem in the world for every human being—from the poorest to the richest, from the sickest to the healthiest—is the same: how to escape the wrath of God that hangs over all humans because of our sin. Love demands that we work to rescue people from the wrath of God" (211).

The motive of compassion has been viewed by some as too anthropocentric, focusing more on human need than on God's command, plan, or love. If the motivation for mission is too exclusively focused on compassion, then missions can easily become dependent on emotional appeals. The next motive redeems and refines the motive of compassion.

The "Love of Christ"

Paul wrote in 2 Corinthians 5:14: "Christ's love compels us . . ." There are several ways to understand the phrase "Christ's love," which can also be translated "the love of Christ":

- Christ's love for the unbeliever: I must bring the unbeliever to the knowledge of Christ's love.
- Christ's love for others mediated through the believer: Christ pours his love for others into my heart; therefore I serve.
- Christ's love for the believer: because Christ loves me, in thankfulness I serve.
- The believer's love for Christ: because I love Christ, I serve.

On the one hand, the context of the passage speaks of the redeeming and reconciling work of Christ (vv. 14b, 18–19), making the first two interpretations seem most prominent. On the other hand, Paul notes that because of Christ's death, we should no longer live for ourselves (v. 15), making gratitude and our love for Christ in the last two interpretations possible. Thus Paul may have all these interpretations in mind (see Harris 1976, 351–54). In verse 11a, Paul notes also a sense of accountability in his ministry: "Since, then, we know what it is to fear the Lord, we try to persuade men." But love is the overriding motivation.

John Wesley rooted "love of benevolence" (or compassion) in the far deeper love of Christ for sinners; "this love constrains him to love every child of man with the love which is here spoken of" (cited in Van den Berg 1956, 99). Gratitude for Christ's love as a motivation is expressed by S. L. Pomeroy, secretary of the American Board, when he wrote in 1853:

> The love of Christ shining out from the cross, has enkindled a responsive love in the heart of the Christian. And one of the earliest emotions of the regenerate soul, commingling itself often with the first swelling tide of gratitude for its own deliverance, is the desire to speak of Christ to others. In this simple desire lies the germ of that great enterprise which carried the gospel through the Roman empire, and is now sending it through the world. . . . It never paralyzes or weakens any subordinate motive; but on the contrary, gives strength and tone to every chord of sympathy, whether for the body or the soul. (cited in Beaver 1968a, 142)

Such love by and for God as a motivation to serve others stands in stark contrast to most other religions. Indian writer and missionary Vishal Mangalwadi notes the lack of volunteerism and sacrificial service by Hindus in comparison to that of Christian missionaries, commenting, "Knowing, loving and serving a transcendent and personal God is at the root of all western volunteerism. Missionaries are usually the most heroic expression of that volunteerism because they give their whole lives to it" (cited in Escobar 2003, 99).

Obedience to Christ's Command

Obedience to the Great Commission, "Go . . . !" is perhaps the most obvious, if not most compelling motivation for mission. Jesus gave his disciples, and thus also the church, the unmistakable missionary mandate to go and preach the gospel to every creature and make disciples of every nation. The command is from him to whom "all authority in heaven and on earth" is given and is valid "to the very end of the age" (Matt. 28:18–20).

During the seventeenth century, the idea that the Great Commission had already been fulfilled by the first apostles faded (Van den Berg 1956, 105). But curiously, Christ's command was not a primary motivation for mission until much later. For the Puritan Reformers of the seventeenth century, "only gradually did the explicit command of Christ begin to play a part in the awakening of the missionary interest" (Van den Berg 1956, 29). Theocratic motives were more prominent. Jonathan Edwards believed that the doctrine of election gives the missionary boldness and assurance that God will save those of his choosing even among the most resistant or unlikely. Missionary activity was participation in the divine plan of predestination (Rooy 1965, 294–309).

The Methodists, on the other hand, rejected Calvinism and felt that the doctrine of predestination undercut the motivation for mission. Wesley claimed that predestination "cuts off one of the strongest motives to all acts of bodily mercy, such as feeding the hungry, clothing the naked, and the like—viz., the hope of saving their souls from death" (cited in Van den Berg 1956, 86). For the Methodists compassion was the primary motive. In either case obedience to God's command to go and preach was assumed.

Obedience to the Great Commission would play a greater role with missionaries such as William Carey and Adoniram Judson. Carey's *Enquiry* argues that Christians are *obligated* to use means for the spread of the gospel and refutes the view that the Great Commission is no longer binding on Christians. Thus many believe that obedience was Carey's primary motive. However, "in the first twenty years after the publication of Carey's *Enquiry* the missionary command continued to play only a very modest part, it was never the one and only motive" (Van den Berg 1956, 165). Van den Berg continues, "Now it is a remarkable fact that not only during the first century of the Church's existence, but also afterwards, the divine command in its explicit form played only a very limited part in the motivation of the missionary task" (176).

From his study of sermons and promotional literature, R. Pierce Beaver concluded that obedience became a powerful incentive only in the nineteenth century (1966, 125). By 1830 Rufus Anderson, who greatly influenced American missionary thinking, held obedience to be the foremost motive (Beaver 1968a, 141). It was not unusual to hear appeals that the commandment of God obligates *all* Christians to volunteer for missionary service unless one has a call from God *not* to go (see sidebar 7.2).

Such appeals to obedience were subject to the critique of legalism, which Robert E. Speer sought to answer in 1902: "Our duty in the matter is determined, not primarily by His command, but by the facts and conditions of life which underlie it. Even if Jesus had not embodied the missionary duty of the Church in the 'great commission,' we should be under obligation to evangelize the world by reason of the essential character of Christianity and its mission to the world" (cited in Beaver 1968a, 144). The simple fact that the Great Commission, as recorded at the end of the four Gospels, is not repeated in any of the Epistles and no other explicit command to preach the gospel to the nations is recorded in the New Testament could well be an indication that sheer obedience is not the primary biblical motivation for mission.

Yet we hear the apostle Paul claiming to be under obligation, having been entrusted with the gospel (Rom. 1:14; Gal. 2:7). This may have related to his specific calling as apostle to the Gentiles. But today in the church there is often a sense of mission being a voluntary matter. Some churches are "mission

SIDEBAR 7.2
J. HUDSON TAYLOR'S SERMON

J. Hudson Taylor, founder of the China Inland Mission, preached these words in 1865 to a large audience in Perth, Scotland, pleading for missionaries to be sent to China.

Do you believe that each unit of these millions has an immortal soul, and that there is "none other name under heaven given among men" save the precious name of Jesus "whereby we must be saved"? Do you believe that He and He alone is "the way, the truth, and the life," and that "no man commeth unto the Father" but by Him? If so, think of the condition of these unsaved souls, and examine yourself in the sight of God to see whether you are doing your utmost to make Him known to them or not.

It will not do to say that you have no special call to go to China. With these facts before you, you need rather to ascertain whether you have a special call to stay at home. If you cannot in the sight of God say you are sure that you have a special call to stay at home, why are you disobeying the Saviour's plain command to go? Why are you refusing to come to the help of the Lord against the mighty? . . .

Before the next Perth conference twelve millions more, in China, will have passed for ever beyond our reach. What are we doing to bring them the tidings of Redeeming Love? (from Taylor and Taylor 1965, 167)

REFLECTION AND DISCUSSION

1. What biblical justification is there for Taylor's plea?
2. In what ways do you agree or disagree with Taylor's understanding of missionary calling?
3. Do you find Taylor's argument persuasive today? Explain your answer.

minded" (it is their "thing"), but others are not. Missions is another line item on the church budget, the short-term mission trip another date on the church calendar. Missionary service is described in terms of a choice for those with a particular interest. Such thinking is entirely inconsistent with the explicit divine mandate emanating from the very lips of Jesus in his parting words to his followers. Obedience may not be the noblest of motives, but it does call the whole church to account as stewards of the gospel with unmistakable marching orders from its Lord.

Divine Calling or Inner Compulsion

The sense of divine calling, supernatural guidance, or even just the sense of inner compulsion has been a powerful motivation for missionaries throughout the generations. This may come through a supernatural vision, a burden of compassion, the sense of Christ's love, or other means and related motives. Personal testimonies often describe such guidance as a burden, as compelling against human reason, or as virtually irresistible. This motivation has the power of being linked not merely to a general sense of need or obligation but directly to the convictions of the explicit divine will for an individual.

The apostle Paul is often cited as a biblical example. Paul originally received the call to be apostle to the Gentiles on the Damascus road at his conversion. This call was then further confirmed as the Holy Spirit spoke through the prophets and teachers in Antioch (Acts 13:1–3). Paul's Macedonian vision is sometimes cited as another example: "Come over to Macedonia and help us!" (Acts 16:9). Paul's missionary calling, however, was not a matter of naked obedience but one that passionately gripped him. He could write, "I am compelled to preach. Woe to me if I do not preach the gospel!" (1 Cor. 9:16b), and speak of "great sorrow and unceasing anguish in my heart" (Rom. 9:2) because his fellow Jews had rejected Christ. We shall examine more carefully the question of the missionary call in chapter 9.

Most of the great personalities of mission history testify to such a sense of calling or inner compulsion as at least part of their missionary motivation. For example, Patrick, missionary to Ireland in the early fifth century, said "I heard calling me the voice of those who dwelt beside the wood of Foclut which is nigh to the western sea, and thus they cried, 'we beseech thee, holy youth, to come and walk again amongst us as before'" (cited in Neill 1964, 56). Or Thomas Coke (1747–1814), the "father of Methodist missions" who traveled to the West Indies and died en route to India in 1814, who claimed, "God Himself had said to me: 'Go to Ceylon'" (cited in Van den Berg 1956, 103).

After citing the example of Charles T. Studd, who passionately gave up a personal fortune to become a missionary to China, Oswald J. Smith asks, "Is that the way you feel? Have you, too, felt the urge? Does the Word of God burn like a fire in your heart? Have you no rest day or night because you do not go?" (2002). Such a conviction or sense of inner compulsion is often considered an indication of calling to missionary service.

This understanding of missionary calling has until recently been considered essential to missionary service within evangelical missions. Traditionally, mission agencies have asked potential candidates to describe their "call" to missions. Though there was usually no single expectation of what that call should be, if the candidate's call was not convincing he or she would seldom be accepted for missionary service (Eskilt 2005).

Extreme and romanticized understandings of the missionary call can be detrimental in at least two ways. Many who were rightly motivated and have genuinely sensed God's leading into missionary service have held back because they lacked a more dramatic experience of calling—the lightning bolt from heaven never came. Others who have become missionaries have suffered an undue burden of failure and the sense of having betrayed their calling when they returned home from missionary service for reasons other than death or retirement. Today most mission agencies have involved application processes that examine not only a candidate's sense of calling but also his or her spiritual gifts, service record, personality traits, emotional stability, team spirit, and more. Such developments are helpful aids when rightly understood and used.

Many in the church view sensational stories of the missionary call as a modern form of hagiography or as sentimental spirituality. But must we not at the same time question the present tendency to reduce missionary service to mere volunteerism? What place is there still for a clear sense of God's guidance regarding a missionary vocation? Are there not many in the church who participate in short-term trips and even long-term service for all conceivable reasons *except* a sense of divine guidance? How many fail to sincerely seek God's guidance or deeper commitments regarding missions? Though God may use the most unlikely circumstances to move his servants into missionary service, can unemployment, self-realization, boredom, or adventure seeking be considered better substitutes for inner compulsion or divine calling attributed to the work of the Holy Spirit?

As we shall see in chapter 9, God gifts and equips certain people in special ways to serve him as cross-cultural servants of the gospel. We may be right in removing some of the romance, idealism, and drama from God's calling regarding missionary service, but we dare not rule out the supernatural guidance of the Holy Spirit.

Doxology: To the Glory of God

We noted that the highest purpose of mission is God's glory: the gospel is to be brought to the nations so that from every people there will be those who become glad worshippers of the King. This purpose in turn could be considered the highest motivation for mission. This is the conviction of John R. W. Stott, who writes, "The exaltation of Jesus Christ to the Father's right hand, that is, to the position of supreme honour, provides the strongest of all missionary incentives" (1992, 366).

Christ himself entered the world, becoming a servant "so that the Gentiles may glorify God for his mercy" (Rom. 15:9). A few verses later Paul writes that he considered his mission to the Gentiles an offering to God (Rom. 15:16). He calls Christians to do all that they do to the glory of God (1 Cor. 10:31). He wrote of his ministry: "All this is for your benefit, so that the grace that is reaching more and more people may cause thanksgiving to overflow to the glory of God" (2 Cor. 4:15). He described his fellow workers as "a glory to Christ" (2 Cor. 8:23 NASB).

The glory of God was central to the *Rule of St. Benedict*, which guided Benedictine monastic life, service, and mission from the early Middle Ages onward (see Heufelder 1983). The doxological motive, often associated with the theocratic motive, was especially prominent among the Puritans and early American mission leaders (Rooy 1965, 282 and 323–28; Van den Berg 1956, 155–56; Beaver 1966, 17–19). "The glory of God is the first and greatest mis-

SIDEBAR 7.3
JUDSON'S MOTIVATION

Adoniram Judson (1788–1850), the first American missionary, wrote a letter to John Hasseltine asking for his daughter Ann's hand in marriage with these words:

> I have now to ask whether you can consent to part with your daughter early next spring, to see her no more in this world; whether you can consent to her departure to a heathen land, and her subjection to the hardships and sufferings of a missionary life; whether you can consent to her exposure to the dangers of the ocean; to the fatal influence of the southern climate of India; to every kind of want and distress; to degradation, insult, persecution, and perhaps a violent death. Can you consent to all this, for the sake of Him who left His heavenly home, and died for her and for you; for the sake of perishing, immortal souls; for the sake of Zion, and the glory of God? Can you consent to all this, in hope of soon meeting your daughter in the world of glory, with a crown of righteousness brightened by the acclamations of praise which shall redound to her Saviour from heathens saved, through her means, from eternal woe and despair? (C. Anderson [1956] 1972, 83).

They married in 1812 and left twelve days later for India and from there on to Burma. Ann experienced a miscarriage en route to Burma, where she would also later bury an eight-month-old son. The hardships of missionary life and caring for Adoniram during his severe seventeen-month imprisonment broke Ann's health.

In 1826, at age thirty-six, she and a six-month-old daughter died. In her life she translated portions of the Bible into Burmese and Thai, and with her husband she planted the seeds of the church in Burma, which would eventually grow to thousands of churches with hundreds of thousands of Christians.

REFLECTION AND DISCUSSION

1. What is the primary motivation for missionary service reflected in Adoniram's letter to Ann's father?
2. Do you feel that the Judsons acted foolishly?
3. What are the biggest differences between the Judsons' motivation and motivation for missionary service today?
4. Times and circumstances of missionary work have dramatically changed since the days of the Judsons. Do you feel that this should also change the nature of missionary motivation today? Explain your answer.

sionary motive in the early [American] National period. Perception of the Church's opportunity to share in the work of redemption was the first grand, exciting concept that captured the imagination of those who early identified with the missionary enterprise" (Chaney 1976, 225). This motive began to discernibly wane by 1810, ironically just as the Protestant missionary movement began to expand (Beaver 1968a, 139–40).

More recently the popular writings of John Piper have rekindled the doxological motive as captured in his phrase, "Missions exist because worship doesn't." Thus worship "is the fuel and the goal in missions" (2003, 17). He continues, "Churches that are not centered on the exaltation of the majesty and beauty of God will scarcely kindle a fervent desire to 'declare his glory among the nations' (Ps. 96:3)" (18).

Eschatological Motivation: With a View to the End

Eschatology, the biblical teaching of the last things and Christ's second coming, has been a powerful motivation for missionary work throughout the history of the church. The eschatological motivation emphasizes that this age is passing, and that a future day will dawn with Christ's return and the full establishment of the kingdom of God. Eschatology gives history today its significance, and mission becomes linked to salvation history. The outcome of mission is not left to chance or dependent on human success or failure. Mission is God's mission and will not fail. The church announces the coming kingdom to the nations, fulfilling the words of Jesus in Matthew 24:14: "And this gospel of the kingdom will be preached in the whole world as a testimony to all nations, and then the end will come" (cf. Mark 13:10). Karl Hartenstein has argued that eschatology is "the strongest motivation for sacrificial love and courageous witness of the church before the world" (cited in Spohn 2000, 101).

A VARIETY OF ESCHATOLOGICAL MOTIVES

Eschatology can motivate for mission in several very different ways. Each of these expressions of eschatological motivation for mission has some element of legitimacy, as well as some element of danger in its extreme form.

First, the statement that the end will not come until the gospel has reached all nations (Matt. 24:14; Mark 13:10) can be understood as a *hope and assurance that the task of mission is not in vain but will prevail*. When Christ returns in glory, the church can be assured that its task has been fulfilled. Eschatology provides hope and confidence in the outcome of mission. As Howard Peskett writes, "It is hard to continue in evangelism and church planting, day after day, year after year, especially in communities of inexplicable hardness, without some sort of hope burning inside you" (1997, 303). As we participate in God's mission, we become part of something infinitely greater and more significant than ourselves. We become God's instrument in fulfilling his plan for the nations from creation to consummation.

Second, the eschatological hope itself is motivation in that it is a message of exceptionally *good news for a world with so little hope*. Life will conquer death. The creation itself will be redeemed with a new heaven and a new earth, a kingdom of peace and righteousness, and a world without pain, suffering, or injustice. The world is now filled with these latter things, and there is little genuine hope that human efforts will ultimately eradicate them. Our efforts are at best stopgap measures. Mission not only entails the announcement of the coming kingdom but is itself a sign of the kingdom that has already been inaugurated with Christ's first coming. This hope, the only hope, must be shared with others. It is good news that the world must hear.

A third motivation for mission raised by eschatology is that of *urgency: the message of salvation must be preached before it is too late.* This view emphasizes that upon Christ's return every person will face the judgment of God. Because all have sinned, all will be found guilty of eternal death unless they have heard the gospel and received forgiveness in Christ. Evangelistic missionary proclamation becomes literally a matter of life and death. Because Christ may return at any time, no effort should be spared in getting out the message of salvation to the largest number of people as quickly as possible.

A fourth form of eschatological motivation is that missionary proclamation becomes a *means of hastening Christ's return.* Matthew 24:14 and Mark 13:10 are so interpreted that Christ's return is contingent upon the church completing the task of world evangelization. In this view missionary proclamation becomes a means to fulfill conditions for Christ's return. Responsibility is placed on the church to fulfill this condition, and in its least thoughtful expressions, makes human effort the key.

ESCHATOLOGICAL MOTIVES THEN AND NOW

The eschatological motivation for mission can be found as early as Pope Gregory the Great (540–604), the first truly missionary pope, who motivated missionaries with the eschatological expectation of the end of the world, which would be hastened by increased missionary activity (Padberg 1995, 350). Seventeenth-century Dutch Reformers viewed the conversion of the Gentiles followed by conversion of the Jews as a necessary condition to Christ's return (Van den Berg 1956, 20). German Pietists, including the Moravians, were motivated by the thought of the coming kingdom, though eschatological motives were not central (Beyreuther 1961, 39). "American missions were the product of the Puritans, and the founding fathers of New England regarded their entire colonial venture from an eschatological viewpoint" (Beaver 1959, 61). Jonathan Edwards (1748) saw the eschatological vision of Zechariah 8:20–22 as a motive for prayer and mission. Eschatology played only a minor role in the motivation for early English mission efforts, of Awakening preachers and Wesleyans. But there was an excitement that such revival might be a sign of the coming kingdom (Van den Berg 1956, 65 and 104).

Early in the nineteenth century eschatology came to play a greater role in mission; "a new enthusiasm took possession of men and women all over Britain, who saw in the incipient missionary work one of the most important signs of the dawn of the Millennium" (Van den Berg 1956, 161). By the 1830s salvation of the perishing in view of an immanent advent of the millennium became the most important motive (Beaver 1968a, 126–27). Millenarian speculations continued to be a great motivation for mission in the nineteenth century; they gradually decreased after the Civil War, but the urgency of saving the perishing heathen remained great (Beaver 1959, 69–70). A host of early mission leaders, especially of the so-called faith missions, strongly advocated mission as a means to hasten the return of Christ. These included such greats as Karl Gützlav (the "Apostle of China"), J. Hudson Taylor (founder of the China Inland Mission), A. B. Simpson (founder of the Christian and Missionary Alliance), Fredrik Franson (founder of the Evangelical Alliance Mission), A. T. Pierson (Student Volunteer Movement), and various Pentecostal mission leaders (D. J. Bosch 1991, 316; Robert 2003, 135; McGee 1986, 95 and 169; 1991, 207–8).

More recently, Arthur P. Johnston writes in the spirit of premillennialism, "The Scriptures have not promised to make man or a society perfect in this present age, yet nothing contributes more to the ultimate needs of the world than evangelism. Nevertheless, *the goal of biblical evangelism is not a Christianized world but a world evangelization that will bring back the King*" (1978, 52, emphasis added). German Lutheran Peter Beyerhaus echoes this sentiment: "Evangelism is the chief contribution of the church to hasten the visible establishment of Christ's Kingdom on earth. Only when this work is complete, will Christ come to redeem the groaning creation from its present bondage" (1975, 294; cf. 1990, 369). One of the incentives for mission agreed upon in the Evangelical-Roman Catholic Dialogue is "to hasten the return of the Lord" ("Evangelical-Roman Catholic Dialogue" 1986, 8).

AN ASSESSMENT OF ESCHATOLOGICAL MOTIVES

Scripture leaves no doubt that the redeeming work of the Lamb of God will in fact purchase men and women from every tribe and language and people and nation (Rev. 5:9; 7:9). Those who respond by receiving the gospel may be a minority (Matt. 7:13), but they will respond. Though the church may be reluctant and though missionaries may be feeble and flawed, of this the church can be assured: God will accomplish his purposes for the nations in this age. This eschatological hope should be great encouragement to persevere in the face of opposition and in spite of human imperfection.

Jesus also exhorts us to work while it is still day, for the night is coming, when we will not be able to work (John 9:4). No one knows the hour or the day of Christ's return (Matt. 24:36), but we do know that when he does come it will be a time of judgment (1 Thess. 1:7–9). When Paul charged Timothy to preach the Word of God in and out of season, and to do the work of an evangelist, he did so with urgency: "In the presence of God and of Christ Jesus, who will judge the living and the dead, and in view of his appearing and his kingdom, I give you this charge" (2 Tim. 4:1). Paul says of his own ministry, "Since, then, we know what it is to fear the Lord, we try to persuade men" (2 Cor. 5:11a). God is patient about Christ's return, "not wanting anyone to perish, but everyone to come to repentance" (2 Pet. 3:9). Our eschatological convictions thus compel us to spread with great urgency the message of Jesus Christ. This attitude, however, should not misguide us to a reckless haste that leads to superficiality in mission.

For a variety of reasons the church today has lost a sense of urgency about mission and Christ's return. But as stated in the Lausanne Covenant, "The promise of his coming is a further spur to our evangelism. . . . We believe that the interim period between Christ's ascension and return is to be filled with the mission of the people of God, who have no liberty to stop before the end" (Article 15).

Can our mission efforts hasten Christ's return? This question calls for a more guarded assessment. First, slogans calling the church to hasten Christ's return easily give the impression that Christ's return is contingent upon human effort. Everett W. Huffard is no doubt correct in claiming that "the American cultural value of success orientation and taking charge of our own destiny makes it very easy for us to assume we can do something to hasten the return of Christ" (1991, 10). The church is God's primary instrument to spread the gospel and fulfill his purposes for the nations in this age, but emphasis is misplaced when the impression is given that if we fail, Christ cannot return and God's plan or timing is thwarted. God remains sovereign, and if one church fails, he will raise up another to accomplish his purposes.

Second, the wording of Matthew 24:14 and Mark 10:13 is not a command but a prophetic statement. Second Peter 3:12a speaks of how believers are to "look forward to the day of God and speed its coming." But we should refrain from overstating the intent of such passages. Richard J. Bauckham sees in this passage the delay of Christ's return because of the Lord's desire that none perish (v. 9). Christian evangelism and lifestyle contribute to more people being saved, thus hastening the return of Christ. "This," he concludes, "does not detract from God's sovereignty in determining the time of the End . . . but means only that his sovereign determination graciously takes human affairs into account" (1983, 325).

However one interprets these passages, the emphasis is clearly less on human responsibility and more on divine plan. Matthew 24:14 and Mark 10:13 indicate that mission, particularly proclamation, is the crucial task of the church in anticipation

> *With the World under his feet, with heaven in his eye, with the gospel in his hand and Christ in his heart, he pleads as an ambassador for God, knowing nothing but Jesus Christ, enjoying nothing but the conversion of sinners, hoping for nothing but the promotion of the kingdom of Christ, and glorying in nothing but in the cross of Christ Jesus, by which he is crucified to the world, and the world to him.*
>
> Henry Venn, 1805
> (cited in Stott 1992, 374)

189

of Christ's return. World evangelization is central to God's purposes in this age. Mission work gives history meaning as it progresses toward Christ's return. "Christian theology, and certainly missiology, must not allow time—and above all the time between the resurrection and the parousia of Christ—to be evacuated of its God-given meaning" (Scherer 1990, 403). The apostle Paul was motivated by this apocalyptic vision and passion for the Lord's return (Aus 1979; Carriker 1993). This should indeed be a motivation for us, not because God depends on us, but rather because we can depend on him to accomplish his purposes through us.

CONCLUSION

Love and compassion are surely the very heart of mission. But alone they can easily degenerate into condescending pity, with a corresponding sense of superiority. Even the deepest compassion for the temporal and the eternal plight of fellow humans is in itself not adequate. It is anthropocentric and subject to corruption.

Obedience to the Great Commission is certainly a biblical motivation, but it is not sufficient alone. A cold obedience apart from love and joy will taint the work and undermine it. The strength of the will to obey must be found in a source greater than the hearing of a command. It is not by chance that the Great Commission comes with the promise of Christ's own authority and abiding presence (Matt. 28:19–20) and the gift of the Holy Spirit (Luke 24:49). Van den Berg affirms the necessity at times of emphasizing obedience, then adds, "But when this necessity arises there is something wrong in the life of the church—just as in a marriage there is something wrong when the duty of mutual love has to be emphasized" (1956, 199).

Calling (including inner compulsion) is certainly a motivation that we find repeatedly in the writings of the apostle Paul. This motive is rooted in God's initiative, God's plan, and God's gifts. Calling will always be confirmed by other spiritual leaders, whereby the visible and public laying on of hands plays no small part (Acts 13:3), and this public act in turn can be an encouragement to the servant who has lost heart or motivation (1 Tim. 4:14; 2 Tim. 1:6). There can be little denying that in the scriptures and throughout the history of mission, divine guidance, calling, and gifting have been a significant motivation for mission.

Both extremes of asceticism, on the one hand, and self-realization, on the other, must be rejected as self-serving motives. Yet Christ himself called true disciples to deny themselves (Luke 14:26–27). Paul wrote in Colossians 1:24, "Now I rejoice in what was suffered for you, and I fill up in my flesh what is still lacking in regard to Christ's afflictions, for the sake of his body, which is the church." In Philippians 3:10, Paul speaks of knowing Christ and "the fellowship of sharing in his sufferings, becoming like him in his death."

These words are worthy of deep consideration. They remind us that although suffering in missionary service does not earn salvation or sanctification, the readiness to suffer in that service, indeed the rejoicing in that suffering, can deepen the relationship to Christ.

Personal edification, satisfaction and fulfillment, church renewal, and other pragmatic benefits are surely welcome by-products and blessings of mission. But when these become primary, mission becomes a means to another end, which is in the last analysis self-serving. This is the very opposite of the spirit of mission, which is the spirit of the Father, who sent his Son entirely selflessly.

The highest motive must remain rooted in the person of God himself: his love for the world, his redemptive work in Christ, and his promise that all nations will hear and that his glory will fill the earth.

8

The Church and Mission

God has chosen to realize his purposes in history—his mission—primarily through a people. As we have seen in the preceding chapters, this people is in our day the church. In this chapter we shall examine the relationship of the church and mission with regard to (1) the missionary nature of the church, (2) the missional church conversation, and (3) the sending structures of mission.

THE MISSIONARY NATURE OF THE CHURCH

The question might fairly be asked, does the church have a mission, or does God's mission have a church? To claim that the church has a mission is to posit that the church has an existence apart from its mission, or at least that the church somehow stands above its mission or decides over its mission. In an institutional sense this is of course true. Institutions exist that are called churches, and these institutions must determine what their mission is. But because the church has been called into existence by God and derives its purpose from him, our understanding must go beyond mere institutional conceptions.

Mission and the Identity of the Church

God has called the church into existence for the very purpose of serving his mission. Jesus himself is the builder of the church, which is *his* church (Matt.

192

16:18). Jesus sends his disciples on a continuation of his mission, to be sent into the world as he was sent (John 20:21). Nothing could be clearer from the book of Acts than this: the church in the power of the Spirit becomes God's instrument to bear witness to the redemptive work of Christ and the coming kingdom. Robert Plummer's careful study of the Pauline epistles concludes that "Paul considered the general apostolic missionary obligation to devolve upon each local congregation. That is, each church, as a whole (not simply individuals within it), inherited the apostles' obligation of making known the gospel" (2006, 48).

"The Church on earth is by her nature missionary since, according to the plan of the Father, she has as her origin the mission of the Son and the Holy Spirit" (AG 2). In this sense the mission of the Triune God must have primacy in our understanding of the church, and the church's very existence and legitimacy are linked to its mission in the world.

Thus church and mission are intimately intertwined. We cannot biblically speak of mission apart from speaking of the church, and we cannot speak of the church apart from speaking also of mission. A missionless church and a churchless mission are theological oxymorons (see sidebar 8.1). As Lesslie Newbigin claimed, "A Church which has ceased to be a mission has lost the essential character of a Church. . . . An unchurchly mission is as much of a monstrosity as an unmissionary Church. . . . No recovery of the true wholeness of the Church's nature is possible without a recovery of its radically missionary character" (1954, 169).

Johannes Blauw was commissioned by the WCC to produce a biblical theology of mission. The resulting work became a classic titled *The Missionary Nature of the Church*, in which he concluded, "Missionary work reflects in a unique way, particularly in its passing boundaries in space and spirit, the very essence of the Church as a Church. It returns (as it were) to its origin,

---

SIDEBAR 8.1
THE MISSIONARY CHURCH

"The Church is by nature missionary to the extent that, if it ceases to be missionary, it has not just failed in one of its tasks, it has ceased to be the Church. Thus, the Church's self-understanding and sense of identity (its ecclesiology) is inherently bound up with its call to share and live out the Gospel of Jesus Christ to the ends of the earth and the end of time" (Kirk 2000, 31).

REFLECTION AND DISCUSSION

1. Do you agree that a church without mission ceases to be the church? Explain your answer.
2. How would you describe the self-understanding of your church in relation to mission?
3. Why do you think that so few churches see mission as central to their identity?

and is confronted with its missionary calling. It is exactly by going outside itself that the Church *is* itself and comes to itself" (1962, 122).

The fact that many churches exist primarily to serve their own needs, relegating mission to a project or line item in the budget, is only testimony to their failure to understand the centrality of mission to their true identity and mission as the basis of their very existence.

Called out *of the World, Placed* in *the World, Sent* to *the World*

Blauw points out the linkage between ecclesiology and missiology when he argues, "A 'theology of mission' cannot be other than a 'theology of the church' as the people of God called *out* of the world, placed *in* the world, and sent *to* the world" (1962, 126). The idea of God calling persons, indeed a people, to himself to in turn be sent into the world is one that can be traced through salvation history.

- Abraham is called apart to be blessed, so that he might become a blessing to the nations (Gen. 12:3).
- Israel, after its deliverance from Egypt, is reminded by the Lord "how I carried you on eagles' wings and brought you to myself. Now if you obey me fully and keep my covenant, then out of all nations you will be my treasured possession. Although the whole earth is mine, you will be for me a kingdom of priests and a holy nation" (Exod. 19:4b–6a).
- Jesus appoints the twelve apostles "that they might be with him and that he might send them out to preach and to have authority to drive out demons" (Mark 3:14b–15).
- Peter echoes the language of Exodus 19 to describe the calling of the church as the new people of God: "But you are a chosen people, a royal priesthood, a holy nation, a people belonging to God, that you may declare the praises of him who called you out of darkness into his wonderful light. Once you were not a people, but now you are the people of God; once you had not received mercy, but now you have received mercy." Peter then continues, "Live such good lives among the pagans that, though they accuse you of doing wrong, they may see your good deeds and glorify God on the day he visits us" (1 Pet. 2:9–10, 12).

God brings his people "to himself" so that as his possession they might be sent into the world. Only through relationship with him are his people empowered and made fit to be light. As they are taken up by his glory, they are able to live for his glory and draw others to glorify God. God's people can fulfill their priestly role among the nations only as they are consecrated and sanctified by God. Like the Twelve, the church is called apart from the world for the purpose of intimate fellowship with Jesus, to be sent again into the world in the name of Jesus as a witness to Jesus and to demonstrate that the kingdom has broken into human history. Apart from this relationship mission is impossible; as Jesus said, "I am the vine; you are the branches. If a man remains in me and I in him, he will bear much fruit; apart from me you can do nothing" (John 15:5).

Election, God's sovereign calling of the church, has often been misinterpreted as an election to privilege, to a special status before God as if God's elect were specially favored over others. This is a perversion of the biblical understanding of election that both Israel and the church today have at times advanced. Jesus, the Son of God, was sent into the world "not to be served, but to serve" on a mission of redemption (Mark 10:45). So too the church is sent into the world not to serve itself but to serve the world, on a redemptive mission of proclaiming the gospel of the kingdom to all nations. We are called to have the same attitude of service and humility that was evidenced in Christ, who surrendered his position of privilege and took on the form of a servant (Phil. 2:5–8).

At the same time, the church is not merely called to be an instrument of the kingdom nor called in a primarily functional sense. The church as the new people of God occupies a special relationship to God as his treasured possession. The church is the bride of Christ whom he loves, gave himself for, and is beautifying for that great wedding day (2 Cor. 11:2; Eph. 5:25–27; Rev. 19:7). Christians' preoccupation for all eternity will be to live as subjects of the King in the eternal kingdom, worshipping and serving the King.

The Church as God's Primary Agent of Mission

It should be abundantly evident from the preceding discussion that the church is God's primary agent of mission in this age. However, in the 1960s and early 1970s the understanding of mission in the WCC was heavily influenced by secularism and theologians such as J. C. Hoekendijk and A. T. Van Leeuwen. They argued that mission is God's work in the world to establish peace, justice, and humanization, and God uses many secular, political, and other means to accomplish this. The mission of the church is to serve the world by discerning God's direct work in the world and aligning with such movements. This viewpoint effectively marginalized the role of the church in mission and virtually ignored the role of God's supernatural working in history.

Though God is almighty and able to work through any means of his choosing, the scriptures are clear that the church is his primary instrument for proclaiming the gospel and realizing his purposes in this age. Surely the church can cooperate with various efforts for justice and compassion that are not immediately associated with the church. But the kingdom is spiritual at its core—the reign of God—and works from this spiritual center outward into lives, churches, communities, and societies. God has chosen to work through kingdom communities comprised of redeemed persons entrusted with the gospel and empowered by the Holy Spirit to be and do what the world *cannot* be or do.

As the gospel is preached among the nations, people repent, believe, and are born again into the kingdom (Mark 1:15; John 3:3–5). New communities are formed as witnesses to the transforming power of the resurrected Christ (Acts 1:8). They live as salt and light in the world glorifying the Father (Matt. 5:13–16). They live to the praise and glory of God in holiness (Eph. 1:4–6), break down barriers dividing people (Eph. 2:11–22), and evidence his wisdom according to his eternal purpose in Christ (Eph. 3:10). Such communities manifesting the kingdom of God can only be the result of the supernatural working of the Holy Spirit. The scriptures tell us of no other people, no other message, no other power, no other movement that is the instrument of God's choosing for fulfilling his purposes in this age as is the church.

The Church as a Sign of the Kingdom

John the Baptist prepared the coming of the Messiah with the proclamation: "Repent, for the kingdom of heaven is near" (Matt. 3:2). The kingdom hope of the Old Testament was about to break into history. Jesus himself began his public ministry with the same message (Matt. 4:17). The message of the kingdom as a present reality as well as a future hope was central to Jesus's teaching. Though direct reference to the kingdom occurs less often in the Epistles than in the Gospels, the same concept permeates the New Testament. God's kingdom is characterized as that place where Christ is acknowledged as Lord, the reign of God transforms all aspects of life, and the powers of evil are defeated. "The proclamation of the Gospel is thus the proclamation of the Lordship of Christ among the nations"; therefore, "mission is the summons of the Lordship of Christ" (Blauw 1962, 84).

We established in chapter 2 that the church is God's kingdom people in this age, and in chapter 4 that the kingdom is the center of mission. In this sense the kingdom of God is the kingpin of church and mission. Mission is about establishing God's reign through the redemptive and transformative work of Christ, and the church is a living sign and witness to that kingdom. The church as God's kingdom people manifests the character of the kingdom in its common life as a redemptive community of love and in its public life as salt and light in the world.

> *The church is, therefore, an ecclesia, a called out assembly whose public life is a sign, witness, foretaste and instrument to which God is inviting all creation in Jesus Christ.*
>
> Alan J. Roxburgh (2004, 3)

But the church is only a sign of that kingdom. It does not and cannot fully realize the kingdom in this age; rather, it lives in the hope of the coming of the kingdom in fullness at Christ's return. As an eschatological community, it anticipates that kingdom. The very life of the church should be a testimony to the glory of the kingdom before the observing world. The message of the church is an invitation to repent and enter that kingdom by receiving the gracious gift of God in Jesus Christ and experiencing a foretaste of the renewal of all things. Newbigin emphasizes a threefold relationship of the church and the kingdom, the people of God being a *sign*, *instrument*, and *firstfruit* of the kingdom: "Each of these three words is important. They are to be a *sign*, pointing men to something that is beyond their present horizon but can give guidance and hope now; an *instrument* (not the only one) that God can use for his work of healing, liberating, and blessing; and a *firstfruit*—a place where men and women can have a real taste now of the joy and freedom God intends for us all" (1994, 33).

In chapter 6 we established that the task of missions is to create kingdom communities among all people. Kingdom communities were described in terms of their three dimensions: the Great Calling (doxology), the Great Commission (evangelism and discipleship), and the Great Commandment (compassion and justice). The mission (singular) of the church may be defined as *being* such a community in word and deed. The task of missions (plural) is the creation and expansion of such communities among all people. The church must authentically *be* what it is *attempting to accomplish* in the world.

THE MISSIONAL CHURCH CONVERSATION

The Gospel and Our Culture Network (GOCN) has developed the concept of the unity of church and mission to yet another level.[1] The earliest usages of the term *missional* in the current sense to describe the activities of the church can be traced back to Francis Dubose (1983) and Charles Van Engen (1991). In the early 1990s the GOCN began using the term *missional church*. But the release in 1998 of *Missional Church: A Vision for the Sending of the Church in North America* marked the first major public discussion using the term. In the words of Alan Roxburgh, the term *missional* or *missional church* has gone "from obscurity to banality in eight short years and people still don't know what it means" (2004, 2). Despite the confusion surrounding its meaning, the missional church discussion has stimulated fresh thinking about the nature of the church and its mission.

According to the original advocates of the concept, the church is to be understood not as an organization with a mission; rather, the church's very identity *is* mission. Mission and church are merged into one. The church is not primarily a sender; rather, the church itself is the sent one, and it is sent on a

---

1. For brief summaries of the "missional church," see Roxburgh (2004) and Van Gelder (2004). For fuller descriptions, see Hunsberger and Van Gelder (1996), Guder (1998), Gibbs (2000), Frost and Hirsch (2003), Minatrea (2004), and a critique by Goheen (2002).

mission that is larger than itself. The mission of God becomes the mission of the church as a whole, and not the mission of particular ministries or emissaries of the church. "In this conversation, mission is no longer understood primarily in functional terms as something the church does. . . . Rather it is understood in terms of something the church is, as something that is related to its nature" (Van Gelder 2004, 437).

Roots

Several developments have led up to this rethinking. Already in 1938 the IMC in its meetings at Tambaram began rethinking the missionary nature of the church, speaking in its report of a "conception of the church as the missionary sent into the world" (cited in Goheen 2002, 481). Works such as Newbigin's *Household of God* (1954) and Blauw's *Missionary Nature of the Church* (1962) more fully developed an understanding of the church in terms of its missionary sending. During the second half of the twentieth century, mission came to be understood less in terms of a task that the church is to fulfill and more in terms of *missio Dei*, which gives birth to the church. These streams merged into the conviction that the church exists as the agent of God's mission. The church does not merely send missionaries; rather, the church itself is sent on God's mission. The church exists for the sake of God's mission and kingdom; thus, ecclesiology must be subordinate to missiology.

Newbigin and others noted in the 1960s that Western culture had become post-Christian and thus a "mission field." Missiologists had long recognized that mission is no longer something to be done exclusively in foreign lands and could no longer be geographically or culturally defined. Old distinctions such as "sending church" and "receiving church" or "mission church" had become anachronous and even harmful. Every church in every place must understand itself as a missional church, and every Christian should understand herself or himself as a missionary. In conciliar circles this thinking made the need for traditional missionary-sending agencies questionable. Upon returning to England after decades of service in India, Newbigin drew attention to the failure of Christendom and to the secularization and religious pluralism of Western culture. Not only is mission everywhere, for God seeks to establish his kingdom everywhere, but a new consciousness was raised for the missionary sending of the church in the West to be a witness for the kingdom in its own context. This spawned the GOCN and the missional church conversation in North America.

Affirmations

We must certainly affirm, as has been demonstrated throughout this volume, that the church is called to mission and that the church finds its very identity in its participation in God's mission. We can thank missional church advocates for returning mission to the center of ecclesiology. Churches everywhere must rediscover their identity in their mission locally and globally, and not in denominational labels, programs, or anything that relegates mission to one of many things the church undertakes. The church does not determine its mission; rather, God's mission determines the church. In an ultimate sense the church does not *do* mission; rather, the church is taken up *by* and participates *in* God's mission.

The missional church conversation also rightly identifies the dangers of overly institutional understandings of the church, which tend to be self-serving and undermine its missionary calling. This conversation exposes functionalistic, managerial, and pragmatic understandings of the church, which are more a product of Western culture than of scripture (see Van Gelder 2000 and 2004). The identity of the church is not to be found in what it does, how large it is, what programs it sponsors, denominational distinctives, or what standing it has in the society. The identity of the church is to be found in its relationship to the Triune God, who has created it as his missionary people.

Furthermore, we are rightly reminded that the church does not exist for itself. As noted above, its election is an election not of privilege but of service. Unfortunately, the church too often has become a consumer-oriented institution serving the needs of its members. But "the church is not a gathering of those who are finding their needs met in Jesus," according to Alan Roxburgh. "This is a terrible debasement of the announcement of the reign of God" (2004, 4).

Finally, it is also a matter of fact that Western culture must be increasingly considered post-Christian. In Western cultural contexts most people no longer share a Christian worldview or Christian values, and the church increasingly exists as a counterculture in contrast to the prevailing society. Thus the church in such contexts must think less in terms of basic evangelism and more in terms of cross-cultural mission if it is to reach its contemporaries with the Christian message. The Western church needs a fresh sense of urgency to live missionally in its post-Christian context. We must confess the tendency for churches to gravitate toward meeting their own needs, retreating into a Christian subculture, and failing to see their primary calling to serve the world as part of their worship of God.

Cautions

At the same time, several cautions must also be raised regarding much of the missional church conversation. First, as we noted in chapter 3, definitions of *missio Dei* vary widely, and the term can be used to define mission in almost any manner. Most advocates of the missional church have defined *missio Dei* very broadly in terms of God's kingdom purposes in the world.

We have argued in chapter 4 that God's sending activity can be scripturally defined as having doxology as the purpose, redemption as the foundation, the kingdom as the center, eschatology as the hope, the nations as the scope, reconciliation as the fruit, and incarnation as the character of God's mission. Our definitions of *missio Dei* must retain biblical clarity and avoid overly broad and vague interpretations.

Second, the reasoning behind the missional church concept draws upon that of the WCC in the 1960s. It was boldly declared at Uppsala that the day of "missions" was past and the day of "mission" had arrived. Mission was no longer to be understood as the church sending missionaries; rather, everything the church does is to be mission. As a result, as we shall see, in many conciliar denominations sending structures such as foreign mission agencies were absorbed into denominational structures, and foreign missions was virtually abandoned as a result of this thinking. It can hardly be said that churches became more missionary in terms of global mission; indeed, the very opposite could be argued. All that the church does *should* in some way flow from and reflect its missionary character. But this principle can in practice be turned on its head so that anything and everything the church does is by definition "mission." It returns us to the old problem that Stephen Neill identified: "If everything is mission, nothing is mission" (1959, 81). When this happens, mission loses.

Third, missional church advocates repeatedly emphasize that the church does not *do* mission, but it is missional by its very nature. Church programs and plans to undertake mission as an activity are downplayed for fear of promoting a "corporate" or "organizational" understanding of the church (doing something on behalf of God). Although there is always the danger of reducing the calling of the church to a form of activism, it is also true that merely proclaiming the church to be missional by nature does not automatically make it missional in practice.

Clearly, not all churches of the New Testament have fulfilled their God-intended mission, though they continue to be called "the church." Every church must consciously discern its mission and intentionally resolve to fulfill that mission in alignment with God's calling as revealed in scripture. Churches failing to fulfill God's mission are in jeopardy of forfeiting their legitimacy and continued existence as Christ's church (e.g., Rev. 2:5; 3:1–2, 15–17). Yes, the church is in its very essence missional; but no, the church does not automatically live and act consistently with that mission. The church must in practice be intentional about living missionally and setting missional priorities.

An early critique of the missional church conversation was that it "remained a relatively theoretic and abstract academic conversation about the church" (Roxburgh 2004, 5). While calling the church to a prophetic, missional task, it offered "little guidance for the positive participation of the church in cultural development" and there was "no mention of ecclesial structures that would prepare the laity for their callings" (Goheen 2002, 486, 488). Fortunately, increasingly this deficit is being addressed with works including practical suggestions and case studies to help churches realize missional transformation (e.g., Minatrea 2004; Hirsch 2006; Stetzer and Putman 2006; and Van Gelder 2007a, 2007b, 2008).

Fourth, missional church advocates generally decry any separation of church and mission (e.g., Van Gelder 2000, 64–65). Because the church does not merely have a mission but is on God's mission, this attitude is fully understandable. The existence of mission structures (such as mission agencies) apart from local churches can reinforce such separation and are thus viewed as "a reflection of deficiencies inherent within the understanding of the church's nature" (Guder 1998, 74–75). However, as we shall discuss later, the specialized task of reaching the nations is complex and can be greatly facilitated through the existence of such agencies. As long as they serve the larger mission of the church, they needn't be understood as a contradiction to the missional nature of the church. On the other hand, by disallowing any separate structure for global or local mission, mission suffers. The cause of mission as intentional outward engagement with the world becomes lost in the regular business of the church and the tasks of pastoral care, administration, and a host of other important concerns.

Fifth, bringing the gospel to yet-unreached peoples holds very little place in the missional church discussion. Although the emphasis on the local witness of the local church in post-Christian societies is a welcome one, one searches the missional church literature almost in vain to find references to bringing the gospel to the nations. Yet, as we demonstrated in chapters 1 and 2, this is one of the central themes of mission in the Bible. The fine distinction between *mission* (singular) and *missions* (plural) is missed by the vast majority of ordinary Christians. Intentional missions, particularly missions to yet-unevangelized peoples, can be lost in all the good things the church now does and calls "mission." While every locality is indeed a "mission field," we must not overlook the fact that there remain hundreds, by some estimates even thousands, of ethno-linguistic people groups that have no gospel witness or indigenous church whatsoever. There remains an urgent place for identifying the task of missions—the creation and expansion of kingdom communities among *all* the peoples of the earth—apart from all the other good and important things that the church can and should do.

THE SENDING STRUCTURES OF MISSION

The biblical mandate of mission includes the bringing of the gospel to yet-unreached peoples and nations. Ultimately, God calls, sends, and sustains such apostolic emissaries. But what means does he use, what is the role of local churches, and what, if any, is the role of mission agencies that have some form of independent organization apart from local congregations? For example, the missional church understanding of the church seeks to merge church and mission into one entity, abhorring any separation of church and mission in either theory or practice. Does there remain any legitimate place for specially formed mission-sending agencies apart from local congregations? What, if any, form of mission society or parachurch agency is theologically or practically justified?

Never before have local congregations been so directly involved in global ministry. International short-term teams abound. Partnerships between congregations spanning continents have become commonplace. Increasingly, churches are taking the initiative in recruiting, training, and sending their own missionaries apart from traditional mission agencies. One study revealed that nearly half of all American churches with over two thousand weekend worshippers act as their own sending agency for some or all of their missionaries and agree or strongly agree that God's instrument of mission is the local church and not mission agencies (Priest 2008).

Though mission agencies in various shapes and forms have historically been the primary vehicle for churches to send and support missionaries, should this continue to be the case? Is there any biblical justification for the existence of mission societies as a parallel structure to local congregations?

Many Ways to Send Missionaries: A Historical Overview

Throughout the history of the global expansion of Christianity, the church has employed various means to facilitate the sending and support of foreign missionaries. In the church of the New Testament, we see that initially the gospel spread through various unintentional means such as persecution (Acts 8:1–4; 11:19–21) and traveling pilgrims (Acts 8:26–40). The first intentional sending of missionaries came many years after Pentecost with the sending of Paul and Barnabas by the church in Antioch (Acts 13:1–3). Paul then recruited additional missionary coworkers from the churches he planted. He was financially supported in part by churches, such as the Philippian church (Phil. 4:15–16), and in part by self-support through the secular work of tentmaking (Acts 18:3; 1 Cor. 9:6). We have relatively little reliable information about the other apostles and their missionary activities.

During the first centuries of Christianity, there were a few missionary bishops such as Irenaeus and Gregory Thaumaturgus, but the gospel continued to spread largely through the informal means of Christian merchants, slaves, soldiers, travelers, and even prisoners of war. We know of no specific missionary-sending organizations. James Scherer notes that with Christianity becoming the state religion of the Roman Empire, "mission was no longer something done by every local congregation. It developed into a separate activity carried on by special agents in remote areas. . . . Since the fourth century mission has been thought of as something quite distinct from the mainstream of the church's life" (1964, 46). Monastic orders became most instrumental in the spread of the gospel as devoted monks traveled, at first primarily on ascetic pilgrimages and then later on intentional trips for evangelism and church planting. Historian Mark A. Noll observes, "The missionary expansion of Christianity was unthinkable apart from the activity of monks" (1997, 99). Unfortunately, it was not beyond the church to at times employ military conquest and coercion to advance the spread of Christianity.

In the age of discovery and European imperialistic expansion, the Roman Catholic Church established the system of patronage, whereby it was the responsibility of the colonizing political potentates to christianize the indigenous peoples in their colonial territories. Missionaries of the various religious orders served under the authority of the given king or magistrate. This system not only failed but led to abuses, so in 1622 the pope formed the Congregation for the Propagation of the Faith, which brought the oversight and direction of mission activities directly under the authority of the church.

The Protestant Reformation was slow in developing a mission movement. The reasons for this are many, but one significant factor was that Protestants had no organizational structure similar to monasticism as a vehicle to carry out the task of foreign missions. Early Pietists and renewal movements saw little hope in the established churches taking up the cause of missions. They were viewed as being indifferent or hostile to the idea. Thus, without official church sanction, such groups formed small societies of the "revived" to advance the cause of foreign missions (Zimmerling 1985; note, however, that the very first Pietist missionaries, Ziegenbalg and Plütschau, were sent under the authority and financing of the Danish king, Friedrich IV, with the Danish-Halle Mission). Brian Stanley calls this the "communitarian-institutional" model (2003, 40).

In seventeenth-century London, congregations had begun forming voluntary societies to promote piety and combat various social evils. Foreign mission societies were formed after this model. Early societies such as the SPCK and SPG were linked with the established church but were generally ineffective in sending missionaries to unreached peoples (A. F. Walls 1996, 243). It would be William Carey's call in 1792 for structures similar to that of the trading companies, even more independent of existing church structures, that would create the vehicle so instrumental in launching the Protestant missionary movement. "The simple fact was that the Church as then organized, whether episcopal, or presbyterian, or congregational, *could* not effectively operate mission overseas. Christians had accordingly to 'use means' to do so" (ibid., 246).

These societies were often interdenominational in nature and frequently led by laypeople. For example, the SPCK was founded in 1698 by five people, four of whom were laymen belonging to the Church of England. The SPCK was viewed with skepticism by clergy and lacked the official support of the

Church of England. Out of this concern under Thomas Bray's leadership (the sole clergyman among the founders of the SPCK), the Society for the Propagation of the Gospel in Foreign Parts (SPGFP) was created in 1701 with the official sanction of the Church and chartered by the king (see Van den Berg 1956, 40–44; and A. F. Walls 1996, 160–72; 2002, 215–35).

Though structurally different and separate from local church or denomination, the success of the societies lay in their ability to connect with local congregations and individual Christians. This was done by activating small groups and forming decentralized auxiliaries. In this sense, far from being isolated from congregational life, they were connected at the grassroots level, giving congregants the opportunity for involvement in mission that traditional church structures were unable to provide. This in turn led to increased numbers in missionary recruitment (A. F. Walls 1996, 250–51). The societies' independence at the same time allowed them to remain entirely focused on the singular task of foreign missions and to not become distracted or encumbered with ecclesial maintenance or other ministries.

The voluntary mission society thus became what Andrew Walls (2002, 232) calls the "organizational engine" of the Protestant missionary movement, the prime and virtually sole vehicle for the explosive growth of the Protestant missionary movement in the nineteenth century. Two broad forms of mission agencies developed. On the one hand were those formed and operated more independently from established denominations, which later included the so-called faith missions. Their missionaries were often less educated, nonordained, nonconfessional, and sometimes tentmakers. On the other hand were denominational mission agencies that were more closely subordinated to the institutional church. Their missionaries were often university educated, confessional, professional, and ordained (Wellenreuther 2004). Nevertheless, even during this "Great Century" of Protestant missions, the promoters of mission remained for the most part a minority of laypeople, and the missionaries were largely nonordained (A. F. Walls 2002, 215–35).

The responsibility of the mission societies and agencies grew to include nearly every aspect of the missionary endeavor: promotion, recruitment, training, deployment, communication, and the facilitation of financial and other support for the missionary. Local congregations gave of their members to become missionary candidates but were otherwise responsible mainly for ongoing prayer and financial support. By the mid-nineteenth century the number of such sending agencies had grown exponentially. They gained expertise and experience in the complexities of mission work, earning the trust of local churches. The difficulties of expense, travel, health, language, and communications made sending and supporting missionaries a seemingly impossible task for a single local congregation to adequately master apart from such agencies. Newer and older mission agencies alike expanded their ministries from primarily evangelism and itinerate church planting to include medicine, education, social work, and a host of other ministries.

Stanley's (2003) excellent discussion of the development of mission-sending structures points out that initially the mission societies were simple structures with a board of directors intended to facilitate the sending and financing of missionaries. But over time the boards took increasing responsibility for decisions related to daily mission work and the emerging churches. "By the 1920s, the denominational missionary societies, especially in the USA, had become big business, relying explicitly on the methods of secular corporations to manage the whole enterprise" (Stanley 2003, 42). The formation of nondenominational faith missions was in part a reaction to such business-oriented approaches to management and fund-raising. Furthermore, whereas denominational agencies tended to become national institutions, many faith missions such as the China Inland Mission became forerunners of truly international agencies with sending bases in various countries.

In the twentieth century numerous more specialized mission agencies emerged, which developed expertise in ministries such as Bible translation, radio broadcasting, and missionary aviation. Globally the number of foreign mission-sending agencies has grown from about 600 in 1900 to 2,200 in 1970 and 4,410 in 2006 (Barrett 2006, 28). Many of these newer agencies have been formed in the majority world, as churches there have become a powerful international missionary-sending force.

By the end of the twentieth century, the situation regarding mission agencies had changed dramatically in both conciliar and evangelical circles. Conciliar churches increasingly questioned the lostness of the unevangelized and the necessity of personal faith in Christ. Humanitarian work gradually took prominence over traditional evangelism. Conciliar churches believed that the nations had been largely reached and the national churches should now be responsible for the further evangelization of their nations. For example, the official report from the WCC assembly at Uppsala in 1966 reads, "The missionary societies originated in a response of a past generation to the call to take the Gospel to the ends of the earth. Changing political, economic and ecclesiastical circumstances demand new responses and new relationships" (Goodall 1968, 35). This shift eventually meant the dismantling of many mission agencies and the redefinition of the role of missionaries. Already in the early 1950s Newbigin had argued that the church is missionary in its very nature and thus decried the dichotomy of church and mission as manifest in the existence of mission societies (1954, esp. 164). This view is echoed by missional church advocates (e.g., Van Gelder 2000, 64–65).

At the same time majority world—especially African—churches called for a moratorium on missions. Not a few mission boards affiliated with conciliar denominations were turned into commissions on ecumenical relations or interchurch aid or absorbed into denominational structures. This reflected the integration of the IMC with the WCC in 1961 at New Delhi, which was based on the convictions that the mission field is everywhere and that all ministries of the church (at home or abroad) should be considered "mission." For example, Scherer argues that the very existence of mission societies resulted in a "legal separation" between church and mission, leading to "un-missionary churches and un-churchly mission" (Scherer 1964, 41–52, esp. 49).

Pierce Beaver has noted how the Presbyterian Church (USA) Board of Foreign Missions was replaced by the Commission on Ecumenical Mission and Relations. As a result, already in 1968 he can state, "It has relatively little to do with direct confrontation with belief and non-belief. A 'sending' enterprise has given way to a 'lending' operation. What now exists is largely a system of interchurch aid" (1968c, 80). Stanley observes, "Placing responsibility for mission squarely on the shoulders of the church seemed the only way to avoid the excesses of society control and the only way in which 'sending' and 'receiving' churches could begin to develop relationships of partnership rather than subordination" (2003, 42). As a result "some [agencies] have internationalized and reinvented themselves so radically that they have effectively ceased to exist as recognizably 'missionary' agencies in the traditional sense, becoming primarily facilitative structures for the management and channeling of interchurch aid, scholarship, training and development programmes, etc." (45). He describes how the London Missionary Society, once the second largest sending agency in Britain, became the Council for World Mission, which in 1999 had only forty-five missionaries but bore responsibility for vast financial resources (ibid.).

As a result of these developments, the number of missionaries sent by conciliar related agencies plummeted. In the wake of the modernist-fundamentalist debates, the number of conciliar-related missionaries began to fall as theological conservatives and fundamentalists lost confidence in denominationally related missions. In 1935 missionaries affiliated with mainline denominational missions comprised 60 percent of the North American missionary force; by 1952 their proportion fell to half and by 1980 to only 10 percent (J. A. Carpenter 1997, 184–85; Coote 1982). Overall, from 1900 to 2000 the percentage of North American missionaries sent by mainline mission organizations dropped from 80 percent to only 6 percent (Pierson 2003, 67; see also W. R. Shenk 1999, 180–81). Evangelicals, on the other hand, continued to maintain the necessity of sending missionaries, and their ranks increased dramatically. The number of conservative North American missionaries grew from under 5,000 in 1935 to over 32,000 in 1980 (J. A. Carpenter 1990; 1997, 184).

However, by the late twentieth century local churches increasingly wanted more direct involvement in foreign missions. This was especially the case in North America. Technological advances reduced the difficulty and cost of international travel and communication, enabling local churches to have more immediate contact with field missionaries and national believers. Through short-term mission trips large numbers of local church members gained personal exposure to mission work. Direct international partnerships were often formed between local congregations on different continents—this often apart from mission agency involvement. Information on mission history, strategy, and cross-cultural ministry became widely available to local churches, which increasingly formed their own opinions about what makes for effective mission work.

By the end of the twentieth century, tensions between local congregations and mission agencies had only grown. An early sign of this was evident in 1971 at a conference of mission leaders at Green Lake, Wisconsin (Linhart 1971; Shepherd 1971; and especially Gordon MacDonald 1971). The legitimacy of parachurch and mission agencies apart from the local church had already been questioned in the early twentieth century by theologians such as A. H. Strong (1909, 890) and missiologists such as Roland Allen ([1912] 1962a, 83; [1927] 1962b, 96). By the end of the century, however, the legitimacy and necessity of the mission agency were being challenged more widely, especially by local congregations directly involved in missions (e.g., W. Phillips 1985; Camp 1995; Rowell 1998).

There had always been local congregations, such as the early Moravian Brethren, the Churches of Christ, and the Plymouth Brethren, that sent missionaries apart from mission agencies. But these were until recently relatively isolated cases. However, by the mid-1980s this practice was becoming widespread and boldly advocated by both large and small churches alike. For example, in 1985 an article appeared in *Evangelical Missions Quarterly* titled "Your Church Can Train and Send Missionaries," which claimed, "The local church is beginning to take its rightful place as the trainer and sender of missionaries. Any church can provide the right kind of help a cross-cultural worker needs before he or she gets on the plane" (W. Phillips 1985, 196–97; see also examples in Siewert 1997).

The term *congregational-direct missions* was coined to describe the movement (M. Phillips 1998). Adherents of this movement perceive mission boards as too bureaucratic, too expensive, too inflexible, unable to respond to the world's rapidly changing situation, and out of touch with (or even condescending toward) the desires of local congregations. Paul Pierson (1998) also attributes this development to a general distrust in American society of institutions, expectation of quick results, and an individualistic ecclesiology. Some have furthermore argued that the very existence of mission boards is unbiblical, illustrating Ralph Winter's observation that Protestants have always been a bit unsure about the legitimacy of such structures (1974, 133).

Most churches continue to send and support missionaries through mission agencies. But they are no longer satisfied to merely "pay and pray." They want more direct involvement in all aspects of mission work and more genuine partnership. Greater accountability and justification for the high cost of sending missionaries through traditional mission agencies are expected (Borthwick 1999). Most mission agencies have attempted—albeit with some difficulty—to address these concerns. New paradigms for the relationship of church and agency are in the making (Guthrie 2002).

The Question of New Testament Precedent

Paul and Barnabas were sent out by the church of Antioch, and they reported back to this church at the conclusion of their first mission journey (Acts 13:1–3; 14:26–28). We find nothing in the New Testament about an independent, formalized structure or organization to promote or facilitate the Pauline mission. Thus it was argued by Allen that there is no basis in the New Testament for the modern mission agency. He maintained that the early church itself was a missionary organization, "consequently there was no special organization for missions in the Early Church; the church organization sufficed. . . . The new modern missionary organization is an addition. . . . With us missions are the special work of a special organization; in the Early Church missions were not a special work, and there was no special organization" ([1927] 1962b, 96). Indeed, he viewed the very existence of mission agencies as a divine condescension (117). More recently, Harry Boer writes, "The missionary society is, scripturally speaking, an abnormality. But it is a blessed abnormality" (1964, 214).

Of course, there is no New Testament example of a mission agency in the modern sense—but then neither are there biblical examples of church buildings, legal incorporation, Sunday schools, youth groups, Christian publishing and media, Christian colleges, seminaries, Christian camps, and many other aspects of church life and ministry that are today taken for granted and greatly used by God. One can more persuasively argue that there is no basis in the New Testament for a single local church being solely and independently responsible for every aspect of the sending, support, and supervision of missionaries or mission activities. The earliest expansion of the church from Jerusalem into the surrounding region was spontaneous and unplanned, in part a result of persecution (e.g., Acts 8:1–8). "These movements of believers were neither planned nor controlled by the church in Jerusalem" (Severn 2000, 322).

The first recorded intentional sending of missionaries came with the aforementioned commissioning of Paul and Barnabas by the Antioch church. But Paul's missionary call did not come through the Antioch church; rather, it had come with his conversion on the Damascus road (Acts 9:15; 22:21). In fact, he had worked previously as a missionary in Arabia, Cilicia, and Syria without even consulting the church in Jerusalem (Gal. 1:17–24; cf. Acts 15:23). The language of Acts 13:1–4 emphasizes more the sending by the Holy Spirit than by the church. Thus it could be argued that the Antioch church merely confirmed and partnered with Paul in a new phase of his missionary work (see Schnabel 2008, 392).

Paul recruited coworkers from other churches (e.g., Acts 16:1–3), but we do not read of these coworkers reporting back to their home churches. Critical decisions regarding the direction of the mission were made by Paul and his team under the direct leading of the Holy Spirit without consulting the church in Antioch (e.g., Acts 16:6–10). The landmark decision regarding Gentiles and the law, which profoundly impacted the Pauline mission, was decided not in Antioch but in Jerusalem (Acts 15:1–34). Intervention of the Antioch church is reported neither in the conflict between Paul and Barnabas nor in the recruitment of Silas as Paul's new missionary partner, though they were both "committed" or "commended" to the Lord, apparently by the Antioch church (Acts 15:35–41). Paul received financial support from churches other than Antioch, such as the church in Philippi (Phil. 4:10–19). When conflict or false teaching arose in the churches Paul planted, he exercised his own apostolic (or missionary) authority over those churches and did not involve the churches in Antioch or Jerusalem in any way.

In fact, judging by Luke's report in Acts, the involvement of the Antioch church in the Pauline mission and in the churches he planted was quite limited. Luke, of course, does not report all the details, and there were no doubt many practical reasons for this limited involvement such as first-century difficulty of travel and communication. Winter is surely correct when he observes of the Pauline missionary band: "No matter what we think the structure was, we know that it was not simply the Antioch church operating at a distance from its home base. It was something else, something different" (1974, 123).

Thus some have claimed that far from being an argument against mission agencies, "the Antioch model is the strongest biblical case for the formation of mission structures to spread the gospel to the regions beyond" (Severn 2000, 324; see also E. F. Murphy 1974; Glasser 1976, 26–27; White 1983; Blincoe 2002; and Plueddemann 2006). Winter (1974), Pierson (2009, 29–40), and others have argued that both mission structures (sodalities) and local congregation structures (modalities) are from a practical viewpoint not only equally legitimate but also equally biblical expressions of the church. Mission structures, distinct from congregational structures, are understood as both theologically and practically justified.

However, much like arguments against mission agencies, one cannot make a case *for* mission agencies based strictly on New Testament precedents. Parallels to modern mission agencies are incidental. Nor can one make a theological case for (or against) agencies based on historical precedent (Camp 1995, 200). Even if an analysis of the report in Acts could demonstrate clearly the relationship between the Antioch church and the Pauline mission, the question remains regarding the extent to which this account is merely a *descriptive* report of practical arrangements or a *normative* pattern to be applied in all churches

209

in all times. Given the enormous differences between the first century and today in travel, communication, resources, church structures, and so on, the debate over biblical precedent for or against sending agencies is historically anachronistic and hermeneutically problematical. In writing Acts, Luke was focused more on the spiritual dynamic of the gospel's progress than on the mechanics of support, accountability, and administration.

Stephen Neill warns of attempting to create a theology of missionary societies as "a theological justification of what we have done in the past and of what we are trying to do in the present" (1959, 82). He claims that this cannot be done because mission agencies are not a necessary part of the existence of the church. They perform a function of the church. To argue theologically for mission agencies would be like arguing theologically for the shape of a baptismal font. You can have a theology of baptism, but not of baptismal fonts! Walls quips that "there never was a *theology* of the voluntary society. The voluntary society is one of God's theological jokes, whereby he makes tender mockery of his people when they take themselves too seriously. The men of high theological and ecclesiastical principle were often the enemies of the missionary movement" (1996, 146).

Nevertheless, the New Testament does contain a clear ecclesiology and a descriptive account of the spread of the gospel. From these teachings and accounts, some broad principles can be deduced, even though they may not offer a dogmatic answer to the current debate about sending structures (Schnabel 2008, 444). In other words, the debate is not strictly pragmatic. It may be ill advised to attempt to formulate a theology of mission agencies per se. But as Walls goes on to say, the mission society has immense theological *implications* (1996, 147). Such questions are answered biblically not by looking for some precedent or exact parallel in the Bible. Rather, we must ask if such structures or systems facilitate the achievement of biblical purposes and principles. Are they *inherently* consistent or inconsistent with the concerns of the New Testament, the advancement of mission, and the values of the kingdom?

Biblical Principles and Theological Considerations

BIBLICAL PURPOSES

We have defined the task of missions as the extension and expansion of kingdom communities among all the peoples of the earth. We also defined doxology as the highest goal of mission, redemption as the foundation, the kingdom of God as the center, eschatology as the hope, the nations as the scope, reconciliation as the fruit, and incarnation as the character of mission. These are the guiding principles. Whatever the structures for missionary sending, they must serve such purposes. Obviously, a wide variety of structures and means can conceivably achieve these ends. Inappropriate structures, however, can compromise or hinder such goals. But the Bible is less concerned with the methods than with the ends and with employing means that are consistent with those ends.

ECCLESIAL PRIMACY

The New Testament is quite clear that the local church is God's primary agent for realizing his purposes in this age. It is only consistent with this understanding that local churches should be intimately and directly involved in the sending of missionaries, whatever structures are used. In the New Testament the calling of missionaries is confirmed by the church (e.g., Acts 13:1–3; 16:1–3; 1 Tim. 4:14). Advances in travel, communication, and resources allow local churches today to be involved in many more ways than were possible in the New Testament church, and such possibilities should surely be utilized. Local churches are rightly taking greater initiative, refusing to leave everything to the mission agency, and expecting direct involvement.

Like most human institutions, mission agencies are in danger of becoming self-justifying ends in themselves (Allen [1927] 1962b, 99–101). But they are only provisional instruments of a higher cause. The church will endure until the day Christ receives it as his bride. All other agencies of the church will pass away—many long before Christ's return. Mission agencies are not to be confused with the church nor considered an expression of the church in any way equal to local congregations (see Camp 1995; Schnabel 2004, 1578–79; 2008, 393). Mission agencies retain their theological justification only to the extent that they *serve* the church in the fulfillment of its missionary calling. On the basis of what George Peters calls "the principle of delegated authority" (1972, 226), churches may choose to create institutions or organizations to facilitate fulfilling its mission.

Paul Beals aptly notes that local churches "are the hub of the missions wheel, while mission agencies are spokes in the wheel helping churches extend their work of world missions. . . . The mission agency is a service organization aiding the local church in its task as the sending agency" (1995, 133). Whereas the mission agency may represent and facilitate the missionary intention of the church, it can never become a substitute for the mission of the church, making mission an appendage of the local church. Much less can the mission agency become an excuse for the local churches to become passive in their missionary responsibility (Gensichen 1971, 174–77). Or as Peters states, "The mission agency ought to be the church's provision, instrument, and arm to efficiently expedite her task. It can neither displace nor replace the church, though it may be called upon to act in place of the church" (1972, 229).

HISTORICAL PRECEDENT

Though historical precedent is not authoritative, it is instructive and we are foolish if we fail to learn from it. Churches, like most human institutions, tend to look out for their own sustenance, needs, and interests. An examina-

211

tion of the expansion of Christianity reveals, as noted, that apart from the early beginnings, global outreach has rarely been facilitated by the sole initiation and sustenance of local churches or denominational structures. Winter (1974) points out that specially formed communities or agencies, structured separately from local congregations, nearly always played a significant if not decisive role in the spread of the Christian faith. In the Middle Ages these communities were the monastic orders. Among Protestants they have been the mission societies. Peters calls this "the principle of selective appointment" (1972, 226–28), whereby we observe in both scripture and history that God repeatedly raises up individuals—often apart from the initial sanction of the church and due to the failure of the church—who are catalysts for renewing passion and vision for missions.

Walls observes that one of the preconditions for sending missionaries was "a form of organization that could supply them, and forge a link between them and their work and the wider church" (A. F. Walls 2002, 221). The mission agency has for two hundred years provided such an organization. Wilbert Shenk's observation is no overstatement: "The modern missionary movement would have been inconceivable apart from the missionary society" (1999, 178). Conversely, it can be observed that where such structures do not exist or are absorbed into general church or denominational ministries, global outreach withers. Given the global expansion of the church today, James Plueddemann argues that "mission agencies will need to expand their focus from evangelism and church planting to mission-agency planting" (2006, 264–65), creating the vehicles for missionary sending by emerging churches.

The sending structures have varied greatly throughout Christian history, often reflecting the social structures of their time: monastic models in early Catholic missions, voluntary society and trading company models in nineteenth-century Protestant missions, and in the twentieth century corporate business models that sometimes resemble multinational corporations. Globalization and other developments have recently resulted in more fluid networking models that are transdenominational and transnational. But in each case these structures differ from local churches and are more highly focused, single-minded, and intentional about fulfilling the Great Commission than a local church can be.

Structures or organizations (i.e., mission agencies) in themselves are not the key to missionary effectiveness. That can be attributed only to God himself working through his people. Allen ([1927] 1962b, 106–7) pointed out a century ago that mission agencies may not only serve to advance the spread of the gospel, but all too often can hinder it when they become too cumbersome, self-justifying, and overly professionalized. But nearly two thousand years of church history is unequivocal: God has seen fit to work primarily through structures that have the singular focus of cross-cultural mission, whereas, generally speaking, churches without such structures fail to significantly advance this cause. Even some of the strongest advocates of the primacy of the church, such as pioneer missiologist Gustav Warneck, have conceded the failure of the institutional church in its missionary obligation and that mission agencies are a practical necessity (Wellenreuther 2004, 179–80). One may debate whether this *should* be the case, or whether it will *remain* the case. Changing times may well demand changed sending structures, but existing structures should not be cast off lightly in the process.

CHRISTIAN UNITY IN MISSION

One of the remarkable fruits of the mission society was that it gave new and unique expression to unity in both the local and the global body of Christ. Christians from various denominations cooperated in the common cause of world mission via mission agencies (A. F. Walls 1996, 247–49). In fact, even the formation of national denominational associations and synods was in part a by-product of unified efforts to promote foreign missions through national societies. Stanley notes, for example, that, "the Baptist Union, until 1903, occupied no more than a few rented offices in the headquarters of the Baptist Missionary Society" (2003, 41). Otherwise, highly independent churches banded together to send and care for missionaries, which they could not do alone.

As many local churches today take responsibility for sending and supporting mission work apart from larger agencies, the danger of an overly independent spirit must be avoided. A congregation can easily have the impression that it can "go it alone" and thereby become oblivious to the larger work of God and the need for cooperation with others. The importance of partnership in mission has become widely recognized, but this recognition has most often applied to international partnerships. The importance of partnership among sending churches must be rediscovered. Congregations must continue to find ways to cooperate with and learn from one another. No single congregation has all the wisdom or resources necessary. Mission agencies have facilitated such partnership and cooperation in the past— doing what one church alone could not do. Other structures may possibly serve the cause of mission in the future. But one thing is clear: every congregation needs other congregations—especially in carrying out the task of global mission. Jesus himself prayed for Christian unity as a key to the world believing in him (John 17:18–23). Participation in the *missio Dei* has no place for ecclesial individualism.

PRACTICALLY INFORMED

If we have given attention to the above considerations, then it should not be considered unduly pragmatic to address this topic frankly on the basis of practicality: What is realistic? What has stood the test of time? What experience have others had? What really works? World mission is a complex undertaking and costly in both financial and human terms. Good stewardship demands that we proceed with wisdom and efficiency. God expects us not only to depend on the supernatural provision of the Holy Spirit; he has also given us the ability to discern and act wisely.

Realistically, the energy of local churches and even denominations tends to gravitate toward ministries of maintenance and pastoral care. These churches normally lack the level of commitment, sacrifice, and single-mindedness necessary to sustain a long-term, cross-cultural mission effort. When mission structures are fully subsumed under congregational structures, mission usually suffers. "Missional church" advocates seek to overturn such tendencies, calling the church to be missional in all its undertakings. But the verdict is still out about whether this can be done, and history gives little warrant for optimism.

Most local congregations simply do not have the resources, personnel, experience, or infrastructure needed to train, send, support, and supervise foreign missionaries on their own. Considerable infrastructure, networking, trust building, and specialized resources are necessary to sustain missionaries and develop wise and effective relationships with national churches around the globe. Good intentions lacking wisdom and missiological insight often result in repeating the errors of history such as paternalism and cultural insensitivity. As Proverbs 19:2 reads, "It is not good to have zeal without knowledge, nor to be hasty and miss the way." Samuel Metcalf adds this concern about local church mission committees acting as mission agencies: "The average committee includes godly, well-meaning, but inexperienced people who go on and off the committee at the whim of church elections. Cross-cultural mission is far too complicated, as well as geographically distant from the supporting church, for the committee to exercise responsibility for field strategy and supervision" (1993, 145).

Even in churches with a weekend attendance of over two thousand, only 28 percent of mission pastors have more than two years missionary experience, and 62 percent have no missionary experience whatsoever (Priest 2008). Smaller churches have even fewer such resources. Even the most experienced missions pastor will not have all the gifts, expertise, or time to coordinate a significant missionary-sending program alone. Not a few churches that have attempted to "go it on their own" apart from any assistance from more experienced agencies have ended up seeking the assistance of such agencies when problems arise. Some congregations have banded together with other local congregations to cooperate in sending missionaries, but such arrangements quickly begin to look very much like traditional mission agencies. Though James Engel and William Dyrness take a critical view of historic mission agencies, they advise local churches against becoming yet another mission board: "Make no mistake about it, a retreat from continued agency/church partnership, no matter how well motivated, virtually guarantees that an independent initiative will face the same challenges and make the same mistakes—without the benefit of the experience missions have acquired" (2000, 128).

Furthermore, direct local church involvement is simply not possible in many restricted-access regions of the world (see Borthwick 1998). Short-term mission trips and projects cannot be allowed to become ends in themselves, geared more toward meeting the needs of the sending church than making a genuine contribution to mission work. Independent, direct involvement in mission can easily lead to the sending church becoming overly invasive in local mission work or even lead to unhealthy manipulation and paternalism. The desire for international partnership has led many churches to naively support distant ministries that lack integrity because they have responded to attractive appeals but lack the cultural insight necessary for discernment.

The desire of churches for more active participation and direct involvement in all aspects of missions is a welcome development. Mission involvement of a congregation should not be limited to a few committee members, occasional prayer, or an annual conference. Today it is possible and desirable for many members of the congregation to gain firsthand exposure to and more personal identification with global mission undertakings. Mission agencies will need to adapt to this new situation if they are to serve the church well in the future. To the extent that agencies are willing and able to adapt, we concur with Eckhard J. Schnabel: "A mission agency is, for pragmatic reasons, the most effective means of initiating and supporting missionary work in distant regions, due to the specialized knowledge in regard to country, culture, language and politics of the particular region" (2004, 1579).

CONCLUSION

The answer is not an "either/or" approach, but rather greater cooperation and mutual appreciation between local church and mission agency in fulfilling the Great Commission. This can result in a synergy of local churches working together closely with mission agencies in a joint effort to advance the kingdom. Darrell L. Guder argues that these two types of structures "must exist in a symbiotic relationship with local congregations and their denominational structures. The apostolic church implies a variety of ways in which its mission is carried out, and thus a variety of structures that a missional ecclesiology must address" (1998, 75). We heartily concur with Bruce Camp when he concludes, "Pragmatically speaking, agencies (independent or denominational) are a gift from God and should be utilized by congregations. However, theologically speaking, they should never be considered as the church in mobile form. Legitimacy ascribed to mission agencies stems from their service with churches, not from usurping the local church's biblical mandate" (1995, 207).

Various models for the church-agency relationship have been proposed, such as a "synergistic (focused) church" (Camp 2003, 239–40) and a "servant-partner" (Hammett 2000) that give the local church primacy while seeking cooperation with mission agencies (see also Beals 1995). As with so many questions relating to contemporary challenges, the Bible does not offer us a simple, easy answer. Rather, we must seek to apply scriptural principles, employ human insight and understanding, and act in the best prayerful wisdom.

9

The Missionary Vocation

The stereotypical image of the missionary in a pith helmet, living in the jungle and teaching "poor natives," is more a caricature from the past than a present reality, though such images die hard. For generations missionaries were the heroes of the church, shrouded in an aura of sacrifice and adventure and serving under compulsion of nothing less than the mysterious "missionary call."

Today not only has the missionary been taken off the pedestal, but the very necessity of sending traditional missionaries and the concept of the "missionary call" are being questioned. Just as the term *mission* has in recent decades been redefined, so too the term *missionary* is being redefined. The number of long-term missionary candidates in North America is falling (Moreau 2004; 2007). According to a survey of 250 students at a Christian liberal arts college, one reason for this trend is the lack of clarity about the nature and necessity of the missionary vocation (Thornton and Thornton 2008).

Like the word *mission*, the term *missionary* does not occur in most English Bibles. Nor has the concept of "missionary" ever been consistently defined throughout the history of the church (Beyerhaus 1969). Like most words its meaning is a matter of convention, which can evolve over time. Nevertheless, our understanding of a missionary as one sent by God on God's mission cannot be considered arbitrary, for the Bible has much to say about such concepts, even if the exact terminology does not appear in the English Bible.

In this chapter we will address four basic questions relating to the concept of missionaries and the missionary vocation: (1) Are cross-cultural missionaries still necessary? (2) Is every Christian a missionary? (3) Is the concept of a missionary call biblical? and (4) Is the New Testament term *apostle* an equivalent of the English term *missionary*?

ARE CROSS-CULTURAL MISSIONARIES STILL NECESSARY?

Development

The global advance of the gospel during the twentieth century was nothing less than astonishing. If the nineteenth century was the "Great Century" for the launching of the Protestant missionary movement, then the twentieth century was the century of explosive church growth internationally, making Christianity a truly global religion. By the mid-1980s the majority of the world's Christians lived in Africa, Asia, or Latin America—on the traditional mission fields.

In the 1960s the ecumenical movement proclaimed that the age of "missions" was thus past. The age of "mission" had come, and now the great task of the church was not the sending of foreign missionaries to unreached peoples but rather that every church be a mission church in its own locale. It was reasoned that in earlier generations foreign, cross-cultural missionaries had been necessary to pioneer the progress of the gospel and establish national churches. But now churches had been planted to some extent in nearly every country of the world. These national churches should be able to complete the task of evangelization in their countries without foreign missionary assistance. The traditional missionary had become obsolete or even harmful. Instead of missionaries, only "fraternal coworkers" were needed.

In the early 1970s calls were heard for a moratorium on missionaries (Underwood 1974; Gatu 1974; Castro 1975; Wakatama 1976). The primary concern was not that the task of missions had been fulfilled, but rather that the national churches needed the freedom to develop apart from missionary dominance. It was argued that as long as missionaries were present and ministries dependent on foreign funding, national leaders would not be fully free to lead nor would churches fully develop and mature. Though the call for moratorium was rarely followed in its radical formulation, some conciliar and mainline mission agencies were restructured into departments of ecumenical relations. The number of missionaries sent by these groups began to drop dramatically. Today most parties agree that partnership and mutual respect, not moratorium, should define the nature of international church relations. Nevertheless, for many the role of the missionary has remained very uncertain.

Furthermore, the growing secularization of Western culture raised awareness of the necessity for the re-evangelization of these traditional missionary-sending countries. Already at the 1938 IMC meeting in Tambaram, Europe and

North America were considered to be mission fields. The theme of the first CWME conference in Mexico City (1963) was "mission on six continents." Thus mission no longer entailed a one-way sending of missionaries from the spiritual "haves" to the "have-nots." Every country is a mission field, every church a mission church, and every Christian a missionary.

Meanwhile, the majority world missionary force also began to grow exponentially (Jaffarian 2004; Wan and Pocock 2009). Some advocated that it is both ineffective and inefficient to continue to send Western foreign missionaries. Funds should be sent to support national evangelists or less expensive majority world missionaries (e.g., Yohannen 1986; Finley 2005). Such partnership made the sending of Western missionaries seemingly unnecessary and even wasteful.

In light of these developments many evangelical churches have also begun reducing support for traditional missionaries. The priority for some shifted to partnerships, short-term mission trips, and support of national evangelists and missionaries. North American mission agencies now support nearly twice the number of non–North American Christian workers as they do long- and middle-term North American missionaries. Meanwhile, in spite of (or perhaps because of) the short-term mission boom, the number of long- and middle-term North American missionaries has over the last ten years plateaued (Moreau 2007; Jaffarian 2008).

Evaluation

Because the face of global Christianity has been transformed, the role of the missionary indeed must be reconsidered. The churches of Africa, Asia, and Latin America have come of age, while traditionally Christian lands have become mission fields. Mission today is truly from everywhere to everywhere. Although in many places the challenge of paternalism and dependency still characterizes church-mission relations, virtually all recognize that the answer lies not in independence but in *inter*dependence. Churches must relate to one another as equal partners in God's mission, each bringing its strengths to the task. Such a stance does not eliminate the role of the foreign missionary, though in many cases it does redefine it.

The image of the missionary today is a diverse one. Many Western missionaries are more involved in leadership development and less in pioneer evangelism. Missionaries from Latin America have a vision of re-evangelizing Europe. The church in China seeks to bring the gospel back to Jerusalem via Central Asia. The typical mission team is increasingly of international composition, and many large mission agencies resemble multinational corporations, with regional offices and training centers around the globe.

Though the church today is truly global, and every locale can be considered a mission field, there are several reasons why the sending of cross-cultural

219

missionaries (from both Western and majority world churches) remains a biblical imperative.

First, whereas the church has indeed been established in most regions or countries of the world, even in many places where the church is numerically large, it remains weak and welcomes foreign missionary assistance. In such places expatriate missionaries are typically involved in ministries such as discipleship, leadership development, theological education, literature production, and infrastructure development. The older churches of the West can conversely be enriched through the input of majority world missionaries. If we understand the task of mission to go beyond mere church growth to include the establishment of kingdom communities, then in such places there remains considerable opportunity for expatriate missionaries.

Second, in many other countries the church remains so small that it is entirely inadequate to the task of evangelizing the nation. Turkey, for example, has a population of some 71 million, who are predominantly Muslim; only 0.56 percent are even nominally Christian (Barrett, Kurian, and Johnson 2001, 2:220), and there are only seven expatriate missionaries per million non-Christians (Barrett, Johnson, and Crossing 2007). In such locations expatriate missionaries often come alongside national workers assisting in evangelism and church-planting ministries.

Third, many people groups remain without any indigenous church or culturally appropriate witness for Christ whatsoever. There is no national church with which to partner; thus, pioneer cross-cultural missionaries are needed. There are approximately 4.4 billion non-Christians and 1.87 billion unevangelized people in the world; "200 major ethnolinguistic peoples each have over 100,000 unevangelized ethnoreligionists in their midst," and there are "1,192 unevangelized ethnolinguistic peoples who have never been targeted by any Christian agencies ever" (Barrett, Johnson, and Crossing 2008). According to another study, approximately one quarter of the world's population—over 1.6 billion people comprising 5,837 people groups—live in a people group of whom less than 2 percent are evangelicals and among whom no active church planting has taken place within the last two years (Holste and Haney 2006). However one might debate such statistics, clearly the need for expatriate, cross-cultural pioneer missionaries continues.

Often within the same district one ethnic group responds to the gospel, while a neighboring ethnic group does not. Countries such as India, Indonesia, and Nigeria are composed of hundreds of ethnolinguistic groups, many having no indigenous church or witness to the gospel. Due to historic ethnic rivalries, one ethnic group may reject the witness of Christians from another nearby neighbor ethnic group. Culturally distant pioneer missionaries will be more effective in such situations.

Fourth, in many places missionaries with technical skills or expertise not available locally are needed. These missionaries might perform such diverse tasks as computer programming, literacy education, Bible translation, agricultural development, and community medicine. Such skills may help advance indigenous ministries, demonstrate compassion, serve the community, and strengthen local economies. Ideally, local people can be trained in such skills, making outside assistance less necessary. But meanwhile outside missionary personnel are needed.

Fifth, unfortunately the world remains ridden with suffering and crises that call for urgent outside assistance and relief. War, famine, refugees, epidemics, and natural catastrophes call for the compassionate response of Christians worldwide. Long-term cross-cultural missionaries who have mastered the local language and culture can serve not only directly as relief workers but also as cultural-bridge persons facilitating communication and ensuring that aid is given in culturally appropriate ways.

Sixth, and finally, the most important reason to continue sending cross-cultural missionaries is the Great Commission itself, which calls the church to be a witness to the ends of the earth (Acts 1:8), to go and make disciples of all nations (Matt. 28:19). So long as there remain people groups without the gospel and so long as kingdom communities have not been established among them, no church is excused from the sending of emissaries in the name of Christ to the outermost places. Although under certain circumstances supporting indigenous workers rather than sending expatriate missionaries may have advantages, there are also many practical difficulties in making this the sole strategy for world evangelization (Ott 1993). More importantly, it would be arrogant to suppose that the Western church (or any other church) can *entirely* delegate the hard work of pioneer evangelism, church planting, and mission to others. The incarnational character of mission and the love of God are manifested not merely by sending money or aid but in the costly sending of our sons and daughters (or even parents and grandparents) to identify with and live among those without Christ.

The Great Commission is mandated with the promise of Christ's presence "to the very end of the age" (Matt. 28:20). Only when the gospel of the kingdom has been preached "in the whole world as a testimony to all nations" will Christ return (Matt. 24:14). The church cannot cease from sending cross-cultural messengers of the gospel to the many yet-unreached peoples until the heavenly vision of worshippers from "every tribe and language and people and nation" (Rev. 5:9; 7:9) has been fulfilled.

This is not to minimize the importance of the mission of every church to be a witness and sign of the kingdom in its own locality. Nor is it to suggest that crossing international borders is always necessary to reach the unreached; many unreached ethnic groups in need of cross-cultural witness live as isolated pockets in the midst of largely Christian communities. We simply maintain that the day of cross-cultural missionary sending is not past, and will not pass until Christ himself returns.

IS EVERY CHRISTIAN A MISSIONARY?

Development

Historically, Protestants and Roman Catholics alike spoke of a missionary vocation whereby an individual received from God a particular calling for full-time missionary service. The person was typically commissioned or ordained by a church and sent to perform missionary work, usually in a foreign country where the spiritual need was greater than in the home country. There were variations on the precise nature of the missionary service, such as "tentmakers" (who supported themselves through secular work) or "home missionaries" (who worked in their country of origin). The "call" was often not well defined. Some served as evangelists, others as doctors or mechanics. But there was generally little question about the existence of such a vocation, which set the missionary apart.

The aforementioned developments in the WCC led to a reconsideration of the nature of the missionary vocation. Already in 1950 Charles Long asked, "If every Christian is called to be a missionary in some sense, in what way can we describe the vocation of those called to be professional missionaries? . . . Do we still dare to maintain that the vocation of a missionary is still uniquely that of one 'sent' to a group other than his own?" (1950, 410). The report from the WCC Uppsala assembly in 1968 declared, "Laymen and women express their full commitment to mission, not primarily through the service they give within the church structures, but pre-eminently through the ways in which they use their professional skills and competence in their daily work and public service" (Goodall 1968, 33).

Kosuke Koyama, a former Japanese missionary to Thailand, defined a missionary in this way: "In the broad sense a missionary is anyone who increases by participation the concretization of the love of God in history" (1974, 128). He goes on to describe government health officials spraying DDT in North Thailand to eradicate malaria-carrying mosquitoes. Because this was a concretization of the love of God, "in this sense, those officers are missionaries" (ibid.).

In North America the GOCN reminds us that Western culture has become a mission field. This organization has called the whole church to more fully engage culture in a prophetic and missionary manner. The missional church is to view itself as God's agent of mission in *all* that it undertakes at home and abroad and is less focused on meeting its own needs than on impacting the world. From this vantage point every Christian is viewed as a missionary.

Today in evangelical circles one increasingly hears the slogan, "Every Christian a missionary!" Brian McLaren, a prolific and popular voice of the emergent church, declares, "Every church a mission organization. Every Christian a missionary. . . . Every neighborhood a mission field" (1998, 142).

Some have argued that the traditional view of missionaries creates a false distinction among Christians. Because every Christian is sent by God into the world, every Christian is to be considered a missionary. If mission is redefined as all that the church does in the world to establish God's kingdom, then a missionary is any person who works toward this end. Milfred Minatrea summarizes the position: "Since every believer is to bear witness, is sent to evidence the veracity of the Gospel message, every believer is on mission. Injustice is done to the term *missionary* when it is reserved only for professional or vocational personnel who cross oceans or other geographic boundaries in their assignment. Missionaries are ones who are sent, and for the New Testament church that includes every believer" (2004, 80–81).

Advocates of "business as mission" have sometimes described international businessmen and women who develop industries, jobs, or profit-making undertakings on behalf of local people as missionaries. Millions of Americans who serve for a few weeks of volunteer service, usually internationally, are called short-term missionaries. This brief overview makes evident the wide range of meanings and usages of the term.

Evaluation

Indeed, all Christians have the responsibility to contribute to the establishment of the kingdom and the fulfillment of the Great Commission wherever they may find themselves, whatever their gifts, and whether they are involved in vocational ministry or not. Every Christian is called to be a witness to Christ (Acts 1:8), to give an account of their hope to those who may ask (1 Pet. 3:15), and to live as salt and light in the world (Matt. 5:13–14).

The false impression that only traditional missionaries have a significant role to play in God's mission and that ordinary Christians should "merely" give and pray must be corrected. The rather condescending view, so often heard, that giving and praying are somehow inferior means of advancing God's mission in fact demeans the value of prayer and the importance of stewardship for God's mission.

Missional church advocates rightly remind us that mission belongs to the very nature of the church and should not be relegated to one among many undertakings or to individual Christians. The church not only sends; the church itself is sent, and every Christian is sent by God as his representative in the world. Calling every Christian a missionary dramatically underlines these truths.

But three problems arise with the slogan "every Christian a missionary." First, as we noted in chapter 8, the missional church ecclesiology can be taken to an unhealthy extreme that overlooks the necessity of intentional mission to the nations. Because the nations are the scope of mission, and because the sending of cross-cultural missionaries remains a necessity (as argued above), churches must include the sending of individuals for cross-cultural ministry as an essential part of their overall mission in the world. Unfortunately, the importance of cross-cultural mission to the nations is being lost in many of America's largest churches (Priest 2008).

Second, the view that every Christian is a missionary has too often been overstated, leading to an opposite unhealthy extreme of devaluing or even abolishing the unique and strategic role of the long-term, cross-cultural missionary. For example, McLaren, disillusioned with traditional mission efforts, envisions a project-centered approach to mission whereby "there will be no career missionaries in the old sense; everyone will work on terms determined by a particular project" (1998, 137). Can the task of missions really be reduced to a series of projects? Can kingdom communities be planted and expanded among all people in this way? How can the concept of genuine, costly incarnational mission be realized with such approaches?

Some local churches have discontinued sending and supporting career missionaries altogether in favor of sending short-term teams and supporting national workers. Ralph Winter wryly observes, "[Missions] has become any Christian volunteering to be sent anywhere in the world at any expense to do anything for any time period" (cited in Hesselgrave 2005, 205). Such a watering down of the missionary task to a least common denominator for which any and every Christian is equally qualified is both practically naive and theologically irresponsible. Such a course will advance neither true partnership in mission nor the discipling of the nations.

The third difficulty with the view "every Christian a missionary" is that it blurs important distinctions in God's gifting and calling of individual believers. Every Christian should be passionately committed to the creation and expansion of kingdom communities locally and globally and applying his or her gifts in some manner to that end. But not every Christian is commissioned and *sent* to create such communities where they do not yet exist (cf. Acts 13:1–3; Rom. 10:15). Every Christian has received spiritual gifts. But as we shall see later, not everyone is gifted as an apostle nor equally gifted to communicate the gospel across cultures (1 Cor. 12:28–29; Eph. 4:11).

Just as it would be neither helpful nor biblical to call every person who performs some aspect of pastoral ministry a pastor, neither is it helpful to call every person who lives missionally or performs some kind of Christian service a missionary. God has given different gifts and different callings corresponding to various tasks of ministry. The challenges of communicating the gospel across cultural and linguistic barriers, of making disciples and establishing healthy kingdom communities in unfamiliar contexts, and of appropriately contextualizing the message and expressions of Christianity demand long-term commitments and exceptional gifts that not every Christian possesses. We see the early church "setting apart" persons for particular ministries— including missionary service—by the laying on of hands (Acts 13:3; 1 Tim. 4:14; 2 Tim. 1:6). This "setting apart" indicates a public affirmation by the church of the divinely appointed role of particular Christians. The laying on of hands in the commissioning of missionaries can be understood as both a mediation of God's sending activity and an authentication of God's calling by the church (so Peters 1972, 221). In this sense clearly not every Christian is a missionary.

If we nevertheless choose to call every Christian a missionary, then we will need to create a new term for the Christian who is specially called, gifted, and commissioned for cross-cultural mission. Otherwise, this unique, essential, and divinely appointed role is at risk of being lost altogether.

IS THE CONCEPT OF A MISSIONARY CALL BIBLICAL?

As we noted in chapter 7, a deep sense of special calling has historically been a significant source of motivation for perhaps the majority of missionaries during the last two centuries. Nearly every missionary "hero" in recent times has articulated some manner of missionary call (see Sills 2008, 179–95). Countless testimonies are heard from missionaries whose clear sense of calling sustained them through difficult and discouraging times when they felt like giving up or that their work was in vain. This calling is usually considered to be supernatural and continuing for an entire lifetime.

Many if not most evangelical mission agencies have expected candidates to be able to articulate in some persuasive manner how God has called them to missionary service, even if the nature of the call remains undefined. Louis R. Cobbs writes, for example, "Throughout history Southern Baptists have expected their missionaries to be called of God. While there has been no great effort to define the term, most Southern Baptists have had a general understanding of what is meant by God's call" (1994, 29).

The WEA Mission Commission conducted a massive international study on missionary attrition asking leaders of mission agencies what they believed to be the most important factors to prevent missionary attrition. "A clear calling to mission work from God" was ranked as most important by 61 percent of newer missionary-sending countries and by 36 percent of older sending countries. However, in data on both avoidable and unavoidable reasons actually given for missionary attrition, "lack of call" ranked only nineteenth on a list of twenty-five reasons (or 1.8 percent of all attrition) for older sending country attrition and second (8 percent) for newer sending countries (W. D. Taylor 1997, 92). Some sense of missionary calling is clearly perceived to be of central importance to missionary service in most evangelical mission agencies.

James Stamoolis asserts, "The actual concept of missions may wax and wane in popularity, but the call of God to be involved in God's mission does not disappear" (2002, 12). But many argue today that the idea of the missionary call *should* disappear. J. Herbert Kane believed in a general call to Christian service, but a generation ago he expressed concisely the contemporary critique when he wrote, "The term *missionary call* should never have been coined. It is not Scriptural and therefore can be harmful" (1974, 41; see more recently K. L. Howard 2003; Moreau, Corwin, and McGee 2004; W. McConnell 2007).

Biblical Precedent

Biblical personalities such as Jesus's twelve disciples received a clear "call" to leave their former occupations for Christ's service (e.g., Matt. 4:19–20; 10:1–2). Paul's call on the Damascus road was quite supernatural and dramatic. At his conversion he received the divine revelation that he would be sent to the Gentiles (Acts 22:21). Later in Antioch the Holy Spirit said, "Set apart for me Barnabas and Saul for the work to which I have called them" (Acts 13:2). Because Paul was called to the Gentile mission at his conversion (Acts 9:15–16; 22:14–15) and had already been active as a missionary in Arabia, Cilicia, and Syria (Gal. 1:15–24), Schnabel (2008, 386–87) argues that Acts 13:1–4 describes not Paul's missionary call but a new ministry assignment (cf. Moreau, Corwin, and McGee 2004, 167–68).

Much like the call of prophets in the Old Testament, such instances can be viewed as exceptional and unique to their place in salvation history. They are rare occurrences in the New Testament. The so-called Macedonian call, which occurred in a vision revealed to Paul (Acts 16:9), is not an example of vocational calling to missionary service (Paul was already a missionary) but rather a singular incident of divine guidance for the apostolic missionary band (Moreau, Corwin, McGee 2004, 168).

Scripture is silent about Paul's numerous other missionary coworkers having received a specific call to mission work. Timothy is recommended for service by his home church in Lystra (Acts 16:1–3), and he was gifted (or confirmed) for ministry by prophetic utterance and the laying on of hands (1 Tim. 4:14; 2 Tim. 1:6). But there is no report of a subjective experience of calling. We know even less about Paul's other coworkers.

Questioning the Missionary Call

During the early centuries of the church, there were relatively few formally commissioned missionaries, yet the gospel spread dramatically through ordinary Christians as they traveled and shared their faith. As church structures became more established, over time a formalized system of vocational ministry and ordination was developed, making a clear distinction between clergy and laity. Prior to the Reformation, most Roman Catholic missionaries were members of religious orders. During the Reformation the teaching of the priesthood of all believers was rediscovered, but, with the exception of smaller Pietist and free church movements, in practice the clergy/laity distinction was retained. Indeed, Lutheran orthodoxy's emphasis on the necessity of an extraordinary call as a prerequisite for a missionary vocation "made real mission impossible" (Aagaard 1987, 16). Though Protestant missionaries were seldom fully ordained, their vocation came to be viewed as similar to that of clergy: a lifetime calling to missionary service involving a commissioning and public recognition by the sending church or body.

Already in the mid-nineteenth century, the necessity of a special missionary call was in a curious way being questioned. Some argued that the universal command of the Great Commission in itself constitutes a foreign missionary call to every Christian. Influential leaders such as J. Hudson Taylor argued that unless one is called to remain at home, every Christian is commanded and qualified to go (Taylor and Taylor 1965, 167). Similar arguments were made by Southern Baptists, the Student Volunteer Movement, and others (Cobbs 1994, 29; Beaver 1968a, 149; Sills 2008, 63–64). James Gilmore (1843–91), a missionary to Mongolia, could say, "In place of seeking to assign a reason for going abroad, I would prefer to say that I have failed to discover any reason why I should stay at home" (cited in Gannett 1960, 33). Keith Green, a popular Christian songwriter and artist of the 1970s, also reflected this view, writing, "In fact, if you don't go, you need a specific calling from God to stay home" (1982, 3).

By the mid-twentieth century qualifications for missionary service became increasingly focused on educational and psychological factors assessed by extensive interview and testing procedures; a subjective call alone was no longer considered sufficient. By the 1960s mission agencies were also creating various associate missionary roles for professionals, short-term workers, and retired people who were not commissioned for career service. The average length of missionary "career" service also steadily declined from twenty-three years in the early twentieth century to about ten years by the end of the century (Cobbs 1994). Missionary service came to be increasingly seen as more a career option than a lifelong calling (Donovan and Myors 1997). Such developments have blurred the nature and necessity of a special missionary call.

Emphasis on a clear, supernatural missionary call has also been criticized for creating an unnecessary hurdle for people otherwise qualified and interested in missionary service. Kane describes the problem in an earlier generation: "Thousands of youth desiring to serve the Lord have waited and waited for some mysterious 'missionary call' that never came. After a time they became weary in waiting and gave up the idea of going to the mission field" (1974, 41). Though this may be less the case today, the mystery of a missionary call remains elusive and confusing to many considering missionary service. In the past the missionary call was generally considered a lifetime calling, often to a single country. In some instances this placed great pressure on missionaries to remain faithful to their call, even though wisdom or obvious circumstances might have dictated a return to their country of origin.

Evaluation

The biblical witness presents a diverse picture of how people may be led into missionary service: some by supernatural calling, others by apparently more ordinary guidance; some for life, others only for a season. Paul was supernaturally called as an "apostle to the Gentiles" (or "nations"; Acts 9:15; Rom. 11:13; Gal. 2:8), indicating a particular cross-cultural or at least cross-ethnic ministry. His entire life was committed to the pioneering spread of the gospel, not limited to one geographical location or people, preaching the gospel wherever Christ was still unknown (Rom. 15:20). Timothy, on the other hand, was for a time Paul's coworker in itinerant pioneer mission work, then for a time settled into a more pastoral ministry in Ephesus, before being summoned to rejoin Paul in Rome (2 Tim. 4:21). Many of Paul's coworkers seem to have been only temporary assistants or emissaries for him (Ollrog 1979).

Today some make a distinction between a calling to vocational ministry, which is more a matter of spiritual gifts and is permanent, and a calling to a specific ministry assignment that may be temporary and change. Vocation in this view is more about what one does and less about where one does it (Bemis 1981; Moreau, Corwin, and McGee 2004, 170). Others maintain that there is a special gifting for cross-cultural ministry, an apostolic calling or vocation, thus making the cross-cultural nature of ministry integral to the vocation.

Throughout biblical history we read of God setting people apart for his service in a special manner. Though surely the prophets, Paul, and the Twelve played unique roles in salvation history, there is no reason to doubt that God continues to set apart people for his service—missionary or otherwise—through supernatural calling. Eckhard J. Schnabel (2008, 385–86) distinguishes between a general call of all Christians to be salt and light in the world (Matt. 5:13–16) and those called to vocational, full-time Christian ministry, citing the call of the Twelve and Paul as a model. As we discuss later, the gift of "apostle" (which can be understood as "missionary") is a "person-gift," seemingly indicating a more comprehensive role or office that God has assigned to certain people. The biblical language of "setting apart" and laying on of hands, as in the case of Timothy, further indicates that such a role was identified and publicly recognized as a special gifting or calling of particular people.

Jesus himself commanded his disciples to pray that the Lord of the harvest *send* workers into his harvest (Matt. 9:38). He is still answering this prayer today. He is the sender, and it is thus perhaps more accurate to speak of a divine "sending" rather than a "calling" to mission work (cf., Rom. 10:14–15).

Given the enormous challenges of missionary service, we should, however, not be surprised that God should in an exceptional way call, set apart, equip, and sustain those he sends. We cannot limit the manner by which the Spirit of God may lead people into his service, nor can we deny the testimony of those who with deep conviction have sensed such a divine call. At the same time, we should refrain from promoting an overly romanticized, formulaic, or dramatized scheme by which God leads or calls people into his service (see sidebar 9.1).

Several common factors, however, can be observed regarding God's guidance of both Paul and Timothy into missionary service. First, we recognize that ultimately it is God who equips, directs, and sends into missionary service. Paul could say he was "an apostle—sent not from men nor by man, but by Jesus Christ and God the Father, who raised him from the dead" (Gal. 1:1). Timothy's ministry was confirmed by prophecy (1 Tim. 1:18). It is not a human decision nor merely a matter of human discernment. God is the one who distributes spiritual gifts and appoints apostles, prophets, teachers, and various ministries to individuals (1 Cor. 12:7–11, 28).

Second, the local church had a role in confirming, if not explicitly articulating, the will of God that a person enter missionary service. Though Paul had received his call at his conversion (Acts 22:21), this call was confirmed by Ananias (Acts 9:15) and the church in Antioch (Acts 13:1–2). Timothy was recommended by the church in Lystra (Acts 16:1–3).

Finally, the missionaries were commissioned by the church through the laying on of hands and prayer (Acts 13:3; 1 Tim. 4:14; 2 Tim. 1:6). This indicated a special anointing of the Spirit, a setting aside for ministry, as well as the public recognition of the person's gifting and spiritual role.

M. David Sills summarizes the various factors that might define and contribute to discerning God's calling into missionary service: "The missionary call

---

SIDEBAR 9.1
WAYS GOD LEADS TO MISSIONARY SERVICE

Walter McConnell rejects the traditional view of a special missionary call but affirms "the 'call' not as a special experience, but as an ordinary way for God to reveal his will to a person, a way that will be recognized and corroborated by the Church" (2007, 213). He suggests the following means by which God might lead a person into missionary service:

1. An unexpected or crisis experience
2. Scripture reading, meditation, and prayer
3. The study of other books
4. The influence of godly people
5. A deep personal concern for the spiritual needs of others
6. A feeling that the person can do no other work
7. Personal recognition of the gifts needed to perform the task
8. Recognition of one's gifts by the church
9. One's personal health
10. Financial support

REFLECTION AND DISCUSSION

1. Do you agree with McConnell's general way of understanding God's guidance into missionary service and his rejection of a special supernatural "call"? Explain the reason for your answer.

2. What biblical or theological support, if any, is there for each of the points McConnell lists as a means through which God might lead a person into missionary service?

3. Describe any important means of God's guidance into missionary service that you feel McConnell overlooked.

includes an awareness of the needs of a lost world, the commands of Christ, a concern for the lost, a radical commitment to God, your church's affirmation, blessing and commissioning, a passionate desire, the Spirit's gifting, and an indescribable yearning that motivates beyond all understanding" (2008, 30).

IS THE NEW TESTAMENT TERM *APOSTLE* AN EQUIVALENT FOR THE ENGLISH TERM *MISSIONARY*?

Because most English translations of the New Testament do not use the word *missionary*, it has been suggested that the biblical office (or gift) of apostle is more or less equivalent to that of a missionary. For example, Michael C. Griffiths writes, "The gift of an apostle may be more generally applied to what we think of today as pioneer missionaries, since the word indicates someone who is sent, with a view to initiating a work, or planting a church" (1985, 164; see also E. F. Murphy 1974; W. D. Taylor 2000b; and Hesselgrave 2005, 215–17). J. C. Lambert writes that the biblical term *apostle* "does not denote a particular and restricted office, but rather a function of a world-wide missionary service to which the Twelve were especially called" (1955, 203). With the giving of the Great Commission, Lambert argues, the Eleven became missionaries.

Others have rejected such equating of terms (Vicedom 1965, 60–88; Blauw 1962, 77–78; W. McConnell 2007). Though the New Testament uses the term *apostle* to describe Barnabas and others, it is argued that the term normally refers to the unique authority of the Twelve and Paul. This is evidenced in the way Paul defends his apostleship as being in no way inferior to the Twelve (1 Cor. 9:1–2; 15:7–10; Gal. 1:11–24). In the case of others called apostles in the New Testament (such as Barnabas, Acts 14:14), it is argued that the term *apostle* does not refer to an office but is merely a general, nontheological term for messenger. Equating the term *missionary* with the biblical term *apostle* could both lead to a false understanding of missionary authority and undermine the unique apostolic authority of the Twelve and Paul.

Johannes Aagaard (1987) has argued that there are in fact two New Testament apostolates. The first is Peter's apostolate, or the "pillar apostolate," which is concerned with mission as the growth of existing churches. The second is Paul's apostolate, or the "traveling apostolate," which is concerned with pioneer mission where the church does not yet exist. These two apostolates thus represent two legitimate types of mission. However useful such a distinction may be, as we shall see, the biblical text does not evidence such differentiation in its use of the term.

People Described as Apostles in the New Testament

In ancient secular literature the Greek term *apostolos* meant simply "messenger, sent one, or envoy." Usage indicated that the envoy went with the authority to represent the king or master. Often it conveyed the sense of being commissioned and being sent overseas (Eicken and Lindner 1975). Forms of the term are found some seven hundred times in the Septuagint to indicate the sending or commissioning of a person for a specific task. The term is used frequently and variously in the New Testament.

Excluding uses of *apostolos* that refer to Christ or an ordinary messenger, there are three kinds of people whom the New Testament calls apostles (see also table 9.1). First, there are the original twelve disciples of Jesus and Paul, who had unique authority in the early church. They were witnesses of the Lord's resurrection (Acts 1:21–22; 1 Cor. 15:3–8). The Twelve were called to become fishers of men (Matt. 4:19–20) and were sent out to preach that the kingdom of God is at hand (Matt. 10:1–5). Paul was called to be an apostle to the Gentiles (Acts 22:21; Rom. 11:13; 1 Tim. 2:7), and performed "signs of a true apostle" (2 Cor. 12:12 NASB). In each case the apostolic calling related to missionary sending.

Most occurrences of the term *apostle* or *apostles* in the Gospels refer to the twelve disciples of Jesus. Luke's usage in Acts, however, shows a transition. Matthias is added to the Twelve to replace Judas (Acts 1:26). Luke uses the term primarily of the Jerusalem apostles (the Twelve), to which Barnabas does not belong (Acts 9:27). But later, after Barnabas and Paul have been sent out on their first missionary journey, Luke calls them both apostles (Acts 14:4, 14). However, they remained distinct from the Jerusalem apostles (Acts 15:2, 4). The twelve apostles hold a unique place in the formation of the church (Eph. 2:20; 3:5) and in salvation history (Rev. 21:14). Through them the word of the Lord has been communicated to the church (Jude 17; 2 Pet. 3:2). The significant number twelve indicates that they symbolically replace the twelve tribes of Israel in the formation of the new people of God, the church (e.g., Matt. 19:28; Rev. 21:14).

Second, the term *apostle* is applied in the New Testament to several people not among the Twelve and other than Paul. Though some English translations read "messenger" or "representative," in the original Greek *apostolos* is used. Those so referenced are Barnabas (Acts 14:14); Apollos (1 Cor. 4:6, 9); Epaphroditus (Phil. 2:25); Titus and other brothers (2 Cor. 8:23); Silvanus (Silas) and Timothy (1 Thess. 2:6); Andronicus and Junias (Rom. 16:7; "outstanding among the apostles," though possibly translated "well known among the apostles"); and possibly James, the Lord's brother (Gal. 1:19).

Most of these references are from Paul's writings. All these people (with the exception of James) were Paul's coworkers and probably ministered alongside Paul on his missionary journeys. Such missionary sending typically involves crossing cultural barriers. Because Paul was at home in both the Hellenistic and the Hebraic cultures where he ministered, Schnabel (2008, 438) argues that the missionary vocation has less to do with crossing cultures and more to do with the geographical sending of the missionary. However, Paul's evangelization of pagans, such as the Lycaonian speakers in Lystra (Acts 14:8–18) and his later ministry in the more Latin cultures of Rome and Spain, would no doubt have involved crossing at least some cultural barriers.

These apostolic workers exercised some measure of authority. For example, Titus and probably Timothy had authority to appoint leaders in the churches (1 Tim. 3:1–13; Titus 1:5), as Paul and Barnabas had done (Acts 14:23). In 1 Thessalonians 2:6, Paul writes that though he and his coworkers are apostles of Christ, they did not assert their authority as apostles. This indicates that they (not only Paul) had authority, which they willingly refrained from exercising. Elsewhere Paul also argues that he and his coworkers had the right to take wives "as do the other apostles" (1 Cor. 9:5). The use of the plural "apostles" in these texts, where none of the original Twelve are present, is clear indication that he considers members of his missionary band to be apostles with at least some of the rights and authority of the other apostles. Wolf-Henning Ollrog (1979, 79–84) makes a distinction between the biblical wording "apostle" and "apostle of the churches" (2 Cor. 8:23; Phil. 2:25). He sees the latter as emissaries or messengers sent by the churches. He concludes, however, that the ministry of the apostles of the church was flexible and that they generally had mission-related assignments (84).

TABLE 9.1
NEW TESTAMENT APOSTLES
(HESSELGRAVE 2005, 218)

Identified	Sent by	Characterized as	To Accomplish
Jesus Christ	God the Father	"the Apostle and High Priest of our profession" (Heb. 3:1 KJV)	Salvation and intercession
The Twelve (including Matthias and Paul)	Christ the Son	"the apostles" (1 Cor. 15:9); "the twelve" (Matt. 10:5); "eyewitnesses of his majesty" (2 Pet. 1:16)	Witness for Christ, proclaim the gospel, disciple the nations, found the church, write portions of the New Testament
Paul, Barnabas, Silas, John Mark, Timothy, Titus, Epaphroditus, and others	Holy Spirit-directed churches and leaders	"Apostles of the churches" (2 Cor. 8:23 margin)	Witness for Christ, proclaim the gospel, disciple the nations, plant churches, and help those engaged in these tasks

But his coworkers in no way possessed the same kind of apostolic authority or salvation-historical significance that he and the Twelve possessed. They had neither witnessed the resurrection of Christ nor had they performed any signs of apostleship. Though they are called apostles, they are clearly in a class different from that of the Twelve and Paul.

Third, there were false apostles who disguised themselves as apostles of Christ. Paul denounces them as "deceitful workmen" and instruments of satanic deception (2 Cor. 11:13–14). Such people apparently had made some claim to apostolic authority, attempting to advance their harmful agenda. In the church of Ephesus there were also those who claimed to be apostles but were not (Rev. 2:2).

This brief survey demonstrates that the term *apostolos* was used flexibly in the New Testament for people beyond the Twelve and Paul. Most if not all of them were Paul's missionary coworkers with limited authority in the churches they planted, but none of them (apart from perhaps the false apostles) claimed authority similar to the Twelve or Paul. It is thus fair to say that the Bible uses the term *apostolos* in such passages to refer to itinerant evangelists, church planters, and helpers in the spread of the gospel to the nations. This is quite similar to the traditional usage of the term *missionary*. Lambert concludes from his analysis, "We are led to the conclusion that the true differentia of New Testament apostleship lay in the missionary calling implied in the name, and that all whose lives were devoted to this vocation, and who could prove by the issues of their labors that God's Spirit was working through them for the conversion of Jew or Gentile, were regarded and described as apostles" (1955, 203).

The Office and Gift of Apostle

The language of Ephesians 4:11 indicates that individual persons are not only given gifts, but the persons *themselves* are given as gifts from God to the church. These offices include apostle, prophet, evangelist, pastor, and teacher.[1] Every Christian has received spiritual gifts for the edification of the church, and all are of equal value (1 Cor. 12:7, 15–25; 1 Pet. 4:10). But the language of Ephesians 4:11 indicates that these particular persons are not merely gifted but occupy *as persons* a larger role or "office" in the church. They have a special calling or vocation unlike others.

Paul certainly used the term in this sense when he calls himself "a servant of Christ Jesus, called to be an apostle and set apart for the gospel of God" (Rom. 1:1; cf. 1 Cor. 1:1; 15:9), even having been set apart in his mother's womb (Gal. 1:15). The language of being "set apart" or "appointed" (Gk. *aphorizo*) emphasizes that, at least for Paul, being an apostle meant more than merely receiving a spiritual gift. Though Paul's personal experience and apostolic authority were no doubt in many ways unique, Ephesians 4 describes persons who are *as persons* also set apart for specific roles in the church, unlike other members of the church.

---

1. Because of the common article in the original Greek text, the offices of pastor and teacher are sometimes considered as one: pastor-teacher.

The term *apostles* in Ephesians 4:11 may refer only to the unique apostolic office of the Twelve and Paul and not to an ongoing office in the church. Later in Ephesians 2:20, Paul writes of "apostles and prophets" who are the foundation upon which the church is built. In 3:5 he notes that the mystery of Christ has been revealed through the apostles and prophets. These passages refer to the unique role of the Twelve and Paul, a possible indication that the reference in 4:11 is also to them alone.

In 4:11, however, Paul includes in the same breath other gifted roles that are clearly of enduring status: evangelists, pastors, and teachers. Similarly Paul mentions the gift of apostleship in 1 Corinthians 12:28–29, where it is included in a list of other enduring gifts such as teaching and administration. He exhorts the Corinthians to "earnestly desire the greater gifts," foremost of which is apostleship (1 Cor. 12:31a; cf. 12:28). If the role of apostle in the church had ceased to exist or was limited only to the Twelve and Paul, this exhortation would make little sense. The reference must be to apostles in the sense of his missionary coworkers. Thus the references to apostles in Ephesians 4:11 and 1 Corinthians 12 are best taken to refer to an ongoing role of apostle in the church.

The presence of false apostles, who were at times accepted in the churches (2 Cor. 11:13; Rev. 2:2), is also evidence that the churches did not limit the role of apostle to the Twelve and Paul. The claims of false apostles would have otherwise been immediately rejected. *Didache* 11:3–6, written in the late first or early second century AD, describes the ongoing existence of apostles as itinerant ministers in the early church, though the authenticity of such apostles was to be tested.

If it is true, as we have argued, that apostles in the sense of missionary messengers of the gospel continue to be among God's person-gifts to the church, then the church should recognize the ongoing role and importance of that calling today. To avoid confusing this term with the unique authority of the original Twelve and Paul, it may be best to speak of *apostolic missionaries*, rather than of modern apostles. Much the same way a church encourages, examines, and sets apart people for church ministry such as deacon, elder, or pastor, so too people should be encouraged, examined, and set apart by the church for apostolic ministry.

The Nature of Apostolic Ministry

Recently the office of apostle has been interpreted in a variety of conflicting ways. For example, some within the Pentecostal and charismatic movements call for a restoration of the "fivefold" ministry of Ephesians 4:11 in the church today, whereby apostleship is defined as a ministry of regional influence and spiritual authority, *not* to be confused with the gift of missionary (see Wagner 2000 and 1999, 105; Cannistraci 1996).

Michael Frost and Alan Hirsch have called for apostolic leadership in the church today. "We would see an apostle as being someone who is moving the church into extension, church planting, crossing frontiers, and embracing significant movements beyond itself" (2003, 170). Beyond this they see the church as a whole exercising an apostolic function. "Some will be called to be apostles, but the whole community is to be apostol*ic*" (ibid.). They then interpret Ephesians 4:7–11 as indicating not church offices (i.e., merely selected persons called to be apostles, prophets, etc.) but that every member of the church is gifted in one of the five mentioned areas. This is not only exegetically questionable but risks again blurring the important distinctions discussed above.

From the preceding discussion of the biblical texts, it is apparent that wherever the term *apostle* is used pertaining to persons other than the Twelve and Paul, it refers to Paul's coworkers on his missionary journeys. Though the primary thrust of these journeys was pioneer evangelism and church planting, "watering" ministries to strengthen the churches was clearly also part of the larger task at hand (1 Cor. 3:5–9). In short, *apostolic ministry was focused on the planting and expansion of kingdom communities among all the peoples of the earth.* Those performing such ministry were generally itinerant, and they exercised only limited authority in the churches. With the exception perhaps of Timothy in Ephesus, Paul's apostolic team never assumed the role of long-term pastor of the churches they planted. Ongoing leadership in the churches was to be entrusted to the local, resident elders or pastors (Acts 14:23; Titus 1:5).

Whereas every Christian and the church as a whole are to be passionately committed to this mission locally and globally, clearly some individuals, whom the New Testament calls apostles, are especially gifted and commissioned to carry out this task.

In Ephesians 4:11 and 1 Corinthians 12:28–29, we note a distinction between apostles and other roles in the church. Apostles are not the same as prophets. Though Paul was a prophet, one who speaks the words of the Lord, as far as we know few of Paul's apostolic coworkers were prophets. Only Silas is explicitly spoken of as being a prophet (Acts 15:32). Apostles are not the same as evangelists. An evangelist (such as Phillip, Acts 21:8) preached the gospel but did not necessarily plant churches as did the apostles. Pastors and teachers served the ongoing care-giving and learning needs of a local congregation. Apostles might provide some initial care and teaching, but such ongoing ministry was quickly assigned by the apostles to local church elders (e.g., Acts 14:23). The apostles kept moving on to pioneer new fields of ministry, though follow-up visits were often necessary to strengthen the young churches.

In Romans 11:13, Paul speaks of himself as "the apostle to the Gentiles" and in Galatians 2:7 of being "entrusted with the task of preaching the gospel to the Gentiles, just as Peter had been to the Jews." He could write to the Corinthians, "Even though I may not be an apostle to others, surely I am to you! For you are the seal of my apostleship in the Lord" (1 Cor. 9:2). This might warrant the idea of being considered an apostle *to* a particular people, for example, Boniface as apostle to the Germans, or Patrick as apostle to the Celts (see Griffiths 1985, 156–57). Persons may be called to be apostolic ministers to a certain people or to various peoples. Scripture describes the apostle as one who normally ministers to a people other than his or her own—they are *sent* from their home church to minister to others.

Use of the Term Missionary *Today*

We have argued that the biblical office of apostle can have a meaning similar to that of the cross-cultural church-planting missionary today. Thus such a missionary vocation, as a particular calling, has biblical warrant.

But what are we to say of other missionary ministries such as compassion and development work or theological education, which differ from our definition of apostolic ministry? What about Christians who serve internationally with organizations such as the Peace Corps? What about Christians who have not been formally commissioned by a church but are secularly employed in a foreign country and seek to be a witness for Christ?

Here again we should avoid being too rigid in such terminology. The central idea behind the concept of apostle is that of being sent as a messenger or emissary. Such people may rightly be considered missionaries to the extent that they have been sent or commissioned by the church, in the name of Christ, and under the guidance of the Holy Spirit to carry out their ministries. We noted in chapter 6 that whereas the center of gravity of the missionary task is evangelism and discipleship, the task of planting and expanding kingdom communities will include many other roles as well.

CONCLUSION

From our discussion we conclude that the questions regarding the missionary vocation are complex. There are many voices and considerable confusion. The scriptures leave room for diverse interpretations, and we must avoid overly dogmatic positions. However, we believe that a strong biblical case can be made for the following theses.

The nature of world Christianity has dramatically changed over the last century, making a reassessment of the role of missionaries necessary. The distinction between sending countries and mission fields has broken down, requiring greater cooperation. International partnership in mission is no longer an option; it is an imperative. Nevertheless, the Great Commission has been neither withdrawn nor fulfilled. There remain yet many peoples unreached by the gospel of Jesus Christ. No church faithful to its Lord can cease to give, pray, and send its daughters and sons for the cause of Christ's global mission.

Every Christian is called to be a witness for Christ, to be salt and light in the world, and to be passionately committed to God's mission. Calling every Christian a missionary may help to emphasize this. But the scriptures also clearly describe different callings and different gifts given to Christians. Some are particularly called and gifted to serve Christ in missionary ministry that crosses geographic and/or ethnic boundaries. Ways must be found to retain this biblical distinction and the importance of the apostolic gifts that God has given the church for the purpose of advancing his mission globally. We should not minimize the challenges involved in cross-cultural ministry, which not only depend on the empowered sending of God but also require specialized training and the supportive prayers of his people.

The question of missionary calling is not clearly answered in scripture. Most clear biblical instances of God's calling on peoples' lives occur in exceptional, salvation-historical situations. It is dangerous to make such experiences normative for others. At the same time, we see in scripture that ordinary individuals are appointed by God and set apart by the church for particular ministries. It is reasonable to believe that the Holy Spirit continues to explicitly set apart men and women for special ministry tasks, including missions. We must, however, avoid confining the leading of the Spirit to a particular method or experience. The collective mind of the church will confirm the calling of individuals for such ministry.

The biblical term apostle *refers not only to the unique position of the Twelve and Paul but also to coworkers in the Pauline band of missionaries.* In this sense the term *apostle* is a rough equivalent to the contemporary term *missionary.* Such people are not merely gifted, but they themselves are God's gift to the church. This role or office was not limited to the early church but is ongoing and should be recognized and valued in the church today.

Because the popular usage of the term *missionary* has become so broad and diverse, we may wish to reintroduce the more biblically defined terminology of *apostolic ministries* and *apostolic missionaries* to describe those who are explicitly appointed by God and commissioned by the church to plant and expand kingdom communities among every people of the earth.

The missionary sending of the church is rooted in the missionary sending of God in Christ. God furthermore calls and equips particular persons for the cross-cultural spread of the gospel and establishment of his church among all peoples. We now turn to the further provision of God for his missionary purposes in the work of the Holy Spirit and examine the spiritual dynamics in mission.

10

Spiritual Dynamics and Mission

The work of missions takes place in the spiritual realm and involves complex issues of spiritual power. All missionaries need a theology of mission that includes a biblical understanding of spiritual dynamics and how they should use God's power to battle their satanic enemy.

WHY ARE SPIRITUAL DYNAMICS AN ISSUE FOR THEOLOGY OF MISSION?

The scriptures are clear that spiritual power is the foundational prerequisite for mission. As he commissioned his disciples to be witnesses of his death and resurrection to all nations, Jesus ordered them to not begin the task until they had received a special infusion of spiritual power (Luke 24:46–49). The book of Acts is the story of the outworking of this power through the ministry of the Holy Spirit (Acts 1:4–8; 3:12; 4:7, 33; 6:8; 19:20). Paul testified that the key to his ministry of preaching the gospel and planting churches was not human wisdom or eloquence in speaking, but God's power working through him (Rom. 15:19; 1 Cor. 2:4–5; 4:20; 2 Cor. 10:4; 1 Thess. 1:5). The New Testament church understood that spiritual power is essential for mission.

Throughout church history missionaries have been consistently aware of their need for spiritual power to fuel their ministries. From the stories of Gregory Thaumaturgus (the "Wonder Worker") in the fourth century to the amazing answers to prayer frequently described by contemporary missionaries, mission history displays a special sensitivity to the role of spiritual dynamics in ministry. Missionaries have always recognized the biblical truth that they are in a *spiritual* war and so have no hope of success unless they are *spiritually* empowered.

However, recent decades have brought an even greater awareness of the need for spiritual power in the face of a wicked, powerful enemy. Several factors have reinforced this fresh emphasis. First, the church has grown fastest and is now largest in the global South, where many cultures have a greater awareness of the spiritual dimension of life and where issues of spiritual power are normal. People in these cultures abound with questions related to spiritual dynamics. If missionaries do not provide biblical answers, these people will look for their answers from other sources. Marguerite Kraft observes that "worldview and human needs are interrelated. Worldview shapes a people's needs; needs shape the worldview. . . . With most of the world heavily involved in spiritual power activities, the initial communication of the gospel must deal with spiritual power" (2002, 280–81). As the church has grown rapidly among cultures and church fellowships that emphasize spiritual power (such as Pentecostal and charismatic churches), mission, in turn, has increasingly emphasized spiritual power.

Second, the worldview of the West itself has changed. New Age, Eastern, and animistic thought have invaded the West, even as the presumptions of modernity have eroded and postmodern assumptions have taken hold. Westerners themselves are more inclined to turn to their "spiritual side" to look for answers than to trust rational objectivity. Western missionaries realize that their more naturalistic worldview and training have not prepared them to respond to the concerns about spiritual dynamics among the people with whom they minister, and so they are more open to approaches that emphasize spiritual power.

> *There are two equal and opposite errors into which our race can fall about the devils. One is to disbelieve in their existence. The other is to believe, and to feel an excessive and unhealthy interest in them. They themselves are equally pleased by both errors, and hail a materialist or a magician with the same delight.*
>
> C. S. Lewis (1961, 3)

Third, some missiologists have expressed frustration at the strategies and methods of the past and have suggested that the key to completing the task of world evangelism includes fresh approaches to employing God's power. As they hear reports from evangelists who emphasize power encounters and as they personally experience prayer walks, identificational repentance, and "strategic-level" spiritual warfare with territorial spirits, many missionaries and missiologists have become convinced that an even greater emphasis on spiritual power is the key to completing the Great Commission.

239

However, many theologians and missiologists have expressed concern over some of these recent approaches. They observe what they perceive to be unbiblical, even animistic, practices in some contemporary strategies and methodologies. Our approach to issues of spiritual dynamics must be rooted in scripture and must respond carefully to cultures oriented around spiritual power. While addressing the felt needs and worldviews of peoples around the world, we must not fall into the trap of adopting a cultural perspective on spiritual power. On the one hand, the materialistic worldview that still dominates most Westerners' mind-sets can lead to downplaying the importance of spiritual dynamics. A proper emphasis on the spiritual dynamics of mission challenges the "practical atheism" of the secular modern age; encourages us to see the world as a spiritual place; challenges the idea that problems can be reduced to psychological, social, physiological, or circumstantial factors; and shows that serious prayer matters (Powlison 1995, 36–37).

On the other hand, worldviews that emphasize the importance of the spirit world can breed animistic beliefs and practices not found in scripture. In either case we can be overly influenced by unbiblical worldviews and slip into a syncretism that Satan can use to sabotage missionary efforts. Although it is important to meet people on their ground in the presentation of the gospel, we must also work to transform their worldview to biblical patterns (Hiebert 2008). Above all, awareness of our need for God's power must transform us into people who are dependent on the Holy Spirit for every aspect of mission.

THE HOLY SPIRIT AND MISSION

The starting place for considering the spiritual dynamics of mission must be recognizing the role of the Holy Spirit. We noted in chapter 3 the role of the Spirit in a trinitarian grounding of mission. The book of Acts is the central New Testament exposition on mission and, not coincidentally, is also the book that puts the greatest amount of attention on the work of the Holy Spirit. As we have seen, mission could not even begin until the disciples had been clothed with the power of the Holy Spirit (Acts 1:8). Mission is impossible without the work of the Spirit, and the work of the Spirit will result in mission.

J. Robertson McQuilkin points out that even though there is general agreement in theory that the Holy Spirit's role in mission is indispensable, "how he goes about his work and how we relate to him are probably the most disputed issues in contemporary missions" (1997, 22). However, generally following McQuilkin (1997), certain aspects of the work of the Holy Spirit seem to be clear.

First, the Holy Spirit is the Spirit of truth (John 14:7; 15:26; 16:13). As the Spirit of truth he reminded the apostles of what Jesus had taught them and directed them as they wrote the New Testament. Today he reminds the church of Jesus's message and guides it in accurately understanding and applying his message (John 14:26; 16:13). He thus provides the message for mission.

Second, the Holy Spirit supernaturally convicts unbelievers and draws them to Christ. Jesus said that the Spirit would convict the world of "sin and righteousness and judgment" (John 16:7–11). He convicts people of the *sin* of their failure to believe in Christ, to believe that Jesus is the only way that they can be *righteous* before God, and to believe that the cross defeated Satan and pronounced ultimate *judgment* on him. Without this convicting work of the Holy Spirit, individuals will not respond to the missionary's presentation of the gospel.

Third, the Holy Spirit regenerates unbelievers (John 3:5–8; Titus 3:5). Bringing men and women to faith in Christ and new birth is not all there is to mission, but it is certainly the focal point of mission. Regeneration of individuals is the prerequisite for planting and discipling churches to maturity and bringing societal transformation. Bringing spiritually dead human beings to new life is the work of the Holy Spirit.

Fourth, the Holy Spirit created the church (1 Cor. 12:13; cf. Acts 2:4 and 11:15), which is both the *root* of mission and the *fruit* of mission. As people come to faith in Christ, they must be discipled into maturing churches. Maturing churches become a launching pad for missionary movements, which have as their goal planting new churches (Acts 13:1–3; 19:10). The church is God's main source and vehicle for mission, and the establishing of new churches is central to the goal of mission.

Fifth, the Holy Spirit empowers and emboldens the church for ministry, especially in the face of persecution (Acts 4:8, 31; 7:55), and gives joy to the persecuted (13:52). The story line of Acts makes clear that the filling of the Holy Spirit enabled fearless witness during persecution, and that God, in turn, used this bold, joyful witness of his persecuted people to spread the gospel (5:42; 6:7; 8:1, 4–8, 12; 16:16–40).

Sixth, the Holy Spirit calls believers into specific missionary service and guides those he has called (Acts 13:3–4; 16:6–10; 26:16–18). All believers are called to engage in the Great Commission, but God specifically calls some to give a significant portion of their lives working cross-culturally (see chap. 9). As they go, the Holy Spirit opens and closes doors to guide them to specific areas of service.

Seventh, as the gospel spreads into pioneer areas around the world, the Holy Spirit sometimes confirms the message through miraculous signs. As we suggested in chapter 2, though the text of Mark 16:9–20 is probably not part of Mark's original manuscript, it almost certainly reflects a reliable ancient tradition consistent with the rest of the New Testament. Mark's account of the Great Commission emphasizes the confirmation of the gospel message with signs. The presence of miraculous signs is not a test for the presence of the Holy Spirit, nor is this passage a promise that all believers would manifest

241

these signs. Rather, Mark records Jesus's promise that as the gospel breaks into new areas around the world, God would at times use the miraculous to demonstrate his power and protect his messengers. The book of Acts (e.g., 3:8; 5:12; 6:8; 8:6; 9:33–43; 14:10; 16:18; 20:12; 28:5–6), reflections in the epistles (e.g., Heb. 2:4), and numerous stories of pioneer missionaries through the centuries demonstrate the work of the Holy Spirit in confirming his message through the miraculous. We will discuss this in more detail below under "Signs and Wonders and Mission."

Of course, the work of the Spirit in giving spiritual gifts (1 Cor. 12; Eph. 4:7–16) and nurturing believers to be increasingly Christlike (Acts 6:3, 5; Gal. 5:22–23) matures the church and thus enhances its missional impact on the world.

Paul frequently speaks of the crucial role of the Holy Spirit in the success of his church-planting ministry (Rom. 15:18–19; 1 Cor. 2:4; 1 Thess. 1:5). Without the empowering work of the Holy Spirit, mission is impossible. Though we dare not limit the Spirit's ministry to demonstrably supernatural works of God, the Spirit's power is necessary for every aspect of missionary work. Without the Spirit's ministry, preaching and teaching will be lifeless. Ministry to human need will become a troublesome duty instead of a display of love and compassion, for the love of God is poured into our hearts by the Spirit (Rom. 5:5). The deprivations and difficulties of missionary life will become burdens to be borne instead of opportunities to see God work. Every phase of missionary work must be done in dependence on the Holy Spirit, infused with the Spirit's power.

Paul also trusted the Holy Spirit in the life of his young churches. He baptized when there was evidence of genuine faith in Christ and appointed elders to lead the young churches. Then he left the leaders to take primary responsibility over their flocks (Acts 13–14; 1 Cor. 1:14–17). Roland Allen "calls missionaries and mission agencies to recover the apostle's bedrock conviction that the Spirit dwells in the church to convict, correct, guide and fortify her" (Howell 1997, 39; Allen [1927] 1962a).

The work of the Holy Spirit is so important to missions that Jesus actually said that it would be to the disciples' *advantage* to have him return to the Father so that the Spirit could begin his indwelling presence in the new age (John 16:7). Apart from the work of the Spirit, advancing the gospel against Satan's kingdom in the new age would be impossible (Luke 24:46–49). Dependence on the Spirit for every aspect of ministry is foundational to the work of mission.

THE KINGDOM AND SPIRITUAL DYNAMICS

If recognizing the role of the Holy Spirit is the starting place for mission, understanding the nature of the present age is the crucial context for depending on his power. God's people live in an age when Jesus has defeated Satan on the cross and inaugurated his rule, but during which Satan is still the active, powerful ruler of a sinful world. This age of conflict is the setting for an ongoing fierce spiritual war, and mission is at the very center of that struggle.

Mission and the "Already-Not Yet" Kingdom

In chapters 2 and 4 we saw that Jesus's first coming inaugurated God's kingdom rule. Jesus announces that in his person "the kingdom of God is in your midst" (Luke 17:20–21 NASB) and that in his driving out demons "the kingdom of God has come upon you" (Matt. 12:28). Paul later speaks of the kingdom as a present reality for believers (Rom. 14:17–18; Col. 1:12–13). However, Jesus makes it equally clear that the kingdom will not be fully and ultimately established until his return to earth (Matt. 16:28; 26:29; Luke 13:28; 21:31). When the disciples ask in expectation if he is about to restore the kingdom to Israel, Jesus refocuses them on the task of witness in the power of the Holy Spirit but does not deny that the kingdom will one day come in its fullness (Acts 1:7–8). The kingdom has "already" been inaugurated but will "not yet" be consummated until Jesus returns.

The "already-but-not-yet" nature of the kingdom means that God's people live in an era of vicious conflict with Satan (fig. 10.1). Because the kingdom has not yet come in its fullness, we live in a time when Satan still has limited rule over the earth. Though Satan's rule in this world is subject to God's overarching permission and power, scripture makes it clear that Satan does presently rule over "human society in rebellion against God" (Yung 2002a, 21). He is the "prince of this world" (John 12:31; 14:30; 16:11), the "ruler of the kingdom of the air" (Eph. 2:2), "the god of this age" (2 Cor. 4:4). Further, he rules a "dominion of darkness" (Col. 1:13), and the whole world is under his control (1 John 5:19). "It would appear that humankind through the Fall gave Satan authority over our lives and our communities" (Yung 2002a, 21), and so he has a certain measure of control over human societies on earth.

FIGURE 10.1:
THIS PRESENT AGE: AGE OF CONFLICT

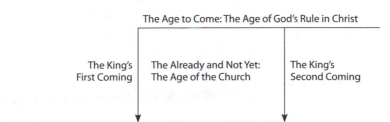

The Age to Come: The Age of God's Rule in Christ

| The King's First Coming | The Already and Not Yet: The Age of the Church | The King's Second Coming |

The Present Age: The Age of Satan's Rule

But when he was on earth Jesus challenged and broke Satan's power over the world. Jesus describes his miracles and exorcisms as binding Satan and plundering his house (Matt. 12:29). His "exorcisms were a sign of the presence of the kingdom of God" (Arnold 1997, 20). As a result of Jesus's life, death, and resurrection, Satan has been driven out (John 12:31), he stands condemned (John 16:11, 33), his works are destroyed (1 John 3:8), and he has fallen in defeat (Luke 10:17–18).

Christ's victory was rooted in "his substitutionary atonement on the Cross. Because the penalty for sin has been paid and judgment averted, sin, Satan and death no longer have any hold over redeemed humanity" (Yung 2002a, 18). By canceling the debt of our sin on the cross and giving us new life, Christ has defeated Satan and his demons, disarmed them, and publicly displayed their powerlessness (Col. 2:13–15; Heb. 2:14–15). "What the kingdom of God means, therefore, is that the hostile alien kingdom of demonic captivity, oppression, poverty and blindness (physical and spiritual) is coming to an end through the ministry of Jesus. He is the bringer of the kingdom of God, for He is the vanquisher of the kingdom of Satan" (Boyd 1999, 84).

Christ's victory at the cross assures us that God is fully in control and that Satan's ultimate destruction is certain when the kingdom comes in all its fullness. The work of mission is the advance of Christ's kingdom and a front line of attack against Satan's kingdom. As God's people proclaim the good news of his kingdom and demonstrate kingdom values in ministry to human need, Christ builds his church and the gates of hell crumble (Matt. 16:18–19; see Strauss 2005). Mission can advance in the assurance of Satan's defeat, the ultimate triumph of Christ, and the establishment of his kingdom in all its fullness on earth. But though he is a defeated foe, Satan is alive, active, and powerful, making this "time between the times" an era of vicious, dangerous conflict (see sidebar 10.1). Because mission is the front line in the attack on Satan's kingdom, spiritual warfare is a central feature of mission.

Spiritual Warfare

"The biblical metaphor of spiritual warfare . . . is a shorthand way of referring to our conflict with" Satan and his demonic spirit forces (Arnold 1997, 26). To successfully wage this war, mission work must go forward with a full awareness of God's control over Satan's limitations, his mode of attack, and believers' resources for battle.

GOD'S CONTROL OVER SATAN

Though believers live in a time of fierce spiritual warfare and though we face a strong enemy, we must never forget that Satan and his demons are created beings and so are limited. Satan is not God. He is not omniscient, omnipresent, or omnipotent. Although we should not underestimate Satan's

SIDEBAR 10.1
D-DAY AND V-E DAY

(adapted from Blue 1999, 72)

The significance for missions of Christ's victory over Satan on the cross has been illustrated by the Allies' success in invading Normandy on D-day in World War II. Once the Allies were successfully ashore and had established a secure beachhead, military experts on both sides knew that Germany's eventual defeat was assured. In fact, a failed attempt by some of Germany's military leaders to assassinate Hitler six weeks after D-day came partially because many in the German high command realized that the war would eventually be lost, and they hoped to install new leadership that could negotiate with the Western Allies. But though the victory in Normandy assured the Allies' eventual success, Germany still had a strong army. A full year of difficult fighting remained, and thousands of men, women, and children would be killed or wounded before the war was over.

In the same way, the death and resurrection of Christ have secured a certain, final victory over Satan, but he is still a strong, vicious, determined enemy. His work to deceive and destroy the nations and harm believers continues to result in great damage. The war will not be over until Christ returns to utterly destroy Satan's work. In the meantime, the work of missions is at the front line of the ongoing battle, as Satan's rule is assaulted and defeated through the advance of the gospel and demonstration of transformational kingdom values.

REFLECTION AND DISCUSSION

1. How does mission work attack Satan's rule?
2. How does the fact of Christ's decisive defeat and certainty of ultimate victory over Satan encourage and motivate you to mission? How does the fact that Satan is still active and powerful sober and prepare you for mission?

power and knowledge (2 Pet. 2:10–12; Jude 8–10), in Christ we have nothing to fear from them.

As a limited, finite creature, Satan is himself fully under God's sovereign control. Martin Luther once said that "the devil is God's devil" to emphasize that God is in control of Satan and his demonic forces. The Bible does not teach a dualistic worldview in which the universe is the scene of a struggle between equally balanced forces of good and evil. Satan and all his demonic forces are not only subject to God, but God even uses the work of demons to accomplish his purposes (Judg. 9:23–24; 1 Sam. 16:14; 2 Sam. 24:1 and 1 Chron. 21:1; 1 Kings 22:19–23; see Powlison 1995, 54–58). Even Satan's most savage attacks are within God's sovereign control and permissive will for our lives (Job 1:12; 2:6; 2 Cor. 12:7–10). No believer can be touched by Satan's attacks unless God allows it (1 John 5:18–19). Believers who are walking in obedience to God need not fear curses, objects or places dedicated to Satan, or people controlled by the demonic. Stephen Lungu of African Enterprise reflects this confidence when he announces to those attending his evangelistic crusades, "You can practice your witchcraft on me but it won't work because I belong to Jesus. . . . I cannot be harmed by curses when walking in obedience to God" (Johnstone 1995, 151).

SATAN'S ATTACKS

Satan and his demonic forces have several weapons in this war. Satan blinds the eyes of unbelievers (2 Cor. 4:4) and snatches the Word away when it is planted in their hearts (Luke 8:12). He gains physical control and oppresses ("demonizes") people, bringing physical harm to those he thus afflicts (Luke 8:26–39; 9:37–43). He tempts (Acts 5:3; 1 Cor. 7:5; 1 Thess. 3:5), accuses and slanders (Rev. 12:10), discourages (1 Pet. 5:6–8), and persecutes (Rev. 2:10) believers. God allowed Satan to disrupt Paul's missionary travel plans (1 Thess. 2:18). At times God even allows Satan to attack believers physically (Job 2:6–7; 2 Cor. 12:7). This, of course, does not mean that all disease is caused by Satan, nor that such disease is outside the permissive will of God. The scriptures give many reasons why God allows disease in the lives of believers.

Spiritual warfare is both personal and corporate. Satan attacks churches, mission agencies, and church-planting movements. He sows the seeds of doubt, mistrust, jealousy, anger, resentment, pride, and envy. He plants grudges and discouragement in hearts. He stimulates opposition from individuals, organizations, social structures, and governments. He brings physical opposition and persecution.

Satan's attacks are intimately intertwined with our own sinful tendencies (the flesh) and the culture in which we live (the world) so that the whole of our lives is spiritual warfare. "Spiritual warfare is a way of characterizing our common struggle as Christians" (Arnold 1997, 27). It is all-encompassing, touching every relationship, every social and cultural situation, and every private and public area of our lives. The secularism of the modern, Western worldview tends to deaden Christ followers to this ongoing but unseen spiritual struggle, leading to "practical atheism" and a sense that all problems are "psychological, social, physiological, or circumstantial" (Powlison 1995, 21, 36, 37). But "both the disenchanted world of modern rationalism and the charmed world of premodern spiritism are wrong" (25). Mission efforts must guard against a tendency to unconsciously depend on wealth, education, the latest missiological strategy, political influence, or technology. Mission is ultimately a spiritual task that must be empowered with spiritual resources.

THE BELIEVERS' RESOURCES

How do believers in this age battle Satan and his forces while advancing the kingdom of God in mission work? "The good news is that we can experience some of the blessings of the age to come right now" (Arnold 1997, 21). These blessings include the presence, power, and gifts of the Holy Spirit; the "ability to break free from the bondage of sin"; and "authority over evil spirits" (ibid.). Jesus has defeated Satan in his "sacrificial death and triumphal resurrection;" consequently, spiritual warfare is primarily "standing in Christ's mighty power" (Van Rheenen 2005, 37–38).

While direct confrontation with demons may be appropriate at times (see below), our primary focus should be on knowing and living out who we are in Christ, yielding our entire lives to God, being transformed into ever-increasing Christlikeness (Rom. 12:1–2; 2 Cor. 3:18), and bringing every thought captive to Christ (2 Cor. 10:3–5). Repentance and confession of sin; practice of the spiritual disciplines of Bible study, prayer, fasting, submission, and thankfulness; devotion to purity and holy living; and loving other believers by practicing the "one another" statements of the New Testament are foundational to spiritual victory (Moreau 1997; Rom. 12:10, 16; 15:7; Gal. 5:13; Eph. 4:2, 32; Col. 3:13; 1 Thess. 5:11; Heb. 10:24–25; 1 Pet. 1:14–16; 5:5; 1 John 1:8–10; 4:7, 11–12). Mission does not advance against Satan's kingdom primarily through the right missiological strategies or technique, abundant finances, or advanced education; it advances through the spiritual power that comes through living as transformed kingdom people in the power of the Holy Spirit.

Paul devotes special attention to how believers fight against their satanic enemy in Ephesians. Foundational is Christ's triumph over all of Satan's forces (1:19–22; possibly 4:8) and the privileged place of triumph that believers share with Christ (2:6). The well-known passage in Ephesians 6:10–20 teaches how to apply these truths. Paul says nothing in these verses about gaining information about demons, casting them out, or dealing with territorial spirits. Rather, "these verses describe the common struggle with evil in the day-to-day lives of Christians" (Arnold 1997, 37). The main point of the passage is that our battle is a *spiritual* battle that can be won only with the *spiritual* resources God gives in salvation. Paul draws his description of the believers' armor from Isaiah (11:5; 49:2; 52:7; 59:16–17), where God is clothed with saving attributes. Each piece of the armor is something God has already accomplished for his people. Each is a realized gospel reality on which believers must act, especially as they proclaim and live out the good news in mission outreach. To battle Satan we, as believers, must (1) be faithful and truthful in our judgments of others and the world around us (Isa. 11:5); (2) do the just, right thing in the face of a sinful world; (3) rest in the security of our peace with God and be ready to announce it to others; (4) trust in God's power, God's Word, and God's way to defeat every one of Satan's attacks personally (temptations) or societally (persecution); (5) live with the confidence that God's saving work will rescue us from our sin in spite of Satan's accusations; and (6) proclaim God's Word to restore the nations to him (Isa. 49:1–6).

Paul's description of this spiritual battle climaxes in his call for prayer for his own missionary outreach (Eph. 6:19–20). Missionary efforts cannot

247

be successful unless they are rooted in humble dependence on God's power and resources. "Victory in spiritual warfare does not come to the proud and self-sufficient" (Moreau 1997, 155). This is a battle waged out of weakness. "Paradoxically, the most aggressive and powerful spiritual warfare must be waged out of great personal brokenness and weakness" (Robb 1999, 148).

PRAYER AND MISSION

If the cornerstone of mission is the power of the Holy Spirit, and spiritual warfare in an age of conflict is the context of mission, then prayer is the way we express our dependence on the Spirit for his enablement in the middle of this vicious struggle. "Prayer is the human conduit of divine energy" (J. R. McQuilkin 1997, 31). "A proper understanding of spiritual warfare informs us that the forces of darkness may be countered and indeed be defeated through prayer. . . . While we may not have complete victory over evil until the return of Christ, we can nevertheless know substantial victory over many of its manifestations here and now" (Yung 2002a, 24).

The New Testament is full of commands and examples of prayer for missions. Jesus commanded his disciples to pray that God would send workers to the harvest field (Matt. 9:38). Paul frequently stresses the importance of prayer for the success of his ministry of outreach. He asks the Colossians to pray for open doors of ministry and clarity in proclamation (Col. 4:3–4) and commends his fellow missionary Epaphras as a man of prayer (Col. 4:12). He implores the Romans to pray for his protection and that his ministry will be accepted (Rom. 15:31–32). He requests that the Thessalonians pray that God's Word will spread rapidly and be honored, and that he and his colleagues will be delivered from those who oppose them (2 Thess. 3:1–2). He urges the Ephesians to pray that he will have the right words to speak and that he will speak them fearlessly (Eph. 6:18–20).

Failure to pray for people to come to Christ, for the gospel to advance, and for "God's will to be done on earth, as it is in heaven" is acceptance of Satan's partial rule in this present age. It is passive support of the enemy. Sometimes the expression *warfare prayer* is limited to praying to cast out demons from individuals or to bind demons who have control

> *Life is war. That's not all it is. But it is always that. Our weakness in prayer is owing largely to our neglect of this truth. Prayer is primarily a wartime walkie-talkie for the mission of the church as it advances against the powers of darkness and unbelief. It is not surprising that prayer malfunctions when we try to make it a domestic intercom to call upstairs for more comforts in the den. . . . Prayer gives us the significance of frontline forces, and gives God the glory of a limitless Provider.*
>
> John Piper (1993, 41)

over places or institutions. However, the concept of warfare prayer must be extended to include all prayer for the destruction of Satan's kingdom and the advance of Christ's rule through the gospel. Patrick Johnstone (1995) encourages believers to move beyond the controversy that surrounds much evangelical discussion of spiritual power in mission and focus on intercession, the primary means of engaging in spiritual warfare throughout church history and today. We must not be ignorant of Satan's devices (2 Cor. 2:11), "nor do we have to know everything about demonism, the occult, the hierarchies of the spirit world, before we dare bind the strong man and spoil his goods (Matt. 12:29)" through prayer (Johnstone 1995, 139).

Prayer is our primary weapon in spiritual warfare, but we must make certain it does not degenerate into a "power tool" (Van Rheenen 2005, 37). The primary purpose of prayer is to build a relationship with God and come into conformity with the will of God, not to manipulate God to use his power on our behalf. "Prayer is not intended to be a vehicle of violence, but a means of fellowship, growth and strength" (Moreau 2002, 267). Prayer should follow the New Testament pattern, focusing on coming to know God and calling on him to use his power to extend the gospel and glorify himself. Believers can also engage in prayer warfare not only by praying *for* those with whom they are sharing the gospel but also by praying *with* them. Prayer with others is an important tool in demonstrating faith in God and assuring them of Christ's love and care. Even individuals who are resistant to the gospel will often welcome prayer on their behalf, opening the door to evangelistic opportunity.

One of the most popular tools in contemporary missions has become the prayer walk. A prayer walk is usually conducted by a group of believers who travel to the site of specific spiritual opposition and pray for God's intervention to break Satan's power, bring people to Christ, and enable the church to display power and purity. Prayer walking does have clear value. First, those participating can gain special insight into the needs of a particular location by being on site and so can pray more insightfully and specifically. Second, prayer walking requires great commitment and focus on the part of those praying and promotes the combined, earnest agreement of all involved. Third, prayer walking is likely to stimulate ongoing prayer from those who have invested time and energy to travel and confront the object of prayer firsthand.

However, Johnstone (1995) calls for a careful examination of prayer walking. If we truly believe in the efficacy of prayer, we do not have to be present at a location for it to be effective. Jesus's healing of the centurion's servant (Luke 7:1–10) illustrates that the greatest kind of faith is exercised when we trust God's presence and power to intervene even when we are not present at the location of concern. Prayer walking also demands "huge expense to the detriment of funding for workers on the front line, the motivation for going can be mixed," it can place a tremendous "drain on the time and energies of workers serving in glamorous places," and it can endanger ministries in sensitive areas (Johnstone

1995, 149). Also, Juliet Thomas (2002a) warns of the cultural insensitivity of some Western Christians whose prayer walks do more harm than good to the gospel. Such people often demonstrate triumphalism in claiming credit for results for which local believers have labored for years, naïveté in reporting conversions that prove to be temporary, cultural insensitivity, and Western superiority.

Believers from the West have much to learn about prayer from their brothers and sisters in Africa, Asia, and Latin America. When the church has access to human resources—such as finances, education, and political influence—it is easy to maintain a subconscious reliance on those human resources instead of God for the success of mission. Believers who live in contexts where they have few human resources for ministry are forced to rely on God alone for protection and proclamation (see sidebar 10.2). That reliance is often demonstrated through a robust prayer life. Of course, it is not wrong to use the resources that God has provided. But a clear indication of the core trust of an individual or church is their prayer life. If we are praying about something, we are ultimately dependent on God for it. If we are not praying about something, we are ultimately depending on some other resource.

SIDEBAR 10.2
THE POWER OF PRAYER

(told to Steve Strauss by Mikael Denbo; see also Cumbers 1995, 214–15)

In 1978, when a communist government controlled Ethiopia, a group of communist youth agitators began to put anti-Christian posters on the wall around an evangelical church in Addis Ababa. When one of the church leaders protested, the agitators announced that the next day officials from the local precinct would come to confiscate the church property. The church leaders contacted as many of the church members as they could, asking them to spend the night in prayer for God's protection for themselves and the building. Many came to the church itself and prayed all night. The next morning, while the people were praying and the leaders were reading scripture to encourage them, the government officials arrived to confiscate the building. But instead of entering the church property, they stood outside and began to argue among themselves over accusations of embezzlement. The officials divided into two angry gangs and became so caught up in their dispute, they forgot all about the church and eventually dispersed. Prayer saved the church, and fifteen people came to Christ as a direct result of experiencing the protection of the property through prayer.

REFLECTION AND DISCUSSION

1. In this story, how does the response of the Ethiopian believers demonstrate their ultimate dependence on God?
2. In what other resources might believers in other contexts have trusted in similar circumstances? What can they learn from these brothers and sisters in Ethiopia?

SIGNS AND WONDERS AND MISSION

Throughout the early days of the church the expansion of the gospel was accompanied by many miraculous works of the Holy Spirit. As we have seen, the book of Acts is full of examples of miraculous works performed by the early followers of Jesus. Paul describes the "signs and miracles" that came "through the power of the Holy Spirit" and accompanied his gospel proclamation in planting the church in the eastern Mediterranean (Rom. 15:18–20). Other New Testament texts demonstrate that the miraculous played a part in the establishment of many of the early churches (2 Cor. 12:12; Gal. 3:5; Heb. 2:4).

Early church history includes many stories of evangelist-missionaries who confronted the demonic and performed miracles as part of their outreach. It is difficult to know how many of the stories of Gregory Thaumaturgus ("Wonder Worker") are legends, but two traditions seem to be rooted in history. First, his tenure as bishop of Pontus was marked by a remarkable turning to Christ. It was said that when he became bishop there were only seventeen Christians in his city, but at the climax of his ministry only seventeen remained who were not Christians. Second, he had a reputation for performing miracles that led directly to significant response to the gospel message (ChristianHistory.net, 2008). Other examples of signs, wonders, and power encounters from church history include Martin of Tours (Sulpitius 1894), Boniface of Germany (Willibald, n.d.), and Ethiopian missionary monks who spread Christian faith in central and southern Ethiopia in the fourteenth and fifteenth centuries (Kaplan 1984; Tamrat 1972, 168). In the early twentieth century Pentecostals prioritized the need for "spectacular displays of celestial power—signs and wonders, healing, and deliverance from sinful habits and satanic bondage" to speed and empower evangelism (McGee 1997, 89).

In the later twentieth century John Wimber (Wimber and Springer 1986) and the Vineyard Movement took the expectation of signs and wonders into mainstream evangelical circles in what has been called the Third Wave of emphasis on the present miraculous work of the Holy Spirit. Wimber suggested that signs and wonders should be part not only of pioneer missionary outreach but also of evangelism in areas that are thoroughly churched. Attracted by Wimber's successes and driven by a passion to adopt strategies that seemed to be working around the world to attract people to the gospel, Charles Kraft (1989, 1995) and Peter Wagner (1988, 1996) of Fuller Seminary incorporated an emphasis on signs and wonders into their own teaching and ministries.

Many agree that *some* kind of evidence of miraculous power seems to follow the expansion of the gospel. We have seen how Mark's account of the Great Commission suggests that miraculous signs would follow the expansion of the gospel into new areas. Was this promise for the apostolic era alone? Stories continue to abound of healings, God's protection from attack, and God's giving unlearned languages in such pioneer evangelistic settings (e.g.,

McGee 1997; Davis 1980, 163–67; Cumbers 1995, 78–82, 128–29). Hwa Yung (2002b) reports that throughout church history but particularly in the past one hundred years, the most effective evangelism in East Asia has been accompanied by signs and wonders.

Church history and the testimony of contemporary missionaries suggest that when the gospel first breaks into a people group or geographic area, the miraculous is frequently present. But the question of how normative such signs and wonders should be for evangelism and outreach where the church is already established and the *necessity* of signs and wonders for a successful church-planting movement is still an issue of debate among evangelicals.

We must remember that miraculous signs can be duplicated by Satan (2 Thess. 2:9). Furthermore, Jesus reserved his harshest criticism for those who *demanded* a miraculous sign as evidence of who he was and as a precondition for trusting him (Matt. 12:39). Perhaps the most balanced conclusion is that any biblical theology of mission must put God's power at the center of effective mission and must emphasize that prayer and dependence on God are foundational to the missionary task. It is never wrong to pray for God's miraculous intervention, trusting him to provide it in his time and his way. It is always wrong to *demand* God's miraculous intervention or to believe that without signs and wonders we cannot be effective in planting the church.

UNSEEN POWERS AND MISSION

Any discussion of spiritual dynamics and mission must address the spirit world that plays such a prominent role in the current age of conflict. The presence and power of these unseen forces is a real part of both biblical theology and the worldview of most of the peoples of the earth.

The Excluded Middle

Paul Hiebert (1982a) has observed that most peoples of the world recognize three levels of reality, which can be illustrated as three tiers (see fig. 10.2). The lowest tier is the empirical, this-worldly, material level, and includes plants, animals, the material world, and other human beings. This level of reality is known through science. All people develop science to understand and control the material world, whether it is simple folk science, such as how to track animals, how to plant crops, or how to build a house, or sophisticated academic fields of science such as chemistry and physics.

The second tier of reality is the level of spirit beings that inhabit the material world; it is this-worldly but unseen and supernatural. According to the worldview of most folk-religious practitioners, this level includes such beings as the "living-dead" ancestors, ghosts, local gods and goddesses, demons, jinn, and angels. In the West most people had an active belief in this level until the early modern age, believing in elves, ghosts, goblins, pixies, and leprechauns;

FIGURE 10.2:
THE EXCLUDED MIDDLE

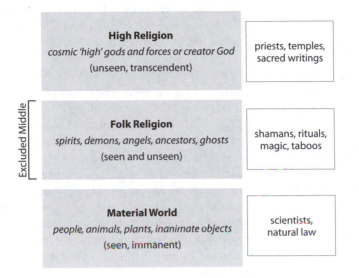

people sought ways to control them for their own benefit. Some Westerners still retain a folk belief in these beings, but most dismiss them as superstition. Many Western Christians have a theoretical belief in angels and demons but practically find little need to consider the beings of this level as relevant to their everyday lives. Finally, the upper tier of reality is the other-worldly, supernatural level. This level includes high, cosmic, personal gods and impersonal cosmic forces, such as karma.

Hiebert points out that, beginning with the Enlightenment, most Westerners increasingly have adopted a two-tier perspective of reality that largely eliminates the middle level. "Science dealt with the empirical world using mechanistic analogies, leaving religion to handle other-worldly matters" (Hiebert 1982a, 43). As Western missionaries carried the gospel around the world, they carried their two-tiered perspective with them. They proclaimed final salvation and a relationship with God (the upper level) and brought Western medicine and developmental improvements (the lower level), but often ignored the middle level. As a result, as Lesslie Newbigin (1966, 18) has noted, Western missions has been one of the most secularizing forces in world history.

But the existence of this middle level is clearly part of a biblical worldview, and it remains extremely important in the lives of most people around the world. Most people understand that the forces of the middle level can bring them great benefit or great harm. They influence most of daily life: disease and health, love and hate, fertility or infertility, prosperity or poverty, victory or defeat. The beings and forces of the middle level must be recognized and dealt with. When missionaries ignored this middle level, many peoples continued to relate to the beings and forces of that level in the old way, untouched by biblical faith in Christ. In some cases people have practiced two kinds of religious faith: a formal religious worship of God and Christ and a folk religion that deals with the spirit world. In other cases a syncretistic blend of the two has developed.

The middle level coexists with modern science without contradiction in the worldview of most societies around the world. For example, many people with a three-tier worldview understand the concept of germs, and they know that they cause disease. But they also often presume that spiritual forces stand behind these naturalistic causes. Modern science may tell the physical *how* of sickness or misfortune, but unseen spiritual forces are considered to be the *why* or ultimate cause of these evils. Unless the spiritual forces are dealt with, merely addressing the outward symptoms (e.g., through modern medicine) will not resolve the deeper problem. Yung (2002a, 6–8) notes that the Western, Enlightenment worldview tends to be dualistic, seeing the spiritual and the naturalistic world operating on two unrelated levels. As a result Western missionaries often are not prepared to engage the worldview of the rest of the world, and new believers from other contexts do not have their most important questions answered.

Mission theology is incomplete without a theology of the excluded middle that is rooted in scripture. This theology must begin with an affirmation of the existence and activity of the spirit world but must stress God's sovereign control over the most powerful beings of the spirit world. It must also include God's concern for issues of the excluded middle, the role spirits play, and how believers should respond to them.

Power Encounter and Truth Encounter

One strategy that has been emphasized for demonstrating God's control over the excluded middle, that is, his authority over Satan in the current age of conflict, is *power encounter*. Most folk religions and the "middle tier" of reality are concerned with issues of power: sickness and health, wealth, status and prosperity, fertility, and control of people and nature. Before people from power-oriented cultures will come to Christ, they often must be convinced that he has the power to address these concerns more effectively than their old religious system. "Power-oriented people require power proof, not simply reasoning, if they are to be convinced" (C. H. Kraft 2000, 775). A power encounter is a confrontation demonstrating that Jesus's power is superior to that of the old gods.

Advocates of power encounter as a missionary strategy point to scripture and church history for support. Moses defeated the gods of Egypt and their magicians through the ten plagues. Elijah confronted the prophets of Baal on

Mount Carmel and proved that Yahweh alone is God. Jesus's ministry was full of encounters with satanic forces demonstrating that he had brought the kingdom of God in power. Paul blinded the sorcerer Elymas on Cyprus, leading to the conversion of the proconsul, Sergius Paulus. Saint Boniface challenged the German god Thor by cutting down a large oak tree and using its wood to build a chapel. Direct confrontation with demonic powers by Ethiopian evangelists opened the door to thousands of conversions in the 1930s (Davis 1980, 150–56). Alan Tippet observed that peoples of the South Pacific frequently came to Christ in the nineteenth and twentieth centuries after confrontations that demonstrated the superior power of the Christian God over their ancestral gods (Tippet 1967). Power encounter clearly has a long history of bringing people to Christ.

> *Truth and power. Power and truth. Always married. Never divorced.*
> David Hesselgrave (2006, 90)

Charles Kraft notes that conversion that comes as a result of dramatic power encounters "does not assure that the movement will be stable and enduring" (2000, 775). Those who choose Christ because they believe he is most powerful may also believe that they can manipulate him—as they tried to manipulate their old gods—to give them the benefits of power that they seek. As soon as they believe the power of another god is more accessible, they may be quick to turn away from Christ. Even in scripture the people who initially turn to God as a result of a power encounter sometimes return to their old gods, as Israel did soon after the Baal was defeated on Mount Carmel. While demonstrating the superior power of Christ may stimulate a church-planting movement, any church established solely on that basis is likely to view Christian faith as simply a new form of animism: a way of manipulating God to gain power and material advantage. New converts who believe that they have simply exchanged one source of power for another are likely to slip into syncretism (Van Rheenen 2005, 37).

Power encounter must always be balanced with truth encounter. It is not enough for people to be persuaded that Christ is more powerful than their old gods. Their belief system and worldview must also be thoroughly transformed. "Syncretism is sometimes occasioned by an over-emphasis on power encounter and a corresponding under-emphasis on truth encounter" (Hesselgrave 2006, 86). Paul was careful to keep power and truth together in his church planting (Rom. 15:19; 1 Cor. 2:1–5; 1 Thess. 1:4–5). Moreau (1997) places biblical truth in the center of a strategy for dealing with Satan. Those who would come to Christ must recognize the biblical truth that they are sinners and that their old lives have separated them from holy God. They must depend on Christ and his work on the cross to make themselves right with God, restore fellowship with God, and rescue them from the power of their old, false gods. Displays of power that God may choose to send will then be grounded in the truth of who God is and what he has done for them. "It's the truth of who God is and who we are in Christ that enables us to fight the enemy, not just a formula" (Moreau 1997, 11).

Although some demonstration of the power of Christ will often be part of a people coming to Christ, power encounter is not always a supernatural confrontation with personal demons. Such conflict does not occur everywhere the church is planted in the New Testament or in church history. God's power is often demonstrated as radically through changed lives and cultures as it is through the supernatural. Power encounter must never degenerate into seeking to manipulate God or sensationalism. Rather, power encounter must emerge from humbly and dependently seeking God to display kingdom power here and now in order to demonstrate God's truth, glorify God, and bring transformation to individuals and societies.

Dealing with Demons

Although power encounter is not always about confrontation with the demonic, one particular type of power encounter involves dealing with those who are afflicted with demons. When the gospel enters a new area, it is not uncommon to face direct confrontation with the demonic. Jesus confronted Satanic forces when he carried the gospel into new regions (Luke 8:26–39). When he sent out his disciples as an extension of his ministry, he prepared them to face similar demonic opposition, both during his earthly ministry and after it (Mark 16:17; Luke 9:1–2; 10:1–24). In the book of Acts, outreach into new areas often included casting out demons (8:7; 16:16–18; 19:12). In fact, most of the demonic expulsions of the New Testament clearly took place in areas of pioneer evangelism and missions. "Exorcism occurs primarily at the

---

SIDEBAR 10.3
ATO KIDAMO'S TESTIMONY

In mid-2008 veteran Ethiopian evangelist Ato Kidamo Machato related stories of his sixty years of evangelistic and missionary experience, including significant pioneer outreach in animistic areas. He recalled hundreds of encounters with demonized people, including different kinds of mediums and sorcerers. When demonized people came to Christ, the demons almost always immediately left the person. These same new believers then renounced Satan and all his works

in a public ceremony proclaiming their new allegiance to Christ. Ato Kidamo's testimony is typical of the experience of many Ethiopian evangelists and missionaries.

REFLECTION AND DISCUSSION

1. In what ways does Ato Kidamo's experience regarding encounters with the demonic illustrate biblical accounts?

border between church and paganism and is primarily a missionary phenomenon" (Skarsaune and Engelsviken 2002, 71; see also Arnold 1997, 108–12). The modern missionary movement has seen a similar pattern of the casting out of demons by evangelists first bringing the gospel into a new region, and new believers renouncing Satan and his demons as a public act to demonstrate conversion (Davis 1980, 179; see sidebar 10.3).

While dealing with the demonic is often part of pioneer missionary work, some have suggested that believers can also be demonized, and that establishing new churches should include casting out demons from believers. Charles Kraft (1992, 1995), Peter Wagner (1996), Jack Deere (1993), Ed Murphy (1992), and others claim to have had many encounters with believers in Christ who manifest signs of demonic control. Though the scripture clearly warns that Satan can gain significant influence in the lives of believers (Acts 5:3; 19:18; Eph. 4:27; 1 Pet. 5:8), it does not give a single clear example of demonized believers or of demons being cast from a true believer (though C. H. Kraft argues otherwise; 2002a, 196). Casting out demons played no part in New Testament instruction on dealing with sin, temptation, and Satan in the life of the believer. Even professing believers dabbling in the occult in newly planted churches did not have demons cast from them (Acts 8:9–24; 19:17–20).

Although the ancient church saw exorcism and renouncing Satan as an important part of conversion, little or no evidence exists of postconversion exorcism (Arnold 1997, 108–12). "The fact that in the New Testament there is no evidence that exorcisms took place within the church but rather seems to have occurred outside the church in evangelistic contexts suggest that the current specialization in exorcisms by some in the church is misdirected at the least" (J. C. Thomas 2002, 54).

Territorial Spirits and Strategic-Level Spiritual Warfare

A recent mission strategy for defeating satanic power is "strategic-level spiritual warfare" (SLSW). Clinton E. Arnold (1997, 146) summarizes SLSW as (1) discerning information about territorial spirits, (2) dealing with the corporate sin of that area, and (3) engaging in aggressive prayer against these spirits. Charles Kraft points out that when speaking of territorial spirits, "we are referring to *the people* more than to the geography" (1995, 131). Proponents of SLSW believe that human sin and allegiance to Satan gives him control over people groups and human institutions. The purpose of SLSW is to wield God's authority to break this satanic power and enlighten minds darkened by the god of this world, opening the way to significant evangelistic advance (2 Cor. 4:4; C. H. Kraft 2002a, 194). Many advocates of SLSW claim that knowing the names of these spirits gives more authority over them. They encourage "spiritual mapping," "researching an area and identifying the spirit(s) in charge so that 'smart bomb' praying may loosen their hold over the people, who may then freely come to Christ" (C. H. Kraft 2002b, 260). SLSW is often accompanied by prayer walks and *identificational repentance*: isolating and repenting past corporate sins of the people or institution controlled by Satan, especially sins that have brought harm to others.

Supporters of SLSW point to scriptural evidence for the existence of territorial spirits. In the Old Testament many of the peoples surrounding Israel perceived that their gods were connected to a specific land or ethnic group (1 Kings 20:23; 2 Kings 5:17; 17:24–31; gods of "high places" are mentioned sixty-three times), and Deuteronomy 32:17 links these false gods to demons. The strongest and most frequently cited scriptural text for territorial spirits is Daniel 10. When the angel Gabriel reached Daniel in answer to his prayer, he told him that he had been delayed by the "Prince of Persia." Biblical scholars generally agree that this is a reference to a spirit being, not a human ruler (Arnold 2000). Demons are also connected to false gods and idols in the New Testament (1 Cor. 10:20). Advocates of SLSW also find evidence of territorial spirits in the belief systems of many people groups around the world, and SLSW practitioners recount examples of spiritual warfare against territorial spirits resulting in people turning to Christ (Wagner 1990b, 1991, 1996).

> *While it is possible that Satan manifests himself more strongly in certain places than in others, there seems to be little biblical warrant for a number of the practices associated with some forms of spiritual warfare which focus on territorial spirits.*
>
> John C. Thomas (2002, 59)

It is clear from the Bible that demons are active and powerful and that believers engaged in mission must practice spiritual warfare against them. Daniel 10 does seem to make a connection between evil spirits and specific people groups, but the text shows no interest in demonic hierarchies or how to battle them. Daniel was not praying against demonic powers and never rebuked them; he was not even aware of the angelic battle until Gabriel informed him (Lowe 1998, 34). Scripture clearly teaches that demonic forces lie behind opposition to the people of God and that demons stand behind the false gods and religious systems of the nations (Deut. 32:17; Ps. 106:37–38; 1 Cor. 10:20; Rev. 18:2). But it gives no teaching about demonic hierarchies or "mapping" their influence.

People groups, ancient and modern, may *believe* that their gods have power and territorial control, but the consistent witness of the Bible is that they are not really gods; the one true God sovereignly rules them and "their" territories (Deut. 4:28; 1 Kings 18:27; Ps. 115:4–8; Isa. 37:18–19; 44:14–20; 45:20; 46:1–2, 6–7; Jer. 16:19–20; 1 Cor. 8:4; Priest, Campbell, and Mullen 1995, 35). The idea of gaining power over beings (spirit or human) by learning names or information about them is common in animistic practice and "is dangerously close to Christian magic" (Moreau 1997, 174), as is seeking to identify geographic centers of spiritual power. "Rather than praying against spirits, then, it is better to pray for God's Spirit to break the rebellious will in human hearts and bring people to repentance before him" (177). The book of Acts, which documents the early spread of the gospel and emphasizes the spiritual dimension of mission, says nothing about attacking territorial spirits. Paul, about whom we have the most information and who encountered demonic opposition and harassment, never attempted to dethrone a territorial spirit or demon. Wagner (1996, 161–224) seeks to demonstrate that Peter and Paul dealt with territorial spirits in Acts and the Epistles. Although the texts he cites demonstrate that the apostles dealt with the demonic, none of them gives evidence that these were *territorial* spirits, and no evidence exists that the apostles sought information about the demons or their territorial "centers of power" in order to defeat them.

Advocates of SLSW have provided evangelical missions with a reminder that evil spirits influence human cultures and stand behind the false religious systems of the world. Likewise, it is always good for God's people to recognize the sins of their ancestors, confess those sins, and seek ways to repair the damage inflicted on others. But an emphasis on identifying and rebuking territorial spirits or making SLSW a foundational evangelistic or missions strategy "demeans the Scriptures: if this strategy is *so* significant, then why is it not found in the Bible?" (Moreau 2002, 268). Finally, the results often attributed to SLSW may have other explanations. "If a group of praying Christians has reached a point where they are attempting to discern and pray down hostile powers in their effort to reach a city for Christ, many other crucial ingredients [for revival and successful proclamation of the gospel] are already in place" including prayer for the lost, unity, confession of personal sin, and sharing the gospel (Arnold 1997, 173–74). These elements of gospel revival are stressed in scripture and must remain the center of our approaches to spiritual warfare.

Curses and Ancestral Spirits

Somewhat related to the concept of territorial spirits is the belief that spiritual power is connected with certain locations, objects, or families. Many peoples believe that spirits are especially present in certain bodies of water, large trees, or mountains, and that charms, amulets, and sacred objects can be imbued with spiritual power. Children may be given over to serve particular spirits, and family lines are presumed to carry special connections to spirit beings and spirit powers. Many evangelicals adopt a modified version of this perspective. They cast out demons from objects, locations, and individuals whose ancestors were involved in the occult. Kraft draws a distinction between this practice and the practices of animists. Animists believe that these objects and family connections inherently *contain* spiritual power; Kraft believes that instead they *convey* the power of Satan because of past actions. Family demons must be banished and satanic power broken from objects, places, and rituals through the power of God (2002b, 296–307). Missionaries sometimes wonder if they should rebuke demons in locations where people have worshipped false gods, whether they should cast demons from new converts whose families had connection to the occult, or whether they and their children are susceptible to satanic influence because they live and work in locations where demons have been worshipped. New converts sometimes wonder if the sacred charms and objects of their past worship still harbor a demonic presence and wonder if they should be destroyed.

David Powlison (1995) and Robert Priest (Priest, Campbell, and Mullen 1995) reject any idea that satanic influence can rest in an object, location, or family through nonmoral means. "The danger lies, not in physical contact with a physical object, but in how a given individual treats an object which has occult meanings for him" (Priest et al. 1995, 45). Objects per se do not have special power, but false worship centered around an object can make a person susceptible to Satan's power. A believer's security must be in Christ himself, not in separation from objects or location dedicated to Satan. Paul's discussion of eating meat offered to idols (1 Cor. 8–10) supports this perspective. Paul makes clear that the context of eating sacrificial meat is the key, not any kind of "demonic contamination" of the meat itself. In one setting, such as a temple feast or celebration, eating such meat involves "fellowship with demons" (1 Cor. 10:18–22). But in another setting, such as a private home, eating sacrificial meat is permissible as long as an unbeliever does not make it an issue of false worship (1 Cor. 10:25–30; see Fee 1987, 475–91).

But while we must be cautious about overly attributing demonic presence to a place, object, or curse, we cannot completely dismiss the idea that demonic presence may be especially active in some locations and associated with certain objects (see sidebar 10.4). At times a person affected by the demonic power of an object is not even aware that it has been dedicated to Satan; that is, the person himself does not attribute that meaning to the object (C. H. Kraft 1995, 126). The demonically afflicted boy of Mark 9:17–27 had been troubled from childhood. Almost certainly the boy's affliction was not the result of his own sin or his personal occult activity. As we have seen, God sometimes allows demonic affliction against his godly, righteous followers (Job; 2 Cor. 12:7; 1 Thess. 2:18). Destruction of objects related to false gods was central to revival in the Old Testament (2 Kings 18:4; 23:4–15), and paraphernalia associated with the occult was destroyed as part of the revival in Ephesus in Acts 19:19. In both cases the implication is that retaining these items was not harmless but dangerous to God's people.

Although we must be careful to avoid the animistic concept that the object itself holds demonic power, we cannot avoid the biblical and contemporary evidence that demons seem to have chosen to associate themselves with cer-

---

SIDEBAR 10.4
DISCIPLESHIP IN EAST AFRICA

In many places in East Africa people worship the spirits of large trees. These spirits are thought to be benevolent, and bringing them offerings is thought to gain their favor to receive a good harvest, more children, protection against an enemy, or other benefits. Imagine that you are discipling a group of new believers in an area where there is such a large tree.

REFLECTION AND DISCUSSION

1. What questions would you ask about the tree and its spirit association?

2. What would you teach from scripture that would address the worldview of these new disciples and their possible past association with the spirit of the tree?

3. How would you address the felt needs of the people that, in the past, may have been met by the spirit of the tree?

4. What, if anything, would you do related to the tree itself?

---

tain objects, places, or families (Bubeck 1975, 147–50). Deliverance from such presence comes through teaching believers the authority of Christ over the demonic world and through "costly and committed intercession" that reflects dependence on God's power, and not on mastering techniques or formulas of exorcism (Johnstone 1995, 161). As an expression of their allegiance to Christ, missionaries should be prepared to lead new believers in renouncing past family connections to the occult, destroying objects dedicated to Satan, and claiming Christ's power in the presence of locations with past demonic connections. Rather than an animistic power game, this is an expression of dependence on the protection that all believers now enjoy through Christ's victory over Satan at the cross.

CONCLUSION

As Great Commission followers of Jesus, we must embark on our mission only in full dependence on the power of the Holy Spirit. We are engaged in a brutal spiritual war. Ultimate victory has already been secured by our Lord at the cross and in the resurrection, but Satan's destructive violence will continue until Christ's return. As we carry the gospel to the nations, we dare not ignore the unseen powers that seek to deceive and destroy, but we need not fear them. Jesus has promised to build his church in the face of this satanic opposition (Matt. 16:18) and has given us all the resources we need to wage this war. Our responsibility is to appropriate those resources through prayer and dependence on the Holy Spirit. Like Grace and Anna in our case study (see next page), we and those to whom we minister must learn the disciplines of repentance, obedience, resisting the devil (1 Pet. 5:9), trusting the sovereignty of God, and living in the truth of who we are in Christ. Above all, we must engage in bold, intense, dependent intercession as the chief spiritual activity of mission. Such prayer demonstrates our utter reliance on the supernatural power of God, the indispensable fuel for biblical mission.

CASE STUDY:
ANNA'S CONFESSION

Grace* was a missionary who served in a Latin American city and held a regular Bible study with a number of women who were professing Christians. One of her Latina friends, Anna, was struggling in her marriage and had a daughter battling anorexia. During one of their Bible studies, Anna shared with the group that her mother and grandmother had been spiritual mediums and that she herself occasionally visited tarot-card readers. Grace encouraged her to confess to God that this was a sin and to ask God to free her from the power that blocked her communion with him. Anna agreed and prayed a prayer of confession. At the end of the prayer, a number of the other women in the Bible study group shared that during Anna's prayer of confession they had heard the neighborhood dogs howling, as if in fear. Later, in a private conversation, Anna further confessed to Grace that she had "fallen in love" with her dance instructor, a man deeply involved in the occult. The two had not yet committed adultery, but she had been making plans to leave her husband and live with this other man. Now, however, she was repentant and wanted to save her marriage. Again she confessed her sin to God. At Grace's encouragement, she broke off all contact with her dance instructor and recommitted herself to her husband and her marriage. A year later Anna's marriage was strong, but her daughter still struggled with anorexia, and another daughter had inherited her ability and interest in telling fortunes.

Grace is faced with the challenge of the spiritual dynamics of mission.

Grace and Anna's story is true, but their names have been changed.

REFLECTION AND DISCUSSION

1. To what extent is Anna's family in satanic bondage because of the actions of her ancestors?
2. Was Anna demonized, and should Grace have exercised spiritual authority to cast evil spirits from her?
3. Was it enough for Anna to confess her sin, or did she need a further infusion of spiritual power to fight temptation and be free from outside spiritual powers?
4. Should Grace have cast a "demon of anorexia" out of Anna's daughter?
5. How did Anna's emotional unfaithfulness and her involvement in the occult relate to each other?

PART 3

Mission in Local
and Global Context

11

Contextualization and Mission

Missions is not just about bringing people to accept the gospel cognitively. Theology of mission is incomplete until it speaks to the gospel's penetration into every aspect of a people's life and worldview. When the good news of Jesus enters a society, those who respond must decide what they will do with many of the old aspects of their culture. Will they celebrate the same holidays and participate in the same rituals? How will they ensure that they have divine favor to find a job, harvest a large crop, or conceive children? Can they use worship forms or rituals from their previous religion to worship Jesus? As missionaries seek to explain the gospel in every new culture, they must determine the best word in the new language to use for the one true God. How will they explain key theological terms such as sacrifice, redemption, holiness, and faith? Every word that they might use from the local language to explain these biblical ideas already comes loaded with meaning from the people's culture and old religion. To what extent can missionaries use local customs, proverbs, and legends to explain biblical truth? How can missionaries explain the gospel and patterns of Christian living without mixing it with *their* own culture? How can they clearly and compellingly communicate the unchanging truths of scripture to the varied, ever-changing contexts of human beings? These are all questions of how we contextualize the gospel.

THE NATURE AND NECESSITY OF CONTEXTUALIZATION

Contextualization means relating the never-changing truths of scripture to ever-changing human contexts so that those truths are clear and compelling. It is the process of engaging culture in all its varied dimensions with biblical truth. Appropriate contextualization shapes the presentation of the gospel and the release of its transforming power in evangelism, lifestyle, church life, and social change. Thus a theology of mission must reflect on the process of contextualization, guiding the church in living out Christian faith in ways that are both faithful to biblical truth and relevant to specific cultural contexts.

The word *contextualization* seems to have been first used by Shoki Coe (1976) to call for connecting the gospel and culture in ways that would go beyond *indigenization* or *adaptation*. Some theologians and missiologists preferred *contextualization* to these older words because it implies the transformation of economic and political structures by the gospel. Evangelicals have generally preferred *contextualization* over other terms because it stresses the inadequacy of simply adapting Western theological forms to non-Western contexts. Instead of merely being influenced by Western forms of Christian faith, every part of culture must be transformed by God's Word itself. Some, however, fear that "contextualizing" the gospel will open the door to watering down or compromising the gospel with culture. Why, then, is contextualization necessary?

Contextualization is necessary for several reasons. First, *whenever* the gospel is presented, it is presented in cultural clothing. Evangelicals rightly root their theology in the Bible, God's unchanging, eternal Word. But only the Bible itself is God's actual revelation of his truth to humankind. Every explanation of the gospel passes through the experience of the person who is sharing it, and that understanding of the gospel is inevitably colored by the person's own culture and personal background. One might say that *every* perception of Christian truth and practice is contextual. The question is not whether we will contextualize the gospel. The question is whether we will do good contextualization or bad contextualization.

Second, when the gospel is presented in ways that ignore the local context, much of culture and life remain unaddressed by biblical truth. Many practices and thought patterns from the old culture and religion are compartmentalized or go underground. Nominal responders to the gospel will accept Christianity on a superficial level, but their core worldview will remain unchanged, and many of their old, unbiblical practices will continue secretly (Hiebert 1987). For example, new believers from an animistic background may attend church on Sunday, but if their Christian faith does not tell them how they can ensure a good harvest or bear children, they may also visit a local shaman to meet these needs. In these cases syncretism develops, not because of contextualization, but from a failure to contextualize. "When we fail to contextualize, we run a much greater risk of establishing weak churches, whose members will turn to non-Christian syncretistic explanations, follow nonbiblical lifestyles, and engage in magical rituals" (Whiteman 1997, 5). Biblically-based contextualization is essential if Christian faith is to take deep root in any culture.

STARTING POINTS FOR CONTEXTUALIZATION: CONTEXT AND SCRIPTURE

The starting point for contextualization is a clear understanding of its key components: context and scripture. What do we mean when we speak of the ever-changing human "contexts" that make contextualization necessary? What exactly are we contextualizing?

Culture and Context

What do we mean by "context"? At the heart of context is culture. Culture is "the more or less integrated systems of ideas, feelings, and values and their associated patterns of behavior and products shared by a group of people" (Hiebert 1985, 30). The most visible aspects of culture are the way people behave and the products they produce (see fig. 11.1). When we enter a different country, we quickly notice that people have different ways of eating, working, and worshipping. We see their different food, clothing, architecture, institutions, and traditions, and we assume that we have identified the basic elements of their culture. But these behaviors and products are the outworking of more basic ideas, values, and feelings, all carefully integrated by a core worldview.

Sometimes missionaries have focused on changing the outward behavior and worship forms of the people with whom they work. If the people begin to attend church, sing Christian songs, recite the denomination's confession of faith, and

FIGURE 11.1:
DIMENSIONS OF CULTURE (HIEBERT 1999, 376)

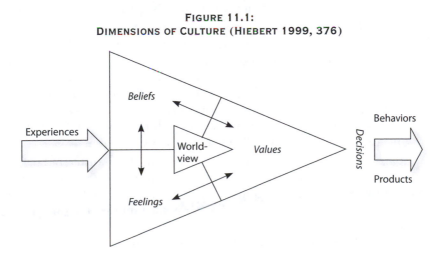

267

change certain moral behaviors (for example, abandon polygamy), the missionaries feel that the culture has become more "Christian." However, it is never enough for the gospel to change the outward behavior of people or even their outward profession of faith. The gospel has not taken hold in a culture until it transforms a culture's inner beliefs, values, feelings, and worldview. Culture is the most obvious and perhaps the most important part of an individual's context.

The gospel is always understood and lived out *within* a culture, but it stands apart from and is distinguished from all cultures. It can be comprehended and applied from within every culture. But because all cultures are human, they are all corrupted by sin. So the gospel must also *challenge* every culture to change and more deeply conform to the will of God.

But context is more than culture. Context includes everything that shapes a society and each individual person (see sidebar 11.1). Context also includes the following components.

- *Religious or Theological Heritage*: Muslims, Hindus, Buddhists, and followers of folk religions each see the world and hear the preaching of a missionary differently. Converts from these religious systems have questions and issues arising from their religious background that need biblical answers. Christians from various denominational backgrounds read the Bible through the grid of their own theological systems. We all view reality through a religious or theological lens, and this shapes our perspective on the context.

- *Historical Era and Current Events*: People look at the world and read scripture conditioned by the times in which they live. Martin Luther was absorbed in his struggles with the Roman Catholic Church and saw the pope in scriptural references to the Antichrist. The events of 9/11 changed the way Christians looked at Muslims and how they read some biblical texts that speak to the differences between Islam and Christian faith.

- *Social, Economic, Educational Group*: Well-educated, middle-class Westerners often do not realize the extent to which their education and socioeconomic condition affects the way they perceive both the world and the Word. People who have a full stomach, a full refrigerator, and a bank account see the world and read the Bible differently than do people who don't know where their next meal is coming from. People with a university education view life and scripture differently than do those who are illiterate but "streetwise" in making their way in life.

- *Age*: Young people in the twenty-first century from different cultures often find they have much in common with one another and share many differences in worldview from their parents' generation. Church leaders who were saved from animistic backgrounds find that the same truths of scripture that changed their worldview have little impact on their grandchildren who are tuning into MTV via satellite TV.

- *Gender*: Men and women are conditioned by their societies in different ways and often have different priorities, values, questions, and concerns. They often perceive different emphases when they read the biblical text.
- *Personal Circumstances*: Personal circumstances such as the loss of a job, a wayward child, the death or sickness of a loved one, or the opposition of an enemy will all affect the impact scripture makes in individuals' lives. Indeed, everything that shapes a society or an individual is part of context.

Gospel and Scripture

If context is more than culture, then what is being contextualized is more than "the gospel." When we speak of contextualizing "the gospel," we often think of identifying a "core" or "kernel" of biblical truth that holds the essence

---

SIDEBAR 11.1
HOW WIDE IS A CONTEXT?

Context can be wide or increasingly narrow. For example, we can legitimately speak of the African context. Sub-Saharan Africa is a vast place with dozens of countries and thousands of different languages and ethnic groups. Nevertheless, many elements of a common worldview characterize most of sub-Saharan Africa, particularly in contrast to a Western worldview or an Asian worldview.

But the African context can be narrowed to speak of one of the dozens of macro-contexts *within* Africa. For example, one could speak of the Ethiopian context. Ethiopia has a two-thousand-year-old written history and an ancient church that was founded in the fourth century. Ethiopians have been united by a common history and Semiticized culture. Ethiopia is a distinctive African context.

But even the Ethiopian context can be narrowed. For example, one could speak of Ethiopian Muslims, who, though sharing many linguistic, cultural, and worldview elements with other Ethiopians, also have a very distinct subculture.

But even Ethiopian Muslims do not form a monolithic context. It is possible to speak even more specifically of the context of Ethiopian nomadic Somali women. The Somali people differ from other Ethiopian Muslims in their language, history, and ethnicity. Nomadic Somalis have a culture and a worldview that are somewhat different from those of urban Somalis. And Somali women have a different way of looking at their world than Somali men do. No matter what country or part of the world one is concerned with, context can be considered from a very wide or a very narrow perspective.

REFLECTION AND DISCUSSION

1. Think through your own context. How might it be described in a very broad way?
2. How is your more specific context different from that of others who share your broad context?

---

of the gospel, or extracting a transcultural truth from this core, and adapting it into a different context. But all the truth of scripture is embedded deeply into the full context of scripture itself (Carson 1987). This includes the cultural contexts in which the biblical writers and their readers themselves lived, be it nomadic Canaanite or first-century Corinthian. Who is to say which aspects of scriptural truth are to be adapted and communicated cross-culturally and which aspects can be dismissed as cultural or contextual scaffolding? One person's list of "nonnegotiable" transcultural truths will inevitably differ from the next person's. Furthermore, the entire counsel of God is relevant to planting and nurturing the church in every context. Rather than isolating the key elements of the gospel and seeking to contextualize them, it seems better, as William Dyrness suggests (1991, 28), to focus on the more comprehensive goal of contextualizing *scripture*. The goal of the missionary is to contextualize the message of scripture so that it speaks clearly and powerfully to every part of the life and worldview of a context. "The Bible itself, rather than any one interpretation of it, is the ultimate locus of transcultural authority" (Vanhoozer 2006, 112).

Contextualization involves not making the message of scripture comfortable but rather speaking clearly to all areas of a context—beliefs, values, emotions. As Andrew Walls (1996) has observed, the gospel should be presented in such a way that believers in Jesus Christ are both *at home* in their culture (the *indigenous* principle) and speak *prophetically* into their context (the *pilgrim* principle). Good contextualization will do both. It will speak the message of scripture into the deepest needs and aspirations of the context. It will speak in ways that stir emotions and stimulate thinking. At the same time, it will challenge values and disturb long-held assumptions. "Good contextualization offends people for the right reasons. . . . When the Gospel is presented in word and deed and the fellowship of believers we call the church is organized along appropriate cultural patterns, then people will more likely be confronted with the offense of the Gospel, exposing their own sinfulness and the tendency toward evil, oppressive structures and behavior patterns within their culture" (Whiteman 1997, 3).

Every culture has elements that conform to God's truth and other elements that violate it. Good contextualization recognizes this good and evil in every culture. It affirms the good in a culture by building links between the Bible and those good elements, speaking clearly and compellingly so that the gospel rings true and sounds authentic in that culture. It challenges the evil in a culture by speaking prophetically from scripture, disturbing those elements of the culture that violate God's truth.

BIBLICAL AND HISTORICAL MODELS

The Bible itself gives us the basis for contextualization. Both the Old and the New Testament include examples of God and his messengers shaping their message to fit the context.

Old Testament

The Old Testament contains few if any examples of God's people adapting his message to communicate more clearly and powerfully to surrounding cultures. However, the Old Testament is full of examples of *God* himself using linguistic, cultural, and religious forms already familiar to his people to reveal himself. The Old Testament "is replete with evidence that God continually used a contextualizing process in his self disclosure of himself to his people" (Glasser 1989, 33). In the Old Testament, God is the primary contextualizer. To be sure, the Old Testament emphasizes that God's people must avoid the idolatry of the surrounding nations and root out any pagan practices that had infiltrated their way of life. But this did not prevent God from using some of the cultural, linguistic, and even religious forms used by these other nations to facilitate Israel's life and worship. But when he did use well-known cultural forms, he filled them with rich, new meaning to communicate divine truth.

> *The story of the patriarchs is, on the one hand, a progressive de-cultur-ization of undesired elements, such as idolatry, sexual immorality, corrupt economic and political practices and, on the other hand, it is an "extension" of other elements from the previous cultural norms or religious forms.*
>
> John Davies (1997, 199)

For example, a primary name for God in Hebrew, El, was the name of the high god of the Canaanite pantheon. God chose to use this word, even though the El of the Canaanites had attributes that were not congruent with his own attributes. He revealed himself as the one true "El" who was qualitatively different from the El of the Canaanites. The act of circumcision originally "was probably a transition rite of puberty but was 'reloaded' with divine content" when God made it the mark of identity for his people, to be performed on all male infants (Davies 1997, 200). God adapted the ancient suzerainty treaty form in the book of Deuteronomy to communicate his covenant relationship with Israel (Craggie 1976). The Old Testament authors frequently make use of mythical figures and language from ancient Near Eastern religion, such as Rahab (Isa. 51:9) and Leviathan (Isa. 27:1; Averbeck 2004, 337–44). The design of the tabernacle and temple had precedents among the nations that surrounded Israel (Kitchen 1977, 54). Both the form and perhaps some of the content of biblical Wisdom literature seems to have been borrowed from surrounding cultures (Davies 1997, 203; Glasser 1989, 47). But probably "the most striking evidence of contextualization in the Old Testament is the manner in which God deliberately and repeatedly shaped the disclosure of himself to this people by using the widely known, ancient phenomenon of covenant" (Glasser 1989, 40). Both the biblical covenants themselves and the preaching styles and object lessons

271

of the prophets who called for loyalty to the covenant were well known in the ancient Near East.

There may also be hints that some of God's people sought to present the one true God in a contextually sensitive way to impact the pagan peoples around them. Jeremiah's call for the Hebrew exiles to contribute to the prosperity and peace of Babylon "involved more than overcoming cultural barriers. It meant living out the faith in a culturally understandable, appropriate manner" (Hesselgrave and Rommen, 1989, 5). This would be the first step in contextualizing the truth of God for the Babylonians to understand and obey. Nehemiah 8:8 says that Ezra and his fellow Levites translated and explained the Book of the Law (given to nomadic and pastoral Israel) hundreds of years later to the returned exiles (who had lived all their lives in Babylon). This is an example of God's truth being translated and contextualized for a group of Hebrews for whom the original message would be quite foreign.

We should note that it has been suggested that Elisha's willingness to allow Naaman to carry Israelite soil back to Syria (presumably on which to build an altar to Israel's God) and to bow in the temple of his king's pagan god was a contextual accommodation to Naaman's worldview. However, this passage raises too many questions and uncertainties for one to conclude that it is a clear example of Old Testament contextualization (see Effa 2007, 310–11; Tennent 2006, 108).

New Testament

We find far more examples of God's revelation being shaped to fit the context for greater clarity and impact in the New Testament than in the Old Testament. Contextualization in the New Testament occurs in at least four ways.

First, the New Testament makes it clear that the gospel was not connected with any one particular culture, specifically the Jewish culture. In the words of Lamin Sanneh, "Christianity affects cultures by moving them to a position short of the absolute, and it does this by placing God at the centre. The point of departure for the church in mission, . . . is Pentecost, with Christianity triumphing by relinquishing Jerusalem or any fixed universal centre, be it geographical, linguistic or cultural, and with the result of there being a proliferation of centres, languages and cultures within the church" (1995, 61).

The church at Antioch was the first place where the disciples were given the name "Christians" (Acts 11:26). The evidence suggests they were given this name because outsiders recognized that the congregation was no mere sect of Judaism. The practices of these people as an assembly of Jews and Gentiles were so unusual that a new name had to be coined for the group (Strauss 2007). In 1 Corinthians 8–10, Paul develops in detail the relationship of form and meaning in bearing witness to the gospel. He clearly demonstrates that there is absolute truth (8:4–6) and that some cultural practices are inherently sinful (10:7–8, 18–20). At the same time, he calls for believers to follow his example of adapting their cultural practices for the sake of the gospel (9:4–5, 12, 14–15, 19–20). Although participation in another culture can be acceptable, participation that becomes false worship must be avoided (10:27–30). Dean Flemming sums up Paul's guidelines on contextualization in 1 Corinthians 8–10: "Because no single cultural expression is ultimate, the gospel is free to come to life in a plurality of cultures and circumstances. Yet because God values all cultures and because the gospel cannot be heard in the abstract apart from a cultural home, God must speak to the Jew as a Jew, to the Greek as a Greek, to the Filipino as a Filipino, to the Gen-Xer as a Gen-Xer. . . . Our articulation of the gospel must be culture-specific, but not culture-bound" (2005, 138).

The Jerusalem Council may be the clearest New Testament illustration of disconnecting the gospel from Jewish culture. The apostles and elders of the church came together to determine whether Jesus's followers must first become culturally, ethnically, and religiously Jews, or whether they could be authentic followers of Christ and remain part of their native cultures. After hearing that God had endorsed the new Gentile converts by giving them the Holy Spirit and performing miracles among them, James concludes that God's acceptance of Gentiles *as Gentiles* was in line with Old Testament prophecy. Gentiles would be welcomed as full disciples of Christ without becoming Jewish proselytes (Acts 15:19). Though this decision was primarily theological, it bears many implications for contextualization (see Strong and Strong 2006).

The second example of contextualization in the New Testament is the way "Jesus and the apostles tailor the gospel message to address different groups of people" (Flemming 2005, 15). Paul's sermons in Acts 13, 14, and 17 are shaped to both build bridges to and challenge the religious assumptions of his listeners in diverse audiences. Twice in Acts, Paul presents the testimony of his conversion. His presentation to a nationalistic Jewish mob is designed to show his close connection to law-abiding Judaism (22:2–5, 12, 19–20) while challenging them with his call to the Gentiles. His message to the Greco-Roman upper class uses a familiar proverb and popular religious themes, while challenging them with the repulsive (to Greco-Romans) notion of resurrection (26:8, 17–18, 20, 23).

The third way the New Testament demonstrates contextualization is found in the apostles' use of words prepackaged with deep meaning, sometimes with pagan religious roots, to communicate spiritual truth. However, in all cases they "reloaded" those words with new meaning (Davies 1997, 209). For example, the *logos* is an impersonal divine principle in Greek philosophy, but John uses it to describe the personal "Word" who was with God and was God himself. John's use of *logos* may find deeper roots as a translation of the Old Testament Hebrew *dbr*, but in either case John is taking a concept already known to his listeners and filling it with new and/or additional meaning to

273

communicate "the unique concept of who Christ is" (Davies 1997, 209). *Theos* is the word used for the Greek "gods" who were really demons (1 Cor. 10:20), but it is also the word used by the Septuagint translators and the writers of the New Testament to describe the one, true, and living God. In Romans 15, Paul uses words common in the mystery cults (*leitourgia*, "sacrifice"; *leitourgon*, "minister"; *thysia*, "libation"; *latreian*, "spiritual worship"; Gilliland 1989, 56) to describe his role as a minister of the gospel.

Fourth, "the New Testament writings themselves are examples of the theological task" (Flemming 2005, 15). The very words of Jesus are recorded in the Gospels (with but few exceptions) not in the original Aramaic he spoke but rather in Greek. This underlines that even Jesus's teaching is translatable (unlike the Qur'an), and that Christianity itself is translatable (see Sanneh 1989). Furthermore, each of the Gospels is a contextual presentation of the Jesus story to a different contextual community. Paul and the other writers of the epistles were missional theologians writing to pastoral issues. They were "doing theology" in missionary situations (D. J. Bosch 1991, 124). The Epistles are not systematic theologies but rather situational applications of God's eternal truth to specific first-century audiences with specific questions and needs.

Even the tendency of the New Testament writers to quote from the Septuagint demonstrates a contextual approach to theologizing. "When Paul uses the Greek Bible, this is already a form of interpretation. The very act of translation means that the original Hebrew terms and ideas frequently take on new connotations when they are expressed in Greek language and terminology" (Flemming 2005, 153–54).

The Bible, and the New Testament in particular, demonstrates that contextualization has been part of the missionary task since the birth of the church.

Mission History

Though the term *contextualization* was not coined until the 1970s, missionaries and theologians have been adapting their presentation of the truths of scripture to diverse human contexts throughout church history. Early church apologists such as Tatian, Justin, and Clement sought to communicate scripture in Greek historical and philosophical categories and answer questions being discussed by Christians with a Greek philosophical background. Cyril and Methodius were missionaries to the Slavic peoples in the ninth century. They translated the scriptures into Slavic in the face of opposition from established church leaders who insisted that only Latin, Greek, and Hebrew were appropriate languages for scripture. Their work opened the door for theologizing to take place outside the Hellenistic culture and worldview of the Greco-Roman world (Sanneh 1989, 73–87).

In the sixteenth and seventeenth centuries, Jesuit missionaries such as Robert de Nobili in India and Matteo Ricci in China used local cultural forms and indigenous religious language to explain Christian truth. The great Protestant missionary movement of the nineteenth and early twentieth centuries involved limited contextualization. But the missionaries' emphasis on vernacular-language scriptures allowed new believers in Africa, Asia, and Latin America to claim Christian faith as their own (Sanneh 2003, 95–130) and stimulated fresh thinking about the opportunities and limits of engaging gospel and culture.

CONTEXTUALIZATION AND SYNCRETISM

What are the limits of appropriate contextualization, and how can we protect the process of contextualization from the danger of syncretism? Syncretism is "the replacement or dilution of the essential truths of the gospel through the incorporation of non-Christian elements" (Moreau 2000b, 924). Some modern scholars are not concerned about syncretism, suggesting that it is a natural, neutral blending of ideas between religions that takes place all the time. "Since all churches are culture-based, every church is syncretistic," they purport (Moreau 2000b, 924; see also Schineller 1992). However, this ignores the biblical emphasis on God's absolute truth, which is the foundation and the measure of all interaction with culture. Both the Old Testament (e.g., Deut. 12:4; Judg. 2:19; 2 Kings 17:16–17) and the New Testament (e.g., 1 Cor. 8–10, see above; Col. 2:8–23, see Arnold 1996) clearly warn God's people against their natural tendency to blend their beliefs and practices with those of the dominant culture in ways that stray outside God-revealed truth and God-acceptable practice.

> *Conversion may include a change in beliefs and behavior, but if the worldview is not transformed, in the long run, the gospel is subverted and the result is a syncretistic Christo-paganism.*
>
> Paul Hiebert (2008, 11)

Some of the work of contextual theologians around the world validates the fear of those who believe that contextualization inevitably leads to syncretism. Advocates of liberation theology, *Minjung* theology, or theologies of decolonialization often seem to find their authority more in economic or political ideologies than in scripture. Some Muslims and Hindus who profess to be followers of Jesus continue to identify themselves as "Muslim" or "Hindu" and practice the same religious forms as other followers of these faiths. Converts from folk religions in Africa or Asia question whether they can reintroduce ancestral practices into their lives and worship. Or, as in the case study at the end of the chapter, even professing evangelicals may use animistic folk practices to address the pressing problems they face in everyday life. When exactly does contextualization slip into syncretism, and how can this be avoided?

Perhaps the major cause for syncretism is a failure of the gospel to penetrate the inner worldview of a culture. "Syncretism often results from devoting

275

too much attention to the outer layers of culture and not enough attention to its inner core or worldview" (Hesselgrave 2006, 76). When missionaries and church leaders focus on changing only the outward behavior of converts, it is likely that the gospel will never change their core beliefs, values, and emotions. Only when the scripture begins to challenge these core assumptions of a culture will the gospel take root in a way that is authentically indigenous but avoids compromise with unbiblical cultural elements.

Another cause for syncretism is an overemphasis on the role of context and a corresponding underemphasis on the role of scripture. After scanning dozens of "ethnic theologies" in the *Dictionary of Third World Theologies*, Kevin J. Vanhoozer notes that "the implication of these many ethnic theologies is that contextual difference may trump textual sameness. Should theology's primary loyalty be to the text or to context? It is not a matter of excluding either element . . . but rather of doing appropriate justice to both" (2006, 105).

How can syncretism be avoided? The most important precaution is an emphasis on scripture as the primary source for all contextual theologizing. Syncretism often creeps into a church when authenticity to the context becomes the most important priority. Context plays an important role as a secondary source, but scripture itself must be the control for acceptable belief and behavior in any context. In the next section we will discuss the role of text and context in more detail.

A second important guard against syncretism is the worldwide church. Although the church in every context has the right and the privilege of self-theologizing (Hiebert 1985, 193–224), no local theology can be incongruent with the theology of the church around the world and throughout the centuries. The more theological exchange that exists between believers from different cultures, socioeconomic groups, ethnicities, and theological traditions, and the more carefully we learn from the theological lessons and mistakes of the past, the less likely it is that a church will slip into syncretism. We will discuss the safeguard against syncretism provided by the global church when we discuss globalizing theology.

A third guard against syncretism is comprehensive, critical contextualization, which addresses the most deeply felt needs of a culture. If practical, everyday needs for protection, blessing, healing, and spiritual power are not addressed, people are likely to blend their old religious practices with their new faith in Christ (Bauer 2008). We will discuss this precaution in the section "What Do We Do with Traditional Practices?"

THE ROLE OF TEXT AND CONTEXT

Different models of contextualization have answered the question of the proper role of text and context in different ways (Bevans 2002). Scott Moreau (2005) groups these different approaches into translation and existential models.

Translation models recognize scripture as the primary source of authority for contextualization. These models see scripture providing the primary message to be contextualized; contextualization is finding the appropriate bridges for communicating this message. *Existential* models regard contextualization as discovering and coming alongside what God is already doing in the preexisting context. Moreau further divides existential models into two main approaches. The first focuses on *culture* and seeks to uncover the way God has revealed himself in the local customs, beliefs, values, and worldview before the gospel arrived. The second focuses on the need for *social change* and focuses on what God is doing to bring justice to marginalized people.

One of the clearest distinctions in these models is the vastly different presuppositions each has about the role of scripture and the role of context. By clarifying the role of both scripture and context, we can develop an approach to contextualization that is biblical and practical.

What Is the Role of Scripture?

Evangelicals who accept the authority of scripture must begin by asking, "What role does the Bible give itself? How does the Bible expect those who read it to respond?" The Bible presents itself as God's revelation for all people. Second Timothy 3:14–17 reminds us that scripture is "God-breathed" and teaches us what we should believe and how we should behave. Second Peter 1:21 tells us that those who wrote the Bible were "carried along" by the Holy Spirit. The presumption of these verses is that the scriptures are God's Word not just for the original audience but also for subsequent generations. Some existential contextualizers make use of the Bible but suggest that it is only a model of successful local theologies in the past, not the authoritative source for theologizing in all contexts. But the Bible is more than a model of God speaking in the past. Scripture presents itself as God's message for all peoples in all eras of history.

Other passages make this even more explicit. Romans 15:4 and 1 Corinthians 10:6, 11 say that the biblical texts written long ago continue to have authority over the beliefs and behaviors of God's people. Biblical characters also used the scriptures written to other generations in other cultures to speak to their times and situations. We have already seen the example of Ezra and the Levites in Nehemiah 8:7–8, which applies scripture written hundreds of years before for a nomadic people to an assembly that had grown up in urban Babylon. Every time a New Testament writer quotes the Old Testament (e.g., Heb. 3:7–4:3), we see that the writers of scripture understood that the Bible is God's authoritative message both for those who first heard it and for them as well.

The Bible contains "everything we need for life and godliness" (2 Pet. 1:3) for God's people of all eras and cultures. Models of contextualization that make contextual authenticity their priority or that find their source of authority in culture or in political or economic ideologies will inevitably become syncretistic. Good contextualization will address all these dimensions of life, but the primary source for addressing them will be found in the Bible. "The lived experience of this or that culture, along with the history and tradition of the church as a whole, has a legitimate role to play as a *secondary* theological source. The primary source, however, must remain Scripture" (Vanhoozer 2006, 106).

A high regard for the text of scripture itself should go hand in hand with a confidence that every culture can sufficiently understand the text of scripture. Though they are divided by culture differences and diverse preunderstandings, all people share enough commonalities that, regardless of their contextual differences, they can all adequately understand the essential truths of scripture (Strauss 2006b, 104–10). The first task for every interpreter of the Bible should be to *seek to read the text the way it was meant to be read*. "An interpreter is not free to import meaning into the biblical text but seeks to be informed by the text" (Ott 2006, 318). Christians of all cultures should make scripture the primary authority in their lives and build their current application of scripture on the foundation of its original message.

What Is the Role of Context?

While strongly emphasizing scripture as the ultimate source for Christian belief and practice, we must be equally careful not to minimize the role of context. Doing theology "is a multidisciplinary activity requiring us not only to exegete the Word but also to exegete the contemporary world" (Netland 2006, 17). Context affects contextualization in at least three ways. First, it influences what we see and what we don't see in the text. Second, context raises questions and issues that need biblical answers. Finally, context helps us effectively communicate the biblical text.

CONTEXT INFLUENCES WHAT WE SEE AND WHAT WE DON'T SEE IN THE BIBLICAL TEXT

Sometimes evangelicals are reluctant to admit that context shapes the way scripture is conceptualized, experienced, and valued. Inevitably, context affects how we *understand* scripture. All students of scripture should begin their Bible study by seeking to read the text the way it was meant to be read, and readers of scripture from every culture can understand the essential truths of every passage of scripture. But because it is impossible to completely separate ourselves from our context, we cannot help but read scripture through the lenses of our own culture, theological background, and personal experience.

Context affects our understanding of the Bible in two ways. First, the lens of context will sharpen some aspects of scripture so that we see things that others miss. "Every culture possesses positive elements, favorable to the understanding of the Gospel" (Padilla 1980, 69). For example, Latin American theologians might have special insight into what the Old Testament prophets teach about justice. Believers who have been refugees will bring personal empathy to texts that refer to famine and exile. Asian Christians have a special sensitivity to passages that teach about honor, "face," and shame.

Second, the lens of context will blur some aspects of scripture so that we miss things that believers from another context see more clearly. "In all cultures there are elements which conspire against the understanding of God's Word" (Padilla 1980, 69). Believers from wealthy, powerful contexts will be less sensitive to aspects of the text that teach about hunger, deprivation, and powerlessness. Believers from individualistic cultures often fail to see biblical insights about living in community. Believers who live in cultures with authoritarian leadership styles may not see everything the scripture teaches about servant leadership.

In these cases the context is not providing the primary *source* for local theology. Rather, context opens (and closes) our eyes to see (or overlook) what is *already there* in scripture, or to see and understand it in a fresh light. "Creative understanding is essentially a matter of understanding the same thing in a different context, thus understanding *more*" (Vanhoozer 2006, 121; see sidebar 11.2).

CONTEXT RAISES QUESTIONS AND ISSUES THAT NEED BIBLICAL ANSWERS

The second role that context legitimately plays in contextualization is to raise questions and issues that need biblical answers. What does the Bible say

---

SIDEBAR 11.2
PREACHING EPHESIANS

When I (Steve) was a new missionary in Ethiopia, I was asked to serve as pastor of an international church for a time. One of my first sermon series was on the book of Ephesians. I preached through Ephesians, primarily using notes that I had from my recent seminary studies.

Years later, while still serving in Ethiopia, I was asked to lead a Bible study on Ephesians. As I studied through the book again, I was amazed at all that was in the text that I had not seen when I was a new missionary. I particularly noticed Paul's emphasis on Christ's lordship over the

spirit world and its impact in the believer's life. Living in a new context had opened my eyes to see things already in the biblical text that I had previously missed.

REFLECTION AND DISCUSSION

1. Think through examples in your own life when you studied a biblical text multiple times and subsequently saw something new in the text that you had missed in an earlier study. How did your changing context affect what you saw and missed?

---

about the problems people are facing, about the questions they are asking, and about their cultural beliefs and practices? For example, African believers might ask, "What does God's Word have to say about initiation rituals for our young people? What does God's Word have to say about honoring our ancestors?" Believers from a Hindu background might ask, "What does the Bible say about the caste system?" Believers from a Muslim background might question, "Should we bow our faces to the ground and pray five times a day?" Believers living in the world's crowded urban areas may ask, "Does the Bible have a theology of the city that answers our questions? Does scripture have anything to say about how believers should respond to the HIV/AIDS pandemic, about the environment, or about economic justice?" Context always raises questions that demand biblical answers.

When context raises questions for theologizing, theologians must be careful that they do not seek biblical answers through simple prooftexting from a few apparently related texts. For example, believers seeking to develop a theology of the city must not simply study verses with the word *city* in them or verses that talk about cities. Careful study rooted in comprehensive biblical theology is required to ensure that the emerging contextual theologies are truly rooted in the intended message of scripture. For example, believers looking for what the Bible teaches about HIV/AIDS will need to study biblical teaching on God's compassion and care for the ostracized, healing, the many reasons God allows disease, God's use of tragedy to bring about good as well as other biblical themes.

A good example of how context raises questions and issues is the recently published *Africa Bible Commentary* (*ABC*, Adeyemo 2006). The *ABC* is a commentary on every book of the Bible written by evangelical African scholars. One can look at any passage in scripture and see how an African Bible teacher has understood and applied the text. But the *ABC* also contains approximately seventy articles on key issues from the African context such as polygamy, initiation rites, HIV/AIDS, *lobola* (bride price), ancestors, tribalism, and the spirit world. The articles give a biblical response to these questions and issues that emerge from the African context. These articles are examples of contextualization that begins with questions from the context but which finds its source of authority in scripture.

Context Helps Us Effectively Communicate the Biblical Message

A third way that context influences theology is by providing bridges to effectively communicate the biblical text. Contextualization is not about making the biblical text less offensive so that people will accept it, but about making the text clearer and more compelling so that people understand and feel it the way it was originally intended to be understood and experienced. Context should inform preaching, teaching, and application of scripture so that it makes the same impact on contemporary hearers as it did on the first readers (Hesselgrave 2006, 85).

For example, Don Richardson (1974, 1981) suggests that every culture contains "redemptive analogies"—such as stories, rituals, proverbs, language games—which are God-ordained bridges to communicate biblical truth. It may be going too far to suggest that God has specifically designed these communication tools within *every* culture. But "since God has created humans in His image, societies all over the world have cultural resources within them to express and understand biblical truths to a good extent without presupposing these cultural elements to carry divine intention" (Chua 2006, 238). Good contextualization asks how biblical truth should be preached, taught, and lived in each context. All followers of Jesus should be lifelong students of the cultures in which they live, looking for effective bridges that communicate God's message with power and clarity.

One of the most effective ways to communicate scripture in any context is to use the stories and proverbs embedded in the people's culture and worldview. Most people in the world learn orally by passing on stories, proverbs, poems, songs, and riddles. Jay Moon (2004) describes proverbs as "sweet talk" that clear away fog in theological communication and root the gospel in vernacular soil. "Storying" is another example of effectively communicating the truths of scripture in the way that most people in the world learn. Chronological Bible storying begins with the Old Testament and uses stories, drama, and song to communicate the truths of scripture (http://www.chronologicalbiblestorying .com). Scott Moreau and Mike O'Rear (2004, 2008) provide an excellent list of resources on the Internet for using stories and proverbs. Good contextualization will recognize the way people most naturally learn and will seek to communicate the truths of scripture using those forms.

WHAT DO WE DO WITH TRADITIONAL PRACTICES?

Contextualized theology will often begin with the text, seeking to most effectively communicate scriptural truth in a particular context. But it will also emerge from the context. As we have already seen, every context raises questions that need to be answered. John Gration (1984) stresses the importance of national church leadership identifying the key contextual questions. He suggests two key questions that will aid the process of determining which issues need a biblical response: (1) How has the gospel been good news in our culture? (2) Where has the gospel not yet touched our culture? This second question should probe specifically into the national (i.e., political), church, and personal realm. Church leaders should then examine the scripture in community to see what it says about this "unfinished agenda" that demands biblical, contextual answers.

Hiebert (1987) proposes a complementary model for dealing with questions and issues that arise from a context and for determining which practices from the local context should be kept and which must be discarded. Rather

281

than thoughtlessly rejecting all old cultural practices or uncritically accepting them, they should undergo a process of *critical contextualization*. Critical contextualization should be done by a group of believers and follows these steps: (1) Exegesis of the culture to make sure that the full meaning and implications of the practice are understood. "The purpose here is to understand the old ways, not to judge them" (Hiebert 1987, 109). (2) Exegesis of scripture, in which a facilitator leads the entire group in a study of relevant scriptures, building an understanding of the text on the original meaning before applying it to the question at hand. (3) Critical response, when the group of believers makes a decision about the future of their old practices based on the teaching of scripture. (4) Implement a contextualized practice (see fig. 11.2).

FIGURE 11.2:
RESPONSES TO TRADITIONAL PRACTICES
(ADAPTED FROM HIEBERT AND MENESES 1995, 169)

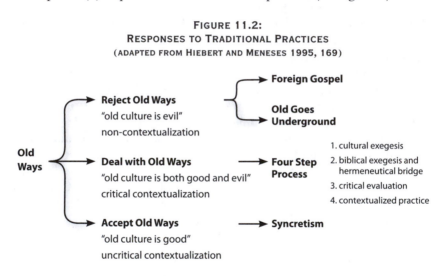

Five different responses are possible in this process of critical contextualization:

Adoption: The old practice is judged not unbiblical and can be retained. For example, believers retain cultural practices when they celebrate national holidays with their non-Christian neighbors, as when Americans enjoy fireworks on Independence Day.

Rejection: The old practice is judged unbiblical and must be rejected completely. For example, believers from an animistic background might decide that they can no longer bring sacrifices to a sacred place to ensure a good crop.

Modification: The group might choose to modify the old practice, giving it a new, Christian meaning. Believers from a Muslim background might choose to continue to kneel and bow their faces to the ground in prayer but explicitly give their worship and prayers to Jesus. Whenever believers write Christian music using the traditional or contemporary music styles of their culture they are modifying a form and giving it Christian meaning.

Substitution: A new symbol or practice is created to substitute for the old. Churches in the United States that hold a "harvest festival" or "costume parade" as an alternative to Halloween are substituting a new ritual as a result of critical contextualization. Believers from an animistic background might reject a traditional initiation ceremony because of its pagan connotation but substitute a different kind of ceremony that initiates young men and women into the responsibilities of Christian adulthood (see the ROPES program at http://tanari.org/index.php?option=com_content&task=view &id=16&Itemid=3).

Toleration: The practice is considered less than the biblical ideal, but changing it immediately would create a greater evil. For example, in some cases polygamy was rejected, and all wives but the first were divorced. As a result, families were torn apart, the divorced wives became social outcasts, and some resorted to prostitution to survive, thus creating a greater evil than polygamy itself. For a transition period a practice may need to be tolerated. But this toleration would only be with a plan that, with adequate teaching or with the introduction of other support systems, the practice would be changed in the future.

Good critical contextualization will ensure that key questions are answered and that old, anti-Christian practices are not simply shifted underground into a syncretistic dualism. The church's emerging theology and ethics will be relevant to its context and rooted in scriptural truth.

CONTEXTUALIZATION THAT CONNECTS: USING THE CULTURE TO COMMUNICATE BIBLICAL TRUTH

How does one actually *do* contextual theology? We have seen that good contextualization draws on scripture as its primary source but recognizes the significant role that context will play in shaping theology and practice. How do text and context practically intersect when we do contextualization?

Dyrness (1991) suggests an "interactional" model of contextualization that emphasizes believers' attempts to apply scripture to the difficult decisions of their everyday lives. The process begins both with the text of scripture and with the context. As obedient believers read scripture, they will reflect on how it relates to their lives and will seek to obey what they have learned. As they begin to live out the reality of the Bible in their context, they will gain even deeper insight into the texts they have read. At the same time, seeking to live obediently to scripture will continually raise further issues and questions that demand biblical answers. That, in turn, will drive them back to scripture to seek answers. "Our understanding of Scripture is conditioned by our environment and shaped by our obedience. . . . Practice, then, inevitably has epistemological significance" (Dyrness 1991, 117).

> *Theology is something that is lived. Doctrinal truth must be not only systematized but also shown; stated, yes, but also staged and even suffered.*
>
> Kevin Vanhoozer (2006, 123)

Two key questions (suggested by Padilla 1983, 87) will fuel this dynamic interchange between text and context and lead to contextualization that connects. First, where has the gospel become a "foreign enclave with no relevance to daily life?" This could be called the *relevance question*. If the church is using language that people do not understand, discussing issues that people do not find significant, or ignoring the questions and problems that concern the people of its culture, it must seek to speak with greater clarity and power into its context. Second, each church should explore where its message has adapted to "the spirit of the age" and become "a mere echo of popular wishful thinking." This can be called the *prophetic question*. Every church must speak prophetically into its culture, challenging the culture's unbiblical assumptions and norms. Good contextualization takes place as believers study scripture and reflect on their context while asking themselves these two questions. This, in turn, will lead to a richer understanding of the text, renewed expression of their faith in meaningful symbols and worship, and fresh attempts to obey, including attempts to influence their context (see fig. 11.3).

Contextualization that connects will always be done in *community*. Christians in the West sometimes imagine that theology should only be written by experts who sit isolated in book-lined libraries. But "the Christian community is the place where the Word of God finds its home and releases its transforming power" (Padilla 1983, 81). The writers of the New Testament and the most influential theologians of Christian history (such as Luther and Calvin) wrote their theology with colleagues and communities of faith while in the middle of active pastoral and evangelistic ministries. Professional theologians can play a key role as facilitators and guides in the process of contextualization, but the entire body of believers should be part of the process.

COMPREHENSIVE CONTEXTUALIZATION

Contextualization covers more than formal theology. It is not enough to find local bridges to communicate key biblical themes and theological categories. It is not enough to evaluate and critically contextualize some of the behaviors and rituals of a culture. Scripture should penetrate every aspect of society and transform every part of culture. All church life and Christian living should reflect scriptural truth in clear and compelling ways. Contextualization must be

FIGURE 11.3:
CONTEXTUALIZATION THAT CONNECTS
(ADAPTED FROM DYRNESS 1991, 30)

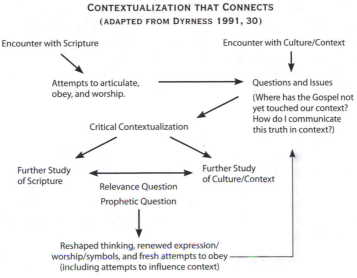

comprehensive. Moreau (2005, 2006) has suggested seven primary dimensions that must be addressed in comprehensive contextualization. Contextualization must speak to:

1. **The Doctrinal or Philosophical Dimension.** Formal beliefs and doctrines must be expressed in ways that make sense in every context. Basic theological questions that every culture asks must be answered: What is the truth about the spirit world, God or the gods, humanity, creation, and the relationship between all of these?

2. **The Ethical/Legal Dimension.** What rules, laws, and guidelines regulate a people's behavior in a culture? The ethical dimensions of a culture are both explicit (e.g., parents giving their teenagers a curfew or laws against running a red light) and implicit (e.g., expectations of appropriate dress for a business meeting). The Bible is full of commands and guidelines for ethical behavior, and believers in every culture must reflect them in their own context. They must also do critical contextualization of the ethical guidelines of their culture and determine whether they should be kept, discarded, adapted, or replaced with an appropriate alternative.

3. **The Mythic or Narrative Dimension.** Myths are the stories in every culture that reflect its core worldview. They may be historically true or false, but the *story as story* is cherished by a culture as reflecting its beliefs and values. For example, Americans value the story of George Washington truthfully admitting he chopped down a cherry tree when he was a boy; whether or not this ever happened historically, this "myth"

285

reflects their cherished value of honesty. Believers in every context must evaluate their society's myths biblically and must also reflect the (historically true) narratives of the Bible in ways that will speak with power and clarity to their cultures. C. S. Lewis's *Narnia* stories are an excellent example of contextualization of biblical truth in mythical form.

4. **The Social or Organizational Dimension.** Anthropologists have recognized a wide range of societal organization structures: associations, kinship, education, and economics. Every one of these social structures should be evaluated biblically through critical contextualization. Leadership styles and education are particularly important to contextualize (Lingenfelter and Lingenfelter 2003; Lingenfelter 2008). Learning styles vary considerably around the world (Chang 1981; Plueddemann 1991). Missionaries must make sure they learn and use local patterns of education and leadership whenever possible and must be especially sensitive about not imposing their own expectations of the best way to learn on new believers.

5. **The Ritual Dimension.** Every culture is full of rituals. Whether it is initiation into the Rotary Club, a local church's pattern for taking the Lord's Supper, or the rite of giving proper honor to the deceased at a funeral, rituals facilitate transitions and symbolize beliefs and values in every society. Westerners may tend to ignore the important place that rituals occupy in their own culture and so devalue their importance in other cultures. It is essential that believers in every culture critically contextualize all their society's rituals. When rituals are simplistically accepted or rejected by a Christian community, syncretism quickly creeps into the church. Cultural rituals must be carefully evaluated and Christian rituals—especially liturgies and worship forms—must be created that are true to scripture and appropriate to each context (see Zahniser 1997).

6. **The Experiential Dimension.** People in every culture understand and explain their encounters with the spirit world in different ways. Many cultures have developed elaborate cosmologies of the spirit world and understand dreams, visions, and ecstatic and prophetic speech as communication from the spirit world. Believers in each context must evaluate these experiences with scripture, reshaping their response to conform to biblical categories of reality and godly behavior.

7. **The Material Dimension.** Next to the doctrinal dimension, the material dimension is probably the area that has been most thoroughly addressed in past discussions of contextualization. It includes art, architecture, clothing, and objects. Beautiful, diverse Christian art, sculpture, clerical vestments, music, and culturally appropriate architecture have developed around the world. The principles of ethnomusicology have been applied to help believers develop musical forms that reflect scriptural

truth and are truly indigenous (e.g., King et al. 2008). Contemporary mission journals and Web sites have specific examples of local art and music to encourage continued contextual development of the material dimension (e.g., Balisky 1997; Hatcher 2001; Chinchen and Chinchen 2002; Jordan and Tucker 2002; Moreau and O'Rear, 2002; www.mislinks .org/practical/arts.htm).

By asking the relevance question and the prophetic question in each of these dimensions, believers can stimulate contextualization that is comprehensive and help ensure that biblical faith connects with every area of their culture.

GLOBALIZING THEOLOGY: LEARNING FROM ONE ANOTHER

One of the rich blessings twenty-first century believers enjoy is living at a time when Jesus's church is truly global. Mature followers of Christ live in every nation on earth and among thousands of distinct people groups. But "what at first glance appears to be the largest world religion is in fact the ultimate local religion" (Robert 2000, 56). The worldwide church exists in many distinct contexts. These many, varied contexts have, in turn, shaped the theology and practice of the church in different ways. Worship styles, theological reflection, and daily Christian living are very different among house church believers in China, rural Africans, American suburbanites, or members of a large urban church in Latin America.

This variety should not trouble us. Instead, it should cause us to rejoice. Part of the blessing of enjoying a universal fellowship of believers is the opportunity to grow and learn from one another. Learning from the worldwide church is not just a privilege; it should be a priority. Because believers in every context will see different aspects of scriptural truth, one way to enrich our understanding of scripture is to learn from one another. The result will be a true globalizing of theology.

> *Perhaps one of the most important functions of contextualization in mission is to remind us that we do not have a privileged position when it comes to understanding and practicing Christianity. It cannot be the exclusive property of any one culture.*
>
> Darrell Whiteman (1997, 4)

Globalizing theology is not "dumbing down" theology to irreducible minimums shared by all Bible-believing Christians. Rather, it is sharing perspectives on theology, worship, and Christian living and learning so that we *enhance* one another's Christian experience. The result will be a more richly hued, deeply textured theology and practice that can be shared by the universal church around the world.

Western Christians often see themselves as the leaders in this theological dialogue. But like any other church, context has blinded Western Christians to some scriptural insights. Believers from the West have as much to learn from their brothers and sisters in other contexts as Christians in Africa, Asia, and Latin America have to learn from them. Believers from every part of the world can enrich their own understanding of scripture and correct their blind spots by interacting with believers from other contexts. The key is humility and a true learner's spirit among all believers. "Every church must learn to be both learner and teacher in theologizing" (Conn 1984, 252).

> *Christians from other cultures can enrich our faith or help us correct our mistakes.*
> Tite Tiénou (1993, 248)

Though rooted in the scriptures, global theologizing recognizes that other contexts must inform the theological process. The first of those other contexts is the *historical legacy of the Christian community through the ages*. Contextual theology does not put so much emphasis on contextual clarity and relevance that it ignores the theologies of past generations. The ancient creeds and the confessions of the church around the world are the crucial repositories of this historical legacy. They are the time-tested articulations of God's eternal truth in the Bible. "They unite the universal church around a common history and serve as examples of theology that is both biblical and relevant" (Strauss 2006a, 155). They are not solely the property of the Western church. They are the heritage of the church wherever it emerges.

But though "theological formulations in the Western tradition are no less true in Africa or Asia than they are in Europe or America . . . they are not necessarily equally relevant, understandable, or adequate in all contexts. Nor are such formulations exhaustive" (Ott 2006, 312). Even the ancient creeds and the well-tested confessions of the church are themselves contextual theologies, shaped by their own historical era. Their articulations of the truth were directed at the problems and issues that Christians at that time faced. They remain crucial reference points as accurate reflections of biblical truth, and every contextual

> *The way forward is not non-Western but* more-*than*-*Western theology.*
> Kevin Vanhoozer (2006, 119)

theology should be deeply informed by these insights from past generations of Bible-believing Christians. But they should never be the starting point for fresh theologizing today. The Bible itself should be that starting point. "We would be fools not to stand on the shoulders of those who have gone before. But then the reason for standing on someone's shoulders is to gain *new* perspectives and to see *further*" into contemporary contextual realities (ibid.).

The ancient creeds and many confessions of the worldwide church "open the door not necessarily for *alternative* but rather for *fuller* theological understanding" (ibid., 315).

Second, global theologizing will be informed by the *diverse perspectives of Christian communities around the world*. Africans will learn from Westerners, Westerners will learn from Asians, Asians will learn from Latin Americans, and Latin Americans will learn from Africans. For example, the African church has much to teach the rest of the worldwide church about joyful dependence on God in the face of deprivation and the importance of living out faith in community. The Latin American church has significant insights to share about economic justice and celebratory worship. The Asian church can pass on what it has learned about relating to other religions as a minority faith. All believers should make it their lifelong goal to learn everything they can from their brothers and sisters from other current cultures.

One way to learn from the global community of faith is to get to know believers from other cultures who are visiting or have moved into our own communities. We can ask them how they came to Christ, how they worship, and about the most serious problems they are facing. We can study scripture with them and observe what they see in the text. A second way to learn from believers in other cultures is to read about how they reflect on the Bible. Sidebar 11.3 includes several current books that share insights from brothers and sisters in other cultures. Reading these books will help globalize our theology more completely.

Not only must each culture learn from believers in other cultures, but Christians must also learn from believers of *different socioeconomic and educational classes* within their own cultures. Wealthy Christians must listen to the biblical insights of poor believers. The more educated can gain insight into the implications of biblical truth from those with less education. Finally, learning from different Christian communities means that believers can learn from *different theological traditions*. Believers from a strong Reformed tradition can profitably listen to and learn from Wesleyans without sacrificing their Reformed com-

---

SIDEBAR 11.3
RESOURCES FOR LEARNING FROM BELIEVERS IN MANY GLOBAL CONTEXTS

- *Africa Bible Commentary* (Adeyemo 2006)
- *Global Dictionary of Theology: A Resource for the Worldwide Church* (Dyrness and Kärkkäinen 2008)
- *God's Global Mosaic: What We Can Learn from Christians around the World* (Chandler 2000)
- *Learning about Theology from the Third World* (Dyrness 1991)
- *Theology in the Context of World Christianity* (Tennent 2007)

mitment or simply seeking to disprove them. The same is true for Pentecostals, dispensationalists, Baptists, or any other theological tradition.

As churches around the world continue to develop local, contextual theologies, global theology will be enriched and enhanced. Sharing these theologies will give the church a richer, fuller understanding of the truth of God contained in scripture and will help protect each local expression of the Body of Christ from syncretism. "The Gospel will be understood in ways the universal church has neither experienced nor understood before, thus expanding our understanding of the kingdom of God" (Whiteman 1997, 4).

CONCLUSION

Mission that is done well must be both true to scripture and authentic for the countless diverse human contexts around the world. Biblical models demonstrate that when God first revealed himself to his people, he spoke in ways that connected with the world in which they lived. The story of Jesus Christ must continue to speak good news into every human situation and impact every part of human society. When the gospel is communicated in ways that do not speak to every area of human experience, weak churches develop that seem irrelevant to their cultures. People in every culture and period of history have the right to hear the gospel in ways that they understand with their minds and feel deeply with their emotions. By rooting all theology and practice in scripture, penetrating to the level of worldview, and interacting with every aspect of context, we can help ensure the emergence of healthy churches that connect with and transform their worlds. The result will be a stronger worldwide church that more fully reflects God's revelation in his Word.

CASE STUDY:
TO CATCH A THIEF

Mike and Sandy* were missionaries in a South American country, where Mike served as a medical doctor in a mission clinic. One morning when Mike was away and the local nurses came to open the clinic, they discovered there had been a break-in. Muddy footprints led to an open bathroom window. The clinic cash box was gone. When Mike returned, the nurses told him that they had reported the theft to the two village government authorities, men who served as the local equivalents to a sheriff and a judge. The two men also happened to be members of the local evangelical church. Mike knew they wouldn't have sophisticated scientific equipment to do a criminal investigation but trusted that they would have culturally appropriate ways to follow up on the crime and discover the thief.

Several days later Mike was talking with one of the nurses and noticed a dirty brick with a plastic bag behind it in the corner of the room where the cash box had been.

"What's that?" he asked the nurse.

"Oh, that's the sheriff's plan for discovering the thief," she answered.

To Mike's shock, when he pulled away the plastic bag, he discovered a human skull with a crown of thorns around the cranium, two cigarettes stuck between the teeth, coca leaves sprinkled around the base, and wax stains on the brick where candles had been burned. The two officials had gone to the local cemetery and dug up some bones. Then they had arranged the skull and other paraphernalia to perform a ritual that they believed would make the thief sick and so force him to return the money.

The story is true, but the names have been changed.

REFLECTION AND DISCUSSION

1. What may have led these Christian believers to perform this animistic practice?
2. How would you advise Mike and Sandy to respond?
3. How might appropriate biblical contextualization address this issue?

Christian Encounter with Other Religions

Toward an Evangelical Theology of Religions

I (Timothy) recall with some fondness my introductory typing class in high school back in 1974. Little did I realize when I took the class how much of my life would be spent typing on a keyboard. The typewriters in those days were manual machines that required considerable effort and timing to master. Learning to type always begins with the "home row" keys, which represent the most frequently used letters in typing. The least used keys are positioned in more remote locations. One of the least used characters, stuck way up at the top of the keyboard above your left hand, was the @ sign. It was used only in the rarest of circumstances, and many of us wondered how it managed to find its way onto the keyboard at all. However, with the advent of e-mail, it quickly went from being the most neglected, somewhat exotic, symbol on the keyboard to its current exalted status as one of the most often used symbols on the board.

This is analogous to what has happened regarding the relationship of Christianity to non-Christian religions. Within the long history of Christendom, other religions were remote and out of reach. Religious diversity in the world is, of course, ancient. However, Western Christians' awareness of other religions generally entered their consciousness only as exotic stories from distant lands. Suddenly, with the emergence of globalization, massive shifts in global immigration patterns, the rise of multiculturalism, the dramatic growth of Christianity in the heartlands of non-Christian faiths, and the events surrounding 9/11, the relationship between Christianity and other religions has become one of the most important issues dominating Christian discourse. Islamic mosques, Hindu temples, and Zen meditation centers are now found in nearly every major city in the Western world. With the collapse of Christendom and the rise of relativistic pluralism, postmodernity, and cultural diversity, we are awash in a sea of competing, and conflicting, truth claims.

The chapter is divided into three major sections. First, the chapter will begin with an exploration of the four most widely held theologies of religion. Second, each of the four positions will be critiqued. Finally, the broad contours of an evangelical theology of religions will be proposed.

THE CLASSIC PARADIGM—AND BEYOND

In 1982 Alan Race published *Christians and Religious Pluralism*, in which he suggested that all theologies of religion operate within three basic paradigms known as pluralism, inclusivism, and exclusivism (to be explained below). This framework was later used and popularized by such well-known writers as Roman Catholic Paul Knitter and Protestant John Hick. Although the paradigm was initially used by pluralists, it was quickly adopted by writers across the theological spectrum, even if not all were happy with the precise language. Evangelicals emerged considerably later in the theology of religions discussion and have, in recent years, raised a number of concerns about the intent of the paradigm and, even more frequently, the adequacy of the language (cf. Netland 1991; 2001, 47–54; Yong 2003). As published elsewhere, we share many of these concerns (Tennent 2002).

In a more recent publication, Knitter (2002) has changed the nomenclature for each of the positions, and he adds a fourth position along the spectrum. He renames the exclusivist position the "replacement model," and the inclusivist position he calls the "fulfillment model." The most important difference for evangelicals is that Knitter has nuanced the "replacement" model by distinguishing between "total replacement," which he attributes primarily to fundamentalists, evangelicals, and Pentecostals, and "partial replacement," which he identifies with the new evangelicals, who, in his view, are more open to the idea of God's presence in other religions and hold a more robust view of general revelation. He cites, for example, Harold Netland as an evangelical scholar who exemplifies the "partial replacement" model (2002, 41). Knitter renames pluralism the "mutuality model" and identifies John Hick with this model. However, Knitter is surprisingly critical of Hick, citing the inherent relativism, the superficiality of analysis, and the reductionistic caricatures that result when one tries to discover common ground among the world's religions. Hick suggests a fourth model that he names the "acceptance model," which draws primarily from postmodernism, George Lindbeck's postliberalism, and the idea of multiple salvations in the writings of Mark Heim.

The growing influence of postmodern and postliberal thought on these discussions necessitates that we move beyond the classic threefold paradigm and analyze four main views as well as the long-needed distinctions within the evangelical view. For the sake of clarity, we will use in the headings both the traditional nomenclature as well as Knitter's more recent language. However, it should be acknowledged at the outset that these four paradigms represent not precise positions but rather a wide variety of more nuanced views that fall along a broad spectrum.

Exclusivism (or the Replacement Model)

The more conservative theologies of religion are generally grouped together in a category known as exclusivism or particularism (sometimes called restrictivism or Christocentric exclusivism). A position is categorized as exclusivistic if it affirms three nonnegotiables. First, exclusivists affirm the unique authority of Jesus Christ as the apex of revelation and the norm by which all other beliefs must be critiqued. In this view, drawing on texts such as John 14:6, Acts 4:12, and 1 John 5:1–12, Jesus is not just one of many lights in the religious cosmos; he is *the* light. Those who are without Christ are, to use the words of the apostle Paul, "without hope and without God in the world" (Eph. 2:12). Second, exclusivists affirm that the Christian faith is centered on the proclamation of the historical death and resurrection of Jesus Christ as the decisive event in human history (Acts 2:31–32). The scriptures declare that "God was reconciling the world to himself in Christ" (2 Cor. 5:19) and "making peace through his blood, shed on the cross" (Col. 1:20). Third, it is believed that salvation comes through repentance and faith in Christ's work on the cross, and no one can be saved without an explicit act of repentance and faith based on the knowledge of Christ (Mark 16:15–16; John 3:16–18, 36).

The most well-known and uncompromising defense of the exclusivistic position was articulated by Hendrick Kraemer in his landmark book *The Christian Message in a Non-Christian World* (1938). The book was written to provoke discussion for the World Missionary Conference in Madras, India, in 1938. Kraemer's work has become a classic exposition of the exclusivist position. He advocates what he calls a "radical discontinuity" between the Christian faith and the beliefs of all other religions. Kraemer refuses to divide revelation into the categories of "general" and "special," which might allow for the possibility of revelation outside the proclamation of the Christian gospel. Kraemer's disdain for general revelation is clearly influenced by Karl Barth. However, to borrow a metaphor from a letter that A. G. Hogg wrote to Lesslie Newbigin in 1937, the Barthian bull pursued the matador of modernism into the china shop and disposed of him there at a destructive cost of many precious things (Sharpe 1971, 70). A proper view of general revelation is certainly one of the more unfortunate losses in Barth's neoorthodoxy.

For Kraemer the incarnation of Jesus Christ represents the "decisive moment in world history" (Kraemer 1938, 74). Jesus Christ is the decisive revelation of God that confronts the entire human race and stands over against all other attempts by other religions or philosophies to "apprehend the totality of existence" (113). Kraemer's attack on what he calls "omnipresent relativism" includes dismantling anything that would chip away at the vast gulf existing between God and the human race. This involves the complete separation of "nature" and "grace," or "reason" and "revelation."

Ron Nash (1994) offers a more contemporary exposition of the exclusivist position. Unlike Kraemer, Nash accepts the distinction between general and special revelation but argues that general revelation "performs the function of rendering man judicially accountable before God" (1994, 21, citing Demarest 1982, 69–70). Nash exposes overly optimistic views of the salvific power of general revelation but does not clearly demonstrate how general revelation might assist or prepare one to receive special revelation.

Exclusivism (or the Partial Replacement Model)

As Knitter has recognized, there are clearly those within the exclusivistic perspective who are not convinced that maintaining the three nonnegotiables necessitates a position of such radical discontinuity or a completely negative assessment of other religions. These views tend to be more optimistic about the role and function of general revelation. While acknowledging that there is no salvation in Hinduism, Buddhism, or Islam, and that general revelation is incapable of saving anyone, some exclusivists nevertheless believe that God provides truths about himself and humanity through general revelation that are accessible to all and that some of these truths have been incorporated into the beliefs of other religions, providing points of continuity whenever there is a consistency with biblical revelation. This view has been advocated by Gerald McDermott (2000) and Harold Netland (2001). This perspective does not see Christian truth as completely detached from truths that may be found through general revelation but nevertheless holds that other religions ultimately fall short and cannot provide salvation because they do not accept the centrality of Christ's revelation and his work on the cross. Furthermore, exclusivists insist that the biblical message calls for an explicit act of repentance and faith in Christ, which is obviously not part of the message or experience of non-Christian religions.[1]

1. For modern treatments of exclusivism, see Newport (1989). For a vigorous defense of exclusivism, but one that ultimately leaves the fate of the unevangelized as a mystery known only to God, see Newbigin (1989).

Some who hold to the three nonnegotiables have also advocated a position known traditionally as fulfillment theology, which arose in the late nineteenth century, although the concept goes back as far as the second century with figures like Justin Martyr and his creative use of the *logos* concept. This use of the term *fulfillment* should not be confused with Knitter's more recent use of the term to describe inclusivism, which will be explored later. Unlike Kraemer's position, the governing idea behind fulfillment theology is to demonstrate the continuity between human philosophies or religions and the supernatural religion of Christianity. While affirming the final revelation of Christ, the fulfillment theologians see God working through philosophy and non-Christian religions to prepare people to hear and respond to the gospel.

> *Do not suppose that God or His people will turn sinners out of heaven and cast them into hell, for God who is Love, never cast anyone into hell, nor ever will do so. It is the foul life of the sinner that will bring him to hell. Long before the end of life brings heaven and hell near to us, there has been set up in every man's heart, according to his good or evil nature, his own heaven or hell.*
>
> Sadhu Sundar Singh (1922, 81)

Fulfillment theology arose out of the nineteenth-century fascination with applying Darwinian ideas of evolution to science, sociology, religion, and ethics. In the writings of Max Müller (1823–1900), the concept of fulfillment robbed Christianity of all claims to revelation, and the origins of religion were viewed as an expression of universal human experience (see M. Müller 1964). All religions were arranged in stages from the lower religions to the higher, monotheistic religions culminating in Christianity. However, there were scholars as well as missionaries who adopted the fulfillment concept within an evangelical framework. The best-known scholar to do this was Monier Monier-Williams (1819–1901) at Oxford. Monier-Williams argued for the supremacy of historical Christianity as divinely revealed. He was convinced that all the other religions of the world would someday crumble as they came into contact with the truth of the Christian gospel. However, he developed a far more positive attitude toward the world religions, arguing that Christianity would be victorious not because it *refuted* all religions but because it *fulfilled* them. He argued that all religions reveal universal, God-given instincts, desires, and aspirations, which are met in the Christian gospel. The missionary community, particularly in India, where they were meeting stiff resistance from Hinduism, latched on to fulfillment ideas and began to explore them in earnest in the early years of the twentieth century. The most notable and articulate expression of fulfillment thought came from missionaries working in India such as T. E. Slater (1902) and J. N. Farquhar (1913), two of the earliest scholars to produce major works that ambitiously set out to compare the doctrines of Hinduism with doctrines in Christianity, demonstrating a fulfillment theme. Farquhar sought to establish a nonconfrontational bridge for the Hindu to cross over to Christianity because, he argued, all the notable features and aspirations within Hinduism find their highest expression and ultimate fulfillment in Christianity. He based the fulfillment theme on Christ's claim in Matthew 5:17 that he had come not to abolish or destroy but to fulfill.

The fulfillment motif among evangelicals was largely snuffed out with the publication of Kraemer's *Christian Message in a Non-Christian World* in 1938, which reasserted a more rigid, uncompromising stance toward world religions. On the liberal side the ongoing rise of rationalistic presuppositions further encouraged evangelicals to close ranks. However, the idea of a radical positive assessment of world religions without relinquishing the supremacy of Christianity found new expression in the second major attitude toward world religions, known as inclusivism.

Inclusivism (or the New Fulfillment Model)

Inclusivism affirms the first two of the three "nonnegotiable" positions held by the exclusivists. Thus, inclusivists affirm without qualification that Jesus Christ is the definitive and authoritative revelation of God. Furthermore, they affirm the centrality of Christ's work on the cross, without which no one can be saved. What distinguishes the inclusivists' position from the exclusivists' is their particular views regarding universal access to the gospel and the necessity of a personal knowledge of and response to Jesus Christ. The inclusivists argue from texts like John 3:16 and 2 Peter 3:9 that God's universal love for the world and his desire to save everyone implies that everyone must have *access* to salvation. Stuart Hackett, an advocate of inclusivism, argues that if every human being has been objectively provided redemption in Jesus Christ through the cross, then "it must be possible for every human individual to become personally eligible to receive that provision" (1984, 244). In other words, universal provision demands universal access. Therefore, since the majority of people in the world do not have a viable access to the Christian message, the inclusivists believe that this access has been made available through general revelation, God's providential workings in history, and even other religions. They affirm that Christ's work on the cross is *ontologically* necessary for salvation, but that it is not *epistemologically* necessary. In other words, you do not need to personally know about Christ to be the recipient of his work of grace on your behalf. Probably the best-known articulation of this view is found in the Vatican II document *Constitution on the Church*: "Those also can attain to everlasting salvation who, through no fault of their own, do not know the Gospel of Christ or his Church, yet sincerely seek God and moved by grace, strive by their deeds to do His will as it is known to them through the dictates of conscience" (*LG* 16).

Inclusivists generally point to examples of God's working outside the covenant with Israel as examples that faith, and even salvation, can be found among Gentiles. Biblical examples that are often cited include Melchizedek (Gen. 14), Rahab (Josh. 2), the Ninevites (Jon. 3), the queen of Sheba (1 Kings 10), and Cornelius (Acts 10), among others. Inclusivists also draw heavily from Paul's statements that "[God] has not left himself without testimony" (Acts 14:17) and that the Gentiles have "the requirements of the law . . . written on their hearts" (Rom. 2:15). They interpret this witness as more than a *preparatio evangelica*, that is, a preparation to receive and respond to the special revelation that follows, but rather as an independent salvific witness because Christ works not only explicitly through the Christian church but anonymously in countless hidden ways to draw people to himself through creation, history, and the testimony of world religions. In short, salvific grace is mediated through general revelation, not just through special revelation.

The belief in universal access to the gospel and the expanded efficacy of general revelation has led inclusivists to make a distinction between a Christian and a believer. Both are saved through the completed work of Christ on the cross. However, the Christian has explicit knowledge of this, whereas the believer has only experienced Christ implicitly and does not even realize that he or she has been saved by Christ. The best-known proponent of inclusivism was the Roman Catholic theologian Karl Rahner, who called these implicit believers "anonymous Christians." A Vatican II statement declared, "Since Christ died for all men, and since the ultimate vocation of man is in fact one, and divine, we ought to believe that the Holy Spirit in a manner known only to God offers to every man the possibility of being associated with his paschal mystery" (*Gaudium et Spes*, sec. 22). Although Vatican II endorsed most of Rahner's theology of religions, it did not officially endorse the notion of an "anonymous Christian." Thus, there remain some differences between the inclusivism of Rahner and the inclusivism of official Roman Catholic dogma. Eugene Hillman (1968) offers a more accessible defense of inclusivism, and Raimundo Panikkar (1964) provides a well-known application of inclusivism specifically to the Hindu context.

Rahner (1981; 1966–83, vols. 5 and 6) maintains that even though the non-Christian religions contain errors, God uses them as channels to mediate his grace and mercy and ultimately to apply the work of Christ. The basis for the explicit-implicit or ontological-epistemological distinction is linked to the Jews themselves. Rahner argues that the believing Jews of the Old Testament were reconciled to God through Christ even though they could not possibly have known about Christ explicitly. Paul, for example, argues that Christ accompanied the Israelites during their wilderness wanderings (1 Cor. 10:4) even though they could not have been explicitly aware of it. This, by extension, is applied to peoples around the world who, although they are living chronologically after Christ, are epistemologically living as if Christ had not yet come. It is for these people in particular that the inclusivists want to hold out hope. Several leading Protestants have followed the new openness exhibited by Vatican II and with some qualifications have fully endorsed inclusivism. Two of the more prominent Protestants who advocate inclusivism are John Sanders (1992) and Clark Pinnock (1992).

Pluralism (or the Mutuality Model)

Pluralism rejects all three of the nonnegotiables held by exclusivists. Pluralists such as Paul Knitter, William Cantwell Smith, W. E. Hocking, and John Hick believe that the world's religions provide independent access to salvation. Conflicting truth claims are reconciled through relocating them from the level of objective, normative truth to subjective experience. Hick writes that world religions merely "embody different perceptions and conceptions of, and correspondingly different responses to, the Real from within the major variant ways of being human" (1989, 240). He goes on to say that world religions all provide what he calls "soteriological spaces" or "ways along which men and women find salvation/liberation/ultimate fulfillment" (ibid.). In short, Christianity is just one among many religions and has no unique claim as the final or authoritative truth. According to the pluralists, Christianity is not necessarily the most advanced religion, and it is not the fulfillment of other religions. Thus all claims to exclusivity have been surrendered through a process of radical relativizing.

Pluralist Gordon Kaufman asserts that exclusivistic views lead to idolatry and render it nearly impossible to take other faiths seriously. Instead, he says, "we must find ways of relativizing and opening up our basic symbol system" (1987, 5). Hick agrees, calling the claim of Christian exclusivity a "myth" that must be radically reconstructed into a statement of personal meaning, not historical fact. Both argue that christocentric views of Christians should be abandoned for a more global-oriented theocentric view that allows all religions to participate as equal players (Hick and Knitter 1987).

Pluralists, unlike exclusivists and inclusivists, do not accept the necessity of demonstrating biblical support for their view because that would cede to Christianity some kind of adjudicating role over other religions. The New Testament may be authoritative for Christians, but the Qur'an holds its own independent authority for Muslims, the Vedas for Hindus, and so forth. For the pluralists the only universal standard of criteria rests in human experience, not in any particular sacred texts. This is in marked contrast to Kraemer and many of his followers, who tended to downplay general revelation altogether. Pluralists go the opposite extreme and either deny special revelation outright or seriously degrade it to a kind of general revelation through universal religious consciousness.

Postmodern, Acceptance Model

This fourth view, as noted above, has not traditionally appeared in the classic three-part paradigm. The acceptance model affirms the postmodern assertion that there are no universal truths to be found, and it is arrogant to assert that such truths may exist. This view also acknowledges that world religions really *are* fundamentally different from one another, and we should quit trying to talk as if they were, on some deeper level, really all the same. According to George Lindbeck (1984), each religion offers a total, comprehensive framework for understanding its view of reality, and any attempt to compare or find common ground is reductionistic. In short, this model affirms the incommensurability of all religions.

Knitter borrows Robert Frost's famous line "good fences make good neighbors" as a metaphor for understanding the acceptance approach. Knitter says, "Religions are to be good neighbors to each other. Each religion has its own backyard. There is no 'commons' that all of them share. To be good neighbors, then, let each religion tend to its own backyard, keeping it clean and neat" (2002, 183). When we talk with our "neighbors," we should do so over the back fence, "without trying to step into the other's yard in order to find what [we] might have in common" (ibid.). The dialogue that plays such a central role in the pluralist/acceptance model is reduced to only "swapping stories" without searching for any commonly shared or universal truths. Lindbeck argues that to say "all religions recommend something which can be called 'love' . . . is a banality as uninteresting as the fact that all languages are spoken" (1984, 42).

Mark Heim (2001), taking the acceptance model to its logical conclusion, notes that the postmodern perspective of this model means that we may really have multiple goals, multiple salvations, and multiple deities to which the various religions are related. He argues this point within the classic doctrine of the Trinity. Since Christians already affirm plurality in God, he notes, perhaps the plurality of religions can fit into the variety of relations that are in God, allowing for what he calls "permanently co-existing truths" and "parallel perfections" (2001, 175).

Through the acceptance model each practitioner can affirm the particularity and exclusiveness of his or her own faith, for God reveals himself not generically but in the diversity of religious particularity. The classic pluralist metaphor of many paths up one mountain has been replaced in the acceptance model with many paths up many different mountains. Jesus, Buddha, Shiva, and Allah are all universal saviors, since none of them represents an exhaustive or exclusive revelation, but all reflect the infinite diversity of the Divine.

EVALUATION OF THE FOUR POSITIONS

Our evaluation will begin with a critique of the four positions as currently outlined and then explore some of the problems with the larger paradigm through which these positions are articulated.

300

Postmodern, Acceptance Model Evaluated

The acceptance model, on the surface, seems to come full circle back to the exclusivist position since it provides a way for Christians to reclaim the language of exclusivism and particularity. However, a closer examination reveals that although the language of particularity has been reclaimed, this masks several major deficiencies inherent in the acceptance model. First, *the model rejects objective revelation as the basis for truth by redefining truth as socially constructed narratives*. This model simultaneously affirms, for example, the exclusive claims of Christianity and Islam and discourages us from considering that one set of claims may be right and the other wrong. Thus, they must *both* be right. However, a closer examination reveals that this claim is only possible through a radical redefinition of truth. For example, a central claim of Christianity is that God became incarnate in Jesus Christ (John 1:14). In Islam such a claim is considered blasphemous, and to affirm it is to commit *shirk* (Surah 17:111; 19:35), the unforgivable sin (*kabirah*). Now, from the perspective of objective truth, either God did become incarnate in Jesus Christ, or he did not. The postmodern answer is to recast truth as a socially constructed metaphor. The word *truth* refers only to a rhetorical, imagining construct and cannot be applied to revelation as in the Christian use of the word. Thus this model cannot even explore the possibility of certain shared truths among religions. There is no shared truth to be known; all we have are individually constructed narratives, shared stories that float autonomously in the sea of religious discourse.

Second, *this model has a very weak view of history*. Some philosophies and religions do not necessitate a robust view of history. For example, a famous Zen Buddhist saying is "if you should meet the Buddha on the road, you should kill him." The point of the rather shocking statement is that the historicity of the Buddha is not important. What matters is the teaching, or *dharma*, that he gave to the world. In contrast, Christianity (like Islam and Judaism) is constructed on specific historical events that are nonrepeatable and therefore unique. For example, Christians assert that the resurrection of Jesus Christ is an event that took place in real history. If Christ was not historically raised, then all the fervent devotion, earnest faith, and worship attributed to Jesus are instantly rendered vain and futile. This is why Paul declares, "If Christ has not been raised, your faith is futile; you are still in your sins" (1 Cor. 15:17). However, the acceptance model is based on a postmodern skepticism regarding history. The actual historicity of the incarnation or the resurrection is regarded suspiciously as either unknown or unknowable. One of the classic problems with postmodernism is that it creates worlds where everything is possible, but nothing is certain. History for the postmodernists is constantly mutable because it never rises above the watermark of an endless series of conjectures and biases. Therefore, the unique claims of religions are all allowed to coexist because none of them can be either denied or verified by history. Lindbeck acknowledges the difficulty that this postmodern proposal poses for a Christian view of history and that it may be some time before Christians can accept his model because we are "in the awkwardly intermediate stage of having once been culturally established but are not yet clearly disestablished" (1984, 134) from the traditional Christian understanding of history.

However, Christianity cannot be separated from history without ceasing to be Christianity. The apostolic faith is not only rooted in history, but it proclaims a historical *telos*, an eschatological goal, to which all history is moving. The eschaton is not *beyond* history but is rather the full manifestation of a new history that has already broken into the present.

Finally, *the antifoundationalist stance inherent in this model leads to an unbridled relativism.* With the twin collapse of truth and history, it becomes impossible to discover any basis for evaluating or adjudicating the various claims of the world's religions. How is someone to decide whether to be a Muslim, a Christian, a Satanist, or nothing at all? Even Lindbeck concedes that the choice is "purely irrational, a matter of arbitrary whim or blind faith" (1984, 130). He acknowledges the need to discover what he calls "universal norms of reasonableness," but he candidly admits that it is unlikely that any such norms can find mutual agreement among the plurality of faiths. The very fact that the advocates of the acceptance model are looking for such norms reveals that the ghost of the Enlightenment or perhaps latent Christendom keeps them from believing their own message. The moment the "universal norms of reasonableness" were found it would, by definition, mark the end of the acceptance model. It is a philosophical solvent that dissolves itself. Pluralists may accept multiple paths, but they at least still envision a *single* mountain and acknowledge that some religious movements exhibit qualities that are moving people *down* the mountain, rather than up. For pluralists *many* religions does not necessarily mean *any* religion. However, the postmodernism of the acceptance model envisions, by its own account, an endless range of mountains, each independent of the other. We are left only with a radical form of relativism among multiple islands of religious autonomy.

Pluralism (or Mutuality Model) Evaluated

The pluralist position has numerous difficulties. First, pluralism does not take seriously the actual claims and practices of those who practice the religions that are being considered. Devout Muslims and Christians, for example, are, despite their differences, all equally disturbed by the pluralist attempt to relativize the particularities of their variant claims. The pluralists claim to see beyond the actual beliefs and practices of religions to some deeper perspective that they, quite paternalistically, have. Those who actually follow these religions are largely unaware that the transcendent claims they have are actually, according to the pluralists, only human projections and perceptions of their own humanity. However, what assurance do we have that the pluralists have found an Archimedean point from which they see all the other religions? Is not pluralism itself a particular stance, drawn from Enlightenment, Kantian philosophy?

Second, *the "God" of the pluralists is so vague that it cannot be known and is, in fact, unknowable.* The pluralist John Hick has forcefully called Christians to abandon a christocentric view of reality. However, in its place he posits a "theocentric" center that is so vague he cannot even use the word *God* to describe ultimate reality lest he offend nontheistic religions like Buddhism and Taoism, which his position insists that he regard with equality. The result is that Hick's "Real" (as he prefers to call the ultimate reality) is broad enough to encompass both the strict theism of Judaism and Islam as well as the atheism of Buddhism and Taoism. Hick's "Real" encompasses both the personal conception of God in Jesus Christ as well as the impersonal conception of God in the *nirguna* Brahman of Hinduism. This resulting fog gives us both a "God" as well as a "no-God" who is unknown and unknowable and about whom we can make no definitive statement because "the Real as it is in itself is never the direct object of religious experience. Rather, it is experienced by finite humankind in one of any number of historically and culturally conditioned manifestations" (Netland 2001, 224).

Third, *the pluralist position is ultimately based on the subjectivity of human experience, not on any objective truth claims.* Human experience is the final arbiter of all truth. Therefore, revelation as revelation is struck down. The deity of Christ, for example, is not an objective truth that calls for our response; rather, it is merely a subjective expression of what Jesus meant to his disciples, which may or may not affect or influence us because every human conceives of truth differently. For example, early in his writings Hick sought to define salvation vaguely as "the movement from self-centeredness to Reality centeredness" (1995, 18).

This kind of unbridled subjectivity that seeks to replace biblical theology based on the assurance of divine revelation with the ever-changing subjectivity of human experience is untenable. For the pluralist religion is no longer about truth as truth but about filling a religious market niche. The question of truth is bracketed off by the pluralists. As George Sumner has observed, "The turban, the prayer wheel and the mantra have all been rendered 'consumer preferences'" (2004, 3).

Inclusivism (or the New Fulfillment Model) Evaluated

The inclusivist position is to be commended for its strong affirmation of the centrality of Jesus Christ and the indispensable nature of his death and resurrection for salvation. Furthermore, inclusivism has keenly discerned how God has worked in the lives of those outside the boundaries of the covenant such as Rahab and Naaman, along with many others. The more positive view of the relationship between general and special revelation is a welcome relief from the complete separation of nature and grace as seen in Kraemer. On this particular point the inclusivists do not necessarily fall outside the parameters of Christian history and tradition. Indeed, Thomas Aquinas advocated a more open attitude toward general revelation with the dictum *Gratia non tollit sed perficit naturam* (grace does not abrogate but perfects nature). However, inclusivists have embraced additional views that are clearly at variance with historic Christian faith.

First, the inclusivists' attempt to drive a wedge between the ontological necessity of Christ's work and the epistemological response of repentance and faith cannot be sustained. Inclusivists can be very selective in their use of biblical data. For example, they often quote the passage in 2 Peter 3:9 that says God is "not wanting anyone to perish" but fail to quote the rest of the verse, which says, "but everyone to come to repentance." God's universal salvific will is explicitly linked to human response. Inclusivists cite Paul's powerful statement about the universality of revelation in Romans 10:18, which says that the "voice" of revelation has "gone out into all the earth," but fail to note that this affirmation is in the context of Paul's saying that "everyone who calls on the name of the Lord will be saved" (Rom. 10:13). Paul goes on to establish a chain that begins with the sending church and the preaching witness, leading to the one who hears, believes, and calls upon the name of the Lord (Rom. 10:14–15). The inclusivists want to separate the links of this chain and argue that the witnessing church is not necessary for believing, that is, implicit saving faith can be present apart from the explicit knowledge of Jesus Christ. However, if the inclusivist position is true, then it would diminish the importance of Christ's commission since it would mean that the non-Christian religions have brought more people to the feet of Christ (implicitly) than has the witnessing church in the world.

Second, for the inclusivists to argue that the object of all genuine faith is implicitly Christ shifts the emphasis from a personal response to Christ to the *experience* of faith regardless of the object of faith. In this view salvation comes equally to the Hindu who has faith in Krishna or the Buddhist who has faith in the eighteenth vow of Amitaba Buddha or the Christian who has faith in Jesus Christ. Moving from the worship of Krishna to the worship of Christ does not involve a turning away from Krishna, but merely a clarification that they were, indeed, worshipping Christ all along. As Knitter says about inclusivism, "The purpose of the church is not to rescue people and put them on totally new roads, rather it is to burn away the fog and enable people to see more clearly and move more securely" (2002, 74). However, Paul says, in Acts 20:21, "I have declared to both Jews and Greeks that they must turn to God in repentance and have faith in our Lord Jesus." What would the inclusivists have recommended to Wynfrith when he confronted the Frisian religion in AD 754?

Would they have counseled Wynfrith to point out that the human sacrifices offered to Njord, the god of the earth, were actually only symbols or types of the Lamb of God? Was Thor really just another name for Jesus Christ (Van Rooy 1985, 9)? This is not to deny that there are examples in the Old Testament of people such as Jethro, Naaman, and Rahab who have faith outside the Jewish covenant, but the object of their faith is explicitly the God of Israel, not the indigenous gods that they formerly worshipped. Paul's famous speech in Acts 17 should not be taken as the construction of a salvific natural theology, but rather as Paul "picking up the inchoate longings of this exceptionally religious people and directing them to their proper object" (Johnson 1992, 319).

Third, *the inclusivist position unduly separates soteriology from ecclesiology*. Inclusivism claims to be a "wider hope" answer to the question, who can be saved? However, the inclusivistic answer focuses on the earnest seeker quite apart from the church as the redemptive community that lives out the realities of the new creation in the present. Only through dramatic theological reductionism can one equate biblical salvation in the New Testament with the individual destiny of a single seeker after God. Karl Rahner responds to this charge by arguing that the church and the sacraments become mysteriously embodied in the communities that gather at the temple or the mosque. Thus, Rahner does not just offer us anonymous *Christians*; he offers us anonymous communities, anonymous scriptures, and anonymous sacraments. Rahner's solution may help to reunite soteriology with ecclesiology, but only by robbing ecclesiology of any meaning, since, in the final analysis, Rahner cannot make a distinction between a Hindu or Islamic community and a Christian one.

Finally, to call Hindus or Muslims or Buddhists "anonymous Christians" has long been regarded as an insult to those within these traditions. It is a latent form of triumphalism to claim that you as an outsider have a better and deeper understanding of other people's religious experience that trumps their own understanding of their actions and beliefs. It is patronizing to tell a devout Hindu who worships Krishna that he or she is really worshipping Christ but is temporarily in an epistemological gap. Could not the Buddhist or the Hindu respond that we as Christians are actually "anonymous Buddhists" or "anonymous Hindus"? Indeed, there are Buddhist and Muslim groups who have made that very claim, including several Islamic groups in Indonesia as well as the better-known view of the Hindu Ramakrishna, who claimed that all the religions of the world are contained within Hinduism.

Exclusivism (or the Replacement/Partial Replacement Models) Evaluated

The strength of the exclusivist position is that it affirms the authority of scripture, the unique centrality of Jesus Christ, and the indispensability of his death and resurrection. Furthermore, exclusivism takes seriously the call to repentance and the need to turn to Jesus Christ as the object of explicit faith. Exclusivism affirms the key tenets of the historic Christian proclamation as delivered to us in the ancient creedal formulations. The problem with exclusivism arises when, in a desire to protect the centrality of these truths, it overextends itself into several potential errors.

First, in a desire to affirm the centrality of special revelation and the particular claims of Christ, exclusivism can fail to fully appreciate God's activity in the pre-Christian heart. It is one thing to affirm that Jesus Christ is the apex of God's self-revelation; it is entirely another to say that Jesus Christ is the only revelation from God. Since all general revelation ultimately points to Christ, exclusivists need not be threatened by these pointers and signs God has placed in creation and in the human heart, which testify to him. God is not passive or stingy in his self-revelation but has left "footprints" behind, whether in the awe-inspiring expanse of the universe or in the recesses of a solitary heart groping after God or in the depths of the reflective human mind as one explores many of the fundamental questions that have gripped philosophers and theologians throughout the ages. In this respect the modified exclusivistic view that Knitter identifies as partial replacement is far better than strict exclusivism.

Second, exclusivists have sometimes taken a defensive posture and been unwilling to honestly engage the questions and objections of those from other religions who are not Christians. The early Christians boldly proclaimed the gospel in the context of a dizzying array of cults, mystery religions, emperor worship, and more. The apostles would have surely found the defensiveness that has often characterized exclusivists as incomprehensible in light of our global mandate. Put simply, the match cannot be engaged if the players remain in the safety of the locker room. The creeds of historic Christianity are not bunkers behind which we hide; they are the basis for a global proclamation.

Third, *exclusivists have often unnecessarily bracketed off non-Christian religions and their sacred texts from the rest of culture.* This has inadvertently created a separation from not only general and special revelation but also between the doctrines of creation and soteriology. The result is what Enlightenment thinker Gotthold Lessing (1729–81) has called the "ugly ditch" that separates the particularities of special revelation and history from the universal knowledge of God rooted in creation and human conscience. However, as has been demonstrated, numerous truths from both general and special revelation have become incorporated into the actual texts and worldviews of other religions (see Tennent 2007, esp. 53–75 and 135–61).

THE CLASSIC AND EXPANDED PARADIGM REVISITED AND EVALUATED

Structural Problems

There are three major structural problems with the classic paradigm that are not sufficiently alleviated by the new nomenclature offered by Knitter.

First, the overall positions within the paradigms have been primarily articulated solely within a *soteriological* framework. In other words, the various positions tend to be the answer to the questions, "Who can be saved?" or "What is the fate of the unevangelized?" Even though these are important questions, if they are asked in isolation, they become theologically reductionistic by separating the doctrine of salvation from the larger creational and eschatological framework from which the doctrine of salvation emerges in the scriptures.

Second, the overall positions within the paradigms have been understood as either validating or negating *particular religious traditions*. Exclusivists and inclusivists are understood to believe in the final supremacy of the Christian *religion*, whereas the pluralists and the postmodernist see the religions of the world on a more level playing field. This perspective is particularly evident in Knitter's description of evangelicals within the total or partial replacement model (exclusivism). Knitter says that the replacement model is calling for a "kind of holy competition between the many religions. . . . Such competition is as natural, necessary, and helpful as it is in the business world. You're not going to sell your product effectively if you present it as 'just as good' as the next guy's. . . . So let the religions compete!" (2002, 31). However, the evangelical view is not to posit that Christianity *as a religion* is superior to all other religions. Evangelicals assert that Jesus Christ is the apex of God's revelation. Christianity, like any other religion, has, at times, been co-opted by cultural forces and become an expression of human rebellion like any other religion. Lesslie Newbigin has reminded us, based on Romans 3:23, that "it was the guardians of God's revelation who crucified the Son of God" ([1978] 1995, 170).

Third, the traditional paradigm emerges out of the Enlightenment project and completely ignores the churches in the majority world, many of which have a very different understanding and experience with religious pluralism. The Enlightenment ushered in a skepticism regarding religious truth that continues to the present. The German philosopher Immanuel Kant (1724–1804) famously defined the Enlightenment as "the emergence of man from his self-incurred immaturity." Kant attempted to construct a universal rational morality that would give rise to a natural religion. He rejected any claims of particularity based on special revelation, thereby opening the doors to a radical kind of relativism regarding religion. Religion was seen as nothing more than a myriad of legitimate alternatives for explaining and interpreting the underlying natural religion that was part of the universal human experience. As the Enlightenment progressed, it became clear that the traditional Christian assertion of objectively received truth revealed propositionally and reliably in the Bible would no longer be countenanced.

This development is to be contrasted with the rise of churches in the majority world, which often takes place in the midst of religious pluralism. George Sumner is correct when he observes that religious pluralism in the West has become the "presenting symptom for a wider epistemological illness in Western Christianity" (2004, 5). In contrast, religious pluralism in the majority world is closer to the context of the first century. Global Christianity is, as a rule, more theologically conservative, less individualistic, and far more experienced in interacting with the actual devoted practitioners of major world religions than is generally the case with Western scholars. Having worked in Asia for twenty years, I (Timothy) have observed that, for the most part, despite living in a context of religious pluralism, majority world Christians view religions not as "comparable religious artifacts" but rather as an actual stimulus to the proclamation of Jesus Christ (Sumner 2004, 3).

Amos Yong's Pneumatological Approach

An alternative approach to the classic paradigm from a conservative theologian has been the proposal by Pentecostal scholar Amos Yong from Regent University. In *Discerning the Spirit(s)* (2000), *Beyond the Impasse* (2003), and *Hospitality and the Other* (2008), Yong has proposed an alternative approach that can be broadly understood as a pneumatological theology of religions. He begins by observing that the way the pluralists have framed a theology of religions as a subset of a generic doctrine of God has become overly optimistic. Likewise, framing a theology of religions as a subset of the doctrine of soteriology is unnecessarily pessimistic. Furthermore, he argues that any theology of religions that is framed by christological categories may position us quite well *defensively* to mute the claims of other religions, but it is less effective in a more *offensive* engagement acknowledging that the particularity of the "Word made flesh" (John 1:14) must also be balanced by the universality of the "Spirit poured-out-on-all flesh" (Acts 2:17). As an alternative Yong proposes that a theology of religions be framed around pneumatology. He is convinced that neglect of the doctrine of the Spirit in Western theology has led to an overly negative perception of the Spirit's work in non-Christian faiths. He explores ways to discern how the Spirit may have extended God's presence and activity in non-Christian religions.

Yong proposes a threefold criterion (divine presence, divine absence, and divine activity) that can enable the church to discern God's presence and work or reject that which is demonic or destructive. In his more recent writings he emphasizes that the Spirit enables Christians to embody the "hospitality of God" by helping us to interact positively as hosts in a religiously plural world. Recalling the multiplicity of tongues on Pentecost, Yong reminds us that even if the religious "other" speaks in a religiously foreign tongue, the Spirit may enable us to understand and discern his presence and work within the other religions.

The strength of Yong's proposal is that his pneumatological approach places the discussion within a much larger theological framework. At the same time, however, Yong's proposal has three main weaknesses. First, it is not sufficiently christocentric. His original proposal was to put forth a more thoroughgoing trinitarian theology of religions that uses pneumatology as a *starting point*. He points out that "any Christian theology of religions that begins pneumatologically must ultimately include and confront the Christological moment" (2003, 103). At the beginning of his proposal he agrees to "bracket, at least temporarily, the soteriological question" (29). However, as his project develops, it seems that he never fully returns to the centrality of Christology and soteriology. In fact, he speaks of Christology imposing "categorical constraints" on his theology of religions (167).

Lacking the anchor that Christology provides, Yong's thesis stands or falls on the basis of the development of a trustworthy set of criteria that can empower the church to distinguish the presence of the Holy Spirit from the presence of demonic and destructive spirits that may be present in the life and thought of the adherents of non-Christian faiths. Unfortunately, his threefold criterion is in the end too ambiguous to provide the assurance that such an ambitious project demands. Even he concedes that "discerning the spirits will always be inherently ambiguous" (2003, 159, 160) and that no religious activity can be neatly categorized as purely divine, human, or demonic (167).

Second, his proposal still does not provide a way to move beyond a dialogue between reified religious traditions and structures. An evangelical theology of religions must demonstrate that the tension is between Christ and all religions; in contrast, his proposal, despite its generosity, inevitably exudes the presumptuous sense that evangelicals believe in the superiority of the Christian *religion*.

Third, Yong's proposal, like the classic paradigm, does not sufficiently take into account the very different ways that religious pluralism is understood and experienced within the global church. He remains determined to find a new theology of religions that will enable evangelicals to have a voice within the larger Enlightenment project. However, in light of the dramatic shift in the center of Christian gravity, it is no longer sufficient to address such a narrow Western audience.

TOWARD AN EVANGELICAL THEOLOGY OF RELIGIONS

The proposal we are setting forth begins by reviewing five standards or benchmarks that any evangelical formulation of a theology of religions must meet.

Five Standards in the Formulation of an Evangelical Theology of Religions

ATTENTION TO NOMENCLATURE

First, labels or nomenclature for various positions must be understood both descriptively and performatively. Any descriptive words or phrases used

309

to describe a position should be accurate and acceptable to those who adhere to the position being named. Unfortunately, positions within interreligious dialogue have often been caricatured rather than honestly engaged. Furthermore, the positions should not just describe what proponents believe in some static way but should also reflect their actions and lives in relationship to those who belong to non-Christian religions. In other words, a theology of religions must have an ethical and relational orientation, not merely a descriptive and doctrinal one.

TRINITARIAN FRAME WITH CHRISTOLOGICAL FOCUS

Second, a theology of religions must be part of a larger trinitarian theology. Quite a few scholars have proposed their theology of religions within a trinitarian framework, but it is important that it also be christocentric. In the final analysis Christology provides the only truly objective basis for evaluating truth claims, whether those claims emerge from within Christianity (intrareligious dialogue) or in response to normative claims from other religions (interreligious dialogue).

PROCLAMATION OF TRUTH

Third, in recent years, increasing numbers of evangelicals have lost confidence in the exclusivity of the gospel message. Indeed, the very word *exclusivism* is avoided because of various negative associations. Furthermore, we have become increasingly accommodating to the relativistic mood of the surrounding culture. Although, as this proposal will reveal, we are not going to suggest retaining the word, our decision is motivated not by an attempt to lessen the "scandal of particularity" but by the desire to create a nomenclature that is more appropriately descriptive without sanding down the rough edges of the gospel message.

We must recognize that we are now proclaiming the gospel within a context where relativity is not merely a theoretical proposal but a moral postulate. One of the most amazing casualties in the contemporary emergence of interreligious dialogue is the absence of the word *truth*, as articulated within a biblical understanding of revelation. Today the tension is increasingly not between truth and falsehood but between tolerance and intolerance. We need to reclaim the language of truth, even if from a position of exile.

PLACING THE DISCUSSION WITHIN A LARGER THEOLOGICAL SETTING

Fourth, an evangelical theology of religions must be placed within a larger biblical and theological context. This standard should not be understood as downplaying the importance of the three nonnegotiables (uniqueness of Jesus Christ, centrality of his death and resurrection, and the need for an explicit response of repentance and faith) affirmed in the traditional exclusivistic position. However, these nonnegotiables must be articulated within the larger context of a doctrine of creation, revelation (general and special), anthropology, the Trinity, Christology, pneumatology, ecclesiology, and, importantly, eschatology. This larger context will also help prevent our theology of religions from being either too individualistic or theologically reductionistic.

THE GLOBAL DIMENSION OF RELIGIOUS PLURALISM AND WORLD CHRISTIANITY

Fifth, an evangelical theology of religions must be articulated within the context of different understandings and perceptions of religious pluralism that are present in the world today. In the West, globalization, immigration, and the collapse of Christendom have given rise to a particular form of modern, religious pluralism that is decidedly relativistic. Religious pluralism is not merely a descriptive fact of our world; it is a "conflict of normative interests" (Soneson 1993, 137). Religious pluralism in the West is generally committed to making all religious discussions a subset of anthropology, which is consistent with the Enlightenment project. Although the postmodern paradigm rejects the Enlightenment's reliance on reason and the notion of inevitable progress, it just as emphatically rejects the notion of revelation. However, in the majority world religious pluralism is more of a *descriptive* fact. Christians in the majority world are accustomed to living side by side with actual practitioners of non-Christian religions, and they have been able to articulate the normative primacy of Christ in the midst of this pluralistic milieu. Any theology of religions articulated today must do so from the perspective of the global church, not of the dwindling community of Enlightenment scholarship.

Building a Theology of Religions on the Restated Classic Paradigm

An evangelical theology of religions need not abandon the widely used classic paradigm, although allowing, as Knitter has proposed, a fourth position to reflect a postmodern perspective is a helpful and important addition to the paradigm. It remains important to use the classic or the modified paradigm since this paradigm remains the starting point of how the discussion has heretofore been framed. However, "the paradigm" needs some renovation if we are to continue to work within it. We will begin by looking at the nomenclature of the paradigm as a whole. In keeping with the first standard, we will suggest terminology that is more descriptive as well as seek to explore what we can learn from the performative practices of each position (see table 12.1). We will then focus exclusively on the traditional evangelical view and demonstrate how the remaining principles will help to strengthen an evangelical theology of religions.

First, *an evangelical theology of religion should embrace more precise and descriptive terms while at the same time recognizing what we can learn from the performative practice of each position in the actual give-and-take of interreligious encounter.* In keeping with the first principle, we propose the following

311

TABLE 12.1
PROPOSED NOMENCLATURE FOR THEOLOGY OF RELIGIONS POSITIONS

Classic	Exclusivism		Inclusivism	Pluralism	
Knitter	Replacement Model		Fulfillment Model	Mutuality Model	Acceptance Model
	Total Replacement	Partial Replacement			
Proposed	Revelatory Particularism		Universal Inclusivism	Dialogic Pluralism	Narrative Postmodernism

changes in the way each of the positions within the paradigm are described. We are earnestly seeking to create a phrase that is not only more descriptively accurate, but also one that adherents of the position can recognize and affirm as their own. Exclusivism should be renamed *revelatory particularism*. The word *revelatory* stresses the importance of revelation (both in scripture and in Jesus Christ) in the evangelical view. An evangelical theology of religions can never relinquish the normative nature of biblical revelation or the final primacy of Jesus Christ. The word *particularism* emphasizes the primacy of Jesus Christ and is more precise than *exclusivistic*, which could be misunderstood to mean the exclusion of people rather than the exclusivity and primacy of Jesus Christ, our intended focus. The word *particularism* also protects the evangelical view from overly robust proposals that are christocentric but also untethered from the historicity of the incarnation in favor of a cosmic Christ, which in practice often becomes disconnected with the apostolic proclamation concerning Jesus Christ.

Inclusivism should be known as *universal inclusivism*. This term emphasizes the universal scope that lies at the heart of inclusivism's claim, trumping even the epistemological need to personally respond to the gospel message. Inclusivism has the performative function of reminding all of us that God's revelation extends beyond the propositions of biblical revelation. The Reformer John Calvin pointed out that God himself "has endued all men with some idea of his Godhead, the memory of which he constantly renews and occasionally enlarges" ([1560] 1960, 43, XX.1.3.1). In this context the Reformer refers to the "sense of the Divine" (*sensus divinitatis*) and the universal "germ of religion" (*semen religionis*). Likewise, in his *Confessions*, Augustine speaks of the "loving memory" of God that lies latent even in unbelievers (1998, 128, 7.17.23). Although we must be careful not to allow general revelation to swallow up special revelation, we must not relinquish the basic truth that there is a continuity between the two and that even in the encounter with other religions, God has not left himself without a witness.

Pluralism should be renamed *dialogic pluralism*, reflecting its performative interest in engaging the religious other with openness and humility. Evangelicals have sometimes been too wary of interreligious dialogue and have taken an overly defensive posture in engaging honest questions and objections from non-Christians. Evangelical writer Gerald McDermott (2000) has ably demonstrated that there are many things we can learn from the honest encounter with practitioners of world religions.

Also, the postmodern "acceptance" model of Knitter should be renamed *narrative postmodernism*. Although much of the postmodern worldview is incompatible with biblical revelation, the performative emphasis on narrative is very helpful. Evangelicals have often equated the biblical message with a short list of doctrinal propositions, unnecessarily separating our proclamation about Christ from the myriad of ways in which the gospel intersects our lives. We must take the individual religious narratives of those we encounter very seriously, even as we seek to connect them to the larger metanarrative of the gospel.

In short, an evangelical theology of religions should embrace the positive performative qualities of each position. We should embrace the "hospitality" of openness characterized by pluralists. We should learn from the inclusivists' eagerness to see that the *missio Dei* transcends the particularities of the church's work of mission and witness in the world. We should take notice of the importance of biblical and personal narrative in the way we communicate the gospel.

The remaining four standards will be applied to the renamed evangelical position known as revelatory particularism.

Second, *revelatory particularism should be articulated within a trinitarian context*. This application of the second standard reminds us that the Christian gospel is unintelligible apart from the doctrine of the Trinity, since the doctrine of the Trinity is both the foundation and the goal of all Christian theologizing. This is the most practical way to keep all inter- and intrareligious discussions within a broad theological frame representing the fullness of the Christian proclamation.

God the Father is the source of all revelation. This fact connects particularism with the doctrine of creation and helps maintain a robust view of general revelation. We can affirm that every religion, in various ways, contains "the silent work of God" (Bavinck 1966, 200). They reflect God's activity in the human heart and the human quest for God. Religions also reflect our unending attempts to flee from God, even in the guise of religious activity. As Calvin Shenk has observed, human religion reflects both "cries for help and efforts of self-justification" (1997, 75). The Reformers insightfully applied the "law and gospel" theme to other religions by noting that other religions can serve one of the classic purposes of "law," namely, they can create such despair and unanswered questions in the life of the adherent that they come to the gospel of God's grace. Terry Tiessen, following the work of Mariasuasai Dhavamony, observes that cosmic religions focus on the revelation of God in creation;

ethical religions reflect that the Divine Absolute makes himself known in the human conscience, and salvific religions are a response to the awareness of the fall and the need for salvation (2007, 167–68).

God the Holy Spirit, as the agent of the new creation, helps to place revelatory particularism within an eschatological context. For Christians salvation is far more than the doctrine of justification. Salvation involves our becoming full participants in the new creation, which is already breaking into the present order. This touches on every aspect of culture.

At the heart of trinitarianism is Jesus Christ, who is the apex of God's revelation and the ultimate standard by which everything is judged. Rather than comparing and contrasting Christianity with other religions, we measure all religions, including Christianity, against the revelation of Jesus Christ, who is the embodiment of the new creation. This is why it is important that an evangelical theology of religions be both trinitarian and christocentric.

This standard has important implications for the practice of interreligious dialogue, which often compares doctrines or experiences between two religions. For example, if a Hindu and a Christian are in a dialogue about the doctrine of karma, the only intelligible response from a Christian would be to relate the doctrine of karma to the Christian proclamation of the grace found in Jesus Christ. If a Muslim and a Christian are in a dialogue comparing Qur'anic and biblical views of revelation, it would only be a form of theological reductionism if the Christian did not point out that, for the Christian, the greatest form of revelation is embodied and personal in Jesus Christ. In short, the Trinity, and Jesus Christ in particular, is the hub from which all the doctrinal spokes of the Christian proclamation radiate. The particularity of Christ is crucial because Christianity has always asserted a quite specific historical intervention by God, which is an "irruption of the timeless into time, by taking on of flesh by the Godhead" (Holloway 1982, 5). God, who is always "Subject," never "object," has voluntarily placed himself, as it were, into the place of "object" for a while to be seen, touched, and observed. Therefore, Christ represents the ultimate revelation of the whole Trinity. Jesus's life and ministry were empowered by God the Holy Spirit, and Jesus declared "anyone who has seen me has seen the Father" (John 14:9).

Third, revelatory particularism embraces a canonical principle asserting that the Bible is central to our understanding of God's self-disclosure. God addresses fallen humanity not only in the Word made flesh but also in the Word that has been inscripturated into the biblical text. Revelatory particularists affirm without qualification that "all Scripture is God-breathed" and therefore "useful for teaching, rebuking, correcting and training in righteousness" (2 Tim. 3:16). The third principle insists that all insights from general revelation, or the particular claims of other religions, must be tested against biblical revelation and against the person and work of Jesus Christ. Firm belief in personal and propositional revelation is the only sure way to deliver us from the abyss of relativism, endless human speculations, or, worse, the notion that religions are nothing more than pragmatic, consumer preferences in a global religious marketplace. As noted earlier, it is not enough to simply state that revelatory particularists affirm the three nonnegotiables. An evangelical theology of religions must be articulated within the larger frame of the entire canonical witness. Furthermore, we should always remember that the gospel is good news to be proclaimed. We are called to be witnesses of Jesus Christ, even in the context of interreligious dialogue.

Fourth, *revelatory particularism positions an evangelical theology of religions within the context of the* missio Dei. In keeping with this principle, it is only through the lens of the *missio Dei* that a theology of religions can be fully related to the whole frame of biblical theology. Central to the *missio Dei* is our understanding that through speech and actions, God is on a mission to redeem and bless all nations. In that sense Kevin Vanhoozer is correct when he argues that God's self disclosure is fundamentally theodramatic. In other words, in Christianity revelation is not transmitted, as in Islam, apart from human culture and context. Instead, God enters into and interacts with human narratives and is thereby set within a *dramatic, missional* context. The gospel is the greatest drama ever conceived. The divine theodrama begins with creation and the human response to God's rule that we call the fall. God responds to the fall by initiating a redemptive covenant with Abraham that includes a commitment to bless all nations. The theater of God's self-disclosure is the stage of human history, which Calvin referred to as the *theatrum gloriae Dei* (a theater of the glory of God, [1560] 1960, 156 and 293, 1.14.20 and 2.6.1). God himself is the primary actor, in both creation, redemption, and in the new creation. God's deliverance of Israel from Egypt represents on a small scale what God intends to do with the entire human race on a deeper level. Vanhoozer points out that as the divine drama unfolded, many dramatic tensions made it difficult to discern how God would keep his promise to Abraham and bless all nations. The death and resurrection of Christ represent the resolution of the tensions (Vanhoozer 2005, 42). Sin and death are defeated, the new creation is inaugurated, and the Spirit is sent to continue unfolding the drama of God's redemptive plan. An evangelical theology of religions should always be set forth within the larger context of the drama of the *missio Dei*.

Finally, *revelatory particularism should be both evangelical and catholic.* By evangelical we mean that we are committed to the centrality of Christ, historic Christian orthodoxy, and the urgency to proclaim the gospel in word and deed, calling the world to repentance and faith. Evangelical faith helps us to remember the center of the gospel. However, we are catholic in the sense that we share a unity with all members of the body of Christ throughout the world. A robust commitment to ecumenism strengthens the whole church as long as it is bounded by the centrality of Christ and the principle of canonicity.

We believe that "the *one* gospel is best understood in dialogue with the *many* saints" (Vanhoozer 2005, 30).

This principle reminds us that the entire global church brings enormous experience and perspective on how to articulate the faith within the context of religious pluralism without being hampered by the governing philosophical assumptions of the Enlightenment. The emergence of the global church represents a unique opportunity to recover biblical catholicity, which, as the Apostles' Creed reminds us, is one of the marks of the true church.

CONCLUSION

Retaining the classic paradigm with these modifications allows us to continue to engage in interreligious discussions within a commonly understood paradigm. However, the more precise nomenclature of the four positions, coupled with the broad outlines on how to build on the position of revelatory particularism, will help to invigorate evangelical involvement in interreligious dialogue and clarify our public witness in the midst of religious pluralism and enable us to remain in consonance with the witness of the global church throughout history and around the world.

13

The Necessity of Mission

Three Uncomfortable Questions

Near the beginning of the twentieth century, a wandering prophet named Asa appeared in southern Ethiopia. Asa traveled among the Wolaytta-speaking people group, claiming to bring a message from the one true God, who had created heaven and earth. The message was that the Wolaytta must stop worshipping the evil spirits and worship God alone. Asa taught the people that they should pray to God, especially on Sundays. He would ritualistically dip his fingers into a bowl of honey and flick the honey toward the sky, indicating that his prayers were to God, not to Satan or the evil spirits. Asa preached a moral code that looked very much like the Ten Commandments, and he prophesied that a foreigner would come to Wolaytta with a book from God. He exhorted his listeners to obey the message of that book. As Asa traveled and preached, many people abandoned their worship of the spirits. Soon the large crowds and enthusiastic following generated by Asa's preaching caught the attention of local government authorities. Asa was arrested for starting an unauthorized political movement and imprisoned. Some time later he died in prison. As far as anyone knows, Asa never heard a clear presentation of the gospel of Christ and never personally trusted Christ as his Savior. Approximately two decades after Asa's dramatic ministry, evangelical missionaries first came to his area of southern Ethiopia. Many of those who responded to their message remembered Asa, and they claimed that their hearts had been prepared for the gospel by his ministry. Today millions of believers in Jesus Christ can be found in that part of Ethiopia. Many of them believe that Asa was their "John the Baptist," who prepared the way for the coming of the message about Christ.[1]

The story of Asa captures some of the most difficult questions with which any theology of mission must grapple. In chapter 12 we suggested that revelatory particularism is the most biblical way of understanding the relationship of Christianity to other religions. Special revelation, especially about the person and work of Christ as revealed in scripture, is the way that God reveals saving truth about himself. Although general revelation reveals much about God and prepares people for the proclamation about Christ, explicit faith in Christ is necessary to appropriate the redemptive work of Christ and eternal salvation. But if this is true, what will be the eternal fate of good, God-fearing people like Asa who have never heard of Christ? Is there no hope for them to be saved? Is explicit, conscious faith in Christ really the only way of salvation?

We will focus on three specific questions that arise when we consider the larger question of the necessity and urgency of mission: (1) Is it too narrow and intolerant to advocate that Christ is the only way to salvation? (2) How could a good and righteous God under any circumstances condemn people to eternal conscious punishment in hell? (3) Is it not unfair of God to condemn people who have never had the opportunity to hear the gospel of Jesus Christ?

Bible-honoring Christians hold differing and nuanced views on these difficult questions. We will attempt to answer them by examining some of the relevant Bible passages. However, we are aware that our discussion will only point us in the direction of a complete answer to these deep issues.

IS CHRIST THE ONLY WAY OF SALVATION? THE QUESTION OF CHRISTIAN UNIQUENESS

As we have seen, neither dialogic pluralism nor narrative postmodernism believes that Christ is the unique way of salvation, the one and only way to have a relationship with God. Both argue that Jesus Christ is just one of many roads to God. Is Jesus truly the one, unique way to salvation?

When we speak about the uniqueness of Jesus Christ, we are not speaking about the uniqueness of the Christian religion, though a case might also be made for that. As we have seen in chapter 12, even Christianity as a religious system must be judged by its faithfulness to biblical revelation, especially revelation about the person of Jesus Christ. Rather than speaking of the superiority of any religious system, we are talking about the uniqueness of the person of Jesus Christ as the one way to God.

---

1. The story of Asa told here is based on accounts told by Ethiopian church leaders to Steve Strauss. It is also found in Davis 1980, 238–39.

In chapter 3 we saw that the Old Testament presents God as utterly unique in comparison to the false gods and idols of the nations. Because he is the only true God, the Old Testament affirms that Israel's God is also the one true God of all nations and people.

Israel lived in a pluralistic world in which each nation, people group, and even city-state had its own gods. These "gods" were presumed to be in competition with one another, even as their people competed with one another. Which god could promise an abundant harvest, victory in war, and a large population? Israel was repeatedly tempted to give a measure of devotion to these other gods in order to assure their own prosperity. The Old Testament law and prophets attacked the idolatrous religions of the surrounding nations as foolish, detestable, and even demonic in comparison to the one true God (e.g., Deut. 32:16–17; Isa. 44:9–20). Because of the danger of being polluted by the worship of other gods, Israel was to destroy everything connected with their worship (Deut. 13:2–3), and anyone found worshipping them was to be put to death (Deut. 17:2–7). Clearly, in the pluralistic world of the Old Testament, none of the gods of the surrounding nations were seen as reflecting the truth of YHWH or providing a genuine experience with the divine.

The world of the New Testament was equally pluralistic, with many cities boasting temples dedicated to Greco-Roman gods, Roman emperors, and a variety of eastern gods. Mystery cults and local animistic beliefs were also common. While many people had their favorite gods, "the opinion of the overwhelming majority was that the competing religions had more or less merit to them," so most people "probably saw no problem in participating in many religions" (Carson 1996, 271).

In this pluralistic world the early Christians embraced the Old Testament perspective that YHWH alone was God. Even more extraordinarily, the New Testament writers boldly included Jesus Christ in the unique identity of the one true God of the Old Testament and insisted that he was the only way of salvation. These claims began with Jesus, who made extraordinary claims for himself by what he said and what he did.

He claimed to bring the fulfillment of the Old Testament (Matt. 5:17).

He exercised the prerogative of definitive reinterpretation of the law (Matt. 5:21–22, 27–28, 31–32, 33–34, 38–39, 43–44).

He claimed universal authority for himself (Matt. 28:18) and eternal authority for his words (Matt. 24:35). He claimed authoritative certainty and validity for his words in the pronouncement formula "truly, truly (*amen, amen*) I say to you" (e.g., John 8:58; Erickson 1991, 434–35).

He claimed the authority to forgive sins in a society where it was clearly acknowledged that only God could forgive sins (e.g., Mark 2:5, 10).

He claimed a unique relationship with God as his Father, including intimate knowledge of God, the ability to do whatever the Father does, the ability to give life, and the prerogative of divine judgment (e.g., Matt. 11:27; John 5:19–23). The way in which Jesus addressed God as his Father "has no parallels in the terms used in Jewish prayers for addressing God" (Erickson 1991, 435).

He received honor, reverence, and even worship reserved for God himself (Matt. 14:33; 28:17; John 5:22–23; 20:28–29).

He frequently took upon himself titles and references to God from the Old Testament (Matt. 21:16 and Ps. 8:1–2; Luke 20:18 and Isa. 8:13–15; John 8:12 and Ps. 27:1; John 10:11 and Ezek. 34:10–22; Ps. 23:1–4). He claimed the authority of YHWH and the Son of Man as universal judge of the nations (Matt. 25:31–46; 26:64; and Dan. 7:9–14; Joel 3:1–12).

He boldly claimed to be the exclusive way to God, the absolute truth, and the unique source of eternal life (John 14:6). In the larger context of John's Gospel, the exclusivism of this verse speaks to both Judaism and pagan religions: (1) Now that Jesus has come, "it is totally inadequate to claim that one knows God, on the basis of the *antecedent* revelation of [the Old Testament], while disowning Jesus Christ" (Carson 1991, 491). Apart from Jesus the way to God taught in the Jewish scriptures was no longer enough. (2) Other religions are "ineffective in bringing people to the true God" (492).

His opponents understood exactly what he was claiming and responded accordingly with attempts to kill him (Matt. 26:65; John 5:17–18).

After his death and resurrection, Jesus's followers extended the audacious claims that Jesus had made about himself. In the fiercely monotheistic environment of first-century Judaism, even the earliest New Testament writers did not hesitate to include Jesus in the unique identity of the one true God without compromising their monotheism. The New Testament writers "include Jesus in the unique divine sovereignty over all things, they include him in the unique divine creation of all things, they identify him by the divine name which names the unique divine identity, and they portray him as accorded the worship which, for Jewish monotheists, is recognition of the unique divine identity" (Bauckham 1998, 26). "Jesus, the New Testament writers are saying, belongs inherently to *who God is*" (45). As a result even the earliest Jewish believers did not hesitate to give Jesus the devotion and worship that was reserved for God alone (Hurtado 2003).

Jesus's unique identity was the basis of the New Testament writers' conviction that salvation now came only through his life, death, and resurrection. One of the core messages of the New Testament is that Jesus is the one way to God. In the monotheistic Jewish context the early apostles preached the exclusive message that it was now only through Jesus that God's forgiveness and salvation could be experienced (Acts 2:38; 4:12; 13:38). In the pluralistic Gentile context they proclaimed that Jesus was the one way to know the transcendent Creator God (Acts 17:24–31). It might even be said that it was precisely *because* of the pluralistic context of the New Testament era that the writers made exclusive claims about Jesus Christ. Precisely because there is only one God, not many, and that one God is passionate about extending salvation to all people, the message that Jesus is the only way to God must be proclaimed (1 Tim. 2:1–7).

Acts 4:12 is particularly significant in proclaiming that Jesus is the unique way to God, even for those who may have some partial revelation of God. Standing before the leaders of the Jewish nation, which worshipped the one true God, Peter boldly proclaimed, "Salvation is found in no one else, for there is no other name under heaven given to men by which we must be saved." Darrell Bock observes that the Greek word order of this verse emphasizes that Jesus is the *only* way of salvation: "There is no one else at all other than Jesus who has the means to provide salvation, even for Jews who have access to God's revelation. . . . There is no other person or god to which to turn" (2007, 194). In the light of the incarnation, crucifixion, and resurrection of Jesus, worship of the one true God is no longer enough. Peter's words speak directly to the question of Christian uniqueness. He is clearly "no advocate of modern notions of religious pluralism" (Witherington 1998, 194). Peter's message is echoed throughout the rest of the book of Acts, which puts a strong emphasis on the *name* of Jesus for salvation (e.g., Acts 2:21, 38; 4:10, 18; 8:12; 9:14–15; 10:43; 15:17; 22:16).

Though every book in the New Testament contributes to understanding the uniqueness of Jesus Christ as the only way of salvation, two stand out as particularly important. Both Colossians and Hebrews have as their major themes the significance of Christ's unique person and work. Colossians was written to deal with a syncretistic heresy that was troubling the Colossian church. Some people in the church were enamored with powerful cosmic forces that they hoped to appease and through whom they hoped to obtain spiritual benefit. "The Christians in Colossae lived in an environment of religious pluralism," with much syncretistic sharing of ideas (Arnold 1996, 311). Instead of tolerating this pluralism and syncretism, Paul attacked it as empty deception inspired by demonic spirits.

In Colossians 1:13, he reminds the Colossians that they have been rescued from the hostile spirit powers' "dominion of darkness." Then, in 1:15–20, he explains that the basis of their rescue was the utterly preeminent Son. The Son is

The one who reveals the invisible God. "The very nature and character of God have been perfectly revealed in him" (O'Brien 1982, 43).

The one who has priority over the entire creation. In this context the word *firstborn* must mean "supreme," not "first in time." Christ existed *before* time and *before* the creation, and he is supreme over the creation since he himself created everything.

Not only the creator of all things generally, but specifically the creator of the spirit forces that now attracted the Colossians. Christ is ultimate, not these "powers."

Sustainer of the creation. Apart from Christ's powerful intervention, the creation would disintegrate into chaos.

Head of the church. The significance of Christ's supremacy over the creation is for those he has redeemed, who are part of his body. He is the one whose resurrection is the basis of all resurrections, giving him supremacy over all.

The one who embodies God in all his fullness. "All the attributes and activities of God—his spirit, word, wisdom, and glory—are perfectly displayed in Christ" (O'Brien 1982, 53).

The one who brings cosmic peace back to the universe, including the pacification of the demonic powers.

In Colossians 2:9–15, Paul argues in more detail why he believes people should not place any competing "gods" next to Christ. The essence of God himself dwells in Christ, "so that He is the essential and adequate image of God" (O'Brien 1982, 111). Believers do not need to give any allegiance to any other spiritual power or authority, "for the one in whom they are complete is Lord and Master of such beings" (114).

> *Christ has not only delivered his people from the domain of darkness, but he has brought them into his kingdom and bestowed on them his salvation.*
>
> Clinton Arnold (1996, 293)

Paul goes on to describe Christ's two-step work of defeating, disarming, and humiliating these hostile, competing spiritual powers. First, God "canceled the written code, with its regulations, that was against us and that stood opposed to us . . . nailing it to the cross." The word translated "written code" was used to describe a certificate of indebtedness. Paul is saying that all humankind was in debt because of our failure to obey the "regulations" of the law (O'Brien 1982, 124–25). When Christ was crucified, our certificate of indebtedness was "nailed to the cross." Christ's death on the cross paid our debt and secured forgiveness of our sins. Second, because our debt has been canceled and our sins forgiven, Satan's power over humankind has been broken. Christ's death "disarmed the powers and authorities," that is, Christ removed the power Satan and his forces had over humanity because of our sin and indebtedness. And having taken away the authority of the powers of darkness on the cross, God "made a public spectacle of them" (Col. 2:15). Using a vivid military picture, Paul says that Christ defeated Satan and his evil spirits so completely that he stripped their weapons and armor and victoriously displayed their weakness and powerlessness.

Christ has given his followers forgiveness, new life, and security against oppressive spiritual forces. How should they respond to his magnificent victory on the cross? They should be completely loyal to him in the face of all competing truth claims, which are simply "hollow and deceptive philosophy" (Col. 2:8). They should avoid becoming entangled in a syncretistic mix with competing religious truth claims and practices (Col. 2:16–23).

The book of Hebrews was written to a group of Jewish believers who were considering abandoning their profession of faith in Christ and returning to Judaism. The main message of the book is that Jesus is superior to all other spiritual powers and any other religious person or system. He is superior in who he is and in the salvation he provides. He is the best revelation of God (1:1–4), superior to all angelic and spirit powers (1:5–14), the one who defeated Satan and freed humanity from its fear of death (2:14–15), superior to Moses (3:1–6), and the best priest (4:14–5:10; 7:23–28). Jesus has established a better covenant (7:22; 8:6–13) with a better sacrifice for sin, his own blood (9:11–14, 23–28; 10:5–18). Because Jesus is absolutely superior, no ground exists for pursuing any other person or religious system. The only acceptable response to Jesus and his work is to steadfastly follow him and hold to him and his salvation (2:1; 3:12–14; 4:14; 6:9–12; 10:19–23, 35–36, 39; 12:1–2, 15; 13:11–15).

> *Confidence in Jesus as the only way of salvation must be done in respectful love, or it will be seen as "in your face" triumphalism.*
>
> William Larkin (2005, 113)

Jesus is absolutely unique in who he is, in his relationship to God the Father, and in his work of providing salvation for humankind (Murray 2005). Anyone who believes that the Bible is God's ongoing revelation to humankind must base his or her understanding of salvation and mission on passages such as these, which directly contradict the pluralistic perspective.

Though evangelicals embrace the uniqueness of Christ and reject religious pluralism as incompatible with the teaching of scripture, we must be careful to avoid arrogant triumphalism in our presentation of Christ to the nations. We live and minister in the context of many cultures and religions. All religious systems are a mixture of truth and falsehood, and adherents of these faiths are equally made in the image of God. We can appreciate what is truthful and noble in other world religions without affirming them as the means of salvation. "Christian exclusivism does not entail that all of the claims of the other religions must be false, . . . that other religions are completely without value, or that Christians cannot learn anything from adherents of other faiths" (Netland 1991, 35). We "must engage in evangelism and apologetics with cultural sensitivity and with attitudes of humility, gentleness, and genuine respect for adherents of other religious traditions," all the while maintaining our conviction about the gospel and Christ (Netland 2005, 160). Peter reminds us that we can maintain a firm conviction and vigorous proclamation that Jesus is the only way to God while displaying gentleness and respect for others (1 Pet. 2:9, 15–17; 3:1–2, 15–16). We must proclaim the uniqueness of Jesus Christ with humility, a willingness to listen and learn, and genuine respect for those to whom we proclaim the gospel.

DOES GOD REALLY CONDEMN PEOPLE TO ETERNAL, CONSCIOUS PUNISHMENT? THE QUESTION OF HELL

Anyone who seriously considers the biblical picture of hell will be horrified with the idea that people will consciously suffer there for eternity. The Bible depicts hell as a place of suffering, isolation, and destruction. How could a loving God condemn anyone to such a place forever? Is *eternal, conscious* punishment truly just for *finite, temporal* sins? How will the saints be able to enjoy heaven knowing that loved ones—or that anyone—is suffering in hell? These questions have troubled thoughtful Christians for centuries, and any theology of mission must consider them. The desire to keep people from suffering in hell is a common motivation for missions. But if God will not really send people to eternal, conscious punishment, why should anyone make the sacrifice to do missions?

Alternatives: Universalism and Conditionalism

Several positions have been suggested as alternatives to the traditional view that those who do not receive God's grace are condemned to eternal, conscious punishment. Two of these alternatives are *universalism*, the belief that God will eventually save all people, and *conditionalism* (also called *annihilationism*), the idea that God's punishment of sinners will end in their extinction, and that they will not exist consciously for eternity.

UNIVERSALISM

Though universalism can be found as far back as Origen (c. 185–c. 254), few Christians doubted the reality of eternal, conscious punishment until the nineteenth century. Friedrich Schleiermacher (1768–1834) was the first influential modern universalist. By the late nineteenth century many Victorian preachers and theologians began to be less concerned with saving people from *punishment* in hell and more concerned with saving them from the *fear* of hell

(Mohler 2004, 24). In the early twentieth century the ecumenical movement turned the focus of missions from proclamation of truth that would lead to salvation to pursuit of enlightened synthesis between religions and social justice. At the Second Vatican Council (1962–65) "sincerity rather than explicit faith in Christ became the ground of salvation" for Roman Catholics who embraced Karl Rahner's idea of "anonymous Christians," that many people would be in heaven who had not explicitly embraced Christ on earth (ibid., 27).

Some universalists do not seek to prove their view on the basis of scripture. Instead, they base their argument on the love of God. God loves all people and wants the best for them; the best thing for all people would be to spend eternity in heaven. This group of universalists usually accepts the results of modern, critical study of the Bible and feels free to regard biblical passages that speak of hell as the mistaken, culturally conditioned ideas of the human authors. Many universalists, like John Hick, are also pluralists who believe that all religions equally reflect ultimate truth and that all are ways of salvation.

But some universalists (who may even identify themselves as evangelicals; Talbot 1999, 2003a, 2003b; Gregory MacDonald 2006) seek to demonstrate their position from scripture. They point to verses that teach God's desire to save all people (Ezek. 33:11; John 3:16; 1 Tim. 2:4; 2 Pet. 3:9), verses that teach that Jesus died to save all or is in some sense the Savior of all people (2 Cor. 5:19; 1 Tim. 4:10; 1 John 2:2), and verses they believe explicitly teach that all will eventually be saved (Rom. 5:18; 11:32; 1 Cor. 15:22; Phil. 2:10–11; Col. 1:20). They readily acknowledge that hell exists, that all people deserve hell, and that unbelievers will spend some time there. However, they believe that hell will be restorative: through the punishment of hell everyone will eventually recognize that they are sinners, come to (postmortem) repentance and faith in Christ, and be saved through the grace of God and the merits of Christ's death. Thomas Talbot insists that this is the only way to reconcile passages that (he believes) teach that all people will be saved with passages that teach the existence of hell.

CONDITIONALISM

An alternative to universalism is the idea that those who die apart from faith in Christ will eventually be annihilated; they will simply cease to exist. Many who hold this position prefer the term *conditionalism* to describe their view because they believe that God created people only with the *potential* to attain eternal existence; they have "conditional immortality." Only when people trust Christ as Savior do they receive permanent immortality. Those who do not trust Christ never receive this immortality and so will eventually cease to exist when they die. Evangelicals who hold this position usually believe that this destruction of those who die apart from Christ will happen after a period of punishment in hell (Edwards and Stott 1988, 313–20; Wenham 1992, 187; Fudge and Peterson 2000; Fudge 1994; see also Morgan 2004, 196).

Conditionalists' strongest argument may be pointing to biblical texts that emphasize future judgment as *destruction* (Matt. 10:28; Rom. 9:22; 2 Thess. 1:9). Conditionalists feel that the logical opposite of receiving eternal *life* is eternal *death*, which they understand to be the eternal end of existence (Rom. 6:23; Rev. 21:8). Conditionalists ask how a just God could punish finite sins with eternal, conscious punishment. Many conditionalists say that the idea of eternal punishment in the Bible (Dan. 12:1–2; Matt. 25:46; 2 Thess. 1:9) refers to *consequences* that last forever, and does not speak of an unending period of time (Fudge and Peterson 2000, 33, 45, 51; Fudge 1994).

Response

Both universalism and conditionalism are very attractive to our human sense of fairness and our horror that people would spend eternity in hell. But what is a biblical response to universalism and conditionalism? We will divide our study into four parts. First, we will note that passages throughout scripture clearly teach that eternal, conscious punishment will be the fate of some people, passages that speak against both universalism and conditionalism. Second, we will take a closer look at scriptural teaching used to support universalism. Third, we will reflect on the love of God and the nature of sin. Finally, we will see the significance of biblical teaching on the nature of hell.

Texts That Teach Eternal, Conscious Punishment

Some core biblical texts seem to affirm eternal, conscious punishment and so speak against both universalism and conditionalism.

Daniel 12:2: Daniel says that the righteous awaken to eternal life and the wicked awaken to eternal *contempt*: "Multitudes who sleep in the dust of the earth will awake: some to everlasting life, others to shame and everlasting contempt." They do not face annihilation, and they do not eventually receive salvation; they face *eternal* disgrace and contempt, suggesting that they are conscious but punished. And as in many of the texts we will see, eternal life and eternal punishment are spoken of as parallels; when "eternal" refers to life and means "an indefinite period of time into the future," it must logically mean the same thing when it refers to death, contempt, or other descriptions of punishment (see below on the meaning of "death" and "destruction"). In this text the wicked will experience contempt, not to the end of time, but "to time without end" (Block 2004, 64).

Isaiah 66:24; Matthew 18:8–9; Mark 9:42–49: These texts speak of eternal *instruments* of punishment, such as fire and worms. It would seem that the instruments would be eternal only if the punishment itself is eternal. The point of Jesus's teaching in Matthew 18 and Mark 9 is that the source of the torment is unending, and it is far better to discipline our lives now than to go to such a place. The implication is that the people are punished there forever.

Matthew 25:41, 46: When Jesus speaks of the righteous going to eternal life and the wicked going to eternal death, life and death are parallel. They each stretch into eternity. It seems clear that Jesus means that both the punishment and life would equally stretch into the infinite future.

Luke 16:19–31: Many suggest that because the parable of the rich man and Lazarus is only a parable, we should not draw explicit teaching about what follows death. While this story is certainly a parable, the entire point of it requires a real place of conscious punishment, and in the parable Abraham gives no hope that the punishment would end in salvation or annihilation.

John 3:36: The opposite of "eternal life" is God's wrath remaining on a person. In John the opposite of eternal life is "perish" (3:16; 10:28), "condemned" (3:18; 5:24, 29), "judgment" (5:22, 30), "death" (5:24), and "die" (6:50). "If salvation and conscious bliss are everlasting, so are perdition and conscious torment" (Yarbrough 2004, 75).

2 Thessalonians 1:8–9: The wicked suffer "*everlasting* destruction." Annihilationists assume that "destruction" and "death" mean "cease to exist" (Edwards and Stott 1988, 316). However, neither the word used for "destruction" (*olethros*) in 2 Thessalonians 1:8–9 nor the other common New Testament word for destruction (*aollymi*) necessarily means "extinction." Rather both words usually refer to the condition of people or objects that have lost the essence of their nature or function, such as land that has lost its fruitfulness, ointment poured out wastefully, wineskins that have holes in them, or the world perishing in the flood. "In none of these cases do the objects cease to exist; they cease to be useful or to exist in their original, intended state. . . . Destruction is similar to a car that has been totaled; it's a heap of wreckage, though all of the metal and plastic that made up the car still exist" (Moo 2004, 105). The best understanding of these words is "ruin." Those who are punished with eternal destruction do not cease to exist; they are eternally ruined. Similarly, the idea of "death" in the Bible is never "cease to exist" but rather "separation." Though the body begins to decompose at physical death, it does not cease to exist. Rather, physical death is the separation of the soul from the body, and spiritual death is the separation of the soul from God.

Revelation 14:9–12: The punishment for those who worship the beast is eternal. Though this speaks specifically of those who worship the beast (and so implies that *some* will suffer conscious punishment forever), "it is just as possible, if not probable, that this passage concerns the final judgment of all unbelievers throughout history who have given allegiance to the ungodly world system" (Beale 2004, 115). In Revelation day and night parallel "forever" (20:10; 22:5). That they find "no rest" parallels the eternal rest of believers in 14:13 (also 4:8). From this text it seems clear that unbelievers will suffer "a punishment of unending restlessness" (Beale 2004, 119).

Revelation 20:10: This verse clearly indicates that Satan, the beast, and the false prophet will suffer eternal, conscious punishment. Some universalists and conditionalists agree that Satan will suffer eternal torment but often say that the beast and the false prophet are institutions, not individuals, so this verse only speaks of the end of oppressive institutions (Fudge 1994, 192). But as Gregory K. Beale points out, "institutions are composed of people, so that if the institution is said to suffer something, so will the people composing the institution" (2004, 127).

Beale concludes: "Revelation 14:11 and 20:10–15 are the Achilles' heel of the annihilationist perspective. Though some argue that the suffering of unbelievers is temporary, the likelihood is that John believed in an endless judgment of the ungodly" (2004, 134).

In addition to these texts, many others imply a decisive, eternal judgment that will not be reversed (Isa. 66:24; Matt. 12:32; 13:42; 24:51; Luke 13:28–30; John 5:28–29; Heb. 6:2; 9:27; 10:27, 31). The consistent witness of scripture seems to be that some people will suffer eternal, conscious punishment for their rebellious rejection of God.

RESPONDING TO TEXTS USED TO SUPPORT UNIVERSALISM

When examined more closely in their context, many of the texts that universalists use to support their position are actually teaching something quite different, such as a universal offer of the gospel, the universal availability and sufficiency of Christ's salvific work, or salvation for all kinds of people (2 Cor. 5:19; 1 Tim. 4:10; Titus 2:11; Heb. 2:9; 1 John 2:2). None of these points is the same as universal salvation. Other texts teach the ultimate universal acknowledgment of Jesus's lordship (Phil. 2:9–11). Those who have trusted him in life will acknowledge him willingly, but those who have rejected him, including hostile spirit forces, will bend the knee under compulsion. Still others are speaking of God's restoration of the creation or of people groups, such as Israel, and not of individual salvation (Acts 3:21; Rom. 9; 11:26, 32; Col. 1:20). Some verses speak of God's passion to save all (1 Tim. 2:4; 2 Pet. 3:9), but "theologians since the early days of the church recognized the need to distinguish between God's 'general' will—his 'desires,' as it were—and his effective will" (Moo 2004, 101). Even though God may desire all people to come to faith in Christ and enjoy fellowship with him for eternity, he leaves them free to reject him.

> *There is no positive evidence anywhere for the view that there will be a postmortem opportunity for salvation.*
> I. Howard Marshall (2003, 65)

Some texts used by universalists, when examined carefully in their broader context, actually include conditions for salvation, conditions not mentioned in the verse itself. For example, Romans 5:18 says that Christ's "one act of righteousness was justification that brings life for all men," but in Romans 3:21–4:25, Paul has already made clear that the only ones who are justified are those who make a decision of faith in Christ. First Corinthians 15:22 says that "in Christ all will be made alive," but in the very next verse Paul qualifies "all" by explaining that only those who belong to Christ will be raised to life.

Scripture never suggests that hell is restorative or that people will receive a chance to repent and trust Christ after death. Instead, the consistent emphasis of scripture is that the decisions we make in this life are decisive for the judgment we face in the next (Matt. 7:13–14; 12:32; 25:41, 46; 26:24; Luke 16:24; John 8:21; Rom. 2:1–16; 2 Cor. 5:10; Gal. 6:7; Heb. 9:27). Finally, "the intensity of the New Testament appeals to people to repent and believe lest they suffer final separation from God is such that it is difficult to believe that this separation is purely temporary and will come to an end" (Marshall 2003, 56). Paul's anguish in Romans 9:1–4; 10:1–2 does not seem to reflect the heart of someone who knows that his people will eventually be saved.

GOD'S LOVE AND HUMAN SIN

The question is often asked, "How could a God of love allow human beings to suffer in hell for all eternity?" The unspoken assumption of this question is that God's love somehow overrides all his other attributes. God is love, but God's love is a perfectly pure love that cannot be understood or defined apart from his holiness, justice, or wrath against the sin that has corrupted his perfect creation. "God's love does not drive his justice. The implementation of God's justice does not undermine his love. God's love and justice cohere" (Morgan 2004, 216). God always acts in ways that perfectly and harmoniously express his love, holiness, wrath against sin, and justice.

If God's love cannot be understood apart from his other attributes, neither can it be understood apart from the seriousness of human sin. Humankind has willfully turned its back on God and chosen to rebel against him, defiling God's perfect purposes and creation. Our modern humanistic values so understate the wickedness of human sin that we are more disturbed by the punishment than by the sin itself. But "sin is actually the ultimate horror of God's universe. Hell is merely the punishment. Sin is the crime. Which is worse, murder or the life sentence? Obviously the crime is worse than the punishment" (Morgan 2004, 210). Sin against an infinitely holy God deserves an infinite punishment. If we took a survey of inmates in prison, we would find that most think their punishment is too great. In the same way, we human beings underestimate the true wickedness of our sin and feel that hell is too great a punishment.

God's love, justice, holiness, and wrath against sin converge on the cross of Christ, the greatest expression of his love (John 3:16; Rom. 5:8; 1 John 4:10). In Christ, God has provided a way that is sufficient and available for all people to be reconciled to him. All who end up eternally separated from God will have already chosen to reject God and separate themselves from him in this life. Hell will be the extension of that decision throughout eternity.

THE NATURE OF HELL

The Bible uses three pictures to describe hell: (1) punishment—just, endless, conscious suffering; (2) destruction—a ruined life; (3) banishment—full and final separation from God (Morgan 2004, 142–51). All three of these pictures coexist in some of the same passages (Matt. 24:45–25:46; 2 Thess. 1:5–10; Rev. 20:14; 21:8). All three are pictures of what is simultaneously true of those in hell. Much of the biblical language that describes hell is metaphorical. For example, hell is described both as "darkness" (Matt. 25:30) and also as a "lake of fire" (Rev. 20:14–15). Understood metaphorically these passages do not contradict each other but are complementary images of punishment, destruction, and banishment.

The biblical pictures of hell merge to reveal hell as the eternal confirmation of decisions people have made in their lives to separate themselves from God. The wrath of God—the punishment of unending restlessness (Rev. 14:11)—that they endure is precisely the separation from God that they have freely chosen. Because people are created to know God, be known by him, and enjoy him forever, eternal separation from God is the ruin of that for which they were created: fellowship with God.

It seems likely that those condemned to hell will willingly *choose* to continue in sinful rebellion against God and separation from him through all eternity (Rev. 16:11). "One reason why the conscious punishment of hell is ongoing is because sin is ongoing" (Carson 1996, 533). The anguish of hell is separation from God, and having never known God and the joy of intimacy with him, those in hell continue in the same self-absorbed rejection that characterized them in life. As C. S. Lewis argues, it seems that "the doors of hell are locked on the *inside*" (1944, 115).

It seems incredible that those in hell would choose to continue in their sin and remain there in rebellion against God. But "what the damned want is to be happy on their own terms. However, that is impossible. The only possible way we can be truly happy is on God's terms. So the damned choose what they *can* have on their own terms, namely, a distorted sense of satisfaction that is a perverted mirror image of the real thing" (J. L. Walls 2003, 121–22).

Some have suggested that the parable of the rich man and Lazarus (Luke 16:19–31) argues against the idea that those in hell choose to remain there. Jerry Walls answers that, though the rich man is miserable, he is more concerned to justify his decisions in life than to truly repent. "The point of the parable is that the rich man is not in hell because he lacks evidence. Just like his brothers, he had available to him Moses and the Prophets. . . . He was indeed informed but declined to act on the truth that was openly before him" (2003, 119).

People make foolish choices in life, reap the negative results, but refuse to admit their error and continue to make the same foolish choices. In the same way, it seems that people in hell will continue to wallow in their rejection and separation from God, digging themselves ever deeper into the misery of separation from God.

Does God Really Condemn People to Eternal, Conscious Punishment?

In his love God has provided a way for all humankind to enjoy eternal fellowship with him. But the Bible's teaching is clear: some people will persist in their rejection of God and as a result *will condemn themselves* to an eternity of separation from him. God will not coerce them into accepting his love, forgiveness, and fellowship. Hell is a real place, and its misery will be the eternal state of all those who reject God's revelation of himself and choose to follow the rebellious inclinations of their own will.

We should remember that Jesus himself talked about hell a great deal. "It is the Lord Jesus, of all persons in the Bible, who consistently and repeatedly uses the graphic images of hell. Is it not clear that he does so precisely to warn people against hell, and to encourage them to repent and believe? Should we not, therefore, do the same?" (Carson 1996, 530). Though scripture contains many valid motivations for engaging in mission (chap. 7), we dare not lose the conviction that people will suffer eternal ruin apart from Christ as one of the reasons that we do so.

WHAT ABOUT THOSE WHO HAVE NEVER HEARD THE GOSPEL? THE QUESTION OF GOD'S FAIRNESS

One of the most troublesome questions any follower of Christ faces is "What about those who have never heard the gospel?" Is it fair for God to condemn to hell people who never had the opportunity to trust Christ? As we have seen, it seems clear that the New Testament teaches that some will be separated from God and punished for their rejection of God through all eternity. But what about those who never explicitly reject the message of Christ? What about people like Asa in the story at the beginning of this chapter? How can God be fair to condemn to eternal punishment people who seek him but who never have the opportunity to hear the gospel? In chapter 12 we saw that universal inclusivism suggests that those who respond in faith to general revelation—even revelation found in non-Christian religions—will receive the benefits of Christ's atoning death. How does revelatory particularism respond to the question of God's fairness? We begin our response by noting what scripture teaches about general revelation. We will then explore the implications of God's justice and consider to what extent anyone has been outside the possibility of a gospel witness.

What Is the Role of General Revelation?

General revelation is "God's communication of himself to all persons at all times and in all places," specifically, what God communicates of himself in nature, history, and the inner being of the human person (Erickson 1983, 153). Historically Christian theology has insisted that general revelation served as

331

"a universal witness to God's existence and character" to all people, but that the only way to be reconciled to God was through "a supernatural revelatory disclosure to a special people," or special revelation (Demarest 1982, 14). What does scripture teach about general revelation?

Psalm 19:1–4: The psalmist says that creation continually points to God's glory, and that no people or language group on earth is exempt from seeing his glory. The latter half of the psalm (vv. 7–14) extols the effects of the special revelation of God's Word, possibly in comparison with the revelation of creation. It is the written Word of God that revives the soul, makes the simple wise, gives joy to the heart and light to the eyes, and brings great reward to God's servants.

Acts 14:14–18: Paul says that in the past God revealed his goodness to his listeners by giving them rain, growing seasons, and joy from the satisfaction of work and good food. God's goodness is clear to all people through the seasons of nature. When he says that in the past God "let all nations go their own way" (v. 16), Paul is saying not that God did not hold the nations responsible for their sin during the Old Testament era but that he had not revealed himself to them as completely as he had to Israel (Harrison 1975, 223). God's full revelation of himself and his calling the nations to a decisive response awaited the coming of Christ and the church's mission to the nations.

Acts 17:22–31: Several aspects of God's general revelation emerge in Paul's sermon to the Athenians. First, the Athenians were worshipping an "unknown god" whom Paul was now about to reveal to them (17:23). This does not mean they were worshipping the one true God in ignorance of his name, but rather that they were hedging their bets by worshipping one extra god they may have missed. Paul tells them that, in fact, they were missing the worship of the one true God. Second, God created the nations and controls their destiny in a way that should lead them to be aware of him and seek him (17:26–27). Third, the creation of human beings as God's "offspring" reveals enough of God to show the foolishness of idolatry (17:29). Fourth, God had "overlooked their ignorance" (v. 30) in worshipping idols in the past. Like Acts 14:14–18, Paul is not saying that God had ignored their sin. Rather, he is pointing to a different time in God's program prior to the gospel's full revelation to the nations. This full revelation had now come in Christ, and its coming required them all to repent and prepare for judgment based on their response to him (17:30–31).

Romans 1:18–32: Romans 1:18–3:20 is Paul's detailed discussion of what God has revealed to all people and how all people have responded to God's revelation. In Romans 1:18–32, Paul focuses on the Gentiles. God has made certain things about himself absolutely plain to all people through creation. All people know that a divine being exists and that he is all-powerful (1:20). This core knowledge about God, however, has been rejected by all people who have chosen to worship the creation instead of the Creator (1:21–22, 25, 28).

Because they rejected what the creation taught them about God, God has allowed them to go their own way and experience the natural consequences of their choice, resulting in a miserable downward spiral of sin (1:24, 26–27, 28–32).

Romans 2:1–16: Even those people who consider themselves more moral than others stand under God's judgment for rejecting his revelation to them. God gives various levels of revelation to different people (2:4, 12). But he holds all people responsible for the level of revelation they have received (2:6–13). Even the Gentiles, who did not receive the special revelation of the Old Testament law, have an inner understanding of certain aspects of God's moral law in their consciences, for which they will be held accountable (2:14–15). All people, even those who think that they are better than other people, have rejected God's revelation and gone their own way into disobedience (2:3–5). God treats all people with complete fairness based on complete truth. He does not show favoritism to one group of people over another (2:2, 11).

What can we conclude from these key texts regarding what is known about God from general revelation? God is a glorious, all-powerful Creator who provides good things and joy for humankind. Because humans reflect God's image, they know that God must be much greater than any idol. His control of nations and history should drive people to seek him. Enough can be known about God through general revelation that people should respond to him and seek him. But in spite of what they should have known about God, human beings have turned their backs on him and have chosen the foolishness of worshipping and serving created things. Some people have received more revelation about God than others, but *all* have turned their backs on him and rejected him. All will be held accountable for the revelation they received of God. During the Old Testament era, God did not reveal himself to the nations as clearly as he did to the nation Israel, but now he is revealing himself clearly in Jesus.

Does scripture itself contain evidence of people who came to Christ through general revelation? The Bible contains examples of non-Jews and non-Christians who came to salvation, but it is likely that these "holy pagans" were all saved by responding to God's special revelation given during their own eras of history, including God's covenants with Adam, Noah, Abraham, and Moses, and perhaps to specific salvific revelation given directly by God. Many Old Testament "holy pagans" were in covenant community with the people of God (e.g., Lot, Jethro, Ruth, Naaman). Others (e.g., Job, Melchizedek, Enoch) were probably responding to special revelation given to the nations in the earliest epochs of human history (e.g., Gen. 3:14–24; 9:1–17). Some so-called holy pagans were probably not redeemed (e.g., Abimelech, Balaam). The magi (Matt. 2:1–12) may well have been responding to revelation in the Hebrew scriptures (Num. 24:17), perhaps passed on through Daniel. Christopher Little surveys the biblical evidence of those who may have come to a saving knowledge of

God through general revelation and concludes that all received special revelation by which they were reconciled to God (2000, 88).

Nothing in the Bible hints that general revelation reveals enough for human beings to become right with God or be reconciled to him (Little 2000, 46). Although some truth about God exists in other religions, and this truth may be a residue of general revelation, scripture contains no indication that this truth is adequate to save followers of other religions, even those who are good, moral people. We must not confuse people who have received salvation and those who, through God's common grace, are otherwise virtuous and have elements of truth and goodness in their culture but are not saved. As we have seen, the general teaching of scripture about other religions is that their gods are not the one true God, that they are "at best . . . nonredemptive, and at worst . . . partaking of the domain of darkness" (Geivett and Phillips 1995, 237; Exod. 20:3–6; 2 Chron. 13:9; Isa. 37:18–19; 40:12–26; Jer. 2:11; 5:7; 16:20; Acts 19:26; 26:17–18; 1 Cor. 1:21; 8:4–6; 10:19–20; Gal. 4:8; Col. 1:13; 1 Thess. 2:16; 2 Thess. 1:8). Though many non-Christian religions have a concept of a high god, some of these concepts are so far removed from biblical teaching about God that we can rightfully question whether they are worshipping the same God (Carson 1996, 291–96).

God's Love for the Lost and His Justice

Earlier in this chapter we saw God's passion to save (John 3:16; 1 Tim. 2; 2 Pet. 3). No biblical text better illustrates God's longing to bring lost people to himself than Luke 15. Jesus tells three stories about the lost being found: the lost sheep, the lost coin, and the lost son. In each parable God is like the one who seeks earnestly for what is lost and is full of great joy when the lost is found. But in the final and most significant parable, the parable of the lost son, the longing of the father for the return of his son is not divorced from the son's repentance. God's passion to save lost people is not disconnected from the need for lost people to come to God in faith and repentance.

Nor is God's love for the lost disconnected from his justice. One of the core biblical descriptions of God is that he is just. He will always do what is right. In Job 34:12, Elihu reminds us that "it is unthinkable that God would do wrong, that the Almighty would pervert justice." God's judgments are always based on truth and righteousness (Rom. 2:2, 5), he is completely impartial in his judgment (1 Pet. 1:17), and he never shows favoritism (Rom. 2:11). God's justice means that his judgments will always be proportional to how much of his truth people have known (Matt. 11:21–24; Luke 12:47–48; 2 Pet. 2:21). All people will receive through all eternity exactly what they deserve based on the lives that they have lived.

The more one studies biblical texts on the justice of God, the more clear it becomes that the biblical writers' greatest concern was not how God could punish sinners eternally and remain just. Their greatest concern was how God could be just and *not* punish sinners immediately and decisively. From a biblical perspective the truly amazing thing is how God can continue to be just and still forgive sin.

Many biblical texts combine God's justice with his love and desire to save. "The Lord is righteous in all his ways and loving toward all he has made" (Ps. 145:17). He is "a righteous God and a Savior" (Isa. 45:21). God delays his judgment on the world because he does not want "anyone to perish, but everyone to come to repentance" (2 Pet. 3:9). Paul explains that it is because Christ has borne the punishment for sin in his death on the cross that God can be both "just and the one who justifies" (Rom. 3:26) those who trust Jesus (Rom. 3:22–26). Because Jesus took God's judgment against sin completely upon himself (2 Cor. 5:21; Heb. 13:11–13; 1 Pet. 2:24; the "cup" in Matt. 26:17–46; Mark 14:12–52; Luke 22:1–53), he will be able to righteously judge all people based on their response to what God has revealed to them of himself.

> *God's judgment settles all moral problems, it does not create them. . . . The biblical writers were not so concerned with how God could be just if he punished the wicked forever, but rather with how God could be just and not punish evildoers immediately.*
>
> Christopher W. Morgan
> (2004, 208)

A story in Genesis vividly portrays God's justice and saving compassion. In Genesis 18 the Lord came to Abraham and shared with him that he was about to destroy Sodom and Gomorrah for their wickedness. Knowing that his nephew, Lot, and his family lived there, in anguish Abraham pleaded for God's mercy. "Will you sweep away the righteous with the wicked?" he asked. "Will not the Judge of all the earth do right?" (Gen. 18:23, 25). In the rest of the story, God goes to extreme measures to extend his mercy to as many people as possible, all the while punishing the wicked and allowing men and women to exercise their free will to accept (e.g., Lot) or reject (e.g., Lot's wife, Lot's sons-in-law) his mercy. Genesis 18:25 reminds us that God will do right in his judgment, with both believers and nonbelievers. When we are inclined to question his justice, he reminds us that he has and will be just and fair, though we do not always understand it.

What about Those Beyond the Hope of a Missionary Witness?

What about those people who have been beyond the possibility of a missionary witness to the gospel? How can God be fair and just in condemning these people if they never had the opportunity to hear the gospel? We may respond in two ways. First, mission history demonstrates that the gospel has penetrated extremely remote areas in unexpected ways. The gospel was being preached in India by the second century, in Ethiopia by the fourth century, and in China by the seventh century. The Irish monk St. Brendan may even have reached North America in the seventh century (Haggerty 2006). We cannot presume that it would have been impossible for missionaries to reach any people who were responsive to general revelation.

Second, though the normal pattern for reaching people with the gospel is through the proclamation of an evangelistic witness (see below on Rom. 10), God could certainly choose to reveal salvific truth about Christ through direct special revelation, such as dreams and visions (Little 2000, 116–31). Scripture records examples of those outside the covenant community of God receiving revelatory dreams from God (e.g., Pharaoh, Abimelech, Nebuchadnezzar), and modern mission history contains stories of non-Christians (especially Muslims) being led to Christ through dreams and visions (Musk 1988; Martin 2004). The justice of God assures us that he will not leave without a witness any person or people group whom he knows would respond to the gospel if it were preached.

The story of Cornelius (Acts 10) provides a model of how this might happen. Cornelius was a faithful follower of God based on what he had learned from his exposure to Judaism. Based on Cornelius's response to what he knew of the one true God, God sent an angelic messenger who told him to contact Peter, who would bring him a further message from God. Cornelius obeyed God's messenger, and God went to dramatic lengths to bring Peter to share the gospel with Cornelius. The story of Cornelius suggests that whenever the Spirit of God prompts a response to God's revelation, God will faithfully provide explicit revelation about the saving work of Jesus.

Can We Then Trust God's Justice and Fairness?

All people have known something about God from general revelation. Different individuals and people groups receive different amounts of God's revelation, but all will be judged based on what they do with the light they receive. God will not hold people accountable for what they do not know, only for what they do know.

God's passion to save lost people assures us that he will do everything he can to bring people to repentance without violating their freedom to reject him. God's justice assures us that he will treat all people with complete fairness and ultimately those who persevere in their rejection will experience the natural consequences of their rejection.

In his mercy and love the Holy Spirit may use general revelation to draw people to seek God, and we must not underestimate God's power to bring a gospel witness to anyone on earth who is prepared to respond to the gospel. The message of Christ is normally spread through the spoken word of a witness or the written word of scripture, but Christ may reveal himself in unusual ways when he so pleases.

SIDEBAR 13.1
A RETURN TO ASA'S STORY

Reread the story of Asa at the beginning of the chapter in light of our discussion of the three difficult questions we discussed. How would you respond if someone asked:

1. Would God accept Asa's faith and obedience and extend salvation to him?
2. Would he condemn him to an eternity in hell even though Asa seems to have responded to general revelation?
3. How can God's fairness and justice be seen in the experience of Asa?

Finally, we simply do not know all the details of perplexing stories of those who may have responded to what God has revealed of himself in general revelation, as in the story of Asa (see sidebar 13.1). Asa apparently spent his last days in a prison in the city of Addis Ababa, a city where the scriptures and a gospel witness were then available. During this time it is entirely possible that he came into contact with a copy of the Bible or with a genuine follower of Christ who could have shared the gospel with him. God does not require that we know the eternal outcomes of situations like Asa's, and we must be careful that we do not build a normative doctrine of salvation or theology of mission on situations about which we lack the whole story. Instead, our theology and practice of mission must be built on the urgency to preach the gospel that we find throughout scripture.

CONCLUSION: THE URGENCY OF MISSION

In Romans 9–11, the apostle Paul is wrestling with the question of why most of the people of Israel had rejected their own Messiah. One reason, he says in Romans 9:30–10:21, is because they freely rejected God's way of salvation and chose to pursue their own way of salvation. They were trying to earn salvation through the law instead of trusting in the work that God had already done to provide them with salvation. The way to salvation is to call on the Lord's name, not to trust in becoming righteous through one's own works or religious ritual.

But if the only way of salvation is by calling on the Lord's name, then it is crucial that the message of salvation through Christ alone be proclaimed around the world. Paul asks a series of questions to show what must happen for a person to call upon the name of the Lord: "How, then, can they call on the one they have not believed in? And how can they believe in the one of whom they have not heard? And how can they hear without someone preaching to them? And how can they preach unless they are sent? As it is written, 'How beautiful are the feet of those who bring good news!'" (Rom. 10:14–15).

Before people can confess Jesus as Lord, they must trust Jesus for salvation. But before they can believe in their hearts that Jesus is the only way of salvation, they must have heard the message about Jesus. Before they can hear the message about Jesus, someone must be sent to proclaim that message to them.

The normal way that God brings people to salvation is through their hearing the message about Jesus Christ and trusting in him. In order for people to hear about and trust Jesus, someone must share the message with them. Therefore, it is urgent that people go and proclaim the gospel message that salvation comes by trusting in Jesus. Paul does not suggest that there is any other way of salvation.

The true scandal of mission is not that evangelicals believe that Jesus is the only way of salvation but that many who claim to believe this are doing little or nothing to spread the gospel to lost people around the world. Paul's passion to preach the gospel controlled his life (Rom. 9:1–4; 10:1; 15:18–21). If we have no reason to believe that any individual will spend eternity with God unless that person puts his or her faith in Christ, then mission becomes the most urgent task of the church and of every individual believer.

Paul goes on to say in Romans 10:15 that people who proclaim the message have "beautiful feet." Paul is quoting Isaiah 52:7, where God promised the captive Israelites that he would return them to their land. When someone brings this good news to the depressed captives, he will be welcomed with great joy because he brings news of deliverance from captivity. In the same way, Paul says, when anyone brings the news of eternal salvation through Jesus Christ, his coming is "beautiful" for those who receive the message. They will greatly appreciate his coming because he has brought them the message that will save them.

Missions is not only the most urgent task facing believers; it is also each believer's greatest joy and privilege. Even as heaven rejoices when one lost person comes to Christ (Luke 15:7, 10, 32), we can share the joy of God himself by sharing the good news with people around us. We each can have the privilege of carrying the transforming message of the gospel to people in need of rescue. Though there are many motivations for missions, we must never forget that people are lost apart from God's grace, and the New Testament pattern for receiving God's grace is clearly the proclaimed message of the cross of Christ. Those who accept the message will be forever grateful that someone cared enough to carry the message to them; that messenger's coming will always be beautiful.

References

Aagaard, Johannes. 1987. "The Double Apostolate (Part I)." *Areopagus* 11 (Fall): 15–18.

Adeyemo, Tokunboh, ed. 2006. *Africa Bible Commentary*. Grand Rapids: Zondervan.

Ad Gentes: On the Mission Activity of the Church. Available online at http://www.vatican.va/archive/hist_councils/ii_vatican_council/documents/vatii_decree_19651207_ad-gentes_en.html.

Aigbe, Sunday A. 1991. "Cultural Mandate, Evangelistic Mandate, Prophetic Mandate: Of These the Greatest Is . . . ?" *Missiology* 19 (1): 31–43.

Allen, Roland. [1912] 1962a. *Missionary Methods: St. Paul's or Ours?* Grand Rapids: Eerdmans.

———. [1927] 1962b. *The Spontaneous Expansion of the Church*. London: World Dominion.

Anderson, Courtney. [1956] 1972. *To the Golden Shore: The Life of Adoniram Judson*. Grand Rapids: Zondervan.

———, ed. 1998. *Biographical Dictionary of Christian Missions*. New York: Macmillan Reference.

AnglicansOnline. 2009. "The Seal of the Society for Propagating the Gospel in Foreign Parts." http://anglicansonline.org/special/spg.html (accessed March 4, 2009).

Aring, Paul Gerhardt. 1971. *Kirche als Ereignis: Ein Beitrag zur Neuorientierung der Missionstheologie*. Neukirchen-Vluyn: Neukirchner Verlag.

Arnold, Clinton E. 1996. *The Colossian Syncretism: The Interface between Christianity and Folk Belief at Colossae*. Grand Rapids: Baker Academic.

———. 1997. *3 Crucial Questions about Spiritual Warfare*. Grand Rapids: Baker Academic.

———. 2000. "Territorial Spirits." In Moreau 2000a.

Augustine. 1998. *Confessions*. Trans. Henry Chadwick. New York: Oxford University.

Aus, Roger. 1979. "Paul's Travel Plans to Spain and the 'Full Number of the Gentiles' of Romans 11:25." *Novum Testamentum* 21 (July): 232–62.

Averbeck, Richard E. 2004. "Ancient Near Eastern Mythography as It Relates to Historiography in the Hebrew Bible." In *The Future of Biblical Archaeology*, ed. James K. Hoffmeier and Alan Millard, 328–56. Grand Rapids: Eerdmans.

Baker, Ken. 2002. "The Incarnational Model: Perception or Deception?" *Evangelical Missions Quarterly* 38 (January): 16–24.

339

Balisky, Lila W. 1997. "Theology in Song: Ethiopia's Tesfaey Gabbiso." *Missiology* 25 (October): 447–56.

Barnett, Mike, and Michael Pocock, eds. 2005. *The Centrality of Christ in Contemporary Missions*. EMS Series, no. 12. Pasadena, CA: William Carey.

Barrett, David B. 2006. "Missiometrics 2006: Goals, Resources, Doctrines of the 350 Christian World Communities." *International Bulletin of Missionary Research* 30 (January): 27–30.

Barrett, David B., Todd M. Johnson, and Peter F. Crossing. 2007. "Missiometrics 2007." *International Bulletin of Missionary Research* 31 (January): 25–32.

———. 2008. "Missiometrics 2008." *International Bulletin of Missionary Research* 32 (January): 27–30.

Barrett, David B., George T. Kurian, and Todd M. Johnson. 2001. *World Christian Encyclopedia: A Comparative Survey of Churches and Religions in the Modern World*. 2nd ed. 2 vols. New York: Oxford University Press.

Bassham, Rodger C. 1979. *Mission Theology, 1948–1975: Years of Worldwide Creative Tension—Ecumenical, Evangelical, and Roman Catholic*. Pasadena, CA: William Carey.

Bate, Stuart. 1994. "Inculturation: The Local Church Emerges." *Missionalia* 22 (August): 93–117.

Bauckham, Richard J. 1983. *Jude, 2 Peter*. Word Biblical Commentary 50. Waco: Word.

———. 1998. *God Crucified: Monotheism and Christology in the New Testament*. Grand Rapids: Eerdmans.

———. 2003. *Bible and Mission: Christian Witness in a Postmodern World*. Grand Rapids: Baker Academic.

Bauer, Bruce L. 2008. "A Response to Dual Allegiance." *Evangelical Missions Quarterly* 44 (July): 340–47.

Bavinck, J. H. 1960. *An Introduction to the Science of Missions*. Phillipsburg, NJ: P&R.

———. 1966. *The Church between Temple and Mosque: A Study of the Relationship between the Christian Faith and Other Religions*. Grand Rapids: Eerdmans.

Beale, Gregory K. 2004. "The Revelation on Hell." In Morgan and Peterson 2004, 111–34.

Beals, Paul A. 1995. *A People for His Name: A Church-Based Missions Strategy*. Rev. ed. Pasadena, CA: William Carey.

Beaver, R. Pierce. 1959. "Eschatology in Early American Missions." In *Basileia: A Tribute to Walter Freytag*, ed. Jan Hermelink and Hans Jochen Margull, 60–75. Stuttgart: Evangelische Missionsverlag.

———. 1966. *Pioneers in Mission: The Early Missionary Ordination Sermons, Charges, and Instructions*. Grand Rapids: Eerdmans.

———. 1968a. "Missionary Motivation through Three Centuries." In *Reinterpretation in American Church History*, ed. Jerald C. Brauer, 113–51. Chicago: University of Chicago.

———. 1968b. *All Loves Excelling: American Protestant Women in World Mission*. Grand Rapids: Eerdmans.

———. 1968c. *The Missionary between the Times*. New York: Doubleday.

Bemis, Kenneth. 1981. "The Myth of the Missionary Call." *Moody Monthly* 81 (March): 49, 55–56.

Berneburg, Erhard. 1997. *Das Verhältnis von Verkündigung und sozialer Aktion in der evangelikalen Missionstheorie*. Giessen: Brockhaus.

Bevans, Stephen B. 2002. *Models of Contextual Theology*. Rev. and expanded ed. Maryknoll, NY: Orbis.

Bevans, Stephen B., and Roger P. Schroeder. 2004. *Constants in Context: A Theology of Mission for Today*. Maryknoll, NY: Orbis.

Beyerhaus, Peter. 1969. "The Ministry of Crossing Frontiers." In *The Church Crossing Frontiers*, ed. Bengt Sundkler, Peter Beyerhaus, and Carl F. Hallencreutz, 36–54. Lund: Gleerup.

———. 1974. *Bangkok '73: Beginning or End of World Mission?* Grand Rapids: Zondervan.

———. 1975. "World Evangelization and the Kingdom of God." In Douglas 1975, 283–95.

———. 1987. *Krise und Neuaufbruch der Weltmission*. Bad Liebenzell: Verlag der Liebenzeller Mission.

———. 1990. "Eschatology: Does It Make a Difference in Missions?" *Evangelical Missions Quarterly* 26 (October): 366–76.

———. 1996. *Er sandte sein Wort: Theologie der christlichen Mission*. Vol. 1: *Die Bibel in der Mission*. Wuppertal: Brockhaus.

Beyreuther, Erich. 1960. "Mission und Kirche in der Theologie Zinzendorfs." *Evangelische Missions-Zeitschrift* 17:65–76.

———. 1961. "Evangelische Missionstheologie im 16. und 17. Jahrhundert." *Evangelische Missions-Zeitschrift* 18:1–10, 33–43.

Bintz, Helmut, ed. 1979. *Texte zur Mission: Mit einer Einführung in die Missionstheologie Zinzendorfs*. Hamburg: Wittig.

Blauw, Johannes. 1962. *The Missionary Nature of the Church: A Survey of Biblical Theology of Mission*. New York: McGraw-Hill.

Blincoe, Robert A. 2002. "The Strange Structure of Mission Agencies—Part I: Still Two Structures after All These Years?" *International Journal of Frontier Missions* 19 (January–March): 5–8.

Block, Daniel I. 2004. "The Old Testament on Hell." In Morgan and Peterson 2004, 43–65.

Blue, Ken. 1999. "D-Day before V-E Day." In Winter and Hawthorne 1999, 72.

Bock, Darrell L. 2007. *Acts*. Baker Exegetical Commentary on the New Testament. Grand Rapids: Baker Academic.

Boer, Harry R. 1964. *Pentecost and Missions*. Grand Rapids: Baker Academic.

Boff, Leonardo. 1988. *Trinity and Society*. Maryknoll, NY: Orbis.

Bonk, Jonathan J. 1991. *Missions and Money: Affluence as a Western Missionary Problem*. Maryknoll, NY: Orbis.

———, ed. 2003. *Between Past and Future: Evangelical Mission Entering the Twenty-first Century*. EMS Series, no. 10. Pasadena, CA: William Carey.

Borthwick, Paul. 1998. "The Confusion of American Churches about Mission: A Response to Paul E. Pierson." *International Bulletin of Missionary Research* 22 (October): 151.

———. 1999. "What Local Churches Are Saying to Mission Agencies." *Evangelical Missions Quarterly* 35 (July): 324–30.

Bosch, David J. 1959. *Die Heidenmission in der Zukunftsschau Jesu: Eine Untersuchung zur Eschatologie der synoptischen Evangelien*. Zürich: Zwingli Verlag.

———. 1980. *Witness to the World: The Christian Mission in Theological Perspective*. Atlanta: John Knox.

———. 1991. *Transforming Mission: Paradigm Shifts in Theology of Mission*. Maryknoll, NY: Orbis.

Bosch, David T. 1969. "'Jesus and the Gentiles'—A Review after Thirty Years." In *The Church Crossing Frontiers: Essays on the Nature of Mission in Honour of Bengt Sundkler*, ed. Peter Beyerhaus and Carl F. Hallencreutz, 3–19. Uppsala: Almquist & Wiksells.

Bowie, Fiona. 1993. "Introduction: Reclaiming Women's Presence." In Bowie, Kirkwood, and Ardener 1993, 1–19.

Bowie, Fiona, Deborah Kirkwood, and Shirley Ardener, eds. 1993. *Women and Missions: Past and Present; Anthropological and Historical*. Providence: Berg.

Boyd, Gregory A. 1999. "God at War." In Winter and Hawthorne 1999, 78–85.

Braaten, Karl E. 2000. "Eschatology and Mission in the Theology of Robert Jenson." In *Trinity, Time, and Church*, ed. Colin E. Gunton, 298–311. Grand Rapids: Eerdmans.

———. 2008. *That All May Believe: A Theology of the Gospel and the Mission of the Church*. Grand Rapids: Eerdmans.

Brandl, Bernd. 1998. *Die Neukirchner Mission*. Cologne: Rheinland-Verlag.

Braun, T. 1992. *Die Rheinische Missionsgesellschaft und der Missionshandel im 19. Jahrhundert*. Erlangen: Ev.-Luth. Mission.

Brechter, Suso. 1969. "Decree on the Church's Missionary Activity." In *Commentary on the Documents of Vatican II*, ed. Herbert Vorgrimler, 4:87–181. New York: Herder & Herder.

Brewster, Tom, and Betty Sue Brewster. 1982. *Bonding and the Missionary Task: Establishing a Sense of Belonging*. Pasadena, CA: Lingua House.

Bria, Ion. 1986. *Go Forth in Peace: Orthodox Perspectives on Mission*. Geneva: World Council of Churches.

341

Bright, J. 1955. *The Kingdom of God in Bible and Church.* London: Lutterworth.

Bubeck, Mark I. 1975. *The Adversary: The Christian versus Demon Activity.* Chicago: Moody.

Bühlmann, Walbert. 1982. *God's Chosen Peoples.* Maryknoll, NY: Orbis.

Bush, Luis. 2000. "AD2000 and Beyond: Toward a Conceptual Model." In *Working Together with God to Shape the New Millennium*, ed. Kenneth B. Mulholland and Gary Corwin, 197–209. EMS Series, no. 8. Pasadena, CA: William Carey.

———. 2003. "AD2000 Movement as a Great Commission Catalyst." In Bonk 2003, 17–36.

Calvin, John. [1560] 1960. *Institutes of the Christian Religion.* Ed. John T. McNeill. Philadelphia: Westminster.

Camp, Bruce K. 1995. "A Theological Examination of the Two-Structure Theory." *Missiology* 23 (April): 197–209.

———. 2003. "A Survey of the Local Church's Involvement in Global/Local Outreach." In Bonk 2003, 121–47.

Cannistraci, David. 1996. *Apostles and the Emerging Apostolic Movement.* Ventura, CA: Regal Books.

Carey, William. [1792] 1961. *An Enquiry into the Obligation of Christians to Use Means for the Conversion of the Heathens.* New facsimile edition with introduction by E. Payne. London: Carey Kingsgate.

Carpenter, Joel A. 1990. "Appendix: The Evangelical Missionary Force in the 1930s." In Carpenter and Shenk 1990, 335–42.

———. 1997. *Revive Us Again: The Reawakening of American Fundamentalism.* New York: Oxford University Press.

Carpenter, Joel A., and Wilbert R. Shenk, eds. 1990. *Earthen Vessels: American Evangelicals and Foreign Missions, 1880–1980.* Grand Rapids: Eerdmans.

Carpenter, John B. 2002. "New England Puritans: The Grandparents of Modern Protestant Missions." *Missiology* 30 (October): 519–32.

Carriker, C. Timothy. 1993. "Missiological Hermeneutic and Pauline Apocalyptic Eschatology." In Van Engen, Gilliland, and Pierson 1993, 45–55.

Carson, Donald A. 1984. "Matthew." In *The Expositor's Bible Commentary*, ed. Frank E. Gaebelein, 8:3–599. Grand Rapids: Zondervan.

———. 1987. "Church and Mission: Reflections on Contextualization and the Third Horizon." In *The Church in the Bible and the World: An International Study*, ed. D. A. Carson, 213–57. Grand Rapids: Baker Academic.

———. 1991. *The Gospel according to John.* Leicester, England: Inter-Varsity.

———. 1996. *The Gagging of God: Christianity Confronts Pluralism.* Grand Rapids: Zondervan.

Castro, Emilio. 1975. "Moratorium." *International Review of Mission* 64 (April): 117–21.

Chae, Daniel Jong Sang. 1997. *Paul as Apostle to the Gentiles.* Carlisle, England: Paternoster.

Chandler, Paul-Gordon. 2000. *God's Global Mosaic: What We Can Learn from Christians around the World.* Downers Grove, IL: InterVarsity.

Chaney, Charles L. 1976. *The Birth of Missions in America.* Pasadena, CA: William Carey.

Chang, Peter. 1981. "Linear and Nonlinear Thinking in Theological Education." *Evangelical Review of Theology* 5 (October): 279–86.

Chapman, Alister. 2009. "Evangelical International Relations in the Post-Colonial World." *Missiology* 37 (July): 355–68.

Chinchen, Del, and Palmer Chinchen. 2002. "Sing Africa!" *Evangelical Missions Quarterly* 38 (July): 286–98.

ChristianHistory.net. 2008. "Gregory Thaumaturgus." http://www.chrisitianitytoday.com/history/special/131christians/thaumaturgus.html (accessed July 25, 2008).

Chua, How Chuang. 2006. "Revelation in the Chinese Characters." In Van Rheenen 2006, 229–41.

Cobbs, Louis R. 1994. "The Missionary's Call and Training for Foreign Missions." *Baptist History and Heritage* 29 (October): 26–35.

Coe, Shoki. 1976. "Contextualizing Theology." In *Mission Trends No. 3: Third World Theologies*, ed. Gerald H. Anderson and Thomas F. Stransky, 19–24. New York: Paulist Press; Grand Rapids: Eerdmans.

Collani, Claudia von. 2006. "Der Ritenstreit und die Folgen für das Christentum." *Zeitschrift für Missionswissenschaft und Religionswissenschaft* 90 (3–4): 210–25.

Conn, Harvie M. 1984. *Eternal Word and Changing Worlds: Theology, Anthropology, and Mission in Trialogue*. Phillipsburg, NJ: P&R.

Coote, Robert T. 1982. "The Uneven Growth of Conservative Evangelical Missions." *International Bulletin of Missionary Research* 6 (July): 118–23.

Corrie, John, ed. 2007. *Dictionary of Mission Theology: Evangelical Foundations*. Downers Grove, IL: InterVarsity.

Costas, Orlando E. 1974. *The Church and Its Mission: A Shattering Critique from the Third World*. Wheaton: Tyndale House.

———. 1979. *The Integrity of Mission*. New York: Harper & Row.

———. 1982. *Christ outside the Gate: Mission beyond Christendom*. Maryknoll, NY: Orbis.

Craigie, P. C. 1976. *The Book of Deuteronomy*. Grand Rapids: Eerdmans.

Cullmann, Oscar. 1950. *Christ and Time*. Philadelphia: Westminster.

———. 1961. "Eschatology and Missions in the New Testament." In *The Theology of the Christian Mission*, ed. G. H. Anderson, 42–54. Nashville: Abingdon.

Cumbers, John. 1995. *Count It All Joy: Testimonies from a Persecuted Church*. Kearney, NE: Morris.

Davies, John G. 1966. *Worship and Mission*. London: SCM.

———. 1997. "Biblical Precedence for Contextualization." *Evangelical Review of Theology* 21 (July): 197–214.

Davis, Raymond J. 1980. *Fire on the Mountains*. Canada: SIM.

Dayton, Edward R. 1987. "Social Transformation: The Mission of God." In Samuel and Sugden 1987, 52–61.

Deere, Jack. 1993. *Surprised by the Power of the Spirit*. Grand Rapids: Zondervan.

Demarest, Bruce A. 1982. *General Revelation: Historical Views and Contemporary Issues*. Grand Rapids: Zondervan.

Donovan, Kath, and Ruth Myors. 1997. "Reflections on Attrition in Career Missionaries: A Generational Perspective into the Future." In W. D. Taylor 1997, 41–73.

Donovan, Vincent. 1978. *Christianity Rediscovered*. Maryknoll, NY: Orbis.

Douglas, J. D., ed. 1975. *Let the Earth Hear His Voice*. Minneapolis: World Wide Publications.

Dubose, Francis M. 1983. *God Who Sends*. Nashville: Broadman.

Dumbrell, William J. 1985. "The Purpose of the Book of Isaiah." *Tyndale Bulletin* 36:111–28.

Dunch, Ryan. 2002. "Beyond Cultural Imperialism: Cultural Theory, Christian Missions, and Global Modernity." *History and Theory* 41 (October): 301–25.

Dyrness, William A. 1983. *Let the Earth Rejoice: A Biblical Theology of Holistic Mission*. Westchester, IL: Crossway.

———. 1991. *Learning about Theology from the Third World*. Grand Rapids: Zondervan.

Dyrness, William A., and Veli-Matti Kärkkäinen, eds. 2008. *Global Dictionary of Theology: A Resource for the Worldwide Church*. Downers Grove, IL: IVP Academic; Nottingham, England: Inter-Varsity.

Edwards, David L., and John R. W. Stott. 1988. *Evangelical Essentials: A Liberal-Evangelical Dialogue*. Downers Grove, IL: InterVarsity.

Edwards, Jonathan. 1748. A humble attempt to promote the agreement and union of God's people throughout the world in extraordinary prayer for a revival of religion and the advancement of God's kingdom on earth, according to scriptural promises and prophecies of the last time. http://www.ccel.org/ccel/edwards/works2.viii.html (accessed November 26, 2008).

Edwards, Wendy J. Deichmann. 2004. "Forging an Ideology for American Missions: Josiah Strong and Manifest Destiny." In W. R. Shenk 2004, 163–91.

Effa, Allan. 2007. "Prophet, Kings, Servants, and Lepers: A Missiological Reading of an Ancient Drama." *Missiology* 35 (July): 305–13.

———. 2008. "The Greening of Mission." *International Bulletin of Missionary Research* 32 (October): 171–76.

Eicken, E. von, and H. Lindner. "Apostle." In *The New International Dictionary of New Testament Theology*. Grand Rapids: Zondervan.

Engel, James E., and William A. Dyrness. 2000. *Changing the Mind of Missions*. Downers Grove, IL: InterVarsity.

Engelsviken, Tormod. 2005. "'Come Holy Spirit, Heal and Reconcile': An Evangelical Evaluation of the CWME Mission Conference in Athens, May 9–16, 2005." *International Bulletin of Missionary Research* 29 (October): 190–92.

Enklaar, Ido H. 1978. "Motive und Zielsetzungen der neueren niederländischen Mission in ihrer Anfangsperiode." In *Pietismus und Reveil*, ed. J. Van den Berg and J. P. Van Dooren, 282–88. Leiden: Brill.

Erickson, Millard J. 1983. *Christian Theology*. Grand Rapids: Baker Academic.

———. 1991. *The Word Became Flesh*. Grand Rapids: Baker Academic.

Escobar, Samuel. 2003. *The New Global Mission: The Gospel from Everywhere to Everyone*. Downers Grove, IL: InterVarsity.

Escobar, Samuel, and John Driver. 1978. *Christian Mission and Social Justice*. Scottdale, PA: Herald.

Eskilt, Ingrid. 2005. "An Analysis of Changing Perspectives on the Understanding of the Missionary Call in the Mission Covenant Church of Norway." PhD diss., Trinity Evangelical Divinity School, Deerfield, Illinois.

"The Evangelical-Roman Catholic Dialogue on Mission, 1977–1984: A Report." 1986. *International Bulletin of Missionary Research* 10 (January): 2–21.

Evangelicals for Social Action. n.d. "Core Values." http://www.esa-online.org/Display.asp?Page=aCoreValues (accessed December 27, 2007).

Farquhar, J. N. 1913. *The Crown of Hinduism*. Oxford: Oxford University Press.

Fee, Gordon. 1987. *The First Epistle to the Corinthians*. The New International Commentary on the New Testament. Grand Rapids: Eerdmans.

Ferguson, James J. 1984. "A Paradigm Shift in the Theology of Mission: Two Roman Catholic Perspectives." *International Bulletin of Missionary Research* 8 (July): 117–19.

Fernando, Ajith. 2007. "Getting Back on Course." *Christianity Today* 51 (November): 40–44.

Finley, Bob. 2005. *Reformation in Foreign Missions*. Longwood, FL: Xulon.

Fishburn, Janet F. 2004. "The Social Gospel as Missionary Ideology." In W. R. Shenk 2004, 218–42.

Flemming, Dean. 2005. *Contextualization in the New Testament: Patterns for Theology and Mission*. Downers Grove, IL: InterVarsity.

Forman, Charles W. 1977. "A History of Foreign Mission Theory in America." In *American Mission in Bicentennial Perspective*, ed. R. Pierce Beaver, 69–140. Pasadena, CA: William Carey.

Frankfurt Declaration on the Fundamental Crisis in Mission. 1970. Available online at http://www.institut-diakrisis.de/fd.pdf.

Freytag, Walter. 1940. "Das Ziel der Missionsarbeit." *Evangelische Missionszeitschrift* 1 (November): 305–8.

———. 1958. "Changes in the Patterns of Western Missions." In *The Ghana Assembly of the International Missionary Council*, ed. R. K. Orchard, 138–48. London: Edinburgh House.

———. 1961. *Reden und Aufsätze*. 2 vols. Munich: Kaiser.

Frost, Michael, and Alan Hirsch. 2003. *The Shaping of Things to Come: Innovation and Mission for the 21st-Century Church*. Peabody, MA: Hendrickson.

Fudge, Edward. 1994. *The Fire That Consumes: The Biblical Case for Conditional Mortality*. Ed. Pete Cousins. Rev. ed. Carlisle, England: Paternoster.

Fudge, Edward William, and Robert A. Peterson. 2000. *Two Views of Hell: A Biblical and Theological Dialogue*. Downers Grove, IL: InterVarsity.

Gannett, Alden A. 1960. "The Missionary Call—What Saith the Scriptures?" *Bibliotheca Sacra* 117 (January–March): 32–39.

Gatu, John. 1974. "Missionary, Go Home." In Underwood 1974, 71–72.

Geivett, R. Douglas, and W. Gary Phillips. 1995. "A Particularist View: An Evidentialist Approach." In *Four Views on Salvation in a Pluralistic World*, ed. Dennis L. Okholm and Timothy R. Phillips, 213–45. Grand Rapids: Zondervan.

Geldenhuys, Norval. 1977. *Commentary on the Gospel of Luke*. Grand Rapids: Eerdmans.

Gensichen, Hans-Werner. 1971. *Glaube für die Welt: Theologische Aspekte der Mission*. Gütersloh: Gerd Mohn.

Gerber, Virgil, ed. 1971. *Missions in Creative Tension: The Green Lake '71 Compendium*. Pasadena, CA: William Carey.

Gibbs, Eddie. 2000. *Church Next: Quantum Changes in Christian Ministry*. Downers Grove, IL: InterVarsity.

Gilliland, Dean S. 1989. "New Testament Contextualization: Continuity and Particularity in Paul's Theology." In *The Word among Us: Contextualizing Theology for Mission Today*, ed. Dean S. Gilliland, 9–31. Dallas: Word.

———. 2005. "Incarnation as Matrix for Appropriate Theologies." In *Appropriate Christianity*, ed. Charles H. Kraft, 493–519. Pasadena, CA: William Carey.

Glasser, Arthur F. 1976. "The Apostle Paul and the Missionary Task." In *Crucial Dimensions in World Evangelization*, ed. Arthur F. Glasser et al., 32–33. Pasadena, CA: William Carey.

———. 1989. "Old Testament Contextualization: Revelation and Its Environment." In Gilliland 1989, 32–51.

Glasser, Arthur F., and Donald A. McGavran. 1983. *Contemporary Theologies of Mission*. Grand Rapids: Baker Academic.

Glasser, Arthur F., with Charles E. van Engen, Dean S. Gilliland, and Shawn B. Redford. 2003. *Announcing the Kingdom: The Story of God's Mission in the Bible*. Grand Rapids: Baker Academic.

Glover, Robert Hall. 1948. *The Bible Basis of Missions*. Chicago: Moody.

Gnanakan, Ken R. 1989. *Kingdom Concerns: A Biblical Exploration Towards a Theology of Mission*. Bangalore: Theological Book Trust.

Goheen, Michael W. 2002. "The Missional Church: Discussion in the Gospel and Our Culture Network in North America." *Missiology* 30 (October): 479–90.

Goodall, Norman. 1964. *Christian Mission and Social Ferment*. London: Epworth.

———, ed. 1968. *The Uppsala Report 1968*. Geneva: World Council of Churches.

Gration, John. 1984. "Willowbank to Zaire: The Doing of Theology." *Missiology* 12 (July): 295–309.

Green, Joel B. 1994. "Good News to Whom? Jesus and the Poor in the Gospel of Luke." In *Jesus of Nazareth, Lord and Christ: Essays on the Historical Jesus and New Testament Christology*, ed. Joel B. Green and Max Turner, 59–74. Grand Rapids: Eerdmans.

Green, Keith. 1982. *Why You Should Go to the Mission Field*. Lindale, TX: Last Days Ministries.

Greene, Colin J. D. 2002. "Trinitarian Tradition and the Cultural Collapse of Late Modernity." In *A Scandalous Prophet: The Way of Mission after Lesslie Newbigin*, ed. Thomas F. Foust et al., 65–72. Grand Rapids: Eerdmans.

Griffiths, Michael C. 1985. "Today's Missionary, Yesterday's Apostle." *Evangelical Missions Quarterly* 21 (April): 154–65.

Guder, Darrell L. 1994. "Incarnation and the Church's Evangelistic Mission." *International Review of Mission* 83 (July): 417–28.

———, ed. 1998. *Missional Church: A Vision for the Sending of the Church in North America*. Grand Rapids: Eerdmans.

Günther, Wolfgang. 2003. "The History and Significance of World Mission Conferences in the 20th Century." *International Review of Mission* 92 (October): 521–37.

Guthrie, Stan. 2002. "New Paradigms for Churches and Mission Agencies." *Mission Frontiers* 24 (January–February): 6–8.

Gutiérrez, Gustavo. 1973. *A Theology of Liberation*. Maryknoll, NY: Orbis.

Haas, Odo. 1971. *Paulus der Missionar*. Münsterschwarzach: Vier-Türme-Verlag.

Hackett, Stuart C. 1984. *The Reconstruction of the Christian Revelation Claim*. Grand Rapids: Baker Academic.

Haggerty, Bridget. 2006. "St. Brendan, The Navigator." http://www.irishcultureandcustoms.com/ASaints/BrendanNav.html (accessed October 27, 2008).

Hahn, Ferdinand. 1965. *Mission in the New Testament*. London: SCM.

Hammett, John S. 2000. "How Church and Parachurch Should Relate: Arguments for a Servant-Partnership Model." *Missiology* 28 (April): 199–207.

Harris, Murray J. 1976. "2 Corinthians." In *The Expositor's Bible Commentary*, ed. Frank Gaebelein, 10. Grand Rapids: Eerdmans.

Harrison, Everett F. 1975. *Acts: The Expanding Church*. Chicago: Moody.

Hartenstein, Karl. 1933. *Die Mission als theologisches Problem*. Berlin: Furche Verlag.

Harvey, John D. 1998. "Mission in Jesus' Teaching." In Larkin and Williams 1998, 39–40.

Hatcher, Mark J. 2001. "Poetry, Singing and Contextualization." *Missiology* 29 (October): 475–87.

Hegeman, David Bruce. 2004. *Plowing in Hope: Toward a Biblical Theology of Culture*. Rev. ed. Moscow, Idaho: Canon.

Heim, S. Mark. 2001. *The Depth of Riches: A Trinitarian Theology of Religious Ends*. Grand Rapids: Eerdmans.

Hengel, Martin. 1983. "The Origins of Christian Mission." In *Between Jesus and Paul: Studies in the Earliest History of Christianity*, ed. Martin Hengel, 48–64, 166–79. London: SCM.

Hesselgrave, David M. 1980. *Planting Churches Cross-Culturally*. Grand Rapids: Baker Academic.

———. 1990. "Holes in 'Holistic Mission.'" *Trinity World Forum* 15 (Spring): 1–5.

———. 1999. "Redefining Holism." *Evangelical Missions Quarterly* 35 (July): 278–84.

———. 2005. *Paradigms in Conflict: 10 Key Questions in Christian Missions Today*. Grand Rapids: Kregel.

———. 2006. "Syncretism: Mission and Missionary Induced?" In Van Rheenen 2006, 71–98.

Hesselgrave, David J., and Edward Rommen. 1989. *Contextualization: Meaning, Methods, and Models*. Grand Rapids: Baker Academic.

Heufelder, Emmanuel. 1983. *The Way to God: According to the Rule of Saint Benedict*. Kalamazoo, MI: Cistercian.

Hibbert, Richard Yates. 2009. "The Place of Church Planting in Mission: Towards a Theological Framework." *Evangelical Review of Theology* 33 (October): 316–31.

Hick, John. 1989. *An Interpretation of Religion*. New Haven: Yale University Press.

———. 1995. *A Christian Theology of Religions: The Rainbow of Faiths*. Louisville: Westminster John Knox.

Hick, John, and Brian Hebblethwaite, eds. 1981. *Christianity and Other Religions: Selected Readings*. Philadelphia: Fortress.

Hick, John, and Paul F. Knitter, eds. 1987. *The Myth of Christian Uniqueness*. Maryknoll, NY: Orbis.

Hiebert, Paul G. 1982a. "The Flaw of the Excluded Middle." *Missiology* 10 (January): 33–47.

———. 1982b. "The Bicultural Bridge." *Mission Focus* 10 (1): 1–6.

———. 1985. *Anthropological Insights for Missionaries*. Grand Rapids: Baker Academic.

———. 1987. "Critical Contextualization." *International Bulletin of Missionary Research* 11 (July): 104–12.

———. 1999. "Cultural Differences and the Communication of the Gospel." In Winter and Hawthorne 1999, 373–83.

———. 2008. *Transforming Worldviews: An Anthropological Understanding of How People Change*. Grand Rapids: Baker Academic.

Hiebert, Paul G., and Eloise Hiebert Meneses. 1995. *Incarnational Ministry*. Grand Rapids: Baker Academic.

Hilary, Mbachu. 1995. *Inculturation Theology of the Jerusalem Council in Acts 15: An Interpretation of the Igbo Church Today*. Frankfurt am Main: Peter Lang.

Hill, Harriet. 1990. "Incarnational Ministry: A Critical Examination." *Evangelical Missions Quarterly* 26 (April): 196–201.

———. 1993. "Lifting the Fog on Incarnational Ministry." *Evangelical Missions Quarterly* 29 (July): 262–69.

Hillman, Eugene. 1968. *The Wider Ecumenism: Anonymous Christianity and the Church*. New York: Herder & Herder.

Hirsch, Alan. 2006. *The Forgotten Ways: Reactivating the Missional Church*. Grand Rapids: Brazos.

Hoekendijk, Johannes Christiaan. 1952. "The Church in Missionary Thinking." *International Review of Mission* 41 (July): 324–36.

———. 1966. *The Church Inside Out*. Philadelphia: Westminster.

———. 1967. *Kirche und Volk in der deutschen Missionswissenschaft*. Munich: Kaiser.

Hoffman, George. 1975. "The Social Responsibilities of Evangelization." In Douglas 1975, 698–709.

Holloway, Richard. 1982. *Signs of Glory*. London: Darton, Longman & Todd.

Holste, Scott, and Jim Haney. 2006. "The Global Status of Evangelical Christianity: A Model for Assessing Priority People Groups." *Mission Frontiers* 28 (January–February): 8–13.

Howard, David M. 2004. "Can a WASP Really Identify with Another Culture?" *Evangelical Missions Quarterly* 40 (April): 178–81.

Howard, Kevin L. 2003. "A Call to Missions: Is There Such a Thing?" *Evangelical Missions Quarterly* 39 (October): 462–65.

Howell, Don N. 1997. "Confidence in the Spirit as the Governing Ethos of the Pauline Mission." In McConnell 1997, 36–65.

———. 1998. "Mission in Paul's Epistles: Theological Bearings." In Larkin and Williams 1998, 92–116.

Huffard, Everett W. 1991. "Eschatology and the Mission of the Church." *Restoration Quarterly* 33 (1): 1–11.

Hunsberger, George R., and Craig Van Gelder, eds. 1996. *The Church between Gospel and Culture*. Grand Rapids: Eerdmans.

Hunter, George R., III. 2000. *The Celtic Way of Evangelism: How Christianity Can Reach the West Again*. Nashville: Abingdon.

Huntington, Samuel P. 1997. *The Clash of Civilizations and the Remaking of World Order*. New York: Touchstone.

Hurtado, Larry W. 2003. *Lord Jesus Christ: Devotion to Jesus in Earliest Christianity*. Grand Rapids: Eerdmans.

Jaffarian, Michael. 2004. "Are There More Non-Western Missionaries than Western Missionaries?" *International Bulletin of Missionary Research* 28 (July): 131–32.

———. 2008. "The Statistical State of North American Protestant Missions Movement from the *Mission Handbook*, 20th Edition." *International Bulletin of Missionary Research* 32 (January): 35–38.

Johnson, L. T. 1992. *The Acts of the Apostles*. Sacra Pagina. Collegeville, MN: Liturgical.

Johnston, Arthur. 1978. *The Battle for World Evangelism*. Wheaton: Tyndale House.

Johnstone, Patrick. 1995. "Biblical Intercession: Spiritual Power to Change Our World." In Rommen 1995, 137–63.

Jongeneel, Jan. 1991. "The Missiology of Gisbertus Voetius: The First Comprehensive Protestant Theology of Missions." *Calvin Theological Journal* 26 (April): 47–79.

———. 1995–97. *Philosophy, Science, and Theology of Mission in the 19th and 20th Centuries: A Missiological Encyclopedia*. New York: Peter Lang.

Jordan, Ivan, and Frank Tucker. 2002. "Using Indigenous Art to Communicate the Christian Message." *Evangelical Missions Quarterly* 38 (July): 302–9.

Kähler, Martin. [1908] 1971. *Schriften zur Christologie und Mission*. Munich: Christian Kaiser.

Kaiser, Walter C., Jr. 1999. "Israel's Missionary Call." In Winter and Hawthorne 1999, 10–16.

———. 2000. *Mission in the Old Testament: Israel as a Light to the Nations*. Grand Rapids: Baker Academic.

Kane, J. Herbert. 1974. *Understanding Christian Mission*. Grand Rapids: Baker Academic.

Kaplan, Steven. 1984. *The Monastic Holy Man and the Christianization of Early Solomonic Ethiopia*. Wiesbaden: Steiner.

Kärkkäinen, Veli-Matti. 2003. *An Introduction to the Theology of Religions*. Downers Grove, IL: InterVarsity.

Kaufman, Gordon D. 1987. "Religious Diversity, Historical Consciousness, and Christian Theology." In Hick and Knitter 1987, 3–15.

King, Roberta, Jean Ngoya Kidula, James R. Krabill, and Thomas A. Oduro. 2008. *Music in the Life of the African Church.* Waco, TX: Baylor University Press.

Kirk, Andrew. 1983. *A New World Coming: A Fresh Look at the Gospel for Today.* Basingstoke, England: Marshall, Morgan & Scott.

———. 2000. *What Is Mission? Theological Explorations.* Minneapolis: Fortress.

Kitchen, Kenneth. 1977. *The Bible in Its World: The Bible and Archaeology Today.* Downers Grove, IL: InterVarsity.

Knapp, Henry M. 1998. "The Character of Puritan Missions: The Motivation, Methodology, and Effectiveness of the Puritan Evangelization of the Native Americans of New England." *Journal of Presbyterian History* 76 (Summer): 111–26.

Knitter, Paul F. 2002. *Introducing Theologies of Religions.* Maryknoll, NY: Orbis.

Köstenberger, Andreas J. 1998a. *The Missions of Jesus and the Disciples according to the Fourth Gospel.* Grand Rapids: Eerdmans.

———. 1998b. "Mission in the General Epistles." In Larkin and Williams 1998, 189–206.

Köstenberger, Andreas J., and Peter T. O'Brien. 2001. *Salvation to the Ends of the Earth: A Biblical Theology of Mission.* Downers Grove, IL: InterVarsity.

Koyama, Kosuke. 1974. "What Makes a Missionary?" In *Mission Trends No. 1: Critical Issues in Mission Today,* ed. Gerald H. Anderson and Thomas F. Stransky, 117–32. New York: Paulist Press.

Kraemer, Hendrik. 1938. *The Christian Message in a Non-Christian World.* New York: Harper & Brothers.

Kraft, Charles H. 1989. *Christianity with Power.* Ann Arbor, MI: Servant Books.

———. 1992. *Defeating Dark Angels.* Ann Arbor, MI: Servant Books.

———. 1995. "'Christian Animism' or God-Given Authority?" In Rommen 1995, 88–136.

———. 2000. "Power Encounter." In Moreau 2000a.

———. 2002a. "Contemporary Trends in the Treatment of Spiritual Conflict." In Moreau et. al. 2002, 177–202.

———. 2002b. "Contextualization and Spiritual Power." In Moreau et al. 2002, 290–308.

Kraft, Marguerite. 2002. "Spiritual Conflict and the Mission of the Church: Contextualization." In Moreau et al. 2002, 276–89.

Kramm, Thomas. 1979. *Analyse und Bewährung theologischer Modelle zur Begründung der Mission.* Aachen: Missio Aktuell.

Kraybill, Donald B. 2003. *The Upside-Down Kingdom.* Scottdale, PA: Herald.

Ladd, George Eldon. [1959] 1992. *The Gospel of the Kingdom.* Grand Rapids: Eerdmans.

Lambert, J. C. 1955. "Apostle." In *International Standard Bible Encyclopedia,* ed. James Orr, 202–4. Grand Rapids, Eerdmans.

Langmead, Ross. 2002. "Ecomissiology." *Missiology* 30 (October): 505–18.

———. 2004. *The Word Made Flesh: Towards an Incarnational Missiology.* New York: University Press of America.

Larkin, William J. 1996. "Mission." In *Evangelical Dictionary of Biblical Theology.* Grand Rapids: Baker Academic.

———. 2005. "The Relevance of Jesus as the Source of Salvation and Mission for the Twenty-First Century Global Context." In Barnett and Pocock 2005, 101–17.

Larkin, William J., and Joel F. Williams, eds. 1998. *Mission in the New Testament: An Evangelical Approach.* Maryknoll, NY: Orbis.

Lausanne Committee for World Evangelization, no. 2. 1978. "The Willowbank Report: Consultation on Gospel and Culture." http://www.lausanne.org/willowbank-1978/lop-2.html (accessed February 27, 2009).

———, no. 21. 1982. "Evangelism and Social Responsibility: An Evangelical Commitment." http://www.lausanne.org/grand-rapids-1982/lop-21.html (accessed November 25, 2008).

Lausanne Covenant. 1974. Available online at http://www.lausanne.org/covenant.

Lausanne Occasional Paper no. 51. 2004. "Reconciliation as the Mission of God." available online at http://www.lausanne.org/documents/2004forum/LOP51_IG22.pdf.

Legrand, Lucien. 1990. *Unity and Plurality: Mission in the Bible.* Maryknoll, NY: Orbis.

Lewis, C. S. 1944. *The Problem of Pain*. New York: Macmillan.

———. 1961. *The Screwtape Letters*. New York: Macmillan.

Lindbeck, George A. 1984. *Nature of Doctrine: Religion and Theology in a Postliberal Age*. Philadelphia: Westminster.

Lindsell, Harold. 1955. *Missionary Principles and Practices*. Westwood, NJ: Revell.

Lingenfelter, Judith E., and Sherwood G. Lingenfelter. 2003. *Teaching Cross-Culturally*. Grand Rapids: Baker Academic.

Lingenfelter, Sherwood. 2008. *Leading Cross Culturally*. Grand Rapids, Baker Academic.

Linhart, George. 1971. "IFMA Missions and Sending (Supporting) Churches—A Pastor's Viewpoint." In Gerber 1971, 52–56.

Little, Christopher R. 2000. *The Revelation of God among the Unevangelized*. Pasadena, CA: William Carey.

———. 2005. *Mission in the Way of Paul: Biblical Mission for the Church in the Twenty-First Century*. New York: Peter Lang.

Livermore, David. 2004. "AmeriCAN or AmeriCAN'T? A Critical Analysis of Western Training to the World." *Evangelical Missions Quarterly* 40 (October): 458–66.

Long, Charles, Jr. 1950. "Christian Vocation and the Missionary Call." *International Review of Missions* 39 (October): 409–17.

Lowe, Chuck. 1998. *Territorial Spirits and World Evangelisation?* Sevenoaks/Kent, Great Britain: Mentor/OMF.

Lutheran World Federation. 2004. *Mission in Context: Transformation, Reconciliation, Empowerment*. Geneva: Lutheran World Federation.

MacDonald, Gordon. 1971. "Report for Pastor Delegates." In Gerber 1971, 372–74.

MacDonald, Gregory. 2006. *The Evangelical Universalist*. Eugene, OR: Cascade Books.

Manila Manifesto. 1989. Available online at http://www.lausanne.org/manila-1989/manila-manifesto.html.

Mare, W. Harold. 1973. "Cultural Mandate and the New Testament Gospel Imperative." *Journal of the Evangelical Theological Society* 16 (3): 139–47.

Martin, George H. 2004. "The God Who Reveals Mysteries: Dreams and World Evangelization." *Southern Baptist Journal of Theology* 8 (1): 60–72.

Marshall, I. Howard. 1985. "New Testament Perspectives on War." *Evangelical Quarterly* 57 (April): 115–32.

———. 2003. "The New Testament Does *Not* Teach Universal Salvation." In Parry and Partridge 2003, 55–76.

Matthey, Jacques. 2005. "Versöhnung im ökumenischen missionstheologischen Diskurs." *Zeitschrift für Mission* 31:174–91.

McConnell, C. Douglas, ed. 1997. *The Holy Spirit in Mission Dynamics*. EMS Series, no. 5. Pasadena, CA: William Carey.

McConnell, Walter. 2007. "The Missionary Call: A Biblical and Practical Appraisal." *Evangelical Missions Quarterly* 43 (April): 210–16.

McDaniel, Ferris L. 1998. "Mission in the Old Testament." In Larkin and Williams 1998, 11–20.

McDermott, Gerald R. 2000. *Can Evangelicals Learn from World Religions?* Downers Grove, IL: InterVarsity.

McElhanon, Kenneth. 1991. "Don't Give Up on the Incarnational Model." *Evangelical Missions Quarterly* 27 (October): 390–93.

McGavran, Donald A. [1970] 1980. *Understanding Church Growth*. Rev. ed. Grand Rapids: Eerdmans.

McGee, Gary B. 1986. *This Gospel Shall Be Preached: A History and Theology of Assemblies of God Foreign Missions to 1959*. Springfield, MO: Gospel Publishing House.

———. 1991. "Pentecostals and Their Various Strategies for Global Mission: A Historical Assessment." In *Called and Empowered: Global Mission in Pentecostal Perspective*, ed. Murray A. Dempster, Byron D. Klaus, and Douglas Petersen, 203–24. Peabody, MA: Hendrickson.

———. 1997. "The Radical Strategy in Modern Mission: The Linkage of Paranormal Phenomena with Evangelism." In McConnell 1997, 69–95.

McKinney Douglas, Lois. 2000. "Single Missionary." In Moreau 2000a.

McLaren, Brian D. 1998. *The Church on the Other Side*. Grand Rapids: Zondervan.

349

McQuilkin, J. Robertson. 1993. "An Evangelical Assessment of Mission Theology of the Kingdom of God." In Van Engen, Gilliland, and Pierson 1993, 172–78.

———. 1997. "The Role of the Holy Spirit in Missions." In McConnell 1997, 22–35.

McQuilkin, Kent. 1990. "Initial Findings in the Major Motivational Factors Influencing Evangelicals to Become Career Missionaries." MA thesis, Trinity Evangelical Divinity School, Deerfield, Illinois.

Meek, Donald E. 2000. *The Quest for Celtic Christianity*. Edinburgh: Handsel.

Merkel, Franz Rudolf. 1920. *G. W. von Leibniz: Eine Untersuchung über die Anfänge der protestantischen Missionsbewegung*. Missionswissenschaftliche Forschungen 1. Leipzig: Hinrichs.

Metcalf, Samuel F. 1993. "When Local Churches Act like Agencies." *Evangelical Missions Quarterly* 29 (April): 142–49.

Minatrea, Milfred. 2004. *Shaped by God's Heart: The Passion and Practices of Missional Churches*. San Francisco: Jossey-Bass.

Miyamoto, Ken Christoph. 2008. "Worship Is Nothing but Mission: A Reflection on Some Japanese Experiences." In Walls and Ross 2008, 157–64.

Mohler, R. Albert Jr. 2004. "Modern Theology: The Disappearance of Hell." In Morgan and Peterson 2004, 15–41.

Montgomery, James H. 1980. *Discipling of a Nation*. Santa Clara, CA: Global Church Growth Bulletin.

Moo, Douglas J. 2004. "Paul on Hell." In Morgan and Peterson 2004, 91–109.

Moon, Jay. 2004. "Sweet Talk in Africa: Using Proverbs in Ministry." *Evangelical Missions Quarterly* 40 (April): 162–69.

Moreau, A. Scott. 1997. *Essentials of Spiritual Warfare*. Wheaton: Shaw.

———, ed. 2000a. *Evangelical Dictionary of World Missions*. Grand Rapids: Baker Academic.

———. 2000b. "Syncretism." In Moreau 2000a.

———. 2000c. "Option for the Poor." In Moreau 2000a.

———. 2002. "Gaining Perspective on Territorial Spirits." In Moreau et al. 2002, 259–75.

———. 2004. "Putting the Survey in Perspective." In *Missions Handbook 2004–2006*, ed. Dotsey Welliver and Minnette Northcutt, 11–64. Wheaton: Evangelism and Missions Information Service.

———. 2005. "Contextualization." In *The Changing Face of World Missions*, by Michael Pocock, Gailyn Van Rheenen, and Douglas McConnell, 321–48. Grand Rapids: Baker Academic.

———. 2006. "Contextualization That Is Comprehensive." *Missiology* 34 (July): 325–35.

———. 2007. "Putting the Survey in Perspective." In *Missions Handbook 2007–2009*, ed. Linda Weber and Dotsey Welliver, 11–75. Wheaton: Evangelism and Missions Information Service.

Moreau, A. Scott, Tokunboh Adeyemo, David G. Burnett, Bryant L. Myers, Hwa Yung, eds. 2002. *Deliver Us from Evil: An Uneasy Frontier in Christian Mission*. Monrovia, CA: MARC World Vision Publications.

Moreau, A. Scott, Gary R. Corwin, and Gary B. McGee. 2004. *Introducing World Missions*. Grand Rapids: Baker Academic.

Moreau, A. Scott, and Mike O'Rear. 2002. "Missions on the Web: Missions and Arts on the Web." *Evangelical Missions Quarterly* 38 (July): 364–71.

———. 2004. "Mission Resources on the Web: And So the Story Goes . . . Web Resources on Storytelling, Myths and Proverbs." *Evangelical Missions Quarterly* 20 (April): 236–42.

———. 2008. "Mission Resources on the Web: A Proverbial Gold Mine." *Evangelical Missions Quarterly* 44 (July): 376–80.

Morgan, Christopher W. 2004. "Annihilationism: Will the Unsaved Be Punished Forever?" In Morgan and Peterson 2004, 195–218.

Morgan, Christopher W., and Robert A. Peterson, eds. 2004. *Hell under Fire: Modern Scholarship Reinvents Eternal Punishment*. Grand Rapids: Zondervan.

Morris, Leon. 1971. *The Gospel according to John*. Grand Rapids: Eerdmans.

Müller, Karl. 1987. *Mission Theology: An Introduction.* Translated from the German by Francis Mansfeld. Nettetal: Steyler.

———, ed. 1997a. *Dictionary of Mission: Theology, History, Perspectives.* Maryknoll, NY: Orbis.

———. 1997b. "Inculturation." In Müller 1997a.

Müller, Max. 1964. *Origin and Growth of Religion.* Varanasi: Indological Book House.

Murphy, Ed. 1992. *The Handbook of Spiritual Warfare.* Nashville, TN: Thomas Nelson.

Murphy, Edward F. 1974. "Missionary Society as an Apostolic Team." *Missiology* 4 (January): 103–18.

Murray, George. 2005. "Is Jesus Christ Really the Only Way?" In Barnett and Pocock 2005, 19–36.

Murray, Stuart. 2001. *Church Planting: Laying Foundations.* Scotsdale, PA: Herald.

Musk, Bill. 1988. "Dreams and the Ordinary Muslim." *Missiology* 16 (April): 163–72.

Myklebust, Olav Guttorm. 1955, 1957. *The Study of Missions in Theological Education.* 2 vols. Oslo: Egede Instituttet.

Nash, Ronald H. 1994. *Is Jesus the Only Savior?* Grand Rapids: Zondervan.

Nazir-Ali, Michael. 1990. *From Everywhere to Everywhere: A World View of Christian Mission.* London: Collins/Flame.

Neely, Alan. 2000. "Incarnational Mission." In Moreau 2000a.

Neill, Stephen. 1959. *Creative Tension.* London: Morrison & Gibb.

———. 1964. *A History of Christian Missions.* Baltimore: Penguin Books.

———. 1966. *Colonialism and Christian Missions.* New York: McGraw-Hill.

Netland, Harold A. 1991. *Dissonant Voices: Religious Pluralism and the Question of Truth.* Vancouver, BC: Regent College Publishing.

———. 2001. *Encountering Religious Pluralism: The Challenge to Christian Faith and Mission.* Downers Grove, IL: InterVarsity.

———. 2005. "Mission and Jesus in a Globalizing World: Mission as Retrieval." In Barnett and Pocock 2005, 145–64.

———. 2006. "Introduction." In Ott and Netland 2006, 14–34.

Newbigin, Lesslie. 1954. *The Household of God.* New York: Friendship.

———. [1963] 1998. *Trinitarian Doctrine for Today's Mission.* Biblical Classics Library. Carlisle, England: Paternoster.

———. 1965. "From the Editor." *International Review of Missions* 54 (October): 417–27.

———. 1966. *Honest Religion for Secular Man.* Philadelphia: Westminster Press.

———. 1969. *The Finality of Christ.* Richmond, VA: John Knox.

———. [1978] 1995. *The Open Secret: An Introduction to the Theology of Mission.* Rev. ed. Grand Rapids: Eerdmans.

———. 1989. *The Gospel in a Pluralist Society.* Grand Rapids: Eerdmans.

———. 1994. *A Word in Season: Perspectives on Christian World Mission.* Ed. Eleanor Jackson. Grand Rapids: Eerdmans.

———. 1997. "The Dialogue of Gospel and Culture: Reflections on the Conference on World Mission and Evangelism, Salvador, Bahia, Brazil." *International Bulletin of Missionary Research* 21 (April): 50–52.

Newport, John P. 1989. *Life's Ultimate Questions.* Dallas: Word.

Niringiye, D. Zac. 2008. "To Proclaim the Good News of the Kingdom (ii)." In Walls and Ross 2008, 11–24.

Noel, Jana. 2002. "Education toward Cultural Shame: A Century of Native American Education." *Educational Foundations* 16 (Winter): 19–32.

Noll, Mark A. 1997. *Turning Points: Decisive Moments in the History of Christianity.* Grand Rapids: Baker Academic.

Oborji, Francis Anekwe. 2006. *Concepts of Mission.* Maryknoll, NY: Orbis.

O'Brien, Peter T. 1982. *Colossians, Philemon.* Word Biblical Commentary. Waco, TX: Word.

———. 1995. *Gospel and Mission in the Writings of Paul.* Grand Rapids: Baker.

Oehler, Wilhelm. 1949. *Geschichte der Deutschen Evangelischen Mission.* Vol. 1. Baden-Baden: Fehrholz.

Ohm, Thomas. 1962. *Machet zu Jüngern: Theorie der Mission*. Freiburg im Breisgau: Erich Wewel.

Okoye, James Chukwuma. 2006. *Israel and the Nations: A Mission Theology of the Old Testament*. Maryknoll, NY: Orbis.

Ollrog, Wolf-Henning. 1979. *Paulus und seine Mitarbeiter*. Neukirchen: Neukirchener Verlag.

O'Sullivan, John L. 1839. "The Great Nation of Futurity." *United States Democratic Review* 6 (23): 426–30. http://cdl.library.cornell.edu/cgi-bin/moa/moa-cgi?notisid=AGD1642-0006-46 (accessed November 25, 2008).

Ott, Craig. 1993. "Let the Buyer Beware: Financially Supporting National Pastors and Missionaries May Not Always Be the Bargain It's Cracked Up to Be." *Evangelical Missions Quarterly* 29 (July): 286–91.

———. 2006. "Conclusion: Globalizing Theology." In Ott and Netland 2006, 309–36.

Ott, Craig, and Harold A. Netland. 2006. *Globalizing Theology: Belief and Practice in an Era of World Christianity*. Grand Rapids: Baker Academic.

Padberg, Lutz von. 1995. *Mission und Christianisierung: Formen und Folgen bei Angelsachsen und Franken im 7. und 8. Jahrhundert*. Stuttgart: Franz Steiner.

Padilla, C. René. 1975. "Evangelism and the World." In Douglas 1975, 116–33.

———. 1980. "Hermeneutics and Culture: A Theological Perspective." In *Down to Earth*, ed. John Stott and Robert Coote, 63–78. Grand Rapids: Eerdmans.

———. 1983. "Biblical Foundations: A Latin American Study." *Evangelical Review of Theology* 7 (April): 79–88.

———. 1985. *Mission between the Times*. Grand Rapids: Eerdmans.

———. 2002. "Integral Mission and Its Historic Development." In *Justice, Mercy, and Humility: The Papers of the Micah Network International on Integral Mission and the Poor (2001)*, ed. Tim Chester, 42–58. Carlisle, England: Paternoster.

Panikkar, Raimundo. 1964. *The Unknown Christ of Hinduism*. London: Darton, Longman & Todd.

Parry, Robin A., and Christopher H. Partridge, eds. 2003. *Universal Salvation? The Current Debate*. Grand Rapids: Eerdmans.

Paton, David M., ed. 1975. *Breaking Barriers: Nairobi 1975; The Official Report of the Fifth Assembly of the World Council of Churches, Nairobi, 23 November–10 December 1975*. Grand Rapids: Eerdmans.

Patterson, James Alan. 1990. "The Loss of a Protestant Missionary Consensus: Foreign Missions and the Fundamentalist-Modernist Conflict." In Carpenter and Shenk 1990, 73–91.

Pentecost, Edward C. 1982. *Issues in Missiology: An Introduction*. Grand Rapids: Baker Academic.

Peskett, Howard. 1997. "Missions and Eschatology." In *Eschatology in Bible and Theology*, ed. Kent E. Brower and Mark W. Elliot, 301–22. Downers Grove, IL: InterVarsity.

Peters, George W. 1972. *A Biblical Theology of Missions*. Chicago: Moody.

Phillips, Mike. 1998. "Congregational-Direct Missions Represented." *Mission Frontiers* 20 (March–April): 43–44.

Phillips, Woody. 1985. "Your Church Can Train and Send Missionaries." *Evangelical Missions Quarterly* 21 (April): 196–201.

Pierson, Paul E. 1998. "Local Churches in Mission: What's Behind the Impatience with Traditional Mission Agencies?" *International Bulletin of Missionary Research* 22 (1998): 146–50.

———. 2003. "Lessons in Mission from the Twentieth Century: Conciliar Missions." In Bonk 2003, 67–84.

———. 2009. *The Dynamics of Christian Mission*. Pasadena: William Carey.

Pinnock, Clark H. 1992. *A Wideness in God's Mercy: The Finality of Jesus Christ in a World of Religions*. Grand Rapids: Zondervan.

Piper, John. 1993. *Let the Nations Be Glad!* Grand Rapids: Baker Academic.

———. 2003. *Let the Nations Be Glad!* 2nd ed. Grand Rapids: Baker Academic.

Plueddemann, James E. 1991. "Culture, Learning and Missionary Training." In *Internationalising Missionary Training*, ed. William Taylor, 217–30. Grand Rapids: Baker Academic.

———. 2006. "Theological Implications of Globalizing Missions." In Ott and Netland 2006, 250–66.

Plummer, Robert L. 2006. *Paul's Understanding of the Church's Mission*. Waynesboro, PA: Paternoster.

Powlison, David. 1995. *Power Encounters: Reclaiming Spiritual Warfare*. Grand Rapids: Baker Academic.

Priest, Robert J. 2008. "U.S. Megachurches and New Patterns of Global Mission." Research report given at Trinity Evangelical Divinity School, June 2008, Deerfield, Illinois.

Priest, Robert J., Thomas Campbell, and Bradford A. Mullen. 1995. "Missiological Syncretism: The New Animistic Paradigm." In Rommen 1995, 9–87.

Race, Alan. 1982. *Christians and Religious Pluralism*. Maryknoll, NY: Orbis.

Rahner, Karl. 1966–83. *Theological Investigations*. 20 vols. New York: Seabury.

———. 1981. "Christianity and the Non-Christian Religions." In Hick and Hebblethwaite 1981, 52–79.

Ramachandra, Vinoth. 1996. *The Recovery of Mission: Beyond the Pluralist Paradigm*. Grand Rapids: Eerdmans.

Ramsey, Arthur Michael. 1960. *An Era of Anglican Theology: From Gore to Temple*. London: Longmans.

Redemptoris Missio: On the Permanent Validity of the Church's Missionary Mandate. Available online at http://www.vatican.va/holy_father/john_paul_ii/encyclicals/documents/hf_jp-ii_enc_07121990_redemptoris-missio_en.html.

Richardson, Don. 1974. *Peace Child*. Ventura, CA: Regal Books.

———. 1981. *Eternity in Their Hearts*. Ventura, CA: Regal Books.

Richelbächer, Wilhelm. 2003. "*Missio Dei*: Basis of Mission Theology or a Wrong Path?" *International Review of Mission* 92 (October): 588–605.

Richter, Martin. 1928. *Der Missionsgedanke im evangelischen Deutschland des 18. Jahrhunderts*. Leipzig: Hinrichs.

Riesner, Rainer. 1998. *Paul: The Early Years*. Grand Rapids: Eerdmans.

Ringma, Charles. 2004. "Holistic Ministry and Mission: A Call for Reconceptualization." *Missiology* 32 (October): 431–48.

Robb, John D. 1999. "Strategic Prayer." In Winter and Hawthorne 1999, 145–51.

Robert, Dana L. 2000. "Shifting Southward: Global Christianity since 1945." *International Bulletin of Missionary Research* 24 (April): 50–58.

———. 2003. *Occupy until I Come: A. T. Pierson and the Evangelization of the World*. Grand Rapids: Eerdmans.

———, ed. 2008. *Converting Colonialism: Visions and Realities in Mission History, 1706–1914*. Grand Rapids: Eerdmans.

Robinson, Martin. 2004. "Pilgrimage and Mission." In *Explorations in a Christian Theology of Pilgrimage*, ed. Craig G. Bartholomew and Fred Hughes, 170–83. Aldershot, England: Ashgate.

Robinson, P. J. 1989. "Some Missiological Perspectives from 1 Peter 2:4–10." *Missionalia* 17 (November): 176–87.

Rommen, Edward. 1993. "The De-theologizing of Missiology." *Trinity World Forum* 19 (Fall): 1–4.

———, ed. 1995. *Spiritual Power and Missions: Raising the Issues*. EMS Series, no. 3. Pasadena, CA: William Carey.

Rooy, Sidney H. 1965. *The Theology of Missions in the Puritan Tradition*. Grand Rapids: Eerdmans.

Rowell, John. 1998. *Magnify Your Vision for the Small Church*. Atlanta: Northside Community Church.

Rowley, Harold H. 1944. *The Missionary Message of the Old Testament*. London: Carey Kingsgate.

Roxborogh, John. 2001. "After Bosch: The Future of Missiology." Princeton Currents in World Christianity Seminar, February 2, 2001. http://www.roxborogh.com/Articles/Missiology%20MAB.doc (accessed August 25, 2005).

Roxburgh, Alan J. 2000. "Rethinking Trinitarian Mission." In W. D. Taylor 2000a, 179–88.

———. 2004. "The Missional Church." *Theology Matters* 10 (September/October): 1–5.

353

Samuel, Vinay, and Chris Sugden, eds. 1987. *The Church in Response to Human Need: Papers from the Consultation on the Church in Response to Human Need, Held in Wheaton, Ill., in June 1983 and Sponsored by the World Evangelical Fellowship*. Grand Rapids: Eerdmans.

Sanders, John. 1992. *No Other Name: An Investigation into the Destiny of the Unevangelized*. Grand Rapids: Eerdmans.

Sanneh, Lamin. 1989. *Translating the Message: The Missionary Impact on Culture*. Maryknoll, NY: Orbis.

———. 1995. "The Gospel, Language and Culture: The Theological Method in Cultural Analysis." *International Review of Mission* 84 (January–April): 47–64.

———. 2003. *Whose Religion Is Christianity? The Gospel beyond the West*. Grand Rapids: Eerdmans.

———. 2008. *Disciples of All Nations: Pillars of World Christianity*. New York: Oxford University Press.

Scherer, James A. 1964. *Missionary Go Home! A Reappraisal of the Christian World Mission*. Englewood Cliffs, NJ: Prentice Hall.

———. 1990. "Why Mission Theology Cannot Do without Eschatological Urgency: The Significance of the End." *Missiology* 18 (October): 395–413.

———. 1993. "Church, Kingdom, and *Missio Dei*." In Van Engen, Gilliland, and Pierson 1993, 82–88.

Schineller, Peter. 1992. "Inculturation and Syncretism: What Is the Real Issue?" *International Bulletin of Missionary Research* 16 (April): 50–53.

Schlatter, Wilhelm. 1916. *Geschichte der Basler Mission, 1815–1915*. Vol. 1. *Die Heimatgeschichte der Basler Mission*. Basel: Verlag der Basler Missionsbuchhandlung.

Schnabel, Eckhard J. 2004. *Early Christian Mission*. 2 vols. Downers Grove, IL: InterVarsity.

———. 2008. *Paul the Missionary: Realities, Strategies and Methods*. Downers Grove, IL: InterVarsity.

Schomerus, H. W. 1935. "Bildung von Kirche als Aufgabe der Mission." *Neue allgemeine Missionszeitschrift* 12 (9): 289–312.

Schreiter, Robert J. 2005. "Reconciliation and Healing as a Paradigm for Mission." *International Review of Mission* 94 (January): 74–83.

Schultz, Richard. 1996. "'Und sie verkündigten meine Herrlichkeit unter den Nationen': Mission im Alten Testament unter besonderer Berücksichtigung von Jesaja." In *Werdet meine Zeugen*, ed. H. Kasdorf and F. Walldorf, 33–53. Neuhausen-Stuttgart: Hänssler.

Scobie, Charles H. H. 1992. "Israel and the Nations: An Essay in Biblical Theology." *Tyndale Bulletin* 43 (2): 283–305.

Seitz, Christopher R. 1991. *Zion's Final Destiny: The Development of the Book of Isaiah*. Philadelphia: Fortress.

Senior, Donald, and Carroll Stuhlmueller. 1983. *The Biblical Foundations for Mission*. Maryknoll, NY: Orbis.

Severn, Frank M. 2000. "Mission Societies: Are They Biblical?" *Evangelical Missions Quarterly* 36 (July): 320–26.

Sharpe, Eric. 1971. *The Theology of A. G. Hogg*. Madras: Christian Literature Society.

Shenk, Calvin E. 1997. *Who Do You Say That I Am? Christians Encounter Other Religions*. Scottdale, PA: Herald.

Shenk, Wilbert R. 1999. *Changing Frontiers of Mission*. Maryknoll, NY: Orbis.

———. 2001. "Recasting Theology of Mission: Impulses from the Non-Western World." *International Bulletin of Missionary Research* 25 (July): 98–107.

———, ed. 2004. *North American Foreign Missions, 1810–1914*. Grand Rapids: Eerdmans.

Shepherd, Jack F. 1971. "Church Mission Relations 'at Home.'" In Gerber 1971, 124–53.

Shorter, Aylward. 1988. *Toward a Theology of Inculturation*. Maryknoll, NY: Orbis.

Sider, Ronald J. 1993. *One-Sided Christianity? Uniting the Church to Heal a Lost and Broken World*. Grand Rapids: Zondervan.

Siewert, John A. 1997. "Growing Local Church Initiatives." In *Mission Handbook 1998–2000: U.S. and Canadian Ministries Overseas*, ed.

John A. Siewert and Edna G. Valdez, 17th ed., 57–72. Monrovia, CA: MARC.

Sills, M. David. 2008. *The Missionary Call.* Chicago: Moody.

Singh, Sadhu Sundar. 1922. *At the Master's Feet.* New York: Revell.

Skarsaune, Oskar, and Tormod Engelsviken. 2002. "Possession and Exorcism in the History of the Church." In Moreau et al. 2002, 65–87.

Slater, Thomas Ebenezer. 1902. *The Higher Hinduism in Relation to Christianity: Certain Aspects of Hindu Thought from the Christian Standpoint.* London: Elliot Stock.

Smith, Oswald J. 2002. "What Constitutes a Call? Is There Any Way of Knowing the Will of God? How Can One Be Sure?" *Frontlines* 1 (Winter). http://www.heartofgod.com/Frontlines1/Articles/Feature.asp (accessed November 26, 2008).

Snyder, Howard A. 1975. "The Church as God's Agent in Evangelism." In Douglas 1975, 327–51.

———. 1991. *Models of the Kingdom.* Nashville: Abingdon.

Sobrino, Jon. 1985. *Spirituality of Liberation: Towards Political Holiness.* Maryknoll, NY: Orbis.

Soneson, Jerome Paul. 1993. *Pragmatism and Pluralism.* Minneapolis: Fortress.

Speer, Robert E. 1902. *Missionary Principles and Practice.* New York: Revell.

Spohn, Elmar. 2000. *Mission und das kommende Reich.* Bad Liebenzell: Liebenzeller Mission.

Stamoolis, James J. 1986. *Eastern Orthodox Mission Theology Today.* Maryknoll, NY: Orbis.

———. 2000. "Orthodox Theology of Mission." In Moreau 2000a.

———. 2002. "The Nature of the Missionary Calling: A Retrospective Look to the Future." *Missiology* 30 (January): 3–14.

Stanley, Brian. 1992. "Planting Self-Governing Churches: British Baptist Ecclesiology in the Missionary Context." *Baptist Quarterly* 34 (October): 378–89.

———. 2003. "Where Have Our Mission Structures Come From?" *Transformation* 20 (January): 39–46.

Stetzer, Ed, and David Putman. 2006. *Breaking the Missional Code: Your Church Can Become a Missionary in Your Community.* Nashville: Broadman & Holman.

Stott, John R. W. 1975. *Christian Mission in the Modern World.* Downers Grove, IL: InterVarsity.

———. 1992. *The Contemporary Christian.* Downers Grove, IL: InterVarsity.

Strauss, Steve. 2005. "Kingdom Living: The Gospel on Our Lips and in Our Lives." *Evangelical Missions Quarterly* 41 (January): 58–63.

———. 2006a. "Creeds, Confessions and Global Theologizing." In Ott and Netland 2006, 140–56.

———. 2006b. "The Role of Context in Shaping Theology." In Van Rheenen 2006, 99–128.

———. 2007. "'And the Disciples Were Called Christians First in Antioch': The Significance of Acts 11:26 for Obeying Jesus in the Church at Antioch and Today." Paper presented at the Evangelical Theological Society Annual Meeting, November 15, 2007, San Diego.

Strong, A. H. 1909. *Systematic Theology.* Vol. 3. Philadelphia: Griffith Rowland.

Strong, David K., and Cynthia A. Strong. 2006. "The Globalizing Hermeneutic of the Jerusalem Council." In Ott and Netland 2006, 129–39.

Sulpitius Severus. 1894. *Life of Saint Martin.* In *A Select Library of Nicene and Post-Nicene Fathers of the Christian Church,* Second Series, Vol. 11. New York. http://www.users.scbsju.edu/~eknuth/npnf2-11/sulpitiu/lifeofst.html#tp (accessed August 21, 2008).

Sumner, George R. 2004. *The First and the Last: The Claim of Jesus Christ and the Claims of Other Religious Traditions.* Grand Rapids: Eerdmans.

Sundermeier, Theo. 2003. "*Missio Dei* Today: On the Identity of Christian Mission." *International Review of Mission* 92 (October): 560–78.

Sundkler, Bengt. 1936. "Jésus et les païens." *Revue d'Histoire et de Philosophie Religieuses* 16:462–99.

Swaisland, Cecillie. 1993. "Wanted—Earnest, Self-Sacrificing Women for Service in South Africa." In Bowie, Kirkwood, and Ardener 1993, 70–84.

Talbot, Thomas. 1999. *The Inescapable Love of God*. Parkland, FL: Universal.

———. 2003a. "Towards a Better Understanding of Universalism." In Parry and Partridge 2003, 3–14.

———. 2003b. "Reply to My Critics." In Parry and Partridge 2003, 247–73.

Tamrat, Taddesse. 1972. *Church and State in Ethiopia, 1270–1527*. Oxford: Clarendon.

Taylor, Dr. Howard, and Mrs. 1965. *J. Hudson Taylor: A Biography*. Chicago: Moody.

Taylor, William D., ed. 1997. *Too Valuable to Lose: Exploring the Causes and Cures of Missionary Attrition*. Pasadena, CA: William Carey.

———, ed. 2000a. *Global Missiology in the 21st Century*. Grand Rapids: Baker Academic.

———. 2000b. "Missionary." In Moreau 2000a.

Tennent, Timothy C. 2002. *Christianity at the Religious Roundtable*. Grand Rapids: Baker Academic.

———. 2006. "Followers of Jesus (Isa) in Islamic Mosques." *International Journal of Frontier Missions* 23 (Fall): 101–15.

———. 2007. *Theology in the Context of World Christianity*. Grand Rapids: Zondervan.

"Theology and Implications of Radical Discipleship." In Douglas 1975, 1294–96.

Thomas, John Christopher. 2002. "Spiritual Conflict in Illness and Affliction." In Moreau et al. 2002, 37–60.

Thomas, Juliet. 2002a. "Issues from the Indian Perspective." In Moreau et al. 2002, 146–51.

———. 2002b. "Worship, Praise, and Prayer." In Moreau et al. 2002, 231–42.

Thomas, M. M. [1972] 2002. "Salvation and Humanization." In *M. M. Thomas Reader*, ed. T. Jacob Thomas, 82–98. Thiruvalla, India: Christava Sahitya Samithy.

Thomas, Norman E. 2005. "Athens 2005: 'Come Holy Spirit—Heal and Reconcile.'" *Missiology* 33 (October): 451–60.

Thornton, Philip, and Jeremy Thornton. 2008. "Why They Don't Go: Surveying the Next Generation of Mission Workers." *Evangelical Missions Quarterly* 44 (April): 204–10.

Tiénou, Tite. 1987. "Evangelism and Social Transformation." In Samuel and Sugden 1987, 175–79.

———. 1993. "Forming Indigenous Theologies." In *Toward the 21st Century in Christian Mission*, ed. James Phillips and Robert Coote, 245–52. Grand Rapids: Eerdmans.

Tippet, Alan R. 1967. *Solomon Islands Christianity*. Pasadena, CA: William Carey.

Tiessen, Terry. 2007. "God's Work of Grace in the Context of the Religions." *Didaskalia* 18 (1): 165–91.

Trites, Allison A. 1977. *The New Testament Concept of Witness*. Cambridge: Cambridge University Press.

Tucker, Ruth A. 1988. *Guardians of the Great Commission: The Story of Women in Modern Missions*. Grand Rapids: Zondervan.

Turaki, Yusufu. 2000. "Evangelical Missiology from Africa: Strengths and Weaknesses." In W. D. Taylor 2000a, 271–83.

Underwood, Joel, ed. 1974. *The Future of the Missionary Enterprise: In Search of Mission, An IDOC Documentation Participation Project*. New York: IDOC International.

Van den Berg, Johannes. 1956. *Constrained by Jesus' Love*. Kampen: J. H. Kok.

Van Engen, Charles. 1991. *God's Missionary People*. Grand Rapids: Baker Academic.

Van Engen, Charles, Dean S. Gilliland, and Paul Pierson, eds. 1993. *The Good News of the Kingdom*. Maryknoll, NY: Orbis.

Van Gelder, Craig. 2000. *The Essence of the Church*. Grand Rapids: Baker Academic.

———. 2004. "From Corporate Church to Missional Church: The Challenge Facing Congregations Today." *Review and Expositor* 101 (Summer): 425–50.

———. 2007a. *The Ministry of the Missional Church: A Community Led by the Spirit*. Grand Rapids: Baker Academic.

———, ed. 2007b. *The Missional Church in Context: Helping Congregations Develop Contextual Ministry*. Grand Rapids: Eerdmans.

———, ed. 2008. *The Missional Church and Denominations: Helping Congregations Develop a Missional Identity*. Grand Rapids: Eerdmans.

Vanhoozer, Kevin J. 1998. *Is There Meaning in This Text?* Grand Rapids: Zondervan.

———. 2000. "The Voice and the Actor." In *Evangelical Futures: A Conversation on Theological Method*, ed. John G. Stackhouse Jr., 61–106. Grand Rapids: Baker Academic.

———. 2005. *The Drama of Doctrine: A Canonical-Linguistic Approach to Christian Theology*. Louisville: Westminster John Knox.

———. 2006. "'One Rule to Rule Them All?' Theological Method in an Era of World Christianity." In Ott and Netland 2006, 85–126.

Van Rheenen, Gailyn. 2005. "Theology of Power." *Evangelical Missions Quarterly* 41 (January): 32–38.

———, ed. 2006. *Contextualization and Syncretism: Navigating Cultural Differences*. EMS Series, no. 13. Pasadena, CA: William Carey.

Van Rooy, J. A. 1985. "Christ and the Religions: The Issues at Stake." *Missionalia* 13 (April): 3–13.

Vatican II. *Gaudium et Spes*. Available at http://www.vatican.va/archive/hist_councils/ii_vatican_council/documents/vat-ii_cons_19651207_gaudium-et-spes_en.html.

Verkuyl, Johannes. 1978. *Contemporary Missiology: An Introduction*. Grand Rapids: Eerdmans.

Vicedom, Georg. 1965. *The Mission of God: An Introduction to a Theology of Mission*. St. Louis: Concordia.

Vriezen, Theodorus Christiaan. 1953. *Die Erwählung Israels nach dem Alten Testament*. Zürich: Zwingli Verlag.

Wagner, C. Peter. 1981. *Church Growth and the Whole Gospel*. New York: Harper & Row.

———. 1988. *The Third Wave of the Holy Spirit: Encountering the Power of Signs and Wonders Today*. Ann Arbor, MI: Vine Books.

———. 1990a. *Church Planting for a Greater Harvest*. Ventura, CA: Regal Books.

———. 1990b. "Territorial Spirits." In *Wrestling with Dark Angels: Toward a Deeper Understanding of the Supernatural Forces in Spiritual Warfare*, ed. C. Peter Wagner and F. Douglas Pennoyer, 73–99. Ventura, CA: Regal Books.

———. 1991. "Territorial Spirits." In *Engaging the Enemy: How to Fight and Defeat Territorial Spirits*, ed. C. Peter Wagner, 43–54. Ventura, CA: Regal Books.

———. 1996. *Confronting the Powers*. Ventura, CA: Regal Books.

———. 1999. *Churchquake: How the New Apostolic Reformation Is Shaking Up the Church as We Know It*. Ventura, CA: Regal Books.

———. 2000. *Apostles and Prophets: The Foundation of the Church*. Ventura, CA: Regal Books.

Wakatama, Pius. 1976. *Independence for the Third World Church: An African's Perspective on Missionary Work*. Downers Grove, IL: InterVarsity.

Walker, David S. 1992. "Preferential Option for the Poor in Evangelical Theology: Assessments and Proposals." *Journal of Theology for Southern Africa* 79 (June): 53–62.

Walls, Andrew F. 1982. "The Gospel as the Prisoner and Liberator of Culture." *Missionalia* 10 (November): 93–105.

———. 1996. *The Missionary Movement in Christian History*. Maryknoll, NY: Orbis.

———. 2002. *The Cross-Cultural Process in Christian History*. Maryknoll, NY: Orbis.

Walls, Andrew, and Cathy Ross, eds. 2008. *Mission in the 21st Century: Exploring the Five Marks of Global Mission*. Maryknoll, NY: Orbis.

Walls, Jerry L. 2003. "A Philosophical Critique of Talbot's Universalism." In Parry and Partridge 2003, 105–24.

Wan, Enoch, and Michael Pocock. 2009. *Missions from the Majority World: Progress, Challenges and Case Studies*. Pasadena: William Carey.

Warneck, Gustav. 1874. "Der Missionsbefehl als Missionsinstruktion." *Allgemeine Missions-Zeitschrift*. Gütersloh: Bertelsmann.

———. 1897–1905. *Evangelische Missionslehre*. 2nd ed. 3 vols. in 5 bks. Gotha: Friedrich Andreas Berthes.

Warner, Clifton D. S. 2000. "Celtic Community, Spirituality, and Mission." In W. D. Taylor 2000a, 491–94.

Warren, Max. 1967. *Social History and Christian Mission*. London: SCM.

Wedderburn, A. J. M. 1988. *The Reasons for Romans*. Edinburgh: Clark.

Weidenmann, Ludwig. 1965. *Mission und Eschatologie*. Paderborn: Verlag Bonifacius Druckerei.

Wellenreuther, Hermann. 2004. "Pietismus und Mission: Vom 17. bis zum Beginn des 20. Jahrhunderts." In *Geschichte des Pietismus*, vol. 4, *Glaubenswelt und Lebenswelten*, ed. Hartmut Lehmann, 166–93. Göttingen: Vandenhoeck & Ruprecht.

Wenham, John W. 1992. "The Case for Conditional Immortality." In *Universalism and the Doctrine of Hell*, ed. Nigel M. de S. Cameron, 161–91. Grand Rapids: Baker Academic.

Werner, Dietrich. 2008. "Evangelism from a WCC Perspective—a Recollection of an Important Ecumenical Memory, and the Unfolding of a Holistic Vision." *International Review of Mission* 96 (July–October): 183–203.

"Wheaton Declaration." 1966. http://www.wheaton.edu/bgc/archives/docs/wd66/b01.html (accessed December 9, 2008).

White, Jerry. 1983. *The Church and the Parachurch: An Uneasy Marriage*. Portland, OR: Multnomah.

Whiteman, Darrell L. 1997. "Contextualization: The Theory, the Gap, the Challenge." *International Bulletin of Missionary Research* 21 (January): 2–7.

———. 2003. "Anthropology and Mission: The Incarnational Connection." *Missiology* 31 (October): 397–415.

Williams, C. Peter. 1990. *The Ideal of the Self-Governing Church: A Study in Victorian Missionary Strategy*. New York: Brill.

Williams, Peter. 1993. "'The Missing Link': The Recruitment of Women Missionaries in Some English Evangelical Missionary Societies in the Nineteenth Century." In Bowie, Kirkwood, and Ardener 1993, 43–69.

Willibald, n.d. *The Life of St. Boniface*. Medieval Sourcebook. http://www.fordham.edu/halsall/basis/willibald-boniface.html (accessed August 21, 2008).

Willmer, Haddon. 2007. "'Vertical' and 'Horizontal' in Paul's Theology of Reconciliation in the Letter to the Romans." *Transformation* 24 (July–October): 151–60.

Wimber, John, and Kevin Springer. 1986. *Power Evangelism*. San Francisco: Harper & Row.

Winter, Ralph, ed. 1973. *The Evangelical Response to Bangkok*. Pasadena, CA: William Carey.

———. 1974. "The Two Structures of God's Redemptive Mission." *Missiology* 1 (January): 121–39.

———. 1975. "The Highest Priority: Cross-Cultural Evangelism." In Douglas 1975, 213–58.

Winter, Ralph D., and Steven C. Hawthorne, eds. 1999. *Perspectives on the World Christian Movement*. 3rd ed. Pasadena, CA: William Carey.

Witherington, Ben. 1998. *The Acts of the Apostles: A Socio-rhetorical Commentary*. Grand Rapids: Eerdmans.

Wood, Rick. 1995. "A Church Planting Movement within Every People: The Key to Reaching Every People and Every Person." *Mission Frontiers* 17 (May–June): 5–6.

Woodberry, Robert D. 2004. "The Shadow of Empire: Christian Missions, Colonial Policy, and Democracy in Postcolonial Societies." PhD diss., University of North Carolina, Chapel Hill.

———. 2006. "Reclaiming the M-Word: The Legacy of Mission in Nonwestern Societies." *The Review of Faith and International Affairs* 4 (Spring): 3–12.

World Council of Churches. 1982. *Mission and Evangelism: An Ecumenical Affirmation*. Geneva: World Council of Churches.

———. 2000. "Mission and Evangelism in Unity Today." http://www.oikoumene.org/en/resources/documents/wcc-commissions/mission-and-evangelism/cwme-world-conference-athens-2005/preparatory-paper-n-1–mission-and-evangelism-in-unity-today.html (accessed December 26, 2007).

Wright, Chris. 1996. "The Old Testament and Christian Mission." *Evangel* 14 (Summer): 37–43.

Wright, Christopher J. H. 2006. *The Mission of God: Unlocking the Bible's Grand Narrative*. Downers Grove, IL: InterVarsity.

Yarbrough, Robert W. 2004. "Jesus on Hell." In Morgan and Peterson 2004, 69–90.

Yohannen, K. P. 1986. *The Coming Revolution in World Missions*. Altamonte Springs, FL: Creation House.

Yong, Amos. 2000. *Discerning the Spirit(s)*. Sheffield: Sheffield Academic.

———. 2003. *Beyond the Impasse: Toward a Pneumatological Theology of Religions*. Grand Rapids: Baker Academic.

———. 2008. *Hospitality and the Other*. Maryknoll, NY: Orbis.

Yoshimoto, Makito. 2005. "The Perspective of the Two Thirds World Churches for World Missions in the 21st Century." In *A New Vision, A New Heart, A Renewed Call: Lausanne Occasional Papers from the 2004 Forum for World Evangelization*, ed. David Claydon, 2:143–51. Pasadena, CA: William Carey.

Young, Edward J. 1972. *The Book of Isaiah*. Vol. 3. Grand Rapids: Eerdmans.

Yung, Hwa. 2002a. "A Systematic Theology That Recognizes the Demonic." In Moreau et al. 2002, 3–27.

———. 2002b. "Case Studies in Spiritual Warfare from East Asia." In Moreau et al. 2002, 138–45.

Zahniser, A. H. Mathias. 1997. *Symbol and Ceremony: Making Disciples across Cultures (Innovations in Mission)*. Monrovia, CA: MARC.

Zangger, Christian D. 1973. *Welt und Konversation: Die theologische Begründung der Mission bei Gottfried Wilhelm Leibniz*. Zürich: Theologischer Verlag Zürich.

Zimmerling, Peter. 1985. *Pioniere der Mission im älteren Pietismus*. Giessen: Brunnen.

Scripture Index

Subject Index

Aagaard, Johannes, 230
Abraham, 7–8, 21, 194
  as blessing to the nations, 11–12, 19, 24, 25, 44, 51, 93
acceptance model, 294, 300–302
Acts, open-endedness of, 52
AD2000 and Beyond Movement, 118
adaptation, 48, 266
Ad Gentes, xvii, xxvi, 66, 102
adoption, into family of God, 85, 97
adoption, of old practices, 282
adventure, mission as, 174–75
Africa, 280, 289
agape, 98
age, 268
age of the Spirit, 23, 25, 27, 44
Aigbe, Sunday, 153
aliens, 10–11, 27, 51
Allen, Roland, xxvi, 116, 124, 126, 146, 207, 208, 242
Alliance for Saturation Church Planting, 118
all nations, 37, 58–59
"already-not yet," 243–44
American Board of Commissioners for Foreign Missions, 115
ancestral spirits, 259–61
ancient suzerainty treaty form, 271
Anderson, Rufus, xxv, 115, 124, 181
Andrews, C. F., 123
Andronicus, 231
angels, 67
Anglican, 170
animism, 240, 258–60, 266, 275

annihilationism, 324, 325–26, 328
"anonymous Christians," 298, 305, 325
anthropology, xx, 56, 124, 311
anticipated eschatology, 92
antifoundationalism, 302
Antioch, 28, 44, 45, 208–9, 272
anti-Westernism, xxvii
apartheid, 134
Apollos, 231
apologetics, xxiv
apostle (term), 218, 228, 230–36, 237
Apostles' Creed, 316
apostolate, xiv
apostolic missionaries, 234, 237
Arabia, 44
Aramaic, 32
archaeological discoveries, in the ancient Near East, 10
ark of the covenant, 11, 21
Arnold, Clinton E., 257
arrogance, 125
art, 286
Asa, 317–18, 337
asceticism, 171–73, 190
Asian church, 289
associate missionary roles, 227
Athanasius, 74
atheism, 303
atonement, 85
Augustine, xxiv, 62, 312
authenticity, 276
autonomy, 302